Effective Teaching Methods

Gary D. Borich
THE UNIVERSITY OF TEXAS AT AUSTIN

MERRILL PUBLISHING COMPANY
A Bell & Howell Information Company
Columbus   Toronto   London   Melbourne

Published by Merrill Publishing Company
A Bell & Howell Information Company
Columbus, Ohio 43216

This book was set in Garamond Light.

Administrative Editor: Jeff Johnston
Production Coordinator: Carol Huston Driver
Cover Designer: Cathy Watterson

Library of Congress Catalog Card Number: 87-63182
International Standard Book Number: 0-675-20962-5
Printed in the United States of America
    2   3   4   5   6   7   8   9 — 92   91   90   89   88

To Kathy
(and all the teachers like her)

Preface

On a poster commemorating the life of the late teacher-astronaut Christa McAuliffe appear these words: "I am the future. I teach." This book is about her future, written for those who will take her place.

Although the legacy of a teacher in space could hardly be imagined only a short time ago, it become a reality—if only for a brief moment. Perhaps less dramatic but no less startling are the many changes that are taking place each day in our classrooms and in the practice of teaching. The classroom of today is a far cry from the classroom of only ten years ago, and this meteoric rate of change is not likely to subside any time soon. Microcomputers, competency testing (for students and teachers), curriculum reform, new state and federal laws, multicultural classrooms, and new teacher certification and degree requirements are but a few of the factors that are working to change the face of schools in America and create special challenges for the beginning teacher. This book has been written to help prepare the beginning teacher to meet these challenges and to discover the opportunities for professional growth and advancement they provide.

To accomplish this, *Effective Teaching Methods* has four simple goals. The first is to provide effective teaching practices derived from a recent 20-year period of research in classrooms. In this research, different teaching practices have been systematically studied for their effects on learners. The results have made it possible to replace many age-old anecdotal suggestions for "good" teaching with modern, research-based teaching practices that are empirically related to positive outcomes in learners. How to use these teaching practices to become an effective teacher is a major focus of this book.

Second, this text describes these effective teaching practices in a friendly, conversational manner. The language of classrooms is an informal language, and there is no reason why a book about teachers in classrooms should not use this language. Therefore, I have tried to talk straight—avoiding complicated phrases, rambling discussions, or pseudoscholarly language. The idea behind each chapter was to get the point across as quickly as possible and in a style that is friendly and readable.

The third goal of this book is to be practical. This book provides positive prescriptive statements about the classroom behavior of teachers by supplying detailed suggestions for how the beginning teacher can engage students in the learning process, manage his or her classroom, and increase student achievement. This text indicates not only *what* to do to obtain these results, but also *how* to obtain them by providing specific, concrete examples and classroom dialogues that illustrate effective teaching practices.

A final goal of this book is to be realistic. Some of what has been written about teaching has been speculative. This book describes what real teachers do in real classrooms and which teaching practices are and are not effective in those classrooms. Nothing in this book is intended to represent pie-in-the-sky theorizing about effective teaching because much of what is presented is the direct result of years of research and observation of effective teaching practices in real classrooms.

These, then, are my four goals: to provide *research-based* effective teaching practices, presented in a *conversational* style, that are *practical* and *realistic.*

Some special features of this book include:

- Beginning and ending chapters on who an effective teacher is (chapter 1) and what an effective teacher does in the classroom (chapter 12)
- A chapter on understanding the important role of individual differences (e.g., prior achievement, intelligence, self-concept, anxiety, disadvantageness, peer group, home and family life) on student learning needs and classroom achievement (chapter 2)
- Two chapters on classroom management, which include the topics of motivation, anticipatory management, and classroom discipline (chapters 9 and 10)
- Two chapters on teaching strategies that explain how to use direct instructional methods, such as lecture, drill and practice, and recita-

tion (chapter 6) and indirect instructional methods, such as group discussion, question and answer, and cooperative learning activities (chapter 7)
- A chapter on teaching methods to use with special types of learners in the regular classroom (e.g., slow, gifted, bilingual, and handicapped) for teaching in today's diverse and multicultural classrooms (chapter 11)

Also provided in this text specifically with the student in mind are:

- End-of-chapter summaries that restate key concepts in an easy-to-follow outline format
- End-of-chapter questions for discussion and practice, and keyed answers in Appendix B
- An annotated list of suggested readings at the end of each chapter that highlight or expand major concepts within the chapter
- An observation instrument for learning how to "see" effective teaching practices in the classroom, illustrated by example dialogues in Appendix C
- A self-report survey instrument for measuring concerns about yourself, the teaching task, and your impact on students (chapter 3 and Appendix A)
- A new procedure for organizing unit and lesson plans that lets the student graphically see the relationship between lessons and unit (chapter 5)

There are many individuals who have contributed to the preparation of this book. Not the least are the many professionals whose naturalistic and quantitative studies of life in classrooms have contributed to the effective teacher described in this text. The work of these professionals have made possible an integration and synthesis of effective teaching practices representing a variety of data sources and methodological perspectives. Although I accept responsibility for the translations of research into practice that I have made, any strengths the reader may see in this approach must be shared with the many individuals who have made them possible.

I would also like to acknowledge those teachers who over the years have shared their insights about the teaching process with me. Among these have been teachers in the Austin, Texas Independent School District, and especially William B. Travis High School, who have provided the opportunity to observe many of the effective teaching methods described in this text. For their helpful reviews of the manuscript, gratitude is extended to Thomas Good, University of Missouri; Gwen Yarger, Syracuse University; Joseph Galbo, California State University at Stanislaus; Roberta Woolover, University of North Carolina; Walter Doyle, University of Arizona; Wayne Mahood, SUNY at Genesco; Grace Kachaturoff, University of Michigan at Dearborn; Susan Bisinger, Northern Illinois University; Jerry Thomas, Southwestern Texas State University; and Robert McNergney, University of Virginia.

Also, I would like to thank Dr. Gerhard Klinzing at the Center for New Learning Methods, University of Tübingen, West Germany, for his insights and source documents used in the preparation of this volume; Kay Smith for her excellent job of editing the manuscript; and Lorraine Sheffield for her typing of the manuscript—without her assitance this project could not have been completed.

GDB
Austin, Texas

Contents

1
The Effective Teacher

What is an effective teacher? How do I become one? How long does it take? These are questions every teacher, young or old, has asked many times over. They are questions that have no simple answers but many different ones. While nothing may seem more challenging and personally rewarding than teaching, teaching is a complex and difficult task. One of the most complex and difficult tasks facing the field of education today is determining exactly what constitutes an effective teacher.

As has been remarked for ages, simple questions do not necessarily have simple answers, nor do they exist in this chapter—or in this book. The goal of this chapter is to introduce you to some of the practices used by effective teachers, practices that are related to positive outcomes in learners. These effective teaching practices do not tell the whole story of what an effective teacher is, but they do form an important foundation for your understanding of the chapters that lie ahead and your becoming an effective teacher. In sub-

sequent chapters we will blend these practices with other activities such as objective writing, lesson planning, teaching strategies, questioning, and classroom management; this provides a rich and comprehensive picture of an effective teacher and, most important to the goals of this book, helps you to become one yourself.

What Is an Effective Teacher?

If you were growing up at the turn of the century, you would find the answer to this question deceptively simple: A good teacher was a good person—someone who met the community ideal for a good citizen, good parent, and good employee. At that time, teachers were judged primarily on their goodness as people and only secondarily on their behavior in the classroom. They were expected to be honest, hardworking, generous, friendly, and considerate and to reveal these qualities in their classrooms by being authoritative, organized, disciplined, insightful, and dedicated. Practically speaking, this meant that in order to be effective all a beginning teacher needed was King Solomon's wisdom, Freud's insight, Einstein's knowledge, and Florence Nightingale's dedication! It became evident that this definition of an ideal teacher lacked clear, objective standards of performance that could be consistently applied across teachers and that educational institutions could use in training future teachers.

This early approach to identifying a good teacher soon gave way to another, which attempted to identify the **psychological characteristics** associated with a good teacher. These characteristics represented the levels of personality, attitude, experience, achievement, and aptitude that were thought necessary to be a good teacher. Personality characteristics (such as achievement-motivation, directness, and anxiety), attitude characteristics (such as motivation to teach, attitude toward children, and attitude toward teaching), experience characteristics (such as years of teaching experience, experience in subject taught, and experience in grade level taught), and aptitude and achievement characteristics (such as scores on ability tests, college grade-point average, and student teaching evaluations) all became tools to help define the good teacher.

Table 1.1 lists some of these psychological characteristics. Since they have a certain intuitive appeal, some of the reasons why they have *not* been particularly useful in defining good teaching are worth mentioning.

Personality

Over the years only a few personality measures have been developed that relate specifically to the practice of teaching. Since most personality measures have been designed to be used in clinical settings to record deviant or abnormal behavior, much of what they measure has been of little help in identifying the positive or "normal" behaviors that may be needed to be an effective teacher. Consequently, the usefulness of many personality tests for predicting a teacher's behavior in the classroom have had to be inferred from their more general success in the field of mental health. Although certain interpersonal, emotional, and coping behaviors are believed to

TABLE 1.1
Commonly studied teacher characteristics

Personality	Attitude	Experience	Aptitude/Achievement
Permissiveness	Motivation to teach	Years of teaching experience	National Teachers Exam
Dogmatism	Attitude toward children	Experience in subject taught	Graduate Record Exam
Authoritarianism	Attitude toward teaching	Experience in grade level taught	Scholastic Aptitude Test
Achievement-motivation	Attitude toward authority	Workshops attended	1. verbal
Introversion-extroversion	Vocational interest	Graduate courses taken	2. quantitative
Abstractness-concreteness	Attitude toward self (self-concept)	Degrees held	Special ability tests, (e.g., reasoning ability, logical ability, verbal fluency)
Directness-indirectness	Attitude toward subject taught	Professional papers written	Grade-point average
Locus of control			1. overall
Anxiety			2. in major subject
1. general			Professional recommendations
2. teaching			Student evaluations of teaching effectiveness
			Student teaching evaluations

be required for effective teaching (Levis, 1987), personality tests, especially of a clinical nature, have provided few insights into the positive social behavior that may be needed for effective teaching in the classroom.

Attitude

Attitude assessments may be either global (e.g., attitude toward the school and the educational system) or specific (e.g., attitude toward a particular task, text, child, or curriculum). In either case, most attempts to measure teacher attitude have suffered from inadequate predictive validity, or the inability to forecast what the teacher with a particular attitude *actually does in the classroom*. Research studies generally have shown the correspondence between attitude and teacher performance in the classroom to be low and nonsignificant (Walberg, 1986; Jackson, 1968). The use of attitude data for measuring teacher effectiveness, therefore, has had to rest on the assumption that attitudes (e.g., positive feelings about teaching) are related to other behaviors (e.g., more organized lesson plans) that are one or more steps removed from the actual process of teaching (Clark & Peterson, 1986). The measurement of teacher attitude in defining effective teaching is more indirect and less credible than is direct observation of the classroom practices that a "good" attitude is supposed to represent.

Experience

Experience variables, such as those outlined in the standard job application form, define the teacher's experience so broadly that they often only sketchily describe those experiences that may be most relevant for performing the day-to-day tasks required in a specific classroom, grade level, or subject area. A teacher's experience with a specific type of curriculum or learner may be more relevant to a teacher's performance than the typical experience data kept in teacher records, such as years of teaching experience, graduate credits earned, or hours of in-service training (Barnes, 1987). The correspondence of such data to actual performance in the classroom generally has been low and nonsignificant, because the data by themselves may represent only a small piece of the "real" experience level of a teacher.

Achievement and Aptitude

Like experience variables, most achievement and aptitude data have been of little value in predicting performance in the classroom. This may be somewhat surprising given the emphasis placed on achievement and intelligence by our society in general. However, regardless of the use of these measures for predicting the performance of students, prior achievement of the teacher as measured by, for example, college grades, rarely has been found to have a strong relationship to the classroom performance of teachers. There is a relatively narrow spread of scores in course grades and college GPAs that typically characterizes the achievement of teachers. Standards set by training institutions usually require teachers to meet some minimum level of achievement, which is usually high enough to make the small variations among beginning teachers irrelevant to actual performance in the classroom.

So, while the definitions of a good teacher turned to more measurable characteristics, these characteristics were often too remote from the teachers' day-to-day work in the classroom to meaningfully contribute to a definition of good teaching. Most notably, these definitions excluded the most important and obvious measure of all for determining good teaching: the performance of the students who are being taught.

A New Direction

In the last two decades a revolution has occurred in the definition of good teaching. Comparisons to community ideals proved unrealistic and unteachable, and the psychological characteristics of teachers proved to be poorly related to what teachers actually did in the classroom. This directed researchers to begin studying the impact of specific teacher behaviors on the specific cognitive and affective behaviors of their students.

The term "good teaching" changed to "effective teaching," and the study of teachers turned to research on their effects on students.

These changes have affected the profession of teaching so dramatically that their effects can now be felt in the reform of teacher training curricula, in the competency testing of teachers, in the education of teacher trainers, and in textbooks, such as this one, on methods of teaching. Perhaps most responsible for this change is the way in which classroom researchers over the past two decades have come to study the nature of teaching. These new ways of studying classroom behavior have made the student and teacher-student interaction the focus of modern definitions of effective teaching.

Linking Teacher Behavior with Student Performance

During the 1960s and 70s new methods of studying teacher-student interactions were being developed. These methods provided a systematic way of studying the interactive patterns of teachers and students. The goal of the researchers who used these methods was to discover those teacher behaviors that were causally related to desirable student outcomes, such as good grades on classroom tests, higher standardized test scores, better attitudes about school and subject, and improved problem-solving skills. Before unveiling the findings from this research and their implications for effective teaching, it may be of interest to see how the research data were obtained using these methods.

The Research Process

To collect data on teacher-student interactions, researchers often used classroom interaction analysis instruments of the type shown in Figure 1.1 and Figure 1.2. These particular instruments were devised by Good and Brophy (1987), although many others, more extensive in scope and number of behaviors measured, also have been used. For these instruments various student-teacher behav-

iors have been chosen for observation. For example, using the response form in Figure 1.1 an observer can code a student's response to a question and then the teacher's reaction and feedback to what the student said. For the tenth interchange recorded on this form, for example, a male student fails to answer a question (0), is criticized by the teacher for not answering (--), and then is given the answer by the teacher (Gives Ans.). Numbers for the interchanges are assigned as they occur, allowing the pattern of question-answer-feedback to be recorded over an entire period. In Figure 1.2 the observer is coding the student performance characteristic which is being praised by the teacher (perseverance, progress, success, good thinking, etc.). In this case individual student identities are recorded by assigning a unique number to each student. For this coding form the praise behavior of the teacher is being observed in relation to the behavior of individual students at the same time that the overall pattern or sequence of action is being recorded (for example, student "8" is praised three times in a row for "perseverance or effort"). Through instruments similar to these, a rich and varied picture of classroom processes could be captured over the course of a research study. Obviously, a single observation of a single class would reveal little in the way of a trustworthy and consistent pattern of behavior, but multiple observation periods extending across different teachers, schools, or school districts could reveal consistent patterns of teacher-student interactions. These patterns of classroom behavior then could be related to student behaviors (such as performance on end-of-year standardized achievement tests, specially prepared classroom tests, and attitude scales) in order to measure the effects of various patterns of teacher-student interaction on student performance.

It was in this manner that patterns of effective classroom teaching began to emerge in studies conducted by different researchers. Although some studies provided results that were contradictory to one another or found no relationships between certain classroom processes and student outcomes, many found patterns of classroom interaction that consistently produced de-

FIGURE 1.1

Coding categories for question-answer-feedback sequences (Good & Brophy, 1987)

Student Sex		
Symbol	Label	Definition
M	Male	The student answering the question is male.
F	Female	The student answering the question is female.
Student Response		
+	Right	The teacher accepts the student's response as correct or satisfactory.
±	Part right	The teacher considers the student's response to be only partially correct or to be correct but incomplete.
−	Wrong	The teacher considers the student's response to be incorrect.
0	No answer	The student makes no response or says he doesn't know (code student's answer here if teacher gives a feedback reaction before he is able to respond).
Teacher Feedback Reaction		
+ +	Praise	Teacher praises student either in words ("fine," "good," "wonderful," "good thinking") or by expressing verbal affirmation in a notably warm, joyous, or excited manner.
+	Affirm	Teacher simply affirms that the student's response is correct (nods, repeats answer, says "Yes," "OK," etc.).
0	No reaction	Teacher makes no response whatever to student's response—he or she simply goes on to something else.
−	Negate	Teacher simply indicates that the student's response is incorrect (shakes head, says "No," "That's not right," "Hm-mm," etc.).
− −	Criticize	Teacher criticizes student, either in words ("You should know better than that," "That doesn't make any sense—you better pay close attention," etc.) or by expressing verbal negation in a frustrated, angry, or disgusted manner.
Gives Ans.	Teacher gives answer	Teacher provides the correct answer for the student.
Ask Other	Teacher asks another student	Teacher redirects the question, asking a different student to try to answer it.
Other Calls	Another student calls out answer	Another student calls out the correct answer, and the teacher acknowledges that it is correct.
Repeat	Repeats question	Teacher repeats the original question, either in its entirety or with a prompt ("Well?" "Do you know?" "What's the answer?").
Clue	Rephrase or clue	Teacher makes original question easier for student to answer by rephrasing it or by giving a clue.
New Ques.	New question	Teacher asks a new question (i.e., a question that calls for a different answer than the original question called for).

FIGURE 1.1

Continued. **Coding Response Form.**

NO.	Student Sex		Student Response									Gives Ans.	Teacher Feedback Reaction				
	M	F	+	±	-	0		++	+	0	-	--		Ask Other	Other Calls	Repeat	Clue	New Ques.
1		✓	✓						✓									
2	✓		✓						✓									
3	✓					✓											✓	
4	✓		✓					✓	✓									
5	✓		✓															
6		✓			✓			✓				✓						✓
7	✓		✓					✓										
8	✓		✓			✓				✓								
9	✓		✓							✓		✓						
10	✓					✓							✓					
11																		
12																		
13																		
14																		
15																		

FIGURE 1.2

Coding form for measuring individual praise (Good & Brophy, 1987).

USE: Whenever the teacher praises an individual student
PURPOSE: To see what behaviors the teacher reinforces through praise, and to see how the teacher's praise is distributed among the students

Behavior Categories	*Student Number*	*Codes*
1. Perseverance or effort; worked long or hard	14	1. 3
2. Progress (relative to the past) toward achievement	23	2. 3,4
3. Success (right answer, high score) achievement	6	3. 3
4. Good thinking, good suggestion, good guess, or nice try	18	4. 3
5. Imagination, creativity, originality	8	5. 1
6. Neatness, careful work	8	6. 1
7. Good or compliant behavior, follows rules, pays attention	8	7. 1
8. Thoughtfulness, courtesy, offering to share; prosocial behavior		8. ___
9. Other (specify)		9. ___

NOTES:

All answers occurred during social studies discussion.
Was particularly concerned about #8, a low-achieving male.

(Codes continue: 10. through 25. ___)

---

sirable student outcomes in the form of higher test scores, increased problem-solving skills, improved attitudes toward subject, etc. From these patterns have come our modern definitions of the effective teacher.

Following are some of the teaching behaviors that researchers generally have agreed contribute to effective teaching irrespective of the context in which the teaching occurs. Later, we will modify these behaviors and add others to them to describe effective teaching at various levels of schooling, in different content areas, and with different types of student populations.

Some Key Behaviors Contributing to Effective Teaching

Approximately 10 teacher behaviors have shown promising relationships to desirable student outcomes, primarily as measured by achievement on classroom and standardized tests. These 10 behaviors have been identified in studies that used the type of classroom interaction instruments illustrated previously. Five behaviors resulting from these studies have strong research support (Rosenshine, 1971b, 1973; Dunkin & Biddle, 1974; Walberg, 1986; Brophy & Good,

1986), and another five have less support but appear logically related to effective teaching. The first five behaviors will be identified as **key behaviors**, because their presence is considered to be essential for effective teaching. The second five will be identified as **catalytic**, or helping, **behaviors** that can occur in various mixtures to help implement the key behaviors. The five key behaviors, which will be referred to throughout this text, are clarity, variety, task orientation, engagement in the learning process, and moderate-to-high rates of success.

Clarity

This behavior refers to how clear and interpretable a presentation is to the class. For example, are the points the teacher is making understandable? Is the teacher able to explain concepts clearly so that the students are able to follow in a logical step-by-step order? Is the teacher's oral delivery to the class clear, audible and intelligible, and free of any distracting mannerisms? One surprising result from research on teacher clarity is that teachers vary considerably on this behavior. That is, not all teachers are able to communicate clearly and directly to their students without wandering, speaking over students' heads, or using speech patterns that impair the clarity of what is being presented. For example, the extent to which the teacher uses vague, ambiguous, or indefinite language (e.g., "might probably be," "tends to suggest," "could possibly happen"), uses overly complicated sentences (e.g., "There are many important reasons for the start of WWII but some are more important than others, so let's start with those that are thought to be important but really aren't"), or gives directions that often elicit student requests for clarification have sometimes been taken as indications of a teacher's lack of clarity (Land & Smith, 1979; Smith & Land, 1981).

Those who teach with a high degree of clarity generally spend less time having to go over material and have their questions answered correctly the first time, allowing more time for instruction. Clarity is a complex behavior because it is related to many other so-called cognitive behaviors, such as a teacher's organization of the content, familiarity with the lesson, and delivery strategies (e.g., whether a teacher uses a discussion, question-and-answer, or small-group format). Nevertheless, both the *cognitive* clarity and *oral* clarity of a teacher's presentation have been found to vary substantially among teachers; this, in turn, has produced differences in student performance on cognitive tests of achievement.

Throughout most of the chapters in this text, and especially in chapters 5, 6, and 7, ways are suggested to help you bring clarity to your lessons.

Variety

This behavior refers to the variability or flexibility of delivery during the presentation of a lesson. It includes, for example, the planned mixing of different classroom behaviors, such as the behaviors measured by the observation systems shown earlier. Research has indicated that the use of variety in instructional materials and techniques, the frequency and variety of reinforcements used, and the types of feedback given to students pay rich dividends in terms of increased student achievement (Brophy & Good, 1986; Brophy & Evertson, 1976).

Perhaps one of the most popular and effective ways of creating variety during instruction is to ask questions. As you will see in chapter 8, many different types of questions can be asked, and when integrated into the pacing and sequencing of a lesson they can provide an effective means of creating meaningful variation within a lesson (Gall et al., 1978; Redfield & Rousseau, 1981). Therefore, the effective teacher needs to know something about the art of asking questions and to have the ability to discriminate among the different types of question formats (e.g., fact questions, process questions, convergent questions, divergent questions). These and related types of questions will be introduced in chapter 8.

Another aspect of variety in teaching is perhaps the most obvious. This involves the use of learning materials, equipment, displays, and space in the classroom and includes the extent to which their visual variety can actually encourage student involvement with lesson content. The display of reading materials, the use of audiovisual devices, the display of maps and globes, the organization of different reference materials—all these contribute to instructional variety, which, in turn, has been found to influence both student achievement on end-of-unit tests and student behavior during instruction. For example, in some studies the amount of disruptive behavior was less in classrooms which had greater variety in classroom activities and materials (Evertson, Sanford, Clements, & Worsham, 1984). Other studies have shown variety to be related to student attention (Lysakowski & Walberg, 1981). Some of the ways to incorporate variety into your lesson plans will be explored in chapters 5, 6, and 7, and the relationship of variety to classroom management is discussed in chapter 9.

Task Orientation

This refers to the degree to which the teacher is achievement-oriented with respect to his or her students and thus provides students with the opportunity to learn. Task-related aspects of this behavior include both the amount of time the teacher spends lecturing, asking questions, and encouraging students to inquire or think independently and the amount of intellectual or cognitive emphasis provided by the teacher. These aspects often manifest themselves in the teacher's concern that all relevant material gets covered and learned as opposed to a preoccupation with procedural matters or an exclusive concern that the students enjoy themselves. Obviously, all teachers want their students to enjoy learning. However, most researchers have agreed that achievement has been higher in classrooms whose teachers espouse *primarily* the former rather than the latter value (Rosenshine, 1983). It follows that classrooms in which teacher-student interactions focus more on intellectual content than process issues (such as how to use materials, or classroom rules and procedures) are more likely to have higher rates of achievement than those that do not. It is also likely that the teachers

in content-oriented classrooms are highly conversant with the content likely to appear on departmental tests and end-of-year standardized achievement tests. This is not to say that these teachers "teach to the test," but that their classroom instruction parallels the instructional goals which guide the construction of tests of student progress. Teachers with a high degree of task orientation are goal-oriented; that is, they know what instructional goals they want to achieve in a given period of time, organize instruction around the goals, and stick steadfastly to the goals in the midst of the distracting and less instructionally relevant activities which pop up from time to time. Perhaps most important, a teacher who is task-oriented has high but realistic expectations with regard to student performance (Brophy & Evertson, 1976). The systematic organization of class content and the use of this organization in the form of well-prepared lesson plans and teaching strategies all are important ingredients of task orientation. These topics are taken up in chapters 4, 5, and 6.

Engagement in the Learning Process

One of the most recently researched teacher behaviors related to student achievement is the amount of learning time devoted to an academic subject; this will be related to a teacher's task orientation and to content coverage. A teacher's task orientation should give the students the greatest possible opportunity to learn the material to be tested. For example, notice in Table 1.2 that rather spectacular results were achieved when the teacher's **task orientation**, or time devoted to an academic subject, was increased. The table shows that increasing the time devoted to an instructional objective from 4 to 52 minutes a day for an average of only 25 school days yielded an increase of more than 25 percentile points on an achievement test. The researchers who recorded these data indicated that while such large differences in instructional time may appear to be unrealistic, they actually occurred in the classrooms in their study. Distinctly different than the amount of instructional time devoted to a topic,

TABLE 1.2

Learning time and student achievement: Example from second-grade reading

Reading Score at First Testing (October)		Student Engaged Time in Reading with High Success Rate		Estimated Reading Score, Second Testing (December)	
Raw Score (out of 100)	Percentile	Total Time Over 5 Weeks (Minutes)	Average Daily Time (Minutes)	Raw Score (out of 100)	Percentile
36	50	100	4	37	39
36	50	573	23	43	50
36	50	1300	52	52	66

Note: An average of twenty-five school days occurred between the first and the second testing.

Source: From Charles W. Fisher et al., *Teaching and Learning in the Elementary School: A Summary of the Beginning Teacher Evaluation Study.* Beginning Teacher Evaluation Study Report VII–I. (San Francisco, Calif.: Far West Laboratory for Research and Development, 1978)

however, is the time students are *actually engaged* in learning the material presented. This has been called the **engagement rate** or the on-task behavior of students.

Engagement rate is the percentage of time devoted to learning when the student is actually on-task, engaged with the instructional materials and activities being presented. The key to understanding engagement rate is the awareness that while a teacher can be task-oriented, providing maximum content coverage and communicating high expectations, the students may not be engaged all of this time (Berliner, 1979; Fisher et al., 1980). This disengagement can involve an emotional or mental detachment from the lesson or both. Off-task behavior may or may not be obvious. When students jump out of their seats, talk, read a magazine, or leave for the restroom, they obviously are not engaged in instruction, however thoroughly it is being presented by the teacher. However, students can also be nonengaged in far more subtle ways, such as looking attentive while their thoughts are many miles away. Correcting this type of nonengagement may be the more difficult task. Several research studies have contributed useful data for increasing learning time and, more important, student engagement. From these data it was possible for Crawford and others (1978) to identify

behaviors that have potential for increasing learning time, which results in increased on-task behavior. The following suggestions have been made:

1. Teachers should have a system of rules that allows pupils to attend to their personal and procedural needs without having to obtain the teacher's permission (Stallings & Kaskowitz, 1974; Brophy & Evertson, 1974).
2. Teachers should move around the room to monitor pupils' seatwork and to communicate an awareness of student progress (Stallings & Kaskowitz, 1974; McDonald, Elias, Stone, Wheeler, & Lambert, 1975).
3. When pupils work independently, teachers should ensure that the assignments are interesting, worthwhile, and easy enough to be completed by each pupil working without teacher direction (Stallings & Kaskowitz, 1974; McDonald et al., 1975).
4. Teachers should minimize such activities as giving directions and organizing the class for instruction by writing the daily schedule on the board, ensuring that pupils know where to go, and what to do (McDonald et al., 1975; Soar & Soar, 1973).
5. Teachers should make abundant use of textbooks, workbooks, and other paper-and-pencil

activities which are at or slightly above a student's current level of functioning (McDonald et al., 1975; Stallings & Kaskowitz, 1974; Brophy & Evertson, 1976).

6. Teachers should avoid "timing errors"; that is, they should prevent misbehaviors from continuing long enough to increase in severity or spread to and affect other children (Brophy & Evertson, 1974, 1976).

These teaching practices, particularly for independent seatwork, have been recommended on the basis of the findings of these and more recent studies (Anderson, Evertson, & Brophy, 1982). These and other more specific ways of increasing the engagement rates of students will be explored in chapters 6, 7, 8, and 9.

Moderate-to-High Success Rate

A crucial aspect of research investigating task orientation and student engagement has been the level of difficulty at which material is presented. Level of difficulty in these studies was measured by the rate at which students could understand and correctly complete exercises pertaining to the material being taught. One possible level of difficulty is that of **high success**, in which the student understands the task and makes only occasional, careless errors; another is **moderate success**, in which the student has partial understanding but makes some substantive errors; and a third is **low success**, in which the student does not understand the task at all. Findings indicate that task orientation and student engagement are closely related to level of difficulty as measured by success rate. The findings consistently point out that instruction producing a moderate-to-high success rate results in increased achievement (Fisher et al., 1980). In addition, research has shown that instruction producing low error rates can contribute to high levels of student self-esteem and to positive attitudes toward the subject matter and the school (Bennett, Desforges, Cockburn, & Wilkinson, 1981). The average student in a typical classroom spends about half of the time working on tasks that provide the opportunity for high success. Researchers have found that students who spend *more than the average* in high-success activities had higher achievement scores, better retention, and more positive attitudes toward school (Brophy & Evertson, 1976; Wyne & Stuck, 1982). These findings have led to at least one suggestion that students spend from 60–70% of their time on tasks that afford the opportunity for moderate-to-high levels of success, that is, that allow for almost complete understanding and only occasional careless errors the first time through the material (Brophy & Evertson, 1976; Rosenshine, 1983).

Moderate-to-high success rates will produce mastery of the lesson content, but, even more important, they will provide an opportunity for the student to apply learned knowledge in some practical way, such as answering questions or solving problems. Exercises providing moderate-to-high success rates allow the individual elements or pieces that are learned to fall into place, thereby providing a crucial final step in the learning process. Many teachers do not devote sufficient time to this stage of learning, which has been found to be particularly crucial for younger students and for those who may be slow learners. Organizing and planning instruction that yields moderate-to-high success rates but at the same time is not boring, repetitive, or time wasting is a key behavior for the effective teacher. You will learn ways to incorporate moderate-to-high success rates into your instruction in chapters 4, 5, and 6, and ways in which you can apply this skill to special learners in chapter 11.

Summary of Key Behaviors

The five concepts—clarity, variety, task orientation, student engagement, and success rate—represent some of the most important behaviors and skills that are central to modern definitions of effective teaching. It would be safe to say that without the knowledge and skill to present lessons that are clear, that incorporate variety, that are task-oriented, and that actually engage students in the learning process at moderate-to-high rates of success, no teacher could be truly effective in producing desirable patterns of student achievement and attitude. It is the objective of the following chapters to present the tools and techniques needed to use these five key elements of effective teaching in your classroom.

Other effective teaching behaviors and a more thorough understanding of those described previously undoubtedly will be discovered by classroom researchers in the years ahead. For the first time, however, research has provided a basis for composing new and more useful definitions of effective teaching and for the training of teachers. The research literature contains additions to and alternatives for these five key behaviors, but they serve well as an organizing framework and backbone of this text. They stand as a practical starting point for defining the effective teacher, the skeleton on which the remainder of this text will construct the heart, mind, and body of the effective teacher.

Earlier it was emphasized that there is no simple answer to "what is an effective teacher?" As has been suggested, there are many behaviors that must be orchestrated into certain *patterns of behavior*. This can be noticed both in the overlapping relationships among the five key behaviors and also in the many other behaviors that may be needed in order to successfully carry out any one behavior or combination of behaviors. Identification of these five behaviors is risky, making teaching appear deceptively simple, as though this were all there were to it. Teaching involves much more than the obvious, however, as the following sections will show.

Some Helping Behaviors Related to Effective Teaching

To begin to flesh out the skeleton, more than five rather general notions of effective teaching are needed. Also necessary are the specifics and details of the behaviors that lead up to making the skeleton come alive. To begin this process, consider some additional behaviors that can be thought of as catalyst, or helping, behaviors for performing the original five key behaviors. These helpers are no less important than the key behaviors themselves; they provide *means of achieving* the key behaviors. The research findings for helping behaviors, while promising, are not as strong and consistent as those identifying the original five behaviors. While there is general agreement as to the importance of these helping behaviors, the research has not been so accommodating as to identify explicitly how these behaviors should be used, nor has it linked these behaviors to student achievement as strongly as the original five. This is why we suspect these behaviors need to be employed in the context of other behaviors to be maximally effective, making them catalysts rather than ends unto themselves. The behaviors include the teacher's use of student ideas, structuring, questioning, probing, and enthusiasm.

Use of Student Ideas

This refers to acknowledging, modifying, applying, comparing, and summarizing students' statements. Note that any one of these activities could be useful in achieving one or more of the key behaviors. Depending on how and when the helping behaviors are applied, the key behaviors can be variously affected. Thus, use of student ideas will be one of several ways to achieve these more general teaching behaviors.

Flanders (1970) described the components of this behavior in the following manner:

Acknowledging: using the student's idea by repeating the nouns and logical connectives expressed by him or her

Modifying: using the student's idea by rephrasing it or conceptualizing it in the teacher's own words

Applying: using the student's idea to teach an inference or take the next step in a logical analysis of a problem

Comparing: using the student's idea by drawing a relationship between it and ideas expressed earlier

Summarizing: using what was said by an individual student or a group of students as a recapitulation of concepts

Although the use of these behaviors in and of themselves has not produced strong relationships with student achievement, it has been noted to increase significantly a student's engagement in the learning process; it is a catalyst helping to achieve the key behavior (Emmer, Evertson, Sanford, Clements, & Worsham, 1984). Consider a brief instructional dialogue that incorporates some of these behaviors.

TEACHER: Tom, what is the formula for the Pythagorean theorem?
TOM: $c^2 = a^2 + b^2$

At this point the teacher could have simply said "Good!" and gone on to the next question. Instead, this teacher continues:

TEACHER: Let's show that on the board. Here is a triangle; now let's do exactly as Tom said. He said: Squaring the altitude, which is a, and adding it to the square of the base, which is b, should give us the square of the hypotenuse, which is c. Would someone like to come up and measure with a ruler the hypotenuse of this triangle and tell us if it equals the square root of c^2?

Which, if any, of the five ways of using student ideas defined previously are in this dialogue? First, by putting Tom's response graphically on the blackboard, this teacher *applied* Tom's answer by taking it to the next step, constructing a proof. Also, by repeating orally what Tom said, the teacher *acknowledged* to the entire class the value of Tom's contribution. And, by having someone come up to prove the correctness of Tom's response, a *summary* of the concept was provided. All this was accomplished from Tom's simple (and only) utterance, "$c^2 = a^2 + b^2$."

Although the use of student ideas looks simple, it takes skill and planning. Even when a teacher's response is unplanned, it requires preparation to be able to notice and to quickly seize upon opportunities to incorporate student ideas into the lesson. In later chapters you will learn how the use of student ideas can be a catalyst in other ways to performing each of the key teaching behaviors.

Research has shown that these five ways of using student ideas, especially when employed in logical sequences, are more strongly and consistently related to student engagement than is acknowledging a student's answer with a simple expression of approval, such as "Good!" (Brophy, 1981). One might argue that the standard phrases that so often are used to acknowledge and reward students, such as "correct," "good," or "right," have become so overused that they no longer convey the reward intended and certainly do not contribute additional content to the instruction. In our example, the teacher was not only *listening* to student ideas but also *using* them to convey lesson content in an alternate or expanded form. In this manner, the use of student ideas can increase the clarity and variety of a lesson as well as promote student engagement in the learning process. Do you think Tom was pleased by what happened? You will learn more about ways of incorporating student ideas into your lessons in chapters 7 and 8.

Structuring

Structuring refers to teacher comments made at the start or end of a lesson for the explicit purpose of organizing what is to come or summarizing what has gone before. When used prior to an instructional activity or question, structuring provides an advance organizer for the students; it aids in their understanding and retention of the material. When used at the conclusion of an instructional activity or question, structuring reinforces learned content and places it in its proper relation to other content. Both these forms of structuring have been found to be related to student achievement and are useful catalysts for increasing the key behaviors (Doenau, 1987; Gage, 1976). Typically, "before" and "after" structuring takes the following form:

TEACHER (at beginning of lesson): O.K., now that we have studied the political and economic climate immediately prior to both WWI and WWII, we will begin a study of the political and economic factors that were present in both periods. Most important, however, we will study those political and economic factors that may precede *any* international or world crisis. First, let's see what these two turbulent times had in common.

TEACHER (at end of lesson): So, we have discovered economic hardship and a feeling of political unrest and insecurity accompanied the periods immediately preceding WWI and II. We might conclude from this that conflicts between nations, such as war, sometimes occur when gains in economic improvements and/or territorial security appear from the vantage of at least one nation to outweigh the human and material costs involved in war. Can you think of other times in history when either of these two factors played a role in the behavior of nations?

This sequence illustrates some of the types of structuring that can occur. One of these is a signal that a shift in direction or content is about to take place. A clear signal alerts students to be attentive to the impending change; without it, some students may confuse new content with old, missing some of the more subtle differences. Signals such as, "Now that we have studied the political and economic climate immediately prior to both WWI and WWII, we will begin to study . . ." help students switch gears and provide a perspective that will make new content more meaningful.

Another type of structuring is the use of emphasis. Can you find a point of emphasis in the previous dialogue? By using the phrase "most important . . .", this teacher is alerting students to the knowledge and understanding that will be expected at the conclusion of this activity. This provides the students with an opportunity to find some way of organizing in advance what is to follow. In this instance the students are given the clue that they should be thinking about the political and economic factors of war that extend *beyond* the two wars discussed in the lesson. This

makes this teacher's final question more meaningful; the students have previously been given a clue that such a question might be raised and that some generalizations that go beyond the concepts discussed are expected. Phrases such as "Now this is important . . .", "We will return to this point later . . .", and "Remember this" are called "verbal markers" and can emphasize your most important points.

The general practice of previewing at the start of a lesson and reviewing at its end has been related to gains in student achievement (Rosenshine & Stevens, 1986). This seems logical, as review activities not only summarize and reinforce what a student already knows but in some instances will be the only time the student is sufficiently engaged, i.e., attentive and actively processing what the teacher says. While it may not be a pleasant fact of life, it is not unusual that a quarter of a class or more is "tuned out" at any one time. Because even mention of the word "review" has special significance to most students, rates of engagement tend to be higher during these periods than at most other times.

Questioning

As could be noted from its use in structuring and its logical relationship to all of the five key behaviors, questioning is an important helping behavior. The art of asking the right questions at the right time is almost ageless, and there is good reason to believe that this art must be included among the most important teacher behaviors. Few other topics have been researched as much as has the teacher's use of questions (Gall et al., 1978; Winne, 1979; Redfield & Rousseau, 1981). For this reason various categories or types of questions have been devised, many of which have overlapping meanings.

While many question categories can be made, some of the more predominant are the following:

direct/indirect questions

low-level/high-level questions

convergent/divergent questions

closed/open questions

fact/concept questions

In addition to these categories, there are different purposes, designed to encourage different mental processes, for which a question can be asked, such as: to test, to problem solve, to guide, to arouse (e.g., curiosity), to encourage (e.g., creativity), to analyze, to synthesize, and to judge.

It is important to distinguish between content questions and process questions. For each of the original five categories of questions listed previously, the category on the left is content-oriented (e.g., direct), while the category on the right is process-oriented (e.g., indirect). This is to say that direct, low-level, convergent, closed, and fact questions are more likely to be posed for the explicit purpose of having the student deal directly with the content taught, as when the teacher asks a question to see if a student can recall and understand specific material. The correct answer in these cases is known well in advance by the teacher and has been conveyed directly in class, in the text, or both. Few, if any, interpretations or alternative meanings of the question are possible. Various researchers have used different words to describe the questions that are listed in this context, such as **direct** (no interpretations of alternative meanings are required), **low-level** (they require only the recall of readily available facts as opposed to generalizations and inferences), **convergent** (different data sources converge on the exact same answer), **closed** (no alternative answers or interpretations are possible), and **fact** (only discrete pieces of well-accepted knowledge need be recalled).

Research has shown that such content-oriented questions are related to student achievement (Armento, 1977). This is not surprising; by some estimates 80% of the questions asked by teachers refer directly to specific content and have readily discernable, unambiguous "right" answers (Brophy & Good, 1974). Perhaps even more to the point is the well-known fact that approximately the same percentage of test items (and behavioral objectives) are written at the recall, knowledge, or fact level (Melton, 1978; Davis & Tinsley, 1967). Test items, behavioral objectives, and the level of the instruction itself all seem to emphasize readily known facts as they are presented in lesson plans, workbooks, and texts. In chapter 8 there is more about content questions and their most appropriate use.

Not all questions are content questions, however. To problem solve, to guide, to arouse, to encourage, to analyze, to synthesize, to judge are also legitimate and useful goals of instruction; they, too, should be reflected in questioning strategies. For these goals, however, content is not an end itself but is a means of achieving what some have called "higher order" ends. Therefore, one can find in the literature reference to questions categorized as **indirect** (interpretation and alternative meanings are possible), **high-level** (the mental processes required are more complex than the simple recall of facts, e.g., making generalizations and inferences), **divergent** (different data sources actually lead to different correct answers), **open** (a single correct answer is not expected or even possible), and **concept** (the processes of abstraction, generalization, and inference are required).

The following are examples of process-oriented questions:

What were the effects of the invention of the cotton gin on cultural values in the South?

From what we know today about atmosphere on the moon, what type of dwelling would be needed to sustain life for one year?

Analyze the effect of recent advances in computer technology on the financial life of the family.

If you were guaranteed a high-paying job for life *or* a free college education, which would you choose? Explain why.

Using examples of your own choosing, compare division with subtraction in ways that illustrate their similar functions.

Research findings on the use of higher order questions have not been as impressive with regard to student achievement as has research on the use of lower order questions (Redfield & Rousseau, 1981). The former does indicate, however, that although gains in student achievement following use of higher order questions have not occurred consistently, positive changes in the *thinking patterns* and *problem-solving strategies* of students frequently occur (Martin, 1979). It is generally recognized that the mental processes of analyzing, synthesizing, and decision making are among those most frequently needed in our adult lives, so the occurrence of these processes as a result of higher order questioning strategies may be justification alone for their use. There is more about higher and lower order questions in chapter 8.

Probing

Probing refers to various statements a teacher makes to encourage students to elaborate upon an answer, either their own or another's. Probing may take the form of a general question but can also include various other expressions that elicit clarification about an answer given, solicit additional information about a response, or redirect a student's response in a more fruitful direction. Probing often is used to shift a discussion to some higher thought level. Generally, student achievement is greatest when eliciting, soliciting, and, if necessary, redirecting occur in cycles in order to systematically lead the discussion to a higher level of complexity, such as when interrelationships, generalizations, and problem solutions are being sought (Zahorik, 1987; Gage, 1976). In this manner a lesson may begin with a simple fact question, and then, by eliciting clarification of student responses, soliciting new information, or redirecting an answer, move to a higher level involving generalizations, abstractions, and the drawing of inferences. A typical cycle might occur in the following manner:

TEACHER: Bobby, what is a scientific experiment?
BOBBY: Well, it's when you test something.

TEACHER: But, what do you test?
BOBBY: Mmm. Something you believe in and want to find out if it's really true.
TEACHER: What do you mean by that?
MARY: He means you make a prediction.
TEACHER: What's another word for "prediction?"
TOM: Hypothesis. You make a hypothesis, then go into the laboratory to see if it comes true.
TEACHER: OK. So a scientist makes a prediction or hypothesis and follows up with an experiment to see if it can be made to come true. Then what?
BILLY: That's the end!
TEACHER: (No comment for 10 seconds and then . . .) Is the laboratory like the real world?
DAVID: The scientist tries to make it like the real world, but it's much smaller, like the greenhouse pictured in our book.
TEACHER: So what must the scientist do with the findings from the experiment, if they are to be useful? (No one answers, so the teacher continues . . .) If something important happens in my experiment, wouldn't I argue that what happened could also happen in the real world?
BOBBY: You mean if it's true in a specific situation it will also be true in a more general situation?
BETTY JO: That's making a generalization.
TEACHER: Good. So we see a scientific investigation usually ends with a generalization. Let's summarize. What three things does a scientific investigation require?
CLASS: A prediction, an experiment, and a generalization.
TEACHER: Good work, class.

Can you find the teacher's soliciting, eliciting, and redirecting behaviors in this dialogue? In chapter 8 you will fully explore dialogues such as this one and learn how to produce them, but a few examples should make clear the concept of probing. Notice that all of the ingredients in this teacher's lesson were provided by the class. The concepts of hypothesis, experiment, and generalization were never defined for the class— the students defined them for themselves with only an occasional "OK" or "Good" to let the students know they were on the right track. The teacher's role was limited to eliciting clarification ("What do you mean by that?"), soliciting additional information ("What's another word for it?"), and redirection ("Is the laboratory like the real world?"). The purpose of this cycle of eliciting, soliciting, and redirection presumably was to promote inquiry, or independent discovery of the content of the lesson. Generally, *retention* of material learned has been greater from inquiry teaching than from formal lecturing methods, although consistent differences in short-term gains in achievement have not always occurred (Ryan, 1973).

Enthusiasm

Enthusiasm refers to the teacher's vigor, power, involvement, excitement, and interest during a classroom presentation. Enthusiasm can be conveyed to students in many ways; the most common include vocal inflection, gesturing, eye contact, and animation. Researchers have usually considered enthusiasm part of a larger category of behavior called **teacher affect**. This larger category includes such behaviors as use of criticism, nonverbal approval, and praise, denoting the degree to which the teacher possesses a warm, nurturing, and encouraging attitude. We have singled out the more specific behavior of enthusiasm from among these because it has been shown to be more consistently related to student achievement (Bettencourt, Gillett, Gall, & Hull, 1983; Rosenshine, 1970a) than are some other behaviors and because of its importance in promoting student engagement in the learning process.

Anyone who has ever been in a classroom in which the instructor's presentation was lifeless, static, and without vocal variety can appreciate the commonsense value of enthusiasm. Unlike the other behaviors discussed previously, however, enthusiasm cannot be fully or accurately revealed in transcripts of teaching behavior or by classroom interaction instruments. Consequently, it is believed that many research instruments often miss the enthusiasm (or lack thereof) that may be apparent in a more holistic view of the classroom. Students, however, are good perceivers of the emotions that lie beneath a teacher's actions and they often respond accordingly. A teacher who is excited about the subject being taught and shows this by facial expressions, voice inflection, gestures, and general movement, whether or not these behaviors are known or even consciously perceived by the teacher, is more likely to hold the attention of students than one who does not exhibit these behaviors. Students take their cue from such behavioral signs and either lower or heighten their engagement with the lesson accordingly. A drab and static presentation, lacking variety, questioning strategies, or use of student ideas is a sure formula for putting students to sleep mentally, if not physically. The very presence of this behavior on the part of the teacher is a message to the students that comparable behavior on their part is acceptable.

Obviously, no one can maintain a heightened state of enthusiasm for very long without becoming totally exhausted emotionally, nor is this what is meant by enthusiasm. A proper level of enthusiasm is far more subtle, and that is perhaps why it has been so difficult to research. A proper level of enthusiasm involves a delicate balance of vocal inflection, gesturing, eye contact, and movement that employs each of these behaviors in only moderate ways; *in combination*, these behaviors send a unified signal to the student of vigor, involvement, and interest. It is the use of these behaviors in moderation and at the right times that conveys the desired message. Timing and the ability to incorporate these behaviors into a consistent pattern will make possible an unspoken behavioral dialogue with students that will be every bit as important as your spoken words. Finally, not to neglect the more general category of teacher affect, letting students know that you are ready to help them by a warm and encouraging attitude is essential if your enthusiasm is to be taken as an honest and sincere expression of your true feelings.

The Need for Multiple Definitions

You may have noticed that we have used the plural when referring to *definitions* of effective teaching. The complexity inherent in finding any single definition of the effective teacher comes from the fact that there can be no *simple* definition. This does not mean that multiple definitions necessarily will contradict one another, but rather that the definition of effective teaching will need to vary according to the age of the student population (for example, elementary, junior high, or secondary), the subject matter (for example, reading versus math), and even the background characteristics of the students being taught (high socioeconomic status versus low socioeconomic status), thereby producing multiple definitions of effective teaching, each of which applies to a particular teaching context. Therein lies one of the major problems with earlier attempts to define effective teaching by describing ideal types or by describing a teacher's personality, attitude, experience, achievement, and aptitude. These attempts failed to consider or even to acknowledge that *different* teaching contexts require *different* teaching behaviors. The complexity and difficulty of learning to teach arises from the complexity of the many and varied decision-making contexts in which teaching must take place. This is why any single definition of effective teaching would be simplistic and, in time, surely would be proven false because of its insensitivity to the different learners, curricula, grade levels, and instructional materials with which teaching and learning must take place. With this admonition concerning the complexity of teaching, it is now time to weave an organized path through this complexity by emphasizing the importance of certain behaviors in several different teaching contexts.

Differences in Teaching Effectiveness Indicators Across SES and Content

In addition to the teaching behaviors that have elicited achievement across a wide variety of students and content, researchers have uncovered other behaviors of special importance to certain types of students and content. Two of the subareas of findings with the most consistent results have been in the areas of teaching low- and high-

socioeconomic status (SES) students and of teaching reading and mathematics.

Teaching Low- and High-SES Students

Although the phrase *socioeconomic status* can represent many different things, generally it is an approximate index of one's income and education level. For the classroom researcher, the SES of a student is determined by the income and education level of his or her parents or, indirectly, by the nature of the school which the student attends (some schools are located in impoverished areas in which the income and education level of the surrounding community is known to be quite low, while other schools are located in more affluent communities). Many schools in impoverished areas qualify for special financial assistance from the Federal government based upon the median income of the parents of those students who attend. These schools, called Chapter I schools, have been considered by researchers to be schools in which the majority of students come from low-SES homes. Since low- and high-SES students are facts of life that are likely to exist for some time, classroom researchers have determined what types of teacher behaviors promote the most achievement in these two types of students. Brophy and Evertson (1976), using a sample of elementary school classrooms, were among the first to provide suggestions for teaching these two types of students. Many of their suggestions have been confirmed by subsequent research as well (Good, Ebmeier, & Beckerman, 1978). A few of the most important teaching behaviors for these two groups are summarized in Table 1.3.

Notice the inclusion of some teaching behaviors that received little mention in the discussion of teaching behaviors in classrooms in which students represented the full range of SES. Teacher affect, for example, seems to be very important in low-SES classrooms as compared to middle- or high-SES classrooms. Notice also that the remaining four behaviors for low-SES classrooms (student responses, overteaching/overlearning, classroom interaction, and individualization) all can be

TABLE 1.3
Important teaching behaviors for low-SES and high-SES students

	Findings for Low-SES Pupils
Teacher Affect	Be warm and encouraging; let students know that help is available.
Student Responses	Elicit response from the student each time a question is asked before moving to the next student or question.
Overteaching/ Overlearning	Present material in small pieces, at a slow pace, with opportunity for practice.
Classroom Interaction	Stress factual knowledge. Monitor student progress. Minimize interruptions by maintaining smooth flow from one activity to another. Help student who needs help immediately.
Individualization	Supplement standard curriculum with specialized material to meet the needs of individual students.
	Findings for High-SES Pupils
Praise and Criticism	Correct poor answers immediately when student fails to perform.
Individualization	Ask difficult questions. Follow prescribed curriculum. Assign homework.
Classroom Management	Be Flexible. Let students initiate teacher-student interaction. Encourage students to reason out correct answer.
Verbal Activities	Engage students in verbal questions and answers.

Based on research by Brophy & Evertson (1976) and Good, Ehmeier, & Beckerman (1978).

seen as special ways of creating student engagement at high rates of success. This, of course, presents a particular challenge when teaching slow learners who may be inattentive and disinterested. On the other hand, behavior that may be inappropriate for low-SES students is valuable and needed in high-SES classrooms. Consistently and promptly correcting inappropriate answers, which could be demeaning and embarrassing to the low-SES student who may already have a poor self-concept, is necessary and efficient for instruction in the high-SES classroom. Also, behaviors such as being flexible and engaging students in extensive

verbal interactions, which could make classroom management and discipline with low-SES groups difficult, can be employed with success in the high-SES classroom. Because much of the research on SES has been conducted in elementary classrooms, it is as yet uncertain to what extent these teaching behaviors apply to the secondary classroom. However, many of the learning characteristics of high- and low-SES students appear to be similar across these school contexts. Therefore, your success as a teacher in a predominately low- or high-SES classroom may depend on your ability to distinguish and be able to execute the different behaviors in Table 1.3. These and other teaching practices for special types of learners will be discussed in chapter 11.

Teaching Reading and Mathematics

Another set of findings pertain to the different teaching behaviors that distinguish reading from mathematics instruction (Good & Grouws, 1979; Brophy & Evertson, 1976). While not all teachers will teach either reading or mathematics, this set of findings may be generalized with some caution to other types of content similar in form and structure to these two subject areas. For example, social studies, history, and language instruction all have high reading content and share some structural features with reading. General science, biology, physics, and chemistry are similar to the science of mathematics in that concepts, principles, and laws all play a prominent role, and visual forms and symbolic expressions are at least as important to understanding these subjects as is the written word. Therefore, some cautious generalizations may be made about the teaching behaviors important both for reading and mathematics instruction and for similar subjects.

Some of the most important of these findings have been summarized in Table 1.4. Notice the two different approaches implied by the behaviors listed. For mathematics instruction a formal, direct approach appears to be most effective. This approach includes maintaining a high degree of structure through close adherence to texts, workbooks, and programmed texts, and maximizing instructional coverage by teaching to the full class as much as possible, minimizing independent work that could diminish the amount of engaged learning time. On the other hand, reading instruction seems to allow for a more interactive and indirect approach to instruction, which utilizes classroom discussions and question-and-answer sessions more frequently than does mathematics instruction.

These approaches, however, are not mutually exclusive of each other, as the preceding paragraph seems to imply. What the research data show is that, in general and over a substantial time period, a more formal, direct instructional approach during mathematics *tends* to influence student achievement positively more than would, say, an inquiry approach. As we have seen, the reverse appears to be true for reading where an explorative, interactive approach that encourages the use of student ideas *tends* to produce better student achievement over time. An important point, however, is that the different approaches represent *degrees of emphasis* and not exclusive strategies. Clearly, at times an inquiry approach will be called for in teaching mathematics just as a lecture approach will be needed in teaching reading. More important than either of these approaches or the behaviors that represent them is the ability of the teacher to be flexible and to know when a change from one emphasis to another is necessary, regardless of the content being taught. In the next chapter there is more about the learners for whom these types of decisions must be made.

Review of Some Important Teacher Effectiveness Indicators

If all that was said in this chapter were reduced to some simple advice to a new teacher that could improve his or her teaching, the result would be a return to a simplistic and flawed definition of the effective teacher. However, if one were to ask about *some* of the indicators of teaching effectiveness that are among the most important for improving student achievement, an answer—or, more correctly, a list of answers—might be possible. The following is a list of some general indicators of effective teaching that are currently supported in the research literature. These have been put in the form of some of the most noticeable things about an effective teacher observed over an extended period of time. These indicators will be used in the chapters ahead to present specific instructional practices that will help you create them in your own teaching. The effective teacher

TABLE 1.4
Important teaching behaviors for math and reading instruction

	Findings for Reading Instruction
Instructional Activity	Devote considerable time to discussing, explaining, questioning, and stimulating cognitive processes during reading instruction.
Interactive Technique	Employ specific cues and questions that require the student to attempt a response during reading instruction.
Questions	Employ thought-provoking questions during reading instruction.

	Findings for Mathematics Instruction
Textbooks and Programmed Workbooks	Use textbooks and programmed workbooks during mathematics instruction and foster task persistence.
Instructional Content	Maximize coverage of instructional content per unit of time during mathematics instruction.
Instructional Organization	Maximize group work during mathematics instruction. Minimize independent work during mathematics instruction, especially that which may interfere with on-task behavior.

Based on research by Brophy & Evertson (1976) and Good & Grouws (1979).

takes personal responsibility for students' learning and has *high expectations*;

matches the difficulty of the lesson with the ability level of the students and *varies* the difficulty when necessary to attain moderate-to-high success rates;

gives students the *opportunity to practice* newly learned concepts and to get feedback;

maximizes instructional time to increase content coverage;

provides direction and control of student learning through *questioning, structuring, and probing*;

uses a *variety of materials and audiovisual aids* to foster use of student ideas and engagement in the learning process;

elicits responses from students each time a question is asked before moving to the next student or question (especially for low-SES);

presents material in *small pieces* at a slow pace with opportunities for *practice* (especially for low-SES);

encourages students to *reason out* the correct answer (especially for high-SES); and

engages students in *verbal questions and answers* (especially for high-SES).

Even though we have described some indicators of the effective teacher, it would be easy to gain the impression that an effective teacher simply is one who has mastered each of the key behaviors and catalysts that have been presented. Unfortunately, teaching involves more than a knowledge of how to perform individual behaviors. Much like an artist who blends color and texture into a painting to produce a coherent impression, so must the effective teacher blend together individual behaviors to form a lasting impression on his or her students. This involves the orchestration or integration of key and catalytic behaviors into meaningful patterns and rhythms that can lead to achieving the goals of instruction. The truly effective teacher knows how to execute individual behaviors with a larger purpose in mind. This larger purpose always requires placing behaviors side by side in ways that accumulate to create an effect greater than could be achieved by the execution of any single behavior or small set of behaviors. This is why teaching involves a sense of timing, sequencing, and pacing that cannot be conveyed by *any* list of behaviors. It is the behaviors that connect these behaviors *together* that are so important to the effective teacher, and it is the combination of curriculum, learning objectives, instructional materials, and learners that provides the decision-making context for the proper connection. Considerable attention will be devoted to this important decision-making context in the chapters ahead.

This chapter has presented some key and catalytic behaviors for becoming an effective teacher. These are not all of what the effective teacher is or does, but they are an important and perhaps the most valid basis for beginning to understand the effective teacher. They will form the backbone and skeleton of the effective teacher. The assembly of the remainder of this complex person, the effective teacher, will be every bit as important as the framework. As you have seen, the major teaching goals representing this framework have been lesson clarity, instructional variety, task orientation, and student engagement at moderate-to-high rates of success. Some of the more specific means of achieving these goals have included the use of student ideas, structuring, questioning, probing, and teacher enthusiasm. The remainder and most important part of the discussion must focus on those teaching practices and decisions that can help you orchestrate these component parts into forms and patterns

that will create a lasting impression on your students. This important task will be addressed in the following chapters.

Summing Up

This chapter has introduced you to the effective teacher. The main points were:

1. Early definitions of effective teaching focused primarily on a teacher's goodness as a person and only secondarily on his or her behavior in the classroom.
2. The psychological characteristics of a teacher—personality, attitude, experience, achievement, and aptitude—do not relate strongly to the teacher's behavior in the classroom.
3. Most modern definitions of effective teaching identify patterns of teacher-student interaction in the classroom that influence the cognitive and affective performance of students.
4. Classroom interaction analysis is a research methodology in which the verbal interaction patterns of teachers and students are systematically observed, recorded, and related to student performance.
5. Five key behaviors for effective teaching and some indicators pertaining to them are

   - Clarity: logical, step-by-step order, clear and audible delivery free of distracting mannerisms
   - Variety: variability in instructional materials, questioning, types of feedback, and teaching strategies
   - Task orientation: achievement (content) orientation as opposed to process orientation, maximum content coverage, and time devoted to instruction
   - Engagement: maintaining on-task behavior, limiting opportunities for distraction, getting students to work on, think through, and inquire about the content
   - Moderate-to-high success rate: 60–70% of time spent on tasks that afford moderate-to-high levels of success

6. Five catalytic behaviors for effective teaching and some indicators pertaining to them are

- Use of student ideas: acknowledging, modifying, applying, comparing, and summarizing students' statements
- Structuring: providing advance organizers at the beginning of a lesson and reinforcing the place of recently learned content in relation to other content at the end of a lesson
- Questioning: using both content (direct) and process (indirect) questions to convey facts and to encourage inquiry and problem solving
- Probing: eliciting clarification, soliciting additional information, and redirecting when needed
- Enthusiasm: exhibiting vigor, involvement, excitement, and interest during classroom presentations through vocal inflection, gesturing, eye contact, and animation

7. The key behaviors appear to be consistently effective across all or most teaching contexts.
8. Other teaching behaviors, such as use of student ideas, structuring, and questioning, may be more important with some learners and objectives than with others.
9. Effective teaching involves the orchestration and integration of key and catalytic behaviors into meaningful patterns to achieve specified goals.

For Discussion and Practice

*1. For the following, place the number *1* beside those indicators that would most likely appear in early definitions of effective teaching based on the characteristics of a "good" person; place the number *2* beside those indicators that would most likely appear in later definitions of effective teaching based on the psychological characteristics of teachers; and place the number *3* beside those indicators most likely to appear in modern definitions of effective teaching based on the interaction patterns of teachers and students.

_____

*Answers for the keyed questions (*) in this and subsequent chapters appear in Appendix B.

_____ is always on time for work
_____ is intelligent
_____ stays after class to help students
_____ works well with those in authority
_____ has plenty of experience at his or her grade level
_____ varies higher with lower order questions
_____ likes his/her job
_____ uses attention-getting devices to engage students in the learning task
_____ is open to criticism
_____ shows vitality when presenting
_____ has worked with difficult students before
_____ always allows students to experience moderate-to-high levels of success
_____ matches the class content closely with the curriculum guide

2. In your opinion, which of the following catalytic behaviors on the right would be *most* helpful in implementing the key behaviors on the left? (The catalytic behaviors may be used more than once across key behaviors, and more than a single catalytic behavior may be used for a given key behavior.) Compare your results with those of another and discuss the reasons for any differences.

Clarity _____   1. student ideas
Variety _____   2. structuring
Task orientation _____ 3. questioning
Engagement in the   4. probing
  learning task _____   5. enthusiasm
Moderate-to-high success rate _____

*3. Using Table 1.3, identify one way in which you would implement each of the following behaviors across high- and low-SES pupils.

Behavior	High-SES	Low-SES
Individualization		
Teacher affect		
Overteaching/ overlearning		
Classroom interaction		

4. Indicate which two teaching effectiveness behaviors you would emphasize if you were teaching

fifth-grade mathematics and which two you would emphasize when teaching fifth-grade reading. Justify your choices from the summary research tables in this chapter.

5. Indicate your perceived strengths in exhibiting the five key and five catalytic behaviors using the following technique described. First, notice the number assigned to each of the key behaviors.

1   clarity
2   variety
3   task orientation
4   engagement in the learning process
5   moderate-to-high rates of success

Now, for each of the following rows of numbers listed, circle the number representing the key behavior in which you perceive yourself to have the greater strength.

1 versus 2	2 versus 4
1 versus 3	2 versus 5
1 versus 4	3 versus 4
1 versus 5	3 versus 5
2 versus 3	4 versus 5

Count up how many times you circled a 1, how many times you circled a 2, a 3, etc., and place the frequencies on the following lines.

1. ____
2. ____
3. ____
4. ____
5. ____

Your perceived greatest strength is the key behavior with the highest frequency, and your perceived least strength is the key behavior with the lowest frequency. In subsequent chapters, underscore material related to your perceived least strength and note the suggested readings related to it.

6. Repeat the paired comparison technique in the same manner for the five catalytic behaviors.

1   use of student ideas
2   structuring
3   questioning
4   probing
5   enthusiasm

| 1 versus 2 | 1 versus 4 |
| 1 versus 3 | 1 versus 5 |

2 versus 3	3 versus 4
2 versus 4	3 versus 5
2 versus 5	4 versus 5

1. ____
2. ____
3. ____
4. ____
5. ____

7. Recall a particularly good teacher you had during your high-school years—and also a particularly poor one. Try to form in your mind a mental image of each one. Now rate each of them on the five key behaviors according to the following format using *1* to indicate that he or she was strong in that behavior, *2* to indicate an average performance, and *3* to indicate that he or she was weak in that behavior. Are the behavioral profiles of the two teachers different? How?

Behavior	Teacher X (good)	Teacher Y (poor)
Clarity		
Variety		
Task orientation		
Engagement in the learning process		
Moderate-to-high success rates		

8. Now do the same thing for the five catalytic behaviors using the same two teachers. Is the pattern the same? What differences in ratings, if any, do you find across key and catalytic behaviors for the same teacher? How would you account for any differences that occurred?

Suggested Readings

Anderson, L. (1987). Opportunity to learn. In M. J. Dunkin (Ed.), *International encyclopedia of teaching and teacher education.* New York: Pergamon.
A brief and authoritative introduction to the key behavior of engagement in the learning process.

Borich, G. (1979). Implications for developing teacher competencies from process-product studies. *Journal of Teacher Education, 30,* 77–86.

An article that reviews the research results of five major classroom observation studies (using classroom interaction analysis) for the purpose of identifying and summarizing effective teaching practices.

Borich, G. (1977). *The appraisal of teaching: Concepts and process.* Reading, MA: Addison-Wesley.

Illustrates the different methods and systems that can be used for evaluating the performance of inservice teachers and addresses some of the measurement issues related to conducting a valid appraisal of a teacher's performance.

Brophy, J. & Evertson, C. (1976). *Learning from teaching: A developmental perspective.* Boston: Allyn & Bacon.

A very readable summary of an extensive classroom research study that contributed much to our modern definitions of effective teaching.

Brophy, J. & Good, T. (1986). Teacher Behavior and Student Achievement. In M. C. Wittrock (Ed.), *Handbook of research on teaching: Third edition.* New York: Macmillan.

An authoritative review of the major findings of the teacher effectiveness research over the past 25 years. Due to its length and wealth of information, this article should be divided into the sections that are of most interest and read over time.

Dunkin, M. & Biddle, B. (1974). *The study of teaching.* New York: Holt, Rinehart and Winston.

An extensive and thorough book reviewing all of the relevant research on teaching effectiveness. The reader will find many easy-to-follow tables summarizing the research results for many specific teaching behaviors (e.g., clarity), which still reflect many of today's more recent findings.

Fisher, C., Berliner, D., Filby, N., Marliave, R., Cahen, L., & Dishaw, M. (1980). Teaching behaviors, academic learning time, and student achievement: An overview. In C. Denham & A. Lieberman (Eds.), *Time to learn.* Washington, DC: National Institute of Education.

A concise and readable summary of much of the important research on task orientation and engagement in the learning process.

Good, T. (1979). Teacher effectiveness in the elementary school. *Journal of Teacher Education, 30,* 52–64.

An excellent summary of effective teaching behaviors for the elementary school teacher derived from some of the most important classroom research studies of the previous decade.

Good, T. & Grouws, D. (1979). Teaching effects: A process-product study in fourth grade mathematics classrooms. *Journal of Teacher Education, 28,* 49–54.

The results of a specific classroom research study in elementary school mathematics that resulted in the identification of several key and catalytic behaviors.

Land, M. (1987). In M. J. Dunkin (Ed.), *International encyclopedia of teaching and teacher education.* New York: Pergamon.

A good overview of the dimensions of teacher clarity and the empirical support for the importance of this key behavior.

Rosenshine, B. & Stevens, R. (1986). Teaching functions. In M. C. Wittrock (Ed.), *Handbook of research on training: Third edition.* New York: Macmillan.

A succinct summary of some of the more generally applicable findings from recent research on teaching effectiveness with particular emphasis on those teaching functions related to student achievement. This article can be used as a short, partial summary of the more lengthy Brophy and Good reading.

2
Understanding Your Students

The previous chapter explained that teaching is not simply the transmission of knowledge from teacher to learner but rather is the *interaction* of teacher with learner. For this reason, effective teaching practices are always relevant to *who* is being taught and under *what* conditions (e.g., curriculum, learning objectives, instructional materials, and learners) the instruction is being provided. This idea appeared in the previous chapter: Some teaching behaviors were found to be more effective with some types of learners (high- vs. low-SES) and content (math vs. reading) than with others. This chapter discusses the decisions you will need to make about *who* you will teach, and in subsequent chapters we will consider the decisions you will need to make about *what* and *how* you will teach.

It was not so very long ago that some teachers thought of their students as blank slates onto which they were to transfer knowledge, skills, and understandings. Their task, as they perceived it, was to be skilled at transmitting to the learner appropriate grade-level content as it appeared in texts, curriculum guides, workbooks, and the academic disciplines. Students were viewed as empty vessels into which the teacher poured the contents of the day's lesson.

It does not take much imagination to see how quickly contradictions could arise from such a simplistic definition of teaching and learning. For example, such a definition cannot explain why some "bright" students get poor grades and some "dull" students get good grades; why some students want to learn while others do not even want to come to school; why some students do extra homework while others do not do any at all; or why some students have attitudes conducive to learning while others talk harshly to their peers about the value of schooling. These are just some of the individual differences existing in every classroom; they will influence the outcome of your teaching, regardless of how adept you may be at transmitting content. Your transmission of knowledge onto the blank slate will be interrupted by more than a few of these individual differences.

Becoming an effective teacher includes not only learning to be knowledgeable about content and how to teach it, but also how to adjust both content and teaching practices to the individual differences that exist among learners. Your understanding of how individual differences affect learning will determine the degree of success you achieve with your teaching objectives. This chapter contains some important facts about the psychology of learners that will be useful in gaining an understanding of, and appreciation for, the many differences in human behavior that lie within every classroom.

Why Pay Attention to Individual Differences?

Any observer in any classroom quickly notices that schoolchildren vary in intelligence, achievement, personality, interests, creativity, and self-discipline as well as in many other ways. Of what consequence is such an obvious observation to teachers? After all, they must teach all the students assigned to them regardless of the extent of the differences. There are two reasons for being aware of the individual differences among learners in a classroom. First, by knowing about and being able to recognize individual differences, a teacher may be able to match or adapt the instructional method to the individual learning needs of the students. Within the same class a teacher may be able to use different instructional approaches with different groups having different learning needs. Second, even when the use of different instructional approaches with different groups may not be possible, it is important to understand the powerful effect that individual differences can sometimes have on instructional methods. When counseling students and consulting with parents and school counselors about the achievement and competencies of those who may be having difficulty learning or be learning above expectations, a teacher must have an understanding of some of the reasons for the behavior being reported. Understanding behavior provides perspective for parents, counselors, and teachers when they wonder why Johnny is not learning, why Mary learns without studying, or why Betty does not even want to learn.

The first purpose for understanding individual differences among learners is to be able to adapt instructional methods to the needs of the learner. Information about a student's intelligence, achievement, personality, and interests, for example, may be used to select the most appropriate teaching style or method for a group of students and a given instructional objective. Researchers are beginning to discover many different content areas and individual differences where the use of different instructional strategies applied to different types of learners has significantly improved their school performance (Corno & Snow, 1986; Cronbach & Snow, 1977). For example, in one instance student-centered *discussion* sessions were found to significantly improve the achievement of highly anxious students while teacher-centered *lecture* classes significantly improved achievement among students with low anxiety (Dowaliby & Schumer, 1973). These results were accounted for by the more informal, nurturing climate accompanying the student-centered discussion, which allowed the highly anxious students to focus more intently on the content, resulting in greater learning. In contrast, the low-anxious students achieved better under the more-efficient direct lecture approach in which greater content coverage was achieved. In another popular example involving the teaching of reading, the *linguistic* approach resulted in higher vocabulary achievement for students *high* in auditory ability, while the *whole-word* approach was more effective for students *low* in auditory ability (Stallings & Keepes, 1970). Here achievement was maximized when the instructional method favored the learners' natural abilities; in this case those who learned best by seeing benefited from the whole-word approach, and the auditory approach was better for those who learned best by hearing.

The general approach to achieving a common instructional goal with learners whose prior achievement, aptitude, or learning styles differ widely is called **adaptive teaching**. Adaptive teaching techniques attempt to apply different instructional strategies to different groups of learners so that the natural diversity that prevails within the classroom does not prevent any learner from reaching the common goal. Two different approaches to adaptive teaching have been reported to be effective (Corno & Snow, 1986). The first approach is specifically to provide the needed prerequisite knowledge, skill, or behavior to those who may need it in order to benefit from the planned instruction. For example, in the first research example cited previously the teacher might first attempt to lower the anxiety of the high-anxious group, so that the lecture method could equally benefit all students. In the second example, the teacher might attempt to raise the auditory (listening) skills of those who may be deficient in them so that both groups could profit equally from the linguistic approach, which due to limitations in time and materials may be the only method available. This approach to adaptive teaching, sometimes called the **remediation approach**, will be successful to the extent the desired prerequisite information, skill, or behavior to overcome a deficiency can be taught within a reasonable period of time. Many times this is not possible or represents an inefficient use of classroom time, and a different approach to adaptive teaching must be taken.

In another approach, sometimes called the **compensatory approach**, an instructional method is chosen that attempts to circumvent or compensate for deficiencies in information, skills, or ability known to exist among learners. With this approach to adaptive teaching, the presentation of content is altered by way of alternate modalities (e.g., pictures vs. words) or by supplementing it with additional learning resources (e.g., games and simulations) and activities (e.g., group discussions, field experiences) to circumvent a fundamental weakness or deficiency. This may involve modifying the instructional technique to include the visual representation of content, using more flexible instructional presentations (e.g., films, pictures, illustrations), or shifting to alternate instructional formats (e.g., self-paced texts, simulations, experience-oriented workbooks) to compensate for known deficiencies and to utilize known strengths. For example, students who are poor at reading comprehension and lack a technical math vocabulary might be taught a unit in geometry almost exclusively by visual handouts; portraying each theorem and axiom graphically emphasizes the visual modality. Others with an adequate reading comprehension and vocabulary level might be allowed to skip this more time-consuming approach and to proceed by learning about the same theorems and axioms from a highly verbalized text, thereby emphasizing the verbal modality.

Notice that this form of adaptive teaching goes beyond the more simple process of ability grouping in which students are divided into slow and fast learners and then presented approximately the same material at different rates. Some research has suggested that differences in academic performance between high and low achievers may actually increase with the use of ability grouping; this creates a loss of self-esteem and motivation for the low group (Good & Stipek, 1983). Adaptive teaching, on the other hand, attempts to achieve the same common goal with all students, regardless of their individual differences, either by building up the knowledge, skills, or abilities required to profit from the planned instruction (remediation) or by circumventing known deficiencies by avoiding instructional methods and/or materials that require heavy use of known weaknesses (compensation). Therefore, adaptive teaching requires an understanding of the students' strongest and weakest areas and the alternate instructional methods that can be utilized to maximize their strongest learning modalities (e.g., visual vs. auditory). A menu of such strategies from which to choose is provided in the chapters ahead. It is also desirable to know some of the areas in which the use of different teaching methods, styles of presentation, and instructional materials have been differentially effective with students of different levels of intelligence, achievement, and learning styles. Some of the most promising instructional alternatives in adaptive teaching include:

High/low vividness of materials

Inductive/expository presentation

Rule-example/example-rule ordering

Inductive/deductive presentation

Teacher-centered/student-centered presentation

Structured/unstructured teaching methods

Lecture/student presentation

Group phonics/individualized phonics instruction

Presence/absence of advance organizers

Programmed/conventional instruction

Each of these teaching methods, styles of presentation, or types of materials has been shown to be more effective for some types of learners than others (Wang & Lindvall, 1984; Cronbach & Snow, 1977), which suggests their potential for adaptive teaching. Curriculum texts in your specific teaching area can help to identify the learners for whom each alternative is most effective and appropriate in terms of achieving your instructional goals.

While the research literature offers many examples of specific content areas in which a particular instructional method in association with a particular student characteristic has enhanced student performance, common sense and classroom experience will suggest many other ways in which teaching can be altered to fit the individual learning needs of students. The point here is that by knowing the students and having a variety of instructional methods available, instruction can be adjusted to learning needs with one of these two methods of adaptive teaching. This calls, however, for a commitment to the belief that there may be no single, best method of teaching that is equally successful with all students. The effective teacher strives to understand the aptitude, achievement, and learning styles of each student in order to choose teaching approaches that are adapted to the learning characteristics of the class members. This chapter contains some of the important aptitude, achievement, personality, peer, and family characteristics

of your students that can affect both their learning and your teaching.

The Effects of General Intelligence on Learning

One of the things everyone remembers about elementary school is how some students seemed to learn so easily, while others had to work so hard. In high school there was an even greater range of "smartness." In a practical sense, we associate the terms *smart; bright; ability to solve problems, learn quickly, and figure things out* with intelligence. Both in the classroom and in life it is obvious that some have more intelligence than others. This observation often has been a source of anxiety, concern, and jealousy among learners. Perhaps because the topic of intelligence can so easily elicit emotions like these, it is the most talked about and least understood aspect of student behavior.

One of the greatest misunderstandings that teachers, parents, and school administrators can have about intelligence is that it is a single, unified dimension. Such a belief is often expressed by the use of word pairs such as *slow/fast, smart/dumb, bright/dull* when referring to different kinds of learners. These phrases indicate that a student is *either* fast *or* slow, bright *or* dull, smart *or* dumb, when, in fact, each of us (regardless of our intelligence) is all of these at one time or another. In other words, on a particular task of a certain nature one may appear to be "slow and dull," but given another task requiring different abilities, that same person may be "fast and bright." How do such vast differences occur within a single individual?

Everyone knows from personal experience in school, hobbies, sports, and interpersonal relationships that degree of intelligence depends on the *circumstances* and *conditions* under which the intelligence is exhibited. Observations such as these have led researchers to study and identify more than one kind of intelligence. This relatively new way of looking at intelligence has led to a better understanding of such contradictions as why Johnny is good in vocabulary but not in mathematics, why Mary is generally good in social studies but specifically bad at reading maps, or why Betty is good at analyzing the reasons behind historical events but poor at memorizing the names and dates that go along with them. Each of these seemingly contradictory behaviors can be explained by the special abilities required by each task. It is these special abilities, on which we all differ, that are the most useful for understanding the learning behavior of students.

There are some controversial issues pertaining to the use of general intelligence tests in schools that you should be aware of when discussing the notion of "intelligence" with parents, other teachers, and school administrators. These issues often strongly divide individuals into two camps. One of these camps represents what has been called the **environmentalist position**. This group criticizes the use of general IQ tests in the schools in the belief that they are culturally biased. This is to say, they believe that differences in IQ scores among groups, such as blacks, Hispanics, and whites, can be attributed largely to social class or environmental differences. They reason that some groups of students, particularly minority students, may come from impoverished home environments in which the verbal skills generally required to do well on intelligence tests are not practiced, and so a significant part of minority students' scores on any IQ test represents the environment in which they grew up and not their true intelligence. They have concluded, and some research has supported this point of view, that the effects of home environment is at least as important as heredity in contributing to one's IQ (Bloom, 1981; Smilansky, 1979). This group believes that intelligence tests are biased in favor of the white middle class who tend to provide their children with more intense patterns of verbal interaction, greater reinforcement for learning, more learning resources, and better physical health during the critical preschool years in which cognitive growth is the fastest.

A second camp has taken what is now called the **hereditarian position**. These individuals, bas-

ing their beliefs on the research and writings of Arthur Jensen (1969), have concluded that heredity rather than environment is the major factor determining intelligence. This group believes that not all children have the same potential for developing the same mental abilities. They contend that programs, such as compensatory education programs that attempt to make up for environmental disadvantages in the early elementary grades through remediation, can have only limited success since the origin of the difference is genetic and not environmental.

Common sense tells us that there is some truth in *both* arguments. However, despite how parents, fellow teachers, and even your own students may feel about them, these issues are highly dependent on the notion of general intelligence and tend to become less relevant in the context of specific abilities. General intelligence tests are not very predictive of anything other than school grades, whereas specific abilities tend to predict not only school grades but also the more important real-life behaviors that school grades are supposed to represent. Tests of general intelligence do not, for example, predict success as a salesman, factory worker, carpenter, or teacher, because they measure few of the abilities that are required to be successful in these occupations. Specific and not general abilities are ultimately responsible for one's success in the real world, so the use of general intelligence test scores for planning instruction, selecting classroom groups, and counseling students and parents about performance deficiencies is not constructive. Knowing your learners' *specific* strengths and weaknesses and altering your instructional goals and activities accordingly will contribute far more to your effective teaching than will categorizing your students' performances in ways that indicate only their *general* intelligence.

The Effects of Specific Abilities on Learning

So far, the role of general intelligence in learning has been discussed and reference made to the value of more specific definitions of intelligence. Such specific definitions and the behaviors they represent are commonly called **aptitudes** or **factors**. As a teacher you are not likely to need to measure these aptitudes in your classroom, but you will need to know that they exist and what their role is in influencing the performance of your students. In some cases students will have already been tested in these areas as part of a larger testing program; in others, the counselor or school psychologist can be requested to measure a specialized aptitude to find the source of a specific learning problem. A general acquaintance with the division of general intelligence into specific aptitudes helps to show how a learner's abilities in specific areas can directly affect the degree of learning that takes place.

Some of the many specialized abilities that have been reliably measured include *verbal comprehension, general reasoning, memory, use of numbers, psychomotor speed, spatial relations,* and *word fluency.* This list of abilities is the result of the work of L. L. Thurstone (1947). Instead of reinforcing the idea of a single IQ score, Thurstone's work led to the development of seven different IQs, each measured by a separate test. In this manner the concept of general intelligence was factored into component parts; it had the obvious advantage that a specific score for a given factor could be related to certain types of learning requirements. Some learning activities require a high degree of memory, such as memorizing long lists of words in preparation for a spelling bee or a vocabulary test. Likewise, spatial relations, use of numbers, and general reasoning ability are essential for high levels of performance in mathematics. Such differences in aptitude become far more useful than general intelligence in explaining to parents why Johnny can get excellent scores on math tests that emphasize number problems ($12 + 2 \times 6 =$) but poor scores on math tests that emphasize word problems (If Bob rows 4 mph against a current flowing 2 mph, how long will it take him to row 16 miles?). Such apparent contradictions become more understandable in light of specific aptitudes.

While Thurstone's dimensions are among the earliest, many others have taken his aptitudes and found still more specific components within them. For example, some content specialists in the field of reading refer to no less than nine verbal comprehension factors indicating ability to do the following:

Know word meanings

See contextual meaning

See organization

Follow thought patterns

Find specifics

Express ideas

Draw inferences

Identify literary devices

Determine a writer's purpose

In other words, a learner's general performance in reading may be affected by any one or a combination of these specific abilities. This list and others like it point up one of the most interesting and controversial aspects of the movement to identify specific aptitudes underlying general intelligence. That is, once aptitudes such as memory, use of numbers, reasoning, verbal comprehension, etc. are defined by their underlying factors, would it not be possible to teach these so-called components of intelligence? It is believed that intelligence is not teachable (or so the hereditarians say), but it seems logical that with proper instruction a learner could be taught to draw inferences, find specifics, and determine a writer's purpose. As the general components of intelligence, such as those defined by Thurstone, become divided into smaller and more specific aptitudes, the general concept of intelligence becomes "demystified"; at least some elements of intelligence are dependent on achievement in certain areas that can be influenced by instruction. Therefore, an added advantage of a multidimensional approach to intelligence is that some specific deficiences once thought to be unalterable can be remedied by instruction.

One of the most recent conceptions of specialized abilities comes from the work of Sternberg (1986). He has been one of the leading proponents of the belief that intelligence, when defined by its underlying components, can be altered through instruction. Sternberg's work has been seminal in forming new definitions of intelligence that allow for intellectual traits, previously believed inherited and unalterable, to be improved through instruction. In short, Sternberg suggests not only that intelligence can be taught but also that the classroom is the logical place to teach it. Look more closely at the theory from which this rather fascinating claim is made.

Sternberg's theory of intelligence is called *triarchic* because it consists of three parts. The first part relates to the individual's internal world that governs thinking. This part of his theory specifies that three kinds of mental processes go on in one's head, processes that are instrumental in planning what things to do, how to learn to do them, and how to actually perform or show intelligence. The first of these three processes is used in planning, monitoring, and evaluating performance of a task. This, in essence, is an "executive" or meta component that tells all other components of our intelligence what to do, just as the boss in a factory keeps things running smoothly by giving directions and orders but who personally does none of the work. Hence, this component's role is purely administrative.

A second component of the internal world of intelligence governs behavior in the actual execution or performance of a task. This component controls the various strategies used in solving problems by, for example, guiding one to the most relevant details of a problem and steering one away from those that are irrelevant. Thus, individuals can become more or less intelligent by learning what details to attend to and which to ignore.

A third component of this internal world of intelligence governs what previously acquired knowledge we bring to a problem. It is here that Sternberg's theory differs most from other concepts of intelligence: Skills involving memory, manipulating symbols, or mental speed are not seen as particularly important to one's intelligence. Instead, it is the previously acquired knowledge that one brings to a problem-solving setting that is more important to thinking intelligently than are these more innate and less alterable characteristics. Sternberg points out that one of the biggest differences found between so-called "experts" and "nonexperts" in the real world is not the mental processes that experts use in performing a task but the previously acquired knowledge they bring to it. The task in explaining intelligence or "expertness," then, is to understand how experts acquire needed information when nonexperts seemingly fail to acquire it.

This notion leads to the second part of Sternberg's triarchic theory. This part specifies at what point in a person's experience intelligence or expertise is most easily acquired. Here, Sternberg proposes that intelligence is the ability to learn and to think with conceptual systems that can be brought to bear upon already existing knowledge. With respect to this point, Sternberg suggests that the opportunity to confront and to learn to deal with novel tasks and situations is one of the most important instructional goals in the learning of intelligent behavior. Sternberg's writings provide many practical exercises and examples of how one can become facile at adapting to, and learning to deal with, novel tasks and situations.

The third part of Sternberg's theory relates intelligence to the external world of the individual. This is where an individual's intelligence can show the most and be altered the quickest. This part of intelligence is governed by how well a person learns to adapt to the environment (e.g., change his or her way of doing things to fit the world), select from the environment (avoid unfamiliar things and choose familiar and comfortable ones), and to shape the environment (change the things in the environment to fit a personal style or way of doing things). Thus, "intelligent" people *learn* to adapt, select, and shape better and more quickly than do "less intelligent" people. Therefore, perhaps the most important aspect of Sternberg's theory is that intelligence is as much a result of how people learn to cope with the world around them as it is a result of the internal mental processes (e.g., memory, symbol manipulation, mental speed) with which they are born.

This notion of coping is never stated more obviously than in 20 characteristics that Sternberg suggests are often impediments to intelligent behavior and, therefore, are often found in the "unintelligent" or the "nonexpert." These are

- Lack of motivation
- Lack of impulse control
- Lack of perserverance and perseveration
- Using the wrong abilities
- Inability to translate thought into action
- Lack of a product orientation
- Inability to complete tasks and to follow through
- Failure to initiate
- Fear of failure
- Procrastination
- Misattribution of blame
- Excessive self-pity
- Excessive dependency
- Wallowing in personal difficulties
- Distractibility and lack of concentration
- Spreading oneself too thin
- Inability to delay gratification
- Inability or unwillingness to see the forest for the trees
- Lack of balance between critical thinking and creative thinking
- Too little or too much self-confidence

From these 20 impediments to intelligent thinking, it should be easy to see why Sternberg believes many aspects of intelligence can and should be taught and why the classroom may be a logical place to convey the attitudes and behaviors that can help learners avoid impediments to intelligent behavior.

The Effects of Prior Achievement on Learning

Closely related to Sternberg's notion of intelligence is the task-relevant prior knowledge and skills of your learners. The phrase *task relevant* emphasizes those facts, skills, and understandings that must be taught if subsequent learning is to occur. Mastery of these behaviors makes possible future learning, so their identification is important not only in planning instruction but also in accounting for why in some situations and for some students learning did not occur. These task-relevant facts, skills, and understandings can sometimes affect learning outcomes even more than do specific behavioral characteristics, such as Sternberg's 20 impediments. These impediments are more conducive to instruction and remediation than are deficiencies in aptitude because they represent the facts, skills, and understandings both of past instruction and those that can be incorporated into future instruction.

Previously taught task-relevant behaviors come in various "shapes" and "sizes." In each content area they will be part of the logical progression of ideas with which a lesson is conveyed. For example, a general-to-detailed, simple-to-complex, abstract-to-concrete, or conceptual-to-procedural order of reasoning may be used. These logical progressions represent a planned structure that identifies at each step of the process the behaviors needed before new learning can take place (e.g., the procedures must come before the concepts, the simple facts before the complex details). In chapters 6 and 7 there will be more about the many possible logical progressions with which teaching can be structured, but for now it is important to appreciate that many task-relevant prior learnings, on which the final outcomes of a lesson or unit will depend, are embedded within these progressions.

This point is illustrated in Figures 2.1 and 2.2 both for an instructional unit on government and for another on writing skills. Regardless of the type of progression that may apply in a specific instance, notice that a breakdown in the flow of learning at almost any point in these progressions will prevent learning from taking place at any subsequent point. Failure to attain concepts at higher levels in the instructional plan, therefore, may not indicate a lack of ability or specialized aptitude but a failure to adequately grasp *task-relevant prior behaviors*. In chapter 5 is a discussion of planning

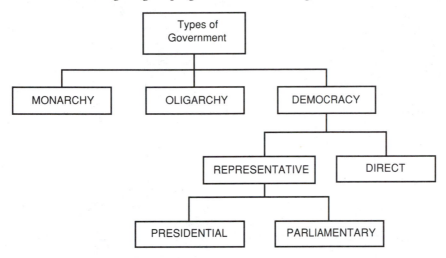

instructional units utilizing a number of different types of "learning structures."

The Effects of Home and Family on Learning

It is well known that there is a close relationship between social class and educational achieve-ment. The effect of one's SES on achievement has been so pronounced in some instances as to lead to the identification of different teaching behaviors for high- and low-SES students; this was noted in chapter 1 (Brophy & Evertson, 1976; Good, Ebmeier, & Beckerman, 1978). Tradition-ally, students from lower class and lower middle-class families have not performed as well on stan-dardized tests of achievement as have students

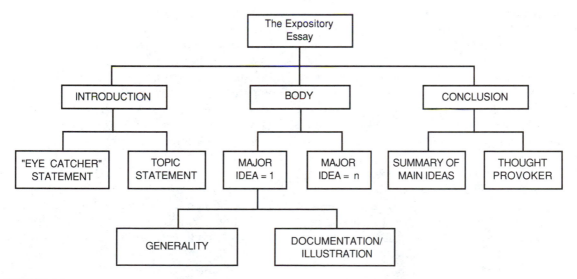

FIGURE 2.2
Organization of content indicating a logical progression for a unit on writing skills

from middle- and upper class families (Levine, 1979). Some of this difference is related to possible differences in the IQ test scores of these groups. However, differences in IQ scores that are unrelated to occupational success is one thing, and differences in the achievement of basic skills in language and mathematics is quite another. These latter differences are so pertinent to success that they immediately become cause for concern. In this regard observers have noted the close relationship among social class, race/ethnicity, and school achievement (National Center for Education Statistics, 1980). Their studies have concluded that, in general, most of the differences in educational achievement that occur by race and ethnicity can be accounted for by social class, *even after the lower socioeconomic status of minority groups are taken into account* (Levine & Havinghurst, 1984). That is, if one knows the socioeconomic status of a group of students, one can predict their achievement with reasonable accuracy. Information about their racial and ethnic group does little to improve the prediction. This indicates the powerful effect social class can have upon the behavior of students in your class. You will see in chapters 9 and 10 that this effect can extend to the affective and emotional makeup of your students as well as to their cognitive achievement.

It is now appropriate to ask "What is it about one's socioeconomic status that creates such large and important differences in the classroom?" and "What can any teacher do to lessen these differences?" Obviously, socioeconomic status—or SES—must stand for something more specific than simply income and education level of students' parents if it is to play such an influential role in student achievement. Researchers have found that associated with income and education level are a number of more meaningful characteristics in which the home and family lives of high- and low-SES families differ. It is these characteristics, an indirect result of income and education, that are thought to influence the achievement of schoolchildren.

One important characteristic that seems to distinguish lower from middle- and upper class children is that the latter are more likely to acquire knowledge of the world outside their home and neighborhood (Hunt, 1979). Through greater access to books, magazines, social networks, and cultural events, and other families that use and value these as learning resources, middle- and upper class students are able to develop their reading and speaking abilities more rapidly. This, in combination with parental teaching (which tends to utilize the formal or elaborated language that trains the child to think independently of the specific communication context), may give the middle- and upper class student an advantage at the start of school. This is in contrast to children who come from lower class homes and whose values and attitudes may emphasize obedience and conformity rather than independent thinking. Researchers who have studied low-SES families report that, generally, they are more likely than middle- and high-SES families to emphasize physical punishment rather than reasoning and to encourage rote learning (memorization, recall of facts, etc.) rather than independent, self-directed learning (Newson & Newson, 1976).

The classroom is the logical place to begin the process of reducing some of the achievement differences that have been noted between lower SES and middle- and upper SES students. Many formal types of interventions from preschools to federally funded compensatory education programs are continuing to reduce the differences. However, these programs and interventions have not made and are not likely to make a major impact on achievement differences among various groups of students with highly divergent home and family life-styles. This leaves the classroom teacher to deal with these differences as a daily fact of life. It is true that the difficulty of planning instruction in the midst of these differences can be overstated, because differences *within* the family behavior of low-SES students sometimes can actually be greater than *between* low- and middle-SES families. However, even admitting that the variation in behavior within a group may sometimes exceed the variability between groups, the general tendencies are clear: The home and family backgrounds of lower and higher SES students differentially prepare them for school. For the effective teacher the task becomes one of planning instruction around these differences in ways that reduce the differences as much as possible.

This will mean various things in various classrooms depending upon the nature of the differences. However, regardless of classroom content and grade level, several important attitudes will make the differences more open to influence by an instructional approach. One of these attitudes is a willingness to incorporate a variety of audiovisual aids and exploratory materials into your lesson, requiring alternative modalities of your students (e.g., sight vs. sound). These could be planned as part of a lesson or as supplementary materials for those who may need alternative ways of seeing the content presented.

Having high expectations and rewarding for intellectual accomplishments—behaviors generally not found in lower SES homes—can be another attitude for reducing achievement differences due to social class. The teacher's role in providing support and encouragement could be instrumental in getting students to realize someone cares about their achievements.

Also, providing opportunities for enlarging students' vocabularies and quality of language through newspapers, periodicals, and popular books can be helpful. In some cases the classroom will be the only place where students can come in contact with these language sources. Emphasizing correct word usage and correcting incorrect linquistic patterns, while respecting the learner's dialect or street language, can also help reduce differences in the verbal performance of students. Correcting without criticizing or embarrassing a student is an art, but one for which there is no substitute in a classroom with diverse language differences. Curriculum specialists generally agree that alternative linguistic forms such as street language and dialects can be used effectively as an intermediate or transitional device for moving students to standard English (Green, 1983).

Finally, the effective teacher has an attitude that seeks opportunities for getting lower SES students to talk about their experiences. One of the most significant differences among students coming from different social classes is that lower SES students have poorer self-concepts than do higher SES students. Getting a student to talk about personal experiences and using these to help attain instructional goals has the double effect of engaging the student's cooperation and interest while showing the students that someone thinks they have something worthwhile to say.

Each of these attitudes, rather than having the lofty goal of changing students' behavior, has the more realistic goal of getting your students ready to learn. Perhaps the most beneficial attitude of all is recognizing that, while no single teacher can remove the powerful influences of family and home life, creating a readiness to learn is the first step in reducing achievement differences attributable to social class.

The Effects of Personality on Learning

In preceding sections were discussed the potential influence on learning of students' general intelligence, specific aptitude, task-relevant prior achievement, and home life. In this section students' personality will be added to this equation.

When words such as *trustworthy, creative, independent, anxious, cheerful, authoritarian,* or *aggressive* are used to describe a student, they refer to an aspect of that student's personality. **Personality** is the integration of all of a person's traits, motives, beliefs, and abilities, including emotional responses, character, and even morals. The notion of personality is indeed broad and, according to some authors, even subsumes intelligence and specialized abilities. It is not necessary to take quite so broad a view of personality in this section, because not all of what is considered to be a part of personality is equally applicable to classroom learning. On the other hand, several aspects of personality are so important that it is difficult to imagine that learning can take place without them. These aspects of personality are sometimes called **traits.**

Traits are considered to represent enduring aspects of a person's behavior that are consistent across a wide variety of settings. Traits are not specific to subject matter content, grade level, or instructional objectives as is the case for aptitude and achievement. This is not to say, however, that variation in content, grade levels, and objectives is unimportant to personality, since many things within an environment, such as a classroom, can trigger some personality traits and not others. In other words, some parts of personalities lie dormant until stimulated to action by some particular perception of the world. This is the reason teachers so often are dismayed to hear, for example, that an aggressive and verbally abusive child in fifth-period social studies is shy and cooperative in someone else's seventh-period mathematics. It also is the reason that some students and teachers may never quite see eye to eye. Fortunately, such personality conflicts are rare; nevertheless, they can be devastating to classroom rapport if left to smolder beneath the surface.

It is believed by some psychologists that different aspects of personality can be dominant at certain periods of our lives. For example, Erikson (1968), who developed a theory on how we form our personalities, hypothesized eight different stages of personality growth, called "crises," between infancy and old age. Three of these stages occur during the school years: The crisis of accomplishment versus inferiority, which occurs sometime during the elementary school years; the crisis of identity versus confusion, which occurs sometime during the adolescent or high-school years; and the crisis of intimacy versus isolation, which occurs in early adulthood.

During this first crisis the student seeks ways of producing products or accomplishments that are respected by others. In this manner the child creates for himself or herself a feeling of worth to dispel feelings of inferiority or inadequacy resulting from living in an adult world. At first such accomplishments may take the easiest course—being good at sports, being good in school, or being helpful at home. For the teacher this is a particularly challenging time, because

student engagement at high rates of success is needed to keep at least some feelings of worth focused in the classroom. Seeing that every student has some successful experiences in the classroom in ways that do not permanently create feelings of ineptness about their ability to perform in school can be an important vehicle for helping students through this crisis.

Erikson's second crisis during the school years is precipitated by the student's need to come to an understanding of self—to find his or her identity, the "real me." One's sex, race, ethnicity, religion, and physical attractiveness can play an important role in producing or failing to produce a consistent and acceptable self-image. This is a process of accepting oneself as one truly is apart from illusions, "make-up," and exaggerations. The process can be painstakingly slow as illusions are stripped away and replaced by realistic conceptions formed by cruel experiences with the real world. Remember the girl or boy who spurned your affections and the hours you spent wondering why? The importance of this stage or crisis for the teacher is to realize that extreme and rapid fluctuations in a student's behavior may be a signal that this turbulent process is taking place. During this crisis students sometimes try out different personalities, taking on all the accoutrements of a particular persona (for example, the "jock," "preppie," "socialite," "Casanova," "model," "tough guy," "feminist"). A strict task orientation can aid in reducing, or at least controlling, the emotional temperature of a classroom, which may look during these times more like the fictitious quality of a movie set than a place for learning. The effective teacher not only understands and has empathy with the conflicting emotions of students at this stage, but also provides the structure and realism needed to help resolve the crisis.

Erikson's third crisis during the school years is that of giving up part of one's own identity in order to develop close and intimate relationships with others. While this stage may for some occur after the high-school years, for most it has its roots there. Forming relationships, especially with the opposite sex, may be one of the most important and traumatic experiences of school. For some students it may represent the only reason for coming to school. It is not unusual for students during this crisis to form emotional relationships with their teachers as well, especially when relationships with their peers are thwarted due to differences in maturity, attractiveness, interests, or even physical size. There are no simple ways to deal with these emotions other than to be aware of them at the time they occur and attempt to both cushion their impact on the student and to channel them into more productive avenues.

Important in all three of the crises will be personality differences due to the anxiety, motivation, and self-concept of the students. Hardly a day goes by when differences from these sources are not observed. Researchers have confirmed the significant influence of each of these three characteristics on learning, their close relationship to one another, and differences among them across social classes.

Anxiety is something that everyone finds uncomfortable, if only because of its debilitating effect on one's ability to get things done. Anxiety about something causes even the simplest of tasks to seem difficult. One feels threatened, fearful of the unknown, and generally tense. Without being consciously aware of it, you have noticed among your acquaintances and perhaps even within yourself at least two types of anxiety. One of these types is an experience of fear or threat related to a particular environmental situation. Very common among these is the anxiety felt before taking a test. This type of anxiety, called **state anxiety** (Spielberger, 1966), represents a condition or state that is *momentary* and produced by some specific stimulus in the environment (e.g., a test, a report card, a speech before the class, a first date). Although levels of state anxiety vary among students as a result of different environmental stimuli, given the right stimulus it can occur at almost any time. There is, however, a positive side to state anxiety: Some state anxiety is a necessary condition for learning. Without some fear of the harmful conditions which could result from a poorly executed lab experiment, Johnny may not be cautious enough to avoid the danger. Without fearing the

negative consequences of a failing grade, Mary may not do the extra preparation required for a passing grade. Without fear of doing poorly in front of his peers, Billy may not organize his speech sufficiently to do well. Therefore, some state anxiety is important to instructional goals. Devices such as grades, report cards, and assignments are generally sufficient to provide the level of state anxiety necessary to motivate one to respond properly.

There is danger in an extreme response to state anxiety. This sometimes occurs when devices such as grades, report cards, and assignments are perceived by students as being more significant than they are, thus unintentionally producing high levels of anxiety. In these instances anxiety levels can reach extremes and the student becomes almost completely immobilized by fear of failure. For example, a student may believe that a "C" on an exam will prevent him or her from entering college, or that doing poorly on a speech will prevent a career requiring oratory ability, or that failing an assignment is a prelude to failing the course. In such instances students perceive the stimulus out of its proper context, the consequences of which can lead to responses such as studying to exhaustion, skipping class the day of the traumatic event, or plagiarizing an assignment.

To prevent extreme levels of state anxiety, the effective teacher communicates clearly and directly the exact value to be placed upon the test, product, or assignment *before* it is given. It is desirable always to provide a variety of tests and assignments for the explicit purpose of creating as large a total context as possible; then any *single* test, product, or assignment is a relatively small part of the total. Reducing the tendency to exaggerate the significance of any single outcome helps to lower state anxiety.

A second type of anxiety found among some students is a general disposition to feel threatened by a wide range of conditions perceived to be harmful. This type of anxiety has been labeled **trait anxiety**, indicating its stability over time. No single stimulus, such as a grade or assignment, can be identified as the source of the anxiety, which results instead from many ill-defined sources. Unlike state anxiety, which all students experience to some degree, this type of anxiety tends *not* to fluctuate within individuals but is found in different amounts from person to person. In other words, this type of anxiety is a fairly stable characteristic of one's personality, with different individuals having different amounts of it.

High levels of trait anxiety seem to go with high motivation and the need to achieve. But, like state anxiety, extremely high levels can be immobilizing, especially when the need to achieve is guided more by a fear of failure (e.g., shame, ridicule by peers, punishment from parents) rather than by a wish to do well. When fear of failure is the primary motive among high-anxious students, more assignments may be completed with more accuracy, but they will be completed in a mechanical, perfunctory way allowing for little more than the most obvious and expected learning outcomes. Research has shown that when motivation to do well among high-anxious students is guided more by a desire to do well (e.g., to "produce a perfect product," "create the spectacular," "gain the respect of others," "tackle the impossible") rather than by a fear of failure, more work is accomplished toward a given end in less time *and* in ways that engage students in discovery types of learning experiences resulting in more creative outcomes (Weiner, 1972).

This suggests that the effective teacher needs to control the learning conditions of high-anxious students. High *state* anxiety requires careful instructions, practice test sessions, and information about the larger context to help lower the anxiety to a point in which it can work for, not against, the student. In the case of high levels of *trait* anxiety, conveying a feeling of warmth, encouragement, and support prior to the assignment can turn fears of failure into more productive motives involving a desire to do well. Structuring the assignment in ways that provide for a *range of acceptable responses* serves to focus the high-anxious student on an obtainable end product and away from general fears of being unable to attain an acceptable level of performance.

A third aspect of personality relevant to Erikson's three crises is that of self-concept, which grows out of interactions with significant others such as parents, teachers, and peers during the course of growing up. These significant others act as mirrors for our behavior. That is, they reflect back the images people create of themselves, sometimes in modified and revised form. When the image that is returned looks good, is acceptable to others, and is consistent with what one wants it to be, a positive self-concept is formed. When the image that is reflected back does not look good, is unacceptable to others, and is inconsistent with beliefs about self, a less favorable self-concept is formed.

The formation of self-concept is perhaps one of the most fascinating aspects of personality. It has captured the attention of many psychologists and researchers who only recently have begun to study the relationship of self-concept to student achievement. While the research thus far is sketchy and focuses only on certain grades and subjects, there are some indications that a positive self-concept may be related to better achievement. For example, a strong relationship was found between poor self-concept and reading disability in the third grade (Bodwin, 1957), and a moderate relationship between self-concept and achievement in the seventh grade (Brookover, Paterson, & Thomas, 1962). The most recent reviews of the self-concept literature generally report modest but consistent relationships to school achievement (Hansford & Hattie, 1982; Kash & Borich, 1978). This research, while not always resulting in impressive relationships between self-concept and achievement, has nevertheless been taken as an encouraging sign that a student's concept of self can affect the extent to which he or she *becomes actively engaged in the process of learning,* even if it is not always strongly related to scores on tests of academic performance.

Whether in studies like those cited previously a positive self-concept influences achievement or whether high levels of achievement tend to create a positive self-concept is not known. However, the intuitive value of having a positive concept of self is so pervasive in our culture that the order of the relationship may not be all that important. An increase in self-concept is believed to have positive results on behavior, either directly on school achievement or indirectly on one's ability to relate to others, to cope with the problems of daily life, and ultimately to be successful in a career or occupation. Such important outcomes are not measured by tests of academic achievement, although performance on school tests might well be a source of raising the self-concept; this, in turn, could influence these important outcomes. This is reason enough for engaging students in the learning process at moderate-to-high rates of success: to provide a mirror with a positive image. It is also one reason why high rates of success are so important to low-SES students, since it is these students who have been found to have the lowest self-concepts and whose home life provides few opportunities for raising them.

The crucial question asked by every student in the process of forming a self-concept is "How am I being perceived?" The answer to this question lies in the student's self-image and impact on significant others in the environment. In the school environment this reflected self-image is derived most often from direct, personal interaction with you, the teacher. As a teacher it is your task to be sensitive to, and to understand, the impact of the images being reflected back by your words and deeds. Clearly, you will not always want to reflect back what your students believe about themselves. On the other hand, any image that is sent back by interactions and performance evaluations should take into consideration that your message may have implications far beyond the specific time and place in which the message is delivered. Often, it may contribute to the ever-growing complement of data which is being used by your students in forming the self-concept they will "wear" for years to come.

Finally, it is not a question of *whether* but of *how* a teacher influences the self-concept of students. You will have this influence, at least for some students, whether you know it or not. Thus,

it is the *quality* of your performance in this role that counts. Good performance on your part begins with your awareness of your own self-concept and its influential role in the formation of your students' self-concept. A teacher's positive concept of self will encourage good self-concepts in students if the teacher allows a warm and encouraging attitude to come through in words and actions. It continues with the realization that students are alike in some respects, like other students in other respects, and unique in still other respects. The effective teacher's performance as a significant other is always guided by a belief in the inherent value of the unique talents and contributions of each individual student. The secret to improving students' self-concepts lies in the process of finding and reflecting back to students the value of their unique talents.

The Effects of the Peer Group on Learning

One of the most powerful but least noted influences on a student's behavior is the peer group. Often considered as the source of a "hidden curriculum," the peer group can influence and even teach how to behave in class, study for tests, converse with teachers and school administrators, and can contribute to the success or failure of an individual's performance in school in many other ways. From the play group in the elementary school to the teenage clique in high school, a student learns from peers how to behave in ways that will be acceptable and that will establish status in the eyes of others.

The power of the peer group in influencing individual student behavior stems from the fact that it is the *voluntary* submission of one's will to some larger cause. While teachers and parents must beg, plead, punish, reward, and cajole to exact the behavior deemed appropriate from their students, sons, and daughters, peer groups need not engage in any of these behaviors to obtain a high level of conformity to often unstated and abstract principles of behavior. Trendy school fashions, new slang words, places to "hang out," acceptable social mates, and respected forms of out-of-school activities are communicated and learned to perfection without lesson plans, texts, or even direct verbalization. Instead, these and other behaviors are transmitted by willing "expressors" and received indirectly by "receptors" who anxiously wish to maintain membership in or gain acceptance to a particular peer group. The power of the peer group to influence the behavior of others was underscored in a survey by John Goodlad in 1984 that was directed to more than 17,000 junior and senior high students in 1000 classrooms across the United States. In Goodlad's survey each student was asked "What is the *one* best thing about this school?" The most frequent response, "my friends," was mentioned more than twice as frequently as any other response, with teachers being mentioned least often.

Friendship patterns are often created through peer groups and sometimes are adhered to with strong commitments of loyalty, protection, and mutual benefit. These commitments create individual peer cultures within a school, cultures that can rival the academic commitments that are made in the classroom and frequently supercede them in importance; studying for a test or completing homework may be sacrificed for the benefit of the peer group. While peer groups can be formed on the basis of many different individual differences—such as intelligence, achievement, personality, home life, physical appearance, and personal and social interests—they commonly are a result of complex combinations of these which are not always discernable to outsiders and sometimes not even to those within the peer group (Epstein & Karweit, 1983). The importance of peer-group characteristics in the classroom lies with the extent to which they can create, promote, and reinforce behaviors that are disruptive to teaching objectives. More specifically, to what extent can the hidden rules, regulations, and rituals often required by a peer group curtail a member's interest in and engagement with the learning process?

Although some peer groups can, and indeed do, create pressure on their members to con-

form to either a passive or a "troublemaker" role in the classroom, they also can promote an increased activity in the learning process. When intelligence, a high need to achieve, and acceptance of responsibility are the basis of a peer group, it well may promote sharp competition and a conformity among its members to achieve in accord with the highest academic standards. Membership in the National Honor Society, ambition to enroll in certain prestigious colleges, and a desire to pursue professional careers are sometimes the "glue" that holds such peer groups together. However, combinations of individual differences can also come together to promote passive learners in which the bare minimum of effort is the desired standard—nothing extra is ever offered or volunteered—or to promote troublemakers whose behavior that can disrupt, intimidate, and provoke is reinforced and may be accorded a special tribute by peer-group members (Lightfoot, 1983). This latter type, contrary to the passive learner who simply is not motivated or successful in school, actually fights against the conformity and routine demands of the classroom by waging a surreptitious war in which all authority figures become targets.

Even though teachers can have little influence in the formation of peer groups, particularly of the troublemaking type, there are several activities that can help dissipate their influence in the classroom. One approach is to rearrange potentially disruptive peer groups into more heterogeneous groups in terms of characteristics and interests, perhaps by arranging with the school counselor to send some members to other classes in return for an equal number of students. Another approach is to divide peer-group members among *other* peer groups within your own classroom. Such a division could be part of a process in which different subgroups are assigned different activities or in which potentially disruptive peer-group members are assigned to different parts of the classroom. In addition, stressing group work in which the groups comprise members from different peer groups can create a dampening of disruptive behavior, especially when equal numbers of learners who are actively engaged in the learning process are assigned to the disruptive group. When different types of individuals are assigned to work cooperatively, group dynamics usually predicts that the group behavior will tend toward a middle ground, preventing members from executing extreme forms of behavior. Finally, the effects of disruptive peer groups can be restricted somewhat by assigning older students to interact with and supervise younger students in a peer-tutoring situation. This is sometimes referred to as cross-age tutoring and has had the effect of increasing pressure for prosocial behavior and reducing pressure for antisocial behavior. There will be more about these and similar techniques in chapter 11, which presents effective teaching practices for special types of learners. There are no simple solutions to the powerful influence on learning that peer groups sometimes can have; in general, the more that individual members of a difficult peer group are placed in contact with members of other peer groups holding values contrary to their own, the more the social setting and group dynamics will tend to control undesirable behavior.

Schools, Neighborhoods, Subcultures, and the Learning Environment

There is no question that the individual differences present among your students, such as those due to variation in intelligence, achievement, personality, home life, and peer group, can have dramatic effects both upon the teaching methods employed and the learning results obtained. So, why place students with such diverse differences within the same classroom? Would it not be more efficient to segregate students according to intelligence and achievement level, personality type, degree of disadvantages due to home life, or even according to the most advantageous peer group? Aside from the impracticality of creating a myriad of homogeneous groups to which students would exclusively belong, the result of such grouping might be quite astounding, if it were tried.

We live, work, and play in a world of such complexity and diversity that it is difficult to imagine what life in such a segregated environment might be like. Our forefathers, however, gave considerable thought to this very question and their answer is contained in the Bill of Rights, which gives every citizen the unqualified right to "life, liberty, and the pursuit of happiness." In a practical and contemporary sense, this constitutional guarantee specifically precludes any attempt to advance a single group at the expense of any other group. It even precludes the segregation of groups when "separate but equal" treatment is accorded them, since even the labeling of groups as different implies inequality, regardless of the motives for forming the groups. These are important constitutional implications for the American classroom; they promote an environment that is not only tolerant of differences among individuals but also is conducive to the integration of diverse types of individuals. This constitutional implication has been referred to as the "pluralistic ideal," and it has become a guide for making many of our most important societal decisions relating, for example, to housing, job opportunity, college and professional school admissions, transportation, elementary and secondary education, and the dispersal of public services. What is not always evident from this constitutional guarantee is that the pluralistic ideal has not only shaped legislation and policies at the national and state level, but it has also provided the rationale for the composition of our neighborhoods, schools, and classrooms. And it is not only limited to cultural and minority issues but also extends to the integration and mixture of all types of individuals, including those marked by the individual differences discussed in this chapter.

It is important to note why the pluralistic ideal is so important and why it has become an insightful constitutional legacy. The pluralistic ideal has two advantages that our forefathers recognized. The first was the realization that our country was and *always would be* a melting pot of enormous diversity. While this original diversity resulted from the many different nationalities and religious persuasions that contributed to our general culture, it later was enriched further by different ethnic groups and most recently by an increasing array of diverse values pertaining to dress, films, life-styles, and politics. With all this diversity, clearly a cultural core would be difficult as a common ground from which to govern all the people. The role of our pluralistic ideal was to acculturate and to socialize vastly different groups to a common, albeit general, core of values, that then could provide the framework of a government. The means of accomplishing this was none other than our Constitution, which promotes the integration and mixing of all individuals in the land regardless of how different they are from the norm. Through the illegality of segregating individuals into any group that by labeling or any other means would limit life, liberty, and the pursuit of happiness or deny maximum individual development, the Constitution encourages and promotes the establishment of a core culture which all individuals adhere to regardless of their personal values and cultural preference. By having to work, live, and play with diverse individuals, at least in our public lives, we have come to establish a common cultural heritage with rules (e.g., paying taxes), loyalties (e.g., going to war), rituals (e.g., observing specified holidays), and laws (e.g., respecting the rights of others) which we all have come to accept regardless of the differences among us.

A second insight reflected in the pluralistic ideal was the shared realization that in a world complicated by a continuing list of social and technological problems (pollution, disease, illiteracy, and congestion, to name only a few), divergent points of view, different abilities, and diverse values would be needed to reduce or eliminate these problems. No simple set of skills, attitudes, temperament, personality, or aptitude could provide all that would be needed to solve our problems. By allowing and encouraging this diversity in human potential, our country has possessed for the better part of its history the most enviable work force in the world, responsible for an impressive array of breakthroughs

in medicine, electronics, energy, and aerospace as well as some of the most creative approaches to problems in health, education, and the behavorial sciences. This has been accomplished as a result of, and not in spite of, the cultural diversity and differences that flourish in our communities, schools, and classrooms as a result of the pluralistic ideal.

To continue this success the effective teacher must carry on the pluralistic ideal by respecting and accepting the diversity of human potential that lies within every classroom. Even more important, such potential must be maximally developed if the pluralistic ideal is to serve us in the future as it has in the past. Flexibility in teaching allows for adapting instruction to students' group-related learning styles, using different instructional approaches in teaching students of differing ethnic and racial backgrounds, and adapting instruction to the concerns and needs of the community. Above all, teaching strategies must emphasize the importance of all students working cooperatively with peers and with the teacher. The remaining portion of this text will explore many ways of accomplishing these important goals.

A Final Word

This chapter discusses some of the individual differences that affect learning and that will determine the degree of success in teaching different types of learners. The list of individual differences has been long and their apparent influence in the learning process great. However, your teaching will be successful to the extent that you become acquainted with the individual differences operating in your classroom and, to the extent possible, are able to adapt your teaching style to accommodate these differences. You have seen in this chapter the considerable influence that students' aptitudes, prior achievements, personalities, home lives, and peer groups can have on their learning. Far from being blank slates onto which you impart knowledge and understanding of your subject matter, your students with all of their individual differences will be an active force in determining your success at transmitting your knowledge and understanding onto the blank slate. In other words, not only your own behavior but also that of your students will affect the extent to which you will be able to successfully execute the key teaching behaviors of clarity, variety, task orientation, and student engagement at moderate-to-high rates of success.

Chapter 1 emphasized the limitation of any single definition of teaching effectiveness. There we saw the multidimensionality of teaching through five key behaviors and some additional catalytic behaviors. Also, we saw how both key and catalytic behaviors could be varied depending on whether high- or low-SES students were being taught and whether instruction was in the area of reading or mathematics. This chapter has emphasized the need to differentially apply key and catalytic behaviors according to the nature of the individual differences of the students. Depending on the nature of students' intellience, prior achievements, personalities, home lives, and peer groups, some key behaviors may predominate in importance over others. Task orientation, for example, may be more important with less able, poorly achieving students who consistently need high degrees of structure to learn than with high-aptitude and with high-IQ students who in many cases can function independently and take responsibility for their own learning. Likewise, low-SES students whose home lives have not emphasized verbal interaction, who have poor self-concepts, and limited records of success in school will need greater amounts of learning time at *high* rates of success than students whose home lives and related academic skills may be far greater and, therefore, can benefit more from *moderate* rates of success. These examples reflect the high degree of flexibility that will always be required in any classroom. The key teaching behaviors and the individual differences of students are important guides as to how to effectively use this flexibility. The remaining chapters of this text will introduce and increasingly develop your skill in executing and orchestrating the key and catalytic behaviors and in learning how to accommodate them to the learning needs of your students.

Summing Up

This chapter introduced you to some of the diverse types of students found in classrooms and their individual differences. Its main points were:

1. Early conceptions of teaching viewed students as empty vessels into which the teacher poured the content of the day's lesson. These conceptions failed to consider the effect of individual differences on learning.
2. A knowledge of the individual differences among learners is important in order to (a) adapt instructional methods to individual learning needs and (b) understand and place in perspective the reasons behind the school performance of individual learners.
3. One misunderstanding that some teachers, parents, and school administrators have about intelligence—or IQ—is that it is a single, unified dimension.
4. Specific aptitudes or factors of intelligence are more predictive of success in school and specific occupations than is general intelligence.
5. Knowing learners' *specific* strengths and weaknesses and altering instructional goals and methods accordingly will contribute to greater learning than will categorizing and teaching them according to their *general* intelligence.
6. Task-relevant prior learning represents the facts, skills, and understandings that must be taught if subsequent learning is to occur. Mastery of task-relevant prior learnings is often required for subsequent learning to take place.
7. Traditionally, students from lower class and lower middle-class families have not performed as well on standardized tests of achievement as students from middle- and upper class families. However, most of the differences in educational achievement that occur by race and ethnicity can be accounted for by social class.
8. An important characteristic that distinguishes lower from middle- and upper class children is that the latter more rapidly acquire knowl-

edge of the world outside their homes and neighborhoods than do lower class children.

9. Low-SES families are more likely than middle- and high-SES families to emphasize physical punishment rather than reasoning and to encourage rote learning (memorization, recall of facts, etc.) rather than independent, self-directed learning.

10. Some instructional strategies for meeting the learning needs associated with low-SES students include: using a variety of audiovisual and exploratory materials that require alternate modalities (e.g., sight vs. sound), having high expectations and rewarding intellectual accomplishments, emphasizing correct word usage and correcting incorrect linguistic patterns, and getting students to talk about personal experiences to improve their self-concepts.

11. Erikson's (1968) three crises are: accomplishment versus inferiority, which occurs sometime during the elementary school years; identity versus confusion, which occurs sometime during the adolescent or high school years; and intimacy versus isolation, which occurs in early adulthood.

12. State anxiety represents a condition that is momentary in time and produced by some specific stimulus in the environment, such as a test.

13. While some state anxiety is necessary for learning, grades, report cards, and assignments generally provide the levels of state anxiety necessary to motivate students to engage in the learning process.

14. Extreme levels of state anxiety can be avoided by placing the value of a specific assignment in perspective with other assignments before it is given and by creating as large a total context of assignments as possible.

15. Trait anxiety represents a condition that is stable within individuals over time but varies among individuals. It is produced by a wide range of ill-defined conditions perceived by an individual to be harmful.

16. High levels of trait anxiety are associated with high motivation and a need to achieve, but extreme levels of trait anxiety are associated with an intense fear of failure which dampens creativity and results in perfunctory, mechanical responses.

17. Extreme levels of trait anxiety sometimes can be avoided by making a range of alternative responses acceptable for a given assignment.

18. Self-concept tends to have only a modest relationship to school achievement but has a strong relationship to active engagement in the learning process and success in one's career or occupation.

19. The concept of self can be improved by finding and reflecting back to the students the value of their unique talents.

20. Peer groups are an influential source of the behavior of learners both in and out of the classroom. Their negative effects may be dissipated by placing the members of potentially disruptive peer groups into more heterogeneous groups and assigning cooperative work assignments within the groups.

21. The pluralistic ideal describes the bringing together of diverse individuals so that (a) a common core of values can be established to provide the framework for a system of cooperation and governance and (b) the unique and individual talents of individuals can be applied to solving the problems common to all.

For Discussion and Practice

*1. In what two ways might you use your knowledge of the individual differences in your classroom to become a more effective teacher?

*2. Given the following list of learners, what types of instructional strategies might you emphasize for each type to meet their learning needs?

high state anxiety

low auditory ability

gifted

---

*Answers for the keyed questions (*) in this and susequent chapters appear in Appendix B.

low SES

poor self-concept

high trait anxiety

unassertive, overassertive, and aggressive

disruptive peer group

3. Describe briefly the environmentalist and hereditarian positions concerning the use of general IQ tests in schools. Devise one counterargument you would use to respond to arguments of an extremist in each camp.

*4. Explain the role that socioeconomic status is believed to play in influencing the score one might attain on a test of general intelligence. If behaviors solely related to socioeconomic status could be eliminated, how might differences among the tested IQ among subgroups of learners change?

5. Identify aptitudes or factors that are likely to be more predictive of success in selected school subjects and occupations than is general IQ.

6. For each of the following give an example of a school subject or content area in which a high score on an aptitude test might be expected to predict a high score on an appropriate test of subject matter achievement.

Aptitude	School subject or content area
verbal comprehension	_____
general reasoning	_____
memory	_____
use of numbers	_____
psychomotor speed	_____
spatial relations	_____
word fluency	_____

7. Give an example of some task-relevant prior knowledge that might be required before each of the following instructional objectives could be taught successfully.
   a. Adding two-digit numbers
   b. Reading latitude and longitude from a map
   c. Writing a four-sentence paragraph
   d. Seeing an amoeba under a microscope
   e. Correctly pronouncing a new two-syllable word
   f. Understanding how the executive branch of government works
   g. Playing ten minutes of basketball without committing a foul
   h. Responding correctly to a fire alarm

   i. Solving the equation $c^2 = a^2 + b^2$
   j. Punctuating two independent clauses

8. What might be some of the home life characteristics of low-SES students that make them consistently score lower than high-SES students on tests of standardized achievement? What are some teaching practices that might shrink differences in standardized achievement due to SES?

*9. Identify one approach that might be used to improve the poor self-concept of a low-SES student.

*10. Which of the following indicators are most representative of state anxiety and which are most representative of trait anxiety?
   a. Looks scared and exhausted before a test
   b. Becomes nervous whenever asked about where he lives
   c. Continuously combs hair and puts on makeup
   d. Has an incessant drive to get into college
   e. Skips school whenever an oral presentation is required
   f. Never fails to complete an extra credit assignment
   g. Always boasts and exaggerates about the number of girls he dates
   h. Copies others' homework often
   i. Wants to become the most respected athlete in the school
   j. Never brings home papers that have received a grade lower than "A"

*11. Identify two reasons why it is important to promote a positive self-concept, even though its relationship to tests of academic achievement may not be strong.

*12. Identify two methods for dealing with a disruptive peer group in your classroom.

13. Explain in your own words what is meant by the phrase "pluralistic ideal." What are some signs in a typical school that show the commitment made by our country, its people, and its government toward this ideal?

Suggested Readings

Bloom, B. (1981). *All our children learning*. New York: McGraw-Hill.
   Shows how learning differences can be greatly reduced with appropriate environmental and instructional conditions.

Epstein, J. & Karweit, N. (1983). (Eds.) *Friendship in school*. New York: Academic Press.

A compilation of different views and school descriptions that vividly portray the peer-group culture comprising the "hidden curriculum."

Good, T. & Stipek, D. (1983). Individual differences in the classroom: A psychological perspective. In G. D. Fenstermacher & J. I. Goodlad (Eds.), *Individual differences and the common curriculum* (82nd Yearbook of the National Society for the Study of Education, Part 7). Chicago: University of Chicago Press.

A review of the many different types of individual differences in the classroom and their known or hypothesized effect on student achievement.

Kash, M. & Borich, G. (1978). *Teacher behavior and pupil self-concept.* Reading, MA: Addison-Wesley.

Illustrates five separate dimensions of the self-concept using autobiographical quotations from well-known individuals, and then reviews the most current research relating to these divisions of the self-concept.

Labov, William. (1972). Academic ignorance and black intelligence. *Atlantic Monthly, 229,* 6, 59–67.

Dispels the myth that there are any meaningful intellectual differences among the races.

Levine, D. (1979). Concentrated poverty and reading achievement in seven big cities. *The Urban Review,* Summer, 63–80.

Convincingly portrays the differences in achievement that are often associated with socioeconomic status.

McClelland, D. C. (1973). Testing for competence rather than for "intelligence." *American Psychologist, 28,* 1–14.

A case against general intelligence and for the measurement of specific skills related to success in school and in the workplace.

Sinclair, K. (1987). Students' affective characteristics. In M. J. Dunkin (Ed.), *International encyclopedia of teaching and teacher education.* New York: Pergamon.

An interesting article on the complex social and emotional behaviors of school learners and their potential effects in the classroom.

Steinberg, R. (1983). Reasoning, problem solving and intelligence. In R. J. Sternberg (Ed.), *Handbook of human intelligence.* New York: Cambridge University Press.

One of the most authoritative sources on new ways of defining and teaching intelligence.

Wang, M. & Lindvall, C. (1984). Individual differences and school learning environments. *Review of research in education, 11,* 161–225.

A summary of some of the most recent research on the individual differences of learners and their effect on what is learned.

3
Instructional Goals and Plans

In chapters 1 and 2 you became acquainted with some of the behaviors expected of you as a teacher and some of the individual differences you can expect among your students. This chapter will combine these two subjects and show how teachers organize their thinking about who, what, and how they will teach. Both the formulation of goals and where they come from will be discussed, as well as the important relationship between goals and the process of planning. First, consider the distinction among aims, goals, and objectives and the use of these concepts in planning and decision-making.

Aims, Goals, and Objectives

The words "aims," "goals," and "objectives" often are used interchangeably without the realization that they have different, albeit related, meanings. **Aims** are general expressions of values that give a sense of direction. They point in a direction that is sufficiently broad to be acceptable to large numbers of individuals, such as "United States taxpayers," "parents," or "the American people." For example, some frequently heard aims are:

> Every citizen should be prepared to work in a technological world.
>
> Every adult should be functionally literate.
>
> Every American should be able to vote as an informed citizen in a democratic society.

Aims such as these serve the important function of expressing values and communicating societal concerns and issues with which large numbers of individuals can agree. The broad generalities that aims represent, however, make their implementation difficult; therefore, to be useful, aims often require greater specification in the form of goals and objectives.

Goals, like aims, provide a sense of direction. Unlike aims, however, they are more specific and can be related more easily to some aspect of the general aims. The previously stated aims might be converted to goals by relating them more specifically to the curriculum in the following manner:

Students should understand the use of the microcomputer.

Students should be able to read and write well enough to become gainfully employed.

Students should know how to choose a candidate and vote in a local election.

Goals bring aims down to earth by connecting them to some tangible aspect of the curriculum (e.g., computer literacy, language instruction, a unit on local government). Although goals are more specific than aims, they are always derived in ways that contribute to the realization of the aim. It will be shown that goals often are formulated at the national or state level by specially convened groups, such as legislators, panels of informed citizens, and curriculum specialists; these groups are charged with the responsibility of establishing school curricula. Some of the most common sources from which goals can be derived are:

School district reports and policies

Faculty handbooks

National curriculum commissions

"Blue ribbon" committee reports

State boards of education

National teacher groups and associations

Textbook committees

Curriculum guides

Courses of study, texts

Needs assessment reports

Objectives carry this process one step further by describing the *specific behavior* the learner is to attain, the *conditions* under which the behavior must be demonstrated, and the *proficiency level* at which the behavior is to be performed. Converting the previous goals to objectives might result in the following:

- Students will, with the use of a microcomputer of their own choosing, produce an edited two-page manuscript free of typographical errors in 15 minutes or less.
- Students will, at the end of the 12th grade, be able to write a 500-word essay with no more than two grammatical and punctuation errors and to read newspapers and magazines without any errors in comprehension.
- Students will, at the end of an eighth-grade unit on government, participate in a mock election by choosing a candidate from the prescribed list, giving three reasons for their choice.

Objectives like these are often included in curriculum guides and the teachers' manuals that accompany textbooks and workbooks. Unfortunately, the objectives are not always well-written and do not always fit a particular class of students or the way the teacher has chosen to organize the content. Therefore, objectives often must be formulated or rewritten to fit individual students, the instructional goals of a school and school district, and a teacher's organizational preferences.

The examples just discussed show that aims are important guides to desired and valued societal ends. But aims cannot be directly measured or observed and, therefore, require greater specification in the form of goals and objectives. Goals bring aims down to the level of the school curriculum, where objectives can tie them to specific behaviors, conditions, and proficiency levels. Some distinctions among aims, goals, and objectives are summarized in Table 3.1.

The Flow of Aims to Goals

In order to allow the greatest amount of flexibility to professionals in the translation of societal aims into goals and objectives at the school level, the *manner of achievement* of those aims is left purposively vague. For this reason goals are an important link between aims and objec-

TABLE 3.1
Aims, goals, and objectives

Category	Description	Examples
Aims	Broad statements of very general outcomes that 1. do not include specific levels of performance 2. do not identify specific areas of the curriculum 3. tend to change infrequently and in response to societal pressure	Become a good citizen Be competent in the basic skills areas Be creative Learn problem solving Appreciate art Develop high-level thinking skills
Goals	More narrowly defined statements of outcomes that 1. apply to specific educational programs 2. may be formulated on an annual basis 3. are developed by program coordinators, principals, and other school administrators	Students receiving Title I reading program services should realize achievement gains on the Iowa Test of Basic Skills.
Objectives	Specific statements of learner behavior or outcomes that state the conditions under which the behavior is to be exhibited (e.g., given a list of 25 vocabulary words at the 8th-grade level) and the proficiency to be attained (e.g., the student will correctly provide synonyms for 20 out of the 25). These behaviors are expected to be attained at the end of a specified time of instruction.	By Friday, the students will be able to recite the names of the months in order. The student will be able to take apart and reassemble correctly a one-barrel carburetor with the tools provided within 45 minutes.

tives because they specify areas of the curriculum to which the societal aims apply. Goals help make aims implementable while leaving flexibility to other professionals whose job it is to specify the *exact behaviors, conditions, and proficiencies* that must be met in order to achieve a given goal within a specific educational context. This second group of professionals includes teachers, principals, and school administrators, whose knowledge of the classroom, the school, and the school district assures that the translation of goals to objectives will be feasible, practical, and in keeping with local needs.

It is essential that the translation of aims, first into goals and then into objectives, be responsive to societal needs and values. This is especially true for educators, because the purse strings of education funding are held by all who make up our society. If a superintendent or school board implements goals too far removed from societal aims—from what the community wants, needs, and values—then the superintendent may find himself or herself out of a job, and the school board may not be reelected. Often it is mistakenly believed that only school administrators are responsible for the curriculum in a school. This is only partially true, because ultimately the general public in local communities has control over the aims upon which goals and objectives are based. Figure 3.1 illustrates the flow of aims to objectives on the "back-to-basics" issue and indicates how public pressure on any national is-

FIGURE 3.1

Back to basics: The flow of aims to objectives

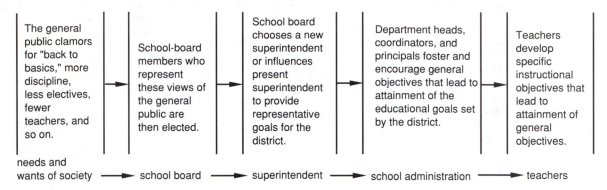

| The general public clamors for "back to basics," more discipline, less electives, fewer teachers, and so on. | School-board members who represent these views of the general public are then elected. | School board chooses a new superintendent or influences present superintendent to provide representative goals for the district. | Department heads, coordinators, and principals foster and encourage general objectives that lead to attainment of the educational goals set by the district. | Teachers develop specific instructional objectives that lead to attainment of general objectives. |

needs and wants of society ⟶ school board ⟶ superintendent ⟶ school administration ⟶ teachers

sue reaches the classroom. This process can also be viewed as a funneling or narrowing of focus, with the general and sometimes abstract aims of society gradually being translated into more specific and manageable components—the goals and objectives—as shown in Figure 3.2.

Two things of particular importance to the classroom teacher are apparent from these illustrations. The first is that objectives must have a close relationship to the goals and a reasonably close relationship to the aims from which they are derived. Thus it is imperative that the classroom teacher charged with the responsibility of writing objectives be knowledgeable about the goals the objectives are supposed to represent. Forming objectives without knowledge of the goals or aims that represent them could place a teacher in a precarious situation when asked to justify the im-

FIGURE 3.2

The funneling of societal aims into objectives

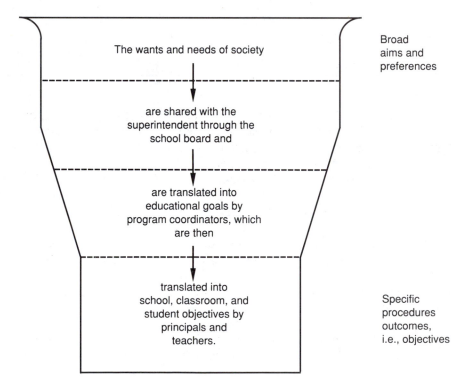

The wants and needs of society

Broad aims and preferences

are shared with the superintendent through the school board and

are translated into educational goals by program coordinators, which are then

translated into school, classroom, and student objectives by principals and teachers.

Specific procedures outcomes, i.e., objectives

portance and value of those objectives to parents, community, school administrators, and students. Generally, adopted textbooks and curriculum guides are valuable sources for preparing objectives that are based on desired goals. On the other hand, because the translation of aims into goals and goals into objectives represents stages at which different individuals must make judgments, human error and bias can produce objectives with relationships to goals and aims that require great leaps of faith. It is important to be aware of the goals from which lesson objectives will be prepared; the teacher must proceed with caution when such a correspondence is not immediately apparent, as might be the case when "borrowing" objectives from nonadopted or out-of-date texts and curriculum guides.

Another aspect of the translation of aims into objectives is the importance of local community prerogatives. While local community values and needs often represent the values and needs of the general public, they may not always be identical to them. School boards and local citizens have the right and responsibility to establish a curriculum that is sensitive to the needs of the community they serve. State-adopted textbooks and curriculum guides generally are chosen to reflect local priorities, but these often are expanded and enhanced by individual school districts in response to specific problems (e.g., the need to teach remedial reading) or areas marked for special emphasis within the curriculum (e.g., critical thinking skills). The effective teacher should be aware of the community priorities that may require a local interpretation of state-mandated curricula or of general societal concerns and values. These community priorities often appear in press reports and television accounts of school issues, in the platforms of school board candidates, and in school district policies that reflect problems of particular concern to a school district (e.g., declining scores on standardized achievement tests, increasing school drop-out rate, unmet needs of the gifted and talented, or moral and ethical issues). A teacher may be expected to address such issues within the context of regular instruction.

That aims, goals, and objectives are related to the process of planning should now be obvious. What teachers see as important to teach comes from aims, goals, and objectives. Although the technical process of lesson planning is treated in a later chapter, it is important to note that course and lesson plans are a direct response to objectives that have been formulated from goals and aims. The content one teaches as well as the methods, materials, and resources one uses will be determined by the aims, goals, and objectives adopted by the school district. The instructional plans and decisions made in the classroom must always reflect these aims, goals, and objectives.

Some Societal Goals for Education in the 1980s and 1990s

In the previous section, a case was made for becoming aware of the aims and goals that provide justification for the classroom objectives. Some important aims and goals at the national level have recently emerged as a result of a number of different policy reports calling for the reform and improvement of our educational system. Five of these reports, issued in 1983, have been particularly instrumental in the revision of both elementary and secondary school curricula and in setting the direction of curriculum reform for the 1990s.* These reports were stimulated in

---

*These reports and the agencies or committees that authored them were: *Academic Preparation for College: What Students Need to Know and Be Able to Do.* (1983). The College Board, 888 7th Avenue, New York, NY 10106; *Action for Excellence: Comprehensive Plan to Improve Our Nation's Schools.* (1983). Education Commission of the States. Task Force on Education for Economic Growth. Denver, CO; *A Nation at Risk: The Imperative for Educational Reform.* (1983). United States National Commission on Excellence in Education. Washington, DC: The Commission; *Educating Americans for the 21st Century:* A plan of action for improving mathematics, science and technology education for all American elementary and secondary students so that their achievement is the best in the world by 1995. (1983). U.S. National Science Board Commission on Precollege Education in Mathematics, Science and Technology. National Science Foundation, Washington, DC; and *Making the Grade: A Report of the Task Force.* (1983). Twentieth Century Fund Task Force on Federal Elementary and Secondary Education Policy. New York: The Fund.

part by a growing disenchantment with the quality of public school education voiced by nearly all segments of our society, including parents, taxpayers, legislators, business and military leaders, and some teacher groups. This disenchantment was not limited to matters of curriculum but extended as well to the quality of teaching, leading in some cases to recommendations for teacher competency testing and new requirements for teacher certification. The five reports taken together, while each registering its own specific concerns, expressed a consensus about what was wrong with American education and what to do about it. For example, there was general agreement across all five of the reports that a back-to-basics approach was needed in our schools. Strengthening curricula in the areas of math, science, English, foreign languages, and social studies was seen as essential. Also, high technology was represented by a call for more computer science and computer literacy, both as separate courses and as adjuncts to other courses. In addition, the reports called for a renewed effort to teach higher order thinking skills, involving the teaching of concepts, problem solving, and creativity; this is opposed to an emphasis on rote memorization and the parroting back of facts, lists, names, and dates divorced from a larger problem-solving context. Not surprisingly, all the reports recommended both the raising of school grading standards and the number of required core courses (as opposed to elective courses) to be taken, especially at the secondary level. This recommendation went hand in hand with the suggestion that colleges should raise their admission requirements by requiring more course work in the core subjects, especially math and foreign language.

Also, the majority of the five reports recommended increasing both the time spent in school (for example, one report suggested a minimum seven-hour school day and 200 days per year of school) and the time spent on homework. The amount of time students would be actively engaged in the learning process would presumably be greater if more courses were taught and greater amounts of time were spent in school.

Time spent on extracurricular and other non-instructional activities was to be reduced accordingly, as would administrative interruptions. These recommendations foreshadowed a tough new policy in which many school districts went on record as wanting to reverse the more flexible curriculum, grading standards, and school management style of the 1960s and 1970s.

The recommendations revealed in these reports were the result of various "blue ribbon" committees composed of informed citizens who were far enough removed from the day-to-day workings of education that they could gain fresh insights into the problems of our nation's schools. For example, by taking a broad view of our nation's educational establishment, these committees were able to note the following:

1. In the past 20 years, many elective and remedial courses have replaced core courses in the areas of mathematics, science, English, and foreign language.
2. Students today are assigned less homework than their counterparts 20 years ago.
3. Scores on almost all Standardized Achievement Tests have been declining steadily (as of 1983), particularly in math and reading. (There is a slight tendency for these scores to be on the rise at this time, perhaps due to the enactment of some of these reforms.)
4. Requirements for graduation have become lower over the years; fewer students than ever before now are taking advanced math, science, and foreign language courses.
5. Proficiency in the basic skills of reading, writing, and arithmetic are at an all-time low; many new business employees and military recruits require training in the fundamentals of reading, writing, and mathematics.

The sum of the major themes of the five reports was the perception that our schools were losing sight of their role in teaching students *how to think*. Traditionally, this was accomplished through the core curriculum (English, math, science, foreign language, and social studies). However, with fewer advanced offerings in these areas and with so much time being spent in remedial activities, teaching children how to think may have been seriously curtailed. The schools, these reports suggested, must reverse this trend by requiring that students receive instruction in both the basic core as well as more advanced areas. Such instruction should require greater amounts of homework, higher testing and grading standards, and higher level thinking skills. Mastering these thinking skills, which involve problem solving, concept learning, decision-making, and making value judgments, are important because they are required both in the world of work and in advanced education and training.

Some of the major goals contained in these recommendations can be summarized in the following ways: Students should

be trained to live and function in a technological world.

possess minimum competencies in reading, writing, and mathematics.

possess high-level thinking, conceptual, and problem-solving skills.

be required to enroll in all of the core subjects each school year to the extent of their abilities.

be trained to work independently and to complete assignments without direct supervision.

improve school attendance and stay in school longer each day and year.

be given more tests that require problem-solving skills and higher grading standards.

Although other goals could have been derived from these reports, the previous list is an example of a broad national consensus that, to varying degrees, is likely to affect the formulation of goals and objectives for some time. Corresponding objectives pertaining to these goals now are being made by state education agencies, school districts, curriculum specialists, and classroom teachers, with the intent of tying these goals to specific areas of the school curriculum. The next chapter will be addressed to the conversion of goals such as these into objectives that can be implemented in the classroom.

Goals, Objectives, and Plans

After this general introduction to aims, goals, and objectives, now consider planning and its relationship to the decisions to be made in the classroom. Planning is the process of deciding what and how the students should learn. It has been estimated that teachers make one such decision on the average of every two minutes while they are teaching (Clark & Peterson, 1986). However, in addition to these "in-flight" decisions (McNair, 1978–79) there are many others that involve setting priorities and making judgments about the form and content of instruction. For example, how much lecturing, questioning, discussing, and testing will be done? How much material will be covered for a specific topic, and how in-depth will the instruction be? The former questions represent planning decisions that involve the *form* or style of teaching; the latter questions involve the *content* of instruction. Many decisions of both form and content must be made before, during, and after teaching a lesson. Planning is the systematic process that aids in both deciding issues of form and content and in setting priorities that establish what things must come before other things.

Chapter 5 discusses unit and lesson plans, which sometimes are confused with the process of planning. Writing or preparing lesson plans (such as topical outlines, lesson blueprints, and written summaries of what you will teach) is the *result* of the planning process, not the process itself. This important distinction explains both why some teacher plans represent little planning and also why some teacher planning never gets put in the form of a plan. Although planning and plan-making (writing out or outlining a lesson) can be separate activities, they function far more effectively when brought together as part of a systematic and related process. The task here and in chapter 5 will be to show how planning and lesson plans can work together to systematically aid instructional decision-making.

The content and form, or the "what" and "how" of your teaching, include choices of many different varieties. These choices are, in fact, so numerous that when left unanticipated, they are made in patchwork-quilt fashion; the resultant teaching is rambling, disconnected, and incoherent. This is one of the reasons why planning is so important. Planning both structures and prioritizes behavior so that only the most effective teaching behaviors for attaining a given objective are employed, which provides the most instruction in the least amount of time. The planning process is necessary also for executing the key behaviors of clarity, variety, task orientation, and student engagement in the learning process at moderate-to-high rates of success. Without good planning there is no assurance that these key behaviors for functioning as an effective teacher will be employed.

Although the preparation of lesson plans will be closely linked to objectives, the process of planning begins with a knowledge of aims and goals acquired from sources such as "blue ribbon" reports, textbooks, curriculum guides, and school district policies. Planning also begins from a knowledge of the learner, of the subject matter that will be taught, and of teaching methods. The gathering of information and the systematic recording of data in these areas are the keys to the planning process. In the previous section we saw the importance of aims and goals; now consider the importance of three remaining inputs to the planning process: knowledge of the learner, knowledge of the subject matter, and knowledge of teaching methods.

The previous chapter showed the importance of understanding learners by becoming acquainted with their learning needs and individual differences. In a review of six separate research studies on planning, Clark and Peterson (1986) discovered that teachers actually spent more of their planning time (an average of 43%) on learner characteristics and information than they did on any other area. Students' intelligence and achievement; anxiety, motivation, and self-concept; their home life and peer-group influences—all these categories provide important information for the planning process. Planning with respect to learners includes consciously noting students' status in these categories and recording significant departures from what might be expected for the class and school. These departures from the norm can signal special learning needs that require the selection of content, materials, objectives, and methods that match the characteristics of the students. Students' intelligence and achievements, personalities, home lives, and peer-group influences are the windows through which the teacher will be able to "see" special learning needs. They also are the psychological characteristics that will reflect the extent to which students are ready and prepared to learn, telling at what level instruction must begin. In chapter 11 there is a close look at the learning needs of a number of special types of students likely to be encountered in classrooms, including the slow, gifted, bilingual, and handicapped learner. The content organization and ordering derived from all these information sources can be instrumental during planning in helping the teacher to select, sequence, and allocate time to various topics of instruction.

A second primary input to the planning process is knowledge of academic discipline or grade level. Undoubtedly you, as a student, have spent much time and effort to become knowledgeable in the subjects you will teach. But, aside from the obvious facts you have learned as a result of your subject matter concentration, a subtle but important aspect of your discipline also has been conveyed to you. You have observed over time, perhaps without realizing it, how textbook authors, your teachers, and subject matter specialists have *organized* concepts in your teaching area. This organization involves how parts relate to wholes, how content is prioritized, how transitions are made between topics, and which themes are major or minor. Figure 3.3 illustrates some of the many different types of content organizations that can be chosen during lesson and

FIGURE 3.3
Some ways of organizing content (Reigeluth, 1983)

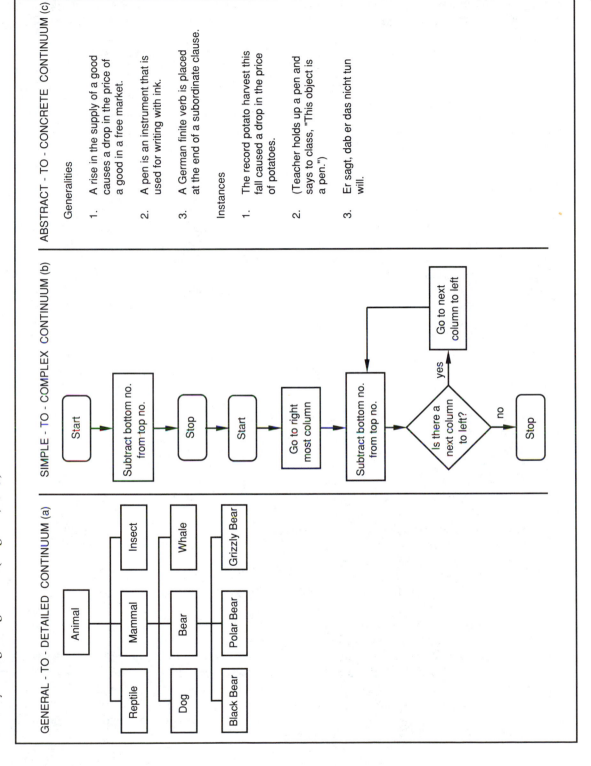

GENERAL - TO - DETAILED CONTINUUM (a)

SIMPLE - TO - COMPLEX CONTINUUM (b)

ABSTRACT - TO - CONCRETE CONTINUUM (c)

Generalities

1. A rise in the supply of a good causes a drop in the price of a good in a free market.

2. A pen is an instrument that is used for writing with ink.

3. A German finite verb is placed at the end of a subordinate clause.

Instances

1. The record potato harvest this fall caused a drop in the price of potatoes.

2. (Teacher holds up a pen and says to class, "This object is a pen.")

3. Er sagt, dab er das nicht tun will.

unit planning. Organizations such as these have been used by teachers, curriculum specialists, and textbook authors to make learning easier, more orderly, and more conducive to retention and later use (Clark & Yinger, 1979). They are usually spelled out by subject matter specialists in textbooks, instructional materials, and curriculum guides pertaining to the subjects or grade levels to be taught. Along with the knowledge of what will be taught, the content organization and ordering derived from these sources can be instrumental during planning in helping select, sequence, and allocate time to various topics of instruction (Clark & Elmore, 1981; Smith & Sendelbach, 1979). Chapter 5 will introduce some ways of recording and using this organization in the preparation of unit and lesson plans.

A third input to the planning process is knowledge of the methods of teaching, such as those that will be discussed in subsequent chapters of this text. Included in the knowledge of teaching methods will be an awareness of different styles of teaching, which are reflected by implementation of the key and catalytic behaviors introduced in chapter 1. Also, included in teaching methods is deciding upon an appropriate pacing or tempo for the instruction (e.g., the speed with which new material will be introduced), the primary mode of presentation (e.g., lecture vs. group discussion), the arrangement of the class (e.g., small groups, full class, independent study), and classroom management procedures (e.g., raise hand, speak out); these are only some of the many dimensions that must be considered. Included in the planning process are both awareness of and purposeful selection of these dimensions of teaching and also how they should be interwoven during the presentation of the subject. Because teaching involves combinations of activities and the orchestration of both key and catalytic behaviors, it must be planned to provide *connections, relationships, transitions,* and *sequences* that make a coherent whole out of the individual bits of knowledge.

An additional aspect of the knowledge of teaching methods is the selection and use of teaching materials. Decisions about textbooks and curriculum materials, workbooks, films, tests, and reference works are crucial to the planning process. Included in the planning process, therefore, is the identification and recording of all the teaching materials and communication media that may be useful in meeting the general goals of instruction. All of these materials may not actually be used, but conscious awareness of their availability will provide the flexibility needed to present a topic effectively to different types of learners. They can also be helpful by connecting specific learning objectives to specific media and materials, which sometimes can pre-organize the teaching task, and make lesson planning easier and less time consuming. Available media and materials will become better known to a teacher as more time is spent in a specific subject area or grade level. Keeping a record of alternative texts, workbooks, media, references, and tests is another important aspect of the planning process.

The four primary inputs to the planning process are summarized as follows:

1. Aims and goals, reflected by, for example, national and state policies and legislation, school district curriculum guides, and adopted textbooks and materials
2. Learner characteristics and individual differences, reflected by student aptitude and achievement; personality traits, including the student's anxiety level, motivation, and self-concept; home life and extent of disadvantagedness; and peer influences in school and neighborhood
3. Knowledge of academic discipline and grade-level curriculum, reflected by organization of content, such as whole-part relationships and sequences; ordering or priorities, such as connections and transitions among and between parts; major and minor themes, such as most important, least important; and content-specific facts, rules, concepts, and abstractions
4. Knowledge of teaching methods, reflected by key and catalytic behaviors, such as clarity, va-

riety, task orientation, and student engagement in the learning process at moderate-to-high rates of success; considerations of pacing, mode of presentation, class arrangement, classroom management; and selection and use of textbooks, media, and materials.

In each of these four areas, a considerable amount of reflection, observation, and, in some cases, data collection is required before lesson plans can be prepared. This is the *process* of planning. The effective teacher actively collects and retains data corresponding to the four primary inputs, either through observation and data collection, as is typical in the case of area 1 (aims and goals) and area 2 (learner characteristics), or by study and review, as is typical in the case of area 3 (knowledge of academic discipline) and area 4 (knowledge of teaching methods). These inputs are important considerations for establishing a planning framework and philosophy that can guide the formulation of objectives and lesson planning.

It is important to note that the planning process being considered thus far does not precede the preparation of each lesson. Instead, it is a process that considers aspects of instruction that are not likely to change over spans of time as long as a semester. Also, this type of planning does not occur at any one point but reflects a teacher's sensitivity to and awareness of a broad spectrum of data that is *continually being emitted* in the school and community in which he or she teaches. Aims and goals at the national and local level constantly are expressed in the newspapers and on television as well as in accounts of school board meetings and special documents authored by the state and school district. Learner characteristics always are in gradual states of flux as the composition of cities and neighborhoods changes with changing industrialization, shifting employment opportunities, and housing and quality of life. For these inputs to the planning process, the data are subtle but continually available on a daily basis; the effective teacher tunes them in and uses them in the planning process.

Decision-Making and Tacit Understanding

Beginning teachers often regard their content and method knowledge to be the result of hard work during their four long years of schooling. To be sure, it is—but not entirely. Knowledge in these areas changes as a result of the *interaction* of extensive "book learning" with experience in the classroom. The way content is organized and prioritized, instructional style, questioning strategies, mode of presentation, and even the content taught and how it is presented can and should be expected to change as a result of a teacher's most recent experiences in the classroom. These experiences and their effects on thinking also are inputs to the planning process. As part of this process an effort should be made both to become consciously aware of and to accept the changes occurring in one's thoughts and feelings from day-to-day experiences in the classroom.

These changes often result from what sometimes is referred to as tacit, or personal, knowledge (Elbaz, 1981; Polanyi, 1958). This knowledge represents those things one knows by *experience* but rarely, if ever, articulates. Through everyday experiences everyone compiles vast amounts of tacit knowledge that can guide actions as effectively as can knowledge gained from books and formal instruction. In most situations tacit knowledge, if acted upon, adds to the quality of planning and decision-making by bringing variety and flexibility to lessons. Tacit knowledge serves to make the planning process less rigid than it sometimes is when conventional and traditional ways of doing things learned from books and formal instruction become so well embedded in one's thinking that they unconsciously become yearly and even lifelong agendas. The point is that day-to-day experiences in the classroom should be as valued an input to the planning process as is more formally acquired knowledge. Incorporating into the lesson planning process the tacitly acquired thoughts, feelings, and understandings acquired from day-to-day experiences will give your teaching the variety, flexibility, and creativity it deserves.

Planning to Eliminate Bias

As strange as it may seem, planning to eliminate bias in classroom teaching can be one of the most significant aspects of becoming an effective teacher. Researchers have recently brought to our attention that, consciously or unconsciously, everyone has biases of one kind or another. When applied in ways that affect only one's own behavior and not that of others, one tends to use the word *preference* instead of *bias*. Preferences are the harmless results of values that are often manifest in the clothes one wears, the car one drives, and the music one listens to. Biases, on the other hand, are not so harmless; they can affect the lives of others in ways that may not always be conducive to their personal growth and well-being. The fact that many biases are covert and unknown at a conscious level makes them even more devastating and difficult to control in the classroom. A teacher's biases can have a significant effect on the growth and development of learners if they are left unchecked. As the previous section has shown, one of the purposes of planning is to raise to a conscious level the thoughts, feelings, and understandings that may have been arrived at tacitly or informally. This process can be used as well to bring to conscious awareness the biases that can influence how and what one teaches.

A particularly alarming case of bias was uncovered by Rist (1970) when he studied a single class of ghetto students from kindergarten through second grade. Rist observed that from the time these students entered kindergarten, they were divided into three groups, "tigers," "cardinals," and "clowns," each seated at a different table. Initial placement into groups in kindergarten was made by the teacher according to SES, using information from registration forms and from interviews with mothers and social workers. The highest status children, called tigers, were seated closest to the teacher and quickly labeled "fast learners." The lowest status children, called clowns, were most removed from the teacher and quickly were led to believe they were "slow learners." In reality, each of the three groups had a mixture of slow and fast learners, but the slow learners seated farthest from the teacher seldom got the opportunity to interact with her, while those closest to the teacher frequently received her attention. Before long the abilities of each group were taken as fact rather than as creations of the teacher, so much so that it was increasingly difficult for the "clowns" to be considered other than slow by their teachers in the following grades. At no time did the teacher seem to be aware that the arrangement was biased or that seating certain students consistently in the back of the room would reduce their contacts with her. Thus, this teacher's bias may have become a self-fulfilling prophecy extending even to subsequent grades and classes as a result of biased labeling during the early years of schooling.

Many other examples of teacher biases have been catalogued in the literature. Brophy and Good (1974), for example, summarized how teachers sometimes unequally respond to high and low achievers by communicating low expectations and thereby accepting and unintentionally encouraging a low level of performance among some students. Brophy and Good identify the following areas in which some teachers were observed to respond differently toward low and high achievers. These teachers tended to:

- wait less time for lows to answer
- give lows the answer after the slightest hesitation
- praise marginal or inaccurate answers of lows
- criticize lows more frequently for having the wrong answer
- praise lows less when the right answer is given
- not give feedback to lows as to why an answer is incorrect
- pay attention to (e.g., smile at) and call on lows less
- seat lows farther from the teacher
- allow lows to "give up" more

Generally, these findings confirm that teachers usually do not compensate for differences between high and low achievers in allowing for more response opportunities and more teacher contact for the latter.

Other types of biases can also affect interactions with students. For example, Gage and Berliner (1984) identified several biased ways in which teachers interact with their students and then analyzed the extent to which experienced teachers actually exhibited these biases in their classroom. Their biases included interacting with or calling on students disproportionately in the following manner:

Seated in front half of class/seated in back half of class

Seated on left-hand side of class/seated on right-hand side of class

Girls/boys

Nice-looking students/average-looking students

More able students/less able students

Minority group members/nonminority group members

In their study these authors calculated the number of student-teacher interactions that would be expected by chance for these classifications, and then from observation determined the actual number of interactions that occurred. Somewhat surprisingly their results showed that *every* teacher showed some form of bias with regard to these categories. In other words, every teacher favored at least one student classification over another by naming, calling on, requiring information from, and otherwise interacting with those in some classification disproportionately to those who were not in that classification. Such biases may be meaningless over a single class period but can have significant and long-lasting emotional impact on students if continued throughout weeks, months, or the entire school year. The accumulated effect of systematic bias in a classroom is an open message to some of the students that they are less desirable and less worthy of attention than others, regardless of how unintentional the bias may be. If the message is received, and it surely will be, the result will be changes in motivation, self-concept, and even anxiety level of some of the students in ways that impede their development and learning.

Bias in the way a teacher interacts with students is undesirable in any form, but it is particularly distasteful when it pertains to students' ethnicity. As we saw in chapter 2, our nation as well as our educational system is based on the ideal of pluralism and respect of individual differences of all types. This means that our classrooms become one of the most, and some would say *the* most, important showplaces of our democratic values. It is disturbing that researchers report that in classrooms with combinations of blacks, Hispanics, Asians, and whites, ethnic biases in student-teacher interactions are not uncommon. In one study of interactions between teachers and Anglo- and Mexican-American students in 429 classrooms in the Southwest, the frequency of interaction consistently favored Anglos in teacher questioning, positive responses, use of student ideas, and praise and encouragement (Civil Rights Commission, 1973). It should be noted that biases also have been known to occur between blacks and Anglos in the inner city, where the bias in student-teacher interactions tended to be reversed, favoring the black majority. Regardless of their direction, biases should be brought to a conscious level and controlled through the planning process. Some suggestions for planning to control bias (suggested by Gage & Berliner, 1984) can include the following:

1. You can plan to spread your interactions as evenly as possible across the categories previously noted by deciding in advance what students you will call on. Since all of these classifications of potential bias can be cumbersome to deal with, choose the one or two categories of bias you know or suspect you are most vulnerable to.

2. If special projects or assignments are to be given only to some of your students, you might want to plan to choose students randomly. This can be accomplished by placing all of your students' names in a jar and having one of your students select the number of individuals needed for the special assignment. This will protect you from inadvertently choosing

the same students and conveying the impression to others that you have "pets."

3. Try consciously pairing students who are opposite in the classification of which you believe you may be biased, e.g., minority, non-minority; more able, less able; easy-to-work with, difficult-to-work with, etc. In this manner, when you interact with one member of the pair you will be reminded to interact with the other. Change one member of the pair occasionally so that your pairing does not become obvious to the class.

4. When a bias is discovered, you may want to develop a code to yourself which reminds you of the bias and then embed the code within your class notes, text, or lesson plan at appropriate intervals. For example, should you discover you systematically favor more able (MA) students over less able (LA) students, place the code *LA* on the margins of your exercise, to remind you to choose a less able student for the next response.

Although the previous suggestions are for controlling bias during your instruction, the planning process is the proper vehicle for identifying potential sources of bias *before they occur* and then planning to deal with them in one or more of these ways. Unless the problem of bias is consciously considered during this phase of your preparation to teach, it is unlikely that it will be dealt with at any later phase.

A Hierarchy of Planning Needs

When you face the planning process for the first time, you will no doubt recognize that some aspects of the teaching task will be of greater concern to you than others. If you are a typical beginning teacher, your thoughts and concerns will at first focus on your own "survival" and only later on the teaching task and your students. Fuller (1969), for example, found that during the early, middle, and late phases of student teaching there was a shift in teaching concerns expressed by undergraduate students majoring in education.

The focus on oneself (e.g., Is my knowledge of the subject adequate? Can I control the class?), shifted to concerns that emphasized the teaching task (e.g., Are there sufficient instructional materials? Is there time to cover all the topics?) and to concerns that emphasized the needs of students (e.g., Are the students learning? How does what I do affect their achievement?). Fuller speculated that concerns for self, task, and student are the natural stages through which most teachers pass, representing a developmental growth pattern extending over months and even years of a teacher's career. Although some teachers may pass through these stages more quickly than others and at different levels of intensity, Fuller suggested almost all teachers can be expected to move from one to another, with the most effective and experienced teachers expressing *student-centered concerns at a high level of commitment*.

There are several other interesting implications to Fuller's "concerns theory." For example, some teachers might be expected to return to an earlier stage of concern, for example, move from a concern for students *back* to a concern for task as a result of suddenly having to teach a new grade or subject, or move from a concern for task *back* to a concern for self as a result of having to teach in a different and unfamiliar school. Also, the second time spent in a stage might be expected to be shorter than the first. And, finally, the three stages of concern need not be exclusive of one another; a teacher could have concerns predominately in one area while still having concerns at lesser levels of intensity in one or both of the other stages.

The implications of Fuller's data also allow for some interesting recommendations for teacher training. If the beginning teacher is preoccupied with concerns of personal adequacy and survival, which appears to be true even to the casual observer, instruction pertaining to these concerns might be presented very early in the teacher training process. This would presume that concerns commonly expressed in the early phase of Fuller's study, such as "Can I control the class?," should be addressed at the beginning of teacher training—perhaps through early teaching and the practicing of classroom management techniques. With these early concerns addressed, concerns pertaining to the teaching task (that is, concerns relating to instructional design, methods of presenting subject matter, and tailoring content to individual needs) would be addressed in the next period of instruction—perhaps through lesson planning and microteaching exercises. Finally, concerns pertaining to the teacher's impact upon students, that is, to producing learning outcomes, assessing achievement, and determining one's own contribution to student behavior, would be addressed in the final phase of training—perhaps through courses in measurement, observation, and practice teaching. Some typical concerns found to pertain to each of these three stages are:

> Self concerns
>> Whether the students really like the teacher or not
>> Feeling under pressure too much of the time
>> Doing well when a supervisor is present
>
> Instructional (task) concerns
>> Lack of freedom to initiate innovative instructional ideas
>> The nature and quality of instructional materials
>> Adequately presenting all of the material
>
> Student needs (impact) concerns
>> Increasing student's feelings of accomplishment
>> Recognizing social and emotional needs of students
>> Challenging unmotivated students

Fuller and Borich (1974) have constructed a 50-item self-report instrument for the assessment of the stage of concern with which a teacher most strongly identifies. The previous items are examples from the instrument, which appears in Appendix A. From a number of studies in which this instrument has been administered to both preservice and inservice teachers, it was possible to construct a hierarchy of planning needs based upon the three stages of the concerns model. This hierarchy suggests the concerns that might be addressed in each of the three stages and lists some of the options available to reduce a high level of concern in any given area. This hierarchy appears in Table 3.2 within a framework for planning suggested by Morine (1973). Table 3.2 provides some suggestions for reducing high levels of anxiety based on some concerns in each of the three stages: self, task, and students. Using the Teacher Concerns Checklist (Appendix A), you can rank from high (totally preoccupied) to low (not concerned) your own level of concern in each of the three stages and then determine with which stage of concern you identify most closely. You can then note your level of concern for each item in Table 3.2. The suggestions in Table 3.2 can then be consulted for those items that most concern you.

Steps in the Planning Process

In an earlier section it was seen that planning consists of gathering and recording information with respect to four inputs to the planning process. This section will deal with how to make decisions pertaining to these inputs prior to the actual preparation of a lesson plan. Recall that the four inputs to the planning process were aims and goals, characteristics of the learner, knowledge of subject matter, and knowledge of teaching methods. Each of these represents a step in the planning process to which can be applied three planning skills: generating alternatives, recognizing value assumptions, and extending or expanding alternatives as needed. For example, it is necessary to generate alternatives, recognize value assumptions, and revise alternatives with respect to each of the following questions:

1. Which aims and goals from among the many should I try to achieve?
2. To which learner needs should I direct my instruction?

TABLE 3.2
Planning aids for three stages of concerns using selected items from the Teacher Concerns Checklist (Appendix A)

Stage	Concern	Generating an Approach	Recognizing the Value Assumptions	Altering or Extending the Approach
SELF	Whether the students really like me	Construct a simple attitude instrument to measure your student's attitudes toward your organization, clarity, and fairness at the end of a major unit. Then try altering your instructional procedures in the areas in which you were rated the lowest until some improvement can be noted. If possible, compare your results with those of another student teacher using the same instrument.	You may want to value your own intuition more than your students' opinions, which may be influenced by factors unrelated to you or your teaching. Keep in mind that some students will be chronic complainers while others are forever silent. Your own instincts may be the best guide to whether your students like you.	Many times the most honest and helpful responses as to how well you are doing are acquired informally rather than from evaluation instruments. Choose a few students of high, average, and low ability and find out how you are doing by asking them the things they thought were the easiest to learn and why, and the things that were the most difficult to learn and why.
	Feeling under pressure too much of the time	Organize your planning time so that a specified amount of time is alloted for planning and organizing each major instructional activity you have responsibility for. Allot more time to your hardest subjects, less to your easiest. Then stick to your schedule.	Feeling some pressure is normal and may even make you perform better by forcing you to "rise to the occasion" when special demands are being placed upon you.	Rotate from lecturing, to question and answer, to assigning seatwork on alternate days or periods thereby reducing the type and amount of planning you must do each day.
	Doing well when a supervisor is present	Ask your supervisor if your first observation can be in a more informal instructional activity, such as tutoring, working with small groups, or	Most supervisors are aware of your anxiety during your first few observations and take this into account in evaluating your performance.	Practice performing three specific instructional activities that are among the most often used in your classroom (e.g., probing, asking a

TABLE 3.2
Continued

Stage	Concern	Generating an Approach	Recognizing the Value Assumptions	Altering or Extending the Approach
SELF		cooperatively teaching with the classroom teacher.		higher-level question, using media to illustrate a point). Then use them at the time you are being observed.
	Clarifying the limits of my authority and responsibility	Ask your supervisor what is expected at your school, and then ask the classroom teacher. Consider all of what both say as the limits of your authority and responsibility.	Often times the limits of behavior can only be defined as a result of trial and error. Increasing in *small degrees* your authority and responsibility over your instructional decisions until a problem is noted is one way to define these limits in concrete ways.	Observe in other classrooms and especially in the classrooms of other student teachers in your department to gain a sense as to how much authority and responsibility is expected.
	Feeling more adequate as a teacher	Recall past microteaching experiences, exercises, or simulations in which you were judged adequate by external standards. Use your performance during these experiences as a baseline for your performance now. Devote time in your classroom to fine tuning these already acquired skills.	Few teachers, even those who are experienced, rarely feel completely adequate, regardless of outward signs to the contrary. The intensity and complexity of the teaching task separates it from most other occupations and makes perfection an unattainable goal for most, if not all, teachers.	Identify those areas in which you have signs you are less adequate than desired. Seek specific references and materials that address those areas and observe other teachers for their behavior in these areas. Then practice what you have learned in small-group settings.
	Being accepted and respected by professional persons	To become a meaningful part of your school, not just another student teacher, accept responsibilities	Student teachers and beginning teachers are, in general, accepted and respected less as a result of their	Let your skills and personality be known outside of your classroom by becoming familar with the members of

TABLE 3.2
Continued

Stage	Concern	Generating an Approach	Recognizing the Value Assumptions	Altering or Extending the Approach
SELF		beyond those you are specifically assigned. With the permission and cooperation of the classroom teacher, try new and innovative ideas even when they require extra or difficult planning. Include the classroom teacher in the planning of these ideas from the very start.	newness and transient nature in the school than are older, more experienced teachers. *Complete* acceptance and respect results from the acquaintance of others with you over time, which may not be sufficient during your student teaching experience.	the various teacher organizations represented at your school, working voluntarily with other teachers who sponsor clubs and activities in which you have an interest, and attending sports functions that are important to your students. The first step of being accepted and respected is being seen and noticed.
TASK	The nature and quality of instructional materials	Catalogue the materials available to you along with the advantages and disadvantages of each. Specifically, note those for which the disadvantages outweigh the advantages and show this to the classroom teacher for possible alternatives.	Inadequate materials do not always translate into inadequate learning, and sometimes may be a result of personal preferences, not inadequate or poor design. How materials are used and what they are supplemented with often can reduce inadequacies.	Pair weak or inadequate materials with other more adequate resources which might compensate, in part, for their poor coverage, accuracy, or difficulty level.
	Maintaining the appropriate degree of class control	Establish specific classroom rules in all important areas, e.g., speaking out, leaving seats, leaving room, talking, neatness, etc. prior to your first teaching day. Hand out and/or display these rules prominently in your classroom.	The amount of class control that is desirable will change according to your objectives and instructional activities. While the teacher must always be in control, there is a degree of control which can be chosen by the	Anticipate and carefully structure in advance those activities that may cause discipline problems, such as discussion sessions, question and answer periods, problem solving exercises— especially those requiring more

TABLE 3.2
Continued

Stage	Concern	Generating an Approach	Recognizing the Value Assumptions	Altering or Extending the Approach
TASK			teacher for a specific objective, such as when students are to explore and discover in small groups versus to listen to you lecture.	student talk.
	Being fair and impartial	Establish your grading standards *before* grading tests and evaluating papers, and stick to it. If changes in your standards seem called for, make them starting on the *next* test or paper, not on the present test or exam.	Oftentimes, concern with being fair and impartial leads to too low a grading standard and over reactions to student complaints. Your own intuition as to your fairness and impartiality may be the best guide—not the opinions of others.	After important tests and papers, ask students if they believe the grade they received accurately represented their knowledge and effort. Use this information and your own judgment to decide if your grading standards or procedures need changing.
	Work with too many students each day	For large classes, vary your instructional procedures each day, e.g., from lectures one day to discussion or question and answer the next. For small groups and tutorials combine similar groups or individuals into a single group and employ peer teaching when possible.	Working with fewer actual students each day, that is, having a reduced class load, may not make instruction easier, since small classes often require more attention to individual needs and can represent a student mix that can be as difficult or more difficult to teach than a larger class.	Identify those in your class who are most in need of special attention. Then, attend to the special learning needs of these individuals, giving special attention to others as time permits and allowing those who are capable to work independently when possible.
	Insufficient time for class preparation	Reserve the first 10 minutes of each class for a review of previous concepts and the last 10 minutes for a	Rarely is there a teacher who has sufficient time for preparation. The fact that teachers generally are not	Use a variety of teaching techniques that make students more responsible for their own learning, such as question-

TABLE 3.2
Continued

Stage	Concern	Generating an Approach	Recognizing the Value Assumptions	Altering or Extending the Approach
TASK		summary of what was just covered. This should reduce the amount of new planning you will have to do each day, while still providing needed instruction and review.	provided sufficient time to prepare during the school day should encourage you to plan as efficiently as possible but not feel guilty for an instructional arrangement that does not include the provision for adequate preparation.	and-answer groups, small-group discussion, research assignments, and seatwork employing exercises and self-instructional workbooks.
	Adequately presenting all of the material	Rearrange content in workbooks and texts so that conceptually similar content is taught at the same time. Emphasizing concepts more than facts will give your students the tools to learn whatever content was not covered on their own at a later time.	This is an often-expressed concern of teachers both experienced and inexperienced. Having the concern itself does not necessarily mean, however, that sufficient material will not be adequately presented. Much of the work of teaching involves making compromises in the use of teaching time and content covered. The nature of the compromise is more important than the fact that a compromise must be made.	Individualize content coverage to the extent possible by providing self-instructional materials and teaching activities at your students' current level of functioning. Ability groups can be formed which avoid unnecessary or unproductive content coverage that may be too easy or too hard for some students.
	The wide diversity of student ethnic and socioeconomic backgrounds	Determine the range of ability in your classroom from standardized achievement scores and ability measures	Diversity of ethnic and socioeconomic backgrounds does not necessarily imply that teaching and learning will be	Use ability grouping based upon prior achievement, motivation, and individual strengths to create

TABLE 3.2
Continued

Stage	Concern	Generating an Approach	Recognizing the Value Assumptions	Altering or Extending the Approach
TASK		recorded on school records. Note from these data if placement changes to higher or lower classes would be in the best interest of the student. Where such changes conform with school policies, refer appropriate students to a school counselor.	more difficult. These are outward signs that may or may not indicate diverse learning needs. Your experience with and the achievement of specific students must determine exactly how diverse the instructional needs are in your classroom.	homogeneous subgroups to which specific materials and objectives can be directed.
	Increasing students' feeling of accomplishment	Use a flexible system of reward and feedback that adjusts your standards and expectations to the students' current level of functioning. In this manner gain or growth from a baseline of each student's own behavior can be used as a source of praise and accomplishment regardless of how the student performs against an objective class standard.	Reward and reinforcement to be meaningful must actually be earned. Simply bestowing undeserved or unearned praise on a student may actually lessen a student's feeling of accomplishment by drawing attention to the fact that something was said that was known to be untrue.	Each week choose a few students from your class to congratulate on having done well by writing them a note on which you identify the work or deed being praised. Singling different students out in this manner over time can often increase the feeling of accomplishment of your entire class.
IMPACT	Diagnosing student learning problems	Assign ample exercises and seatwork activities during the first few days and weeks of school in order to obtain a reasonable sample of your students' performance with	Diagnosing the learning problems of individual students may be beyond the scope and even expertise of most teachers. Although learning problems at the class level must be dealt with	Choose students with the most severe learning problems and arrange a learning center where the students can go to obtain special reference material, media, exercises, and peer

TABLE 3.2
Continued

Stage	Concern	Generating an Approach	Recognizing the Value Assumptions	Altering or Extending the Approach
IMPACT		respect to grade-level expectations. Large discrepancies should be brought to the attention of the school counselor. Smaller discrepancies can be your individualized agenda for working with these students the remainder of the year.	through your lesson planning, diagnosing the special learning needs of individual students may not be practical in the average classroom and such needs when obvious may best be dealt with by bringing them to attention of the counselor, special educators, or school administrators.	tutoring geared to their special problems. Their work at the center can also be used to further diagnose their learning problem.
	Challenging unmotivated students	At the beginning of the year record each student's personal interests and unique experiences. Where possible, select materials and assignments for poorly motivated students that match their interests and experiences.	Some students may remain unmotivated regardless of what is done to accommodate their interests in the classroom. For these students the reasons for their lack of motivation may lie outside your classroom and out of your control.	Choose learning materials for unmotivated students that are visually oriented and concrete in nature. Allow them more flexibility to substitute these materials for regular school curricula.
	Whether students apply what they learn	At the end of each major unit of instruction include a real-world problem-solving exercise whose solution calls for the practical application of some of the concepts you have taught.	Oftentimes being able to successfully apply what one "knows" requires extensive interactions with problems in the real world. While school must help prepare individuals for the real world, being able to actually apply school concepts with efficiency and proficiency must, in part, be the result of	Assign action research projects, experiments, demonstrations, and fieldwork to help relate classroom learning to the types of problem-solving contexts in which this learning will be most likely used.

TABLE 3.2
Continued

Stage	Concern	Generating an Approach	Recognizing the Value Assumptions	Altering or Extending the Approach
IMPACT			experience outside the domain and control of any one classroom.	
	Slow progress of certain students	When slow progress persists, test to see if remediation is indicated and, if so, assign remedial work in place of regular school assignments until some progress is made.	Slow progress is a fact of life for some students, calling for patience and understanding from the teacher. Slow progress, if it persists, may require a lowering of standards so that what was once considered slow for a particular student may now be considered acceptable.	Examine the alternative modes of instruction that may exist in your school, such as a "low ability" track, remedial programs, or federally-funded districtwide programs that provide special instruction or materials for slow learners. Use these when the problems of the learner match the objectives of the program.
	Helping students to value learning	Relate learning to real-world accomplishments wherever possible, indicating the cause and effect relationship between them. Use examples that support the fact that knowledge, in a sense, is "power" by indicating the knowledge of individuals that preceded and made possible modern-day inventions, discoveries, and personal successes.	To value is to have a deep and unwavering belief in something. Such a belief comes from many different experiences over years of someone's life. School is only one context in which the value of learning can and should be taught. Others are the home, workplace, and community.	Incorporate into your planning ways in which learning can be made fun, exciting, or unusual. Games, simulations, and group projects, for example, can encourage students to value learning for its own sake if they are planned in a way that leads to discoveries within oneself and a greater understanding of self.
	Recognizing the social and emotional needs of students	Social and emotional needs in the classroom are rarely	Practically all students have social and emotional	A warm and nurturing attitude toward your students

TABLE 3.2
Concluded

Stage	Concern	*Generating an Approach*	*Recognizing the Value Assumptions*	*Altering or Extending the Approach*
IMPACT		indicated by major episodes or events but rather are often marked by seemingly inconsequential forms of behavior that communicate a larger message. Follow up unusual expressions of need or distress through observation and direct student contact to determine if a social or emotional need is being expressed that hinders the learning process.	needs, only some of which will be debilitating to the learning process. Although social and emotional needs are important to recognize, seldom can they be met in the instructional context of the classroom.	can reduce some of their most important emotional needs by providing a climate of acceptance, security, and understanding in which learning can occur.

3. What should I teach, and in what ways can I organize the content (e.g., establish sequences, make transitions, highlight important points, interweave themes), to produce the maximum amount of learning in the least amount of time?
4. How can I orchestrate various teaching methods (e.g., questioning strategies, testing, class arrangement) to meet my objectives?
5. What instructional media and materials should I use to present the content and to test to see if it has been learned?

For each question there will be many possible alternatives. Selecting an instructional goal, determining to which learner characteristics instruction will be directed, organizing content for maximum learning and retention, and selecting instructional methods and materials—all require planning skills that must reduce the alter-natives to those that are the most practical and effective. These planning skills include the ability to generate alternatives, recognize value assumptions contained in the choice of alternatives, and extend or change previously chosen alternatives when needed. Although examples have been given of these planning skills in regard to the teacher concerns listed in Table 3.2, these skills are sufficiently important to emphasize their use here also. Consider how these skills can be used as an organizing framework for planning and, as will be explained in a subsequent chapter, as the basis for writing lesson plans.

As mentioned earlier, planning begins with a broad aim and ends in a specific course of action expressed in the form of an objective. Between the beginning and end, planning generates and distinguishes among alternative courses of action, recognizes the values implied by each course of action, and as needed, revises the alternatives chosen.

Generating Alternatives

Generating alternative courses of action is one of the first steps of good planning. For example, one must choose among different instructional goals to select the learner characteristics to which the instruction will be tailored, organize the content to be taught, and select the teaching methods and instructional materials with which to convey this content. For each of these tasks there are choices to be made. Some possibilities can be eliminated due to their impracticality for a specific set of learners, lack of resources, or the time required for achieving the desired end. Others, however, will stand out as viable alternatives for certain types of learning needs, given the resources and time available. The first step in planning, then, is to describe more than a single alternative course of action and to check each alternative course of action against what is practical considering the content to be taught, the learning needs in the classroom, and the time and resources at hand.

This step of the planning process is illustrated with some following example alternatives.

Some possible instructional goals (from curriculum guide and textbook):
1. Teach facts regarding . . .
2. Teach appreciation of . . .
3. Teach analytical thinking in . . .
4. Teach how to make decisions about . . .

Some possible learning needs (from previous testing, prior classroom assignments, and informal observation):
1. Remediate deficiencies
2. Improve problem solving
3. Acquire new skills

Possible content organizations (from curriculum guide, text, subject matter references, and tacit knowledge):
1. Simple-to-complex ordering
2. Most interesting to least interesting ordering
3. First step to last
4. General to specific

Some possible methods (from knowledge of teaching methods):
1. Independent, programmed learning
2. Question and answer
3. Small-group discussion
4. Lecture and recitation

Taken together, these alternatives are examples of the complex set of decisions involving goals, learners, content, and methods that must be made prior to nearly every lesson plan. The alternatives listed under each of these planning process inputs will depend on what is practical and feasible for both the learners in the classroom and also the subject being taught. What is practical and feasible will depend on the goal chosen, the time available for instruction in a certain goal area, the characteristics of the students who must achieve the goal, and the resources (i.e., workbooks, media, and tests) available to assist in formulating the instruction. For this lesson four different goals appear possible, three different learning needs have been identified, four organizational patterns seem applicable to the goals, and four instructional methods or combination of methods have been selected as possible ways of delivering the content to the learner. The alternatives for goals come from external sources, such as curriculum guides and adopted textbooks, indicating desirable aims and goals. The alternatives for learners come from student test data, prior student performance on exercises and assignments, and informal observations of the learning needs of the students in your classroom. Alternatives pertaining to content organization come from a review of and familiarity with the subject matter content and its organization. Alternatives for methods come from texts, coursework, inservice training, and classroom experience, from which you have gained a knowledge of teaching.

Recognizing Value Assumptions

Although a consideration of data pertaining to the four planning process inputs will suggest specific alternatives under each category, there is the matching up of goals, learning needs, content, and methods to consider. Goals must be matched with learning needs, which are then tied to a specific organizational pattern and instructional arrangement to make the most appropriate goal-learning need-organization-method match. For example, the teaching of facts to remediate deficiencies using a simple-to-complex ordering in small groups may be a reasonable matching. Likewise, teaching skills to improve the problem-solving performance of students on weekly quizzes using a general-to-specific organization in a discussion format might be another. Clearly, not all possible goals can be achieved, learning needs met, or organizations and methods used. The point of this phase of planning is simply to *lay out the possibilities,* not to see that each and every possibility is achieved. The time and resources available in any one classroom will preclude such a broad approach to instruction. On the other hand, such a laying out of the possibilities in accord with the four planning process inputs permits a practical matching up of alternatives at the time of lesson planning. This provides the opportunity to *prioritize* different goal–learning need–organization–method matches, so that while not all matches may be practical within a limited time frame, other matches can be pursued in order of priority over longer periods as time and resources permit. One of the most important results of efforts at prioritizing various goal–learning need–organization–method matches is the recognition of the *value assumptions* that any such ordering will imply. For example, if the teaching of analytical skills to improve problem solving using a most-complex-to-least-complex organization in a lecture format is of highest priority, this implies that time and resources may not be available to teach the facts needed to remove existing deficiencies. Such a recognition of the values implied by this choice, and their conflict with other value sources such as those of the school and community, may encourage a reconsideration of the selection and perhaps result in the division of time and resources more evenly among various matches.

This part of the planning process is successful to the extent that it promotes consideration and reconsideration of *all the instructional alternatives* that are practical and available. Matching and prioritizing are planning activities that encourage, and ideally force, an active consideration of the values, implications, and consequences of the decisions that are made. Recognizing the values implied by a choice is one of the most effective means of promoting thoughtful deliberation and, when necessary, reconsideration of the alternatives that are chosen.

Revising Alternatives

Not all instructional alternatives need be identified during the planning process. Alternatives also can be chosen as a result of feedback received as to the consequences of implementing previously selected alternatives. A particular goal–learning need–organization–method match has been selected with a certain end result in mind (e.g., improved basic skills, greater problem-solving ability, more creativity). When that match proves not to be a useful means to the behavior described, it should be altered to establish a tighter and more observable connection between the match and the end it was chosen to achieve. Shifting to other organizational patterns, teaching methods, or learning needs are typical ways of adjusting the match to improve the outcome when feedback from work samples, tests, and class performance indicate the intended result is not being attained. Therefore, it is important to remember that feedback from the observation and measurement of learners represents another and equally important input to the planning process. Sensitivity to these data will provide the most effective means of monitoring the consequences of the instructional decisions that are made—and of revising them as needed. This planning process is shown in Figure 3.4.

A Final Word

Earlier in this chapter the important distinction was made between the process of planning and

FIGURE 3.4
Stages of the planning process

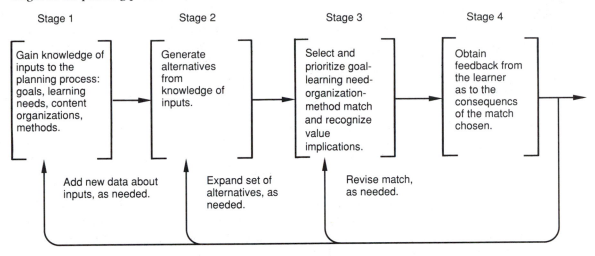

that of writing lesson plans. While it is true that planning would be a sterile and ineffective exercise if it did not culminate in lesson plans, it is equally true that lesson plans would be sterile and ineffective unless preceded by a consideration of goals, learning needs, content, and teaching methods. This chapter has presented some of the data sources pertaining to these inputs and some of the ways in which possibilities could be generated and matched to form the basis for a lesson or unit plan. Without an awareness of these alternatives, created through the conscious deliberation of all the relevant inputs to the planning process, there is likely to be no rational structure to the resulting lesson plans.

The following chapter will present one other crucial link to the development of lesson plans. This is the concept of *objectives,* which will serve as a critical link between the planning concepts introduced in this chapter and the preparation of lesson plans to be addressed in chapter 5. Recall that while aims and goals were useful inputs to the planning process, they were far too general to be of use in the preparation of lesson plans, because they do not indicate either how to carry out an alternate course of action or how to determine if the alternate course was effective. This will be the role of objectives in which spe-

cific behaviors, the conditions under which the behaviors are to be achieved, and the level of proficiency at which the behavior is to be performed will be identified. It is this important link in the planning process which will be discussed in the following chapter.

Summing Up

This chapter introduced you to instructional goals and plans. Its main points were:

1. The words *aims, goals,* and *objectives* often are used interchangeably but have different meanings.
2. Aims are expressions of societal values that point in a direction that is sufficiently broad to be acceptable to large numbers of individuals.
3. Goals bring aims down to earth by connecting them to some tangible aspect of the school curriculum.
4. Objectives are more specific than goals and describe the specific behavior a learner is to attain, the conditions under which the behavior must be demonstrated, and the pro-

ficiency level at which the behavior is to be performed.

5. Aims are translated into goals and goals into objectives by a process of funneling or narrowing.

6. Local community prerogatives expanding or enhancing societal aims may establish a curriculum sensitive to the learning needs of a particular community.

7. With the publication of five specially commissioned reports in 1983, American education began a period of reform that called for

- strengthening of the curriculum in the areas of math, science, English, foreign language, and social studies;
- renewed effort to teach higher-order thinking skills;
- raising school grading standards;
- higher college admission standards; and
- more work in the core subjects, especially math and foreign language.

8. Planning is the process of deciding what and how teachers want their students to learn. The preparation of lesson plans, often confused with the process of planning, is the *result* of this process.

9. Planning both structures and prioritizes behavior so that only the most effective teaching behaviors for attaining a given objective are employed, providing the most instruction in the least amount of time.

10. The four primary inputs to the planning process are:

- aims and goals,
- learner characteristics and individual differences,
- knowledge of academic discipline and grade level content, and
- knowledge of teaching methods.

11. Knowledge of aims and goals is reflected by national and state policies and legislation, school curriculum guides, and adopted texts.

12. Knowledge of learner characteristics and individual differences is reflected by student aptitude and achievement data, student anxiety, motivation and self-concept levels, home life indicators, and peer-group influences.

13. Knowledge of academic discipline and grade level content is reflected by a knowledge of content and its organization.

14. Knowledge of teaching methods is reflected by the key and catalytic behaviors for effective teaching, teaching strategies that encompass these behaviors, classroom management techniques, and use and selection of instructional media and materials.

15. Tacit knowledge is knowledge derived from personal experience which rarely, if ever, gets articulated. Tacit knowledge is useful in the planning process for revising teaching practices and making the planning process less rigid.

16. Almost every teacher shows some type of bias in interacting with students, which may be avoided by

- consciously spreading interactions across categories of students predetermined to represent a known bias,
- randomly selecting students for special assignments,
- covertly pairing students who are opposite in the classification of which one may be biased and then interacting with both members of the pair, and
- coding class notes to remind one to call on the classifications of students toward which one may be biased.

17. Most teachers express concerns related to self (e.g., Do students like me?), related to the teaching task (e.g., Is my coverage of content adequate?), and related to their impact on students (e.g., Are the students learning?). Self, task, and student concerns appear to be natural stages which most teachers pass through (and occasionally revisit), representing a developmental growth pattern ex-

tending over months and even years of a teacher's career.

18. To be effective, the process of planning must generate and distinguish among alternative courses of action, recognize the values implied by each course of action, and revise the alternative courses of action chosen as needed.

19. Generating and distinguishing among alternative courses of action means identifying the different goals, learners, content organizations, and teaching methods that may be relevant to the classroom.

20. Recognizing the values implied by each course of action means examining various goal–learning need–organization–method matches for their practicality and conflict with school and community priorities.

21. Revising the alternatives chosen means altering the goal–learning need–organization–method match based on feedback pertaining to its effectiveness in the classroom.

For Discussion and Practice

*1. Distinguish aims from goals by placing an *a* to the left of each aim and a *g* to the left of each goal.
_____ To be able to live in a technological world
_____ To know how to add, subtract, multiply, and divide
_____ To appreciate the arts, both nationally and internationally
_____ To know the historical reasons for WW II
_____ To work together cooperatively
_____ To know parliamentary procedure
_____ To be able to read a popular magazine
_____ To experience literature from around the world
_____ To understand the rudiments of health and hygiene
_____ To know how to swing a tennis racket

2. Take one of the aims identified in the previous question and (1) translate it into a goal and then (2) translate that goal into an objective. Check to be sure your objective is responsive to the aim from which it was derived.

3. In your own words, indicate some of the differences you see between aims, goals, and objectives. How are they the same?

4. Give an instance of a local community prerogative that might be used to expand or enhance statewide curriculum goals in each of the following communities having these characteristics:
   a. The average standardized reading achievement in the fourth grade is 2.7.
   b. The average IQ is 117.
   c. The dropout rate in high school last year was 42%.
   d. One out of 10 adults in the surrounding community is believed to have received treatment for substance abuse in the past year.
   e. The teen suicide rate is among the highest in the state.
   f. The school sits within "a stone's throw" of the top three computing manufacturers in the world.
   g. Many students who want to go to the state college cannot get in because their SAT math scores are too low.

*5. Name five recommendations for the reform of American education shared by most of the national policy reports issued in 1983.

*6. If you had to sum up in a single phrase the most general and agreed-upon problem with our schools as seen by the authors of the policy reports of 1983, what would it be?

7. Identify five changes that you now see being implemented in our schools as a result of the national policy reports and of local and state efforts to reform school curricula. Which, if any, do you *not* agree with, and why?

8. In your own words, how would you convince another teacher (who disagrees with you) that lesson plans are the *result* of the planning process, not the process itself? What benefits to your teaching might result from seeing the process of planning differently from plan making (preparing lesson plans)?

*9. What are the four inputs to the planning process, and where would you go to get information about each?

10. If tacit, or personal, knowledge is known only through experience and cannot be found on the pages of a textbook or in a college lecture, what are some examples of tacitly-acquired knowledge that a new teacher might have at the end of his or her first full day of teaching?

*11. Gage and Berliner (1984) identify a number of ways your interactions with students can be biased. Name four of these and then add one of your own that is not mentioned by Gage and Berliner.

*12. Identify four procedures for reducing or eliminating the biases you may have when interacting with your students.

*13. Name Fuller's three stages of concern and give an original example of a concern *you* have in each of the three areas.

14. Complete The Teacher Concerns Checklist in Appendix A according to the instructions provided. After completing the checklist, label each of the concern statements as pertaining to self, task, or impact, using your own judgment as to what statements belong in which category. (If you wish, form subgroups to discuss each item and arrive at a consensus.) Now, calculate your average score within each of the three categories to determine the relative intensity of your concerns in each of these three areas. How does your score in each of the three areas compare with the average of the class?

*15. Teachers A, B, C, and D have the following profile of scores on The Teacher Concerns Checklist.

	Self	Task	Impact
Teacher A	low	medium	high
Teacher B	high	medium	low
Teacher C	low	medium	high
Teacher D	high	low	high

One teacher has been teaching for four months, another has taught the same subject in the same school for eight years, another has taught in the same school for eleven years but just recently has been assigned to teach a subject never taught before, and the fourth teacher has taught in the same school for six years but just recently was declared "surplus" and reassigned to the same subject in an inner city vocational school. Which teacher would most likely have which profile, according to Fuller's concerns theory.

16. Using ideas from Fuller's concerns theory, how might you rearrange the course you are now taking? How might you extend your ideas to the design of a new undergraduate teacher training curriculum?

17. For a particular lesson at your grade level or in your content area construct a list of alternative goals, learning needs, ways of organizing the content, and teaching methods. Choose one alternative from each category to create a goal–learning need–organization–method match that you feel should be of highest priority in your classroom or that you would like to teach most. Now, construct another match of next highest priority (which may use some of the same alternatives). Construct a third match, if possible.

18. Consider for a moment the two or three matches you have constructed for the previous question. What educational values did you assume were important when choosing your match of highest priority? What educational values did you assume were important when choosing your match of next highest priority?

Suggested Readings

Clark, C. & Yinger, R. (1979). Teachers' thinking. In P. L. Peterson & H. J. Walberg (Eds.), *Research on teaching.* Berkeley, CA: McCutchan.
This article contains many good examples of how teachers' thinking influences planning and instruction.

Joyce, B., Hersch, R., & McKibbin, M. (1983). *The structure of school improvement.* New York: Longman.
Some constructive suggestions on how to improve American education based on many of the same insights reported in the national policy reports of 1983.

Mayer, R. *Goal analysis.* (1972). Belmont, CA: Fearon.
An interesting and informative booklet on how to write goals and a technique for deciding which are most important.

McCutcheon, G. (1980). How do elementary school teachers plan? The nature of planning and influences on it. *Elementary School Journal, 81,* 4–23.
An informative guide for elementary teachers on how to plan and what forces influence the planning process.

National Commission of Excellence in Education. (1983). *A nation at risk: The imperative for educational reform.* Washington, DC.: U.S. Department of Education.
The premiere and most-talked-about policy report of 1983, detailing many critical insights and an agenda for reforming American education to the end of the century.

Shavelson, R. (1987). Planning. In M. J. Dunkin (Ed.), *International encyclopedia of teaching and*

teacher education. New York: Pergamon.
An overview of teacher planning and its relationship to effective teaching.

Yinger, R. (1979). Routines in teacher planning. *Theory into Practice, 18,* 163–169.
Some typical scenarios describing how teachers plan and what influences what they plan.

Zahorik, J. (1975). Teacher's planning models. *Educational Leadership, 33,* 134–139.
A description of several practical approaches to lesson and unit planning—from the teacher's perspective.

4
Instructional Objectives

In the previous chapter, the importance of goals and aims was stated by including them as inputs to the planning process. In this chapter their importance is emphasized in the description of a procedure by which general goals and aims can be converted to specific instructional strategies and outcomes. Earlier it was noted that the strength of goals and aims is that they provide a general direction for curriculum reform, state and national mandates, and local school district policies. Their weakness, however, is that they are not necessarily tied to a specific curriculum and do not provide either the strategies for attaining a particular end result or the means of knowing when that end is successfully achieved. Recall that part of the character of aims and goals is that they can be activated in different ways according to the needs of specific learners in the context of specific curricula and with respect to local community values. These three factors—learners, curricula, and values—play an important role in how aims and goals are interpreted

and become operational within a particular school district and classroom. By the selection and preparation of objectives, the classroom teacher plays an active role in translating aims and goals into specific classroom strategies and outcomes.

Objectives assist the classroom teacher in planning and organizing instruction in ways that in the long run will save instructional time, avoid redundancy, and ensure that critical learning needs are addressed. Unfortunately, some teachers waste a lot of time because they do not have clear objectives for themselves or for their students. These teachers often do not know where they are going with their instruction and so cannot know when, or even if, they have arrived at a desired destination. Objectives not only tie classroom activities to desired goals at the district, state, and national levels but they also bring specificity and concreteness to the activities performed in the classroom.

The use of objectives has been an emotionally charged topic and has resulted in much confusion. Fortunately, many of the emotional arguments and much of the confusion can be disregarded as a product of overzealous proponents of the behavioral objectives movement of the 1960s and 1970s. This movement did much to highlight the use of objectives, but it also frightened many teachers and administrators into believing that no teacher could be accountable and no instruction truly effective unless every lesson is planned in painstaking detail using behavioral objectives. As with any new idea, there were those who became extreme advocates, sometimes making major issues out of minor details and vice versa as was the case when elaborate systems, training materials, and stringent rules were devised for writing behavioral objectives. Unfortunately, many of these behavioral objectives systems focused attention on the *form* in which objectives were to be written to the exclusion of *how* and *when* objectives could best be used. To make matters worse, teachers were sometimes compelled to write behavioral objectives for all the areas of the curriculum they taught, whether or not such an exercise could clarify instructional goals, improve instructional methods, or identify unmet learning needs. At the heart of the problem was the mistaken belief that simply by establishing objectives all learning problems would disappear when, in fact, objectives can only be a means for *organizing one's thinking* about who, what, and how to teach. They cannot do the teaching for the teacher, nor does their use guarantee that teaching and learning will become any easier or better. In some areas the instruction may already be well organized, precluding a need to write objectives, while in other areas objectives may be helpful in clarifying goals, selecting instructional methods, and identifying the desired outcomes.

Although every teacher should know how to write objectives, they should be used in situations in which the time and effort devoted to them will have the most benefit for both teacher and students. Beginning teachers probably profit most from the preparation of behavioral objectives because they have devoted little previous thought to clarifying goals, selecting instructional

methods, and identifying learning outcomes within the context of daily lessons and unfamiliar curriculum. Experienced teachers, on the other hand, seldom actually write down behavioral objectives because the repetition of the teaching task over time has imprinted for them a mental image of most of the ingredients any well-written objective would have contained (Morine-Dershimer, 1977). Also, experienced teachers are much more able to alter and generalize key instructional elements from one lesson or topic to another, precluding the need to think through an instructional approach each time a minor variation is called for. Experienced teachers often develop a repertoire, or menu, of instructional approaches which can be adapted almost at a moment's notice to fit the purposes of a particular lesson. For the experienced teacher, teaching is like playing a musical instrument, where only so many notes can be played. The experienced teacher has learned how to play the notes well so that any new piece can be learned quickly and easily by interconnecting some of the same themes, rhythms, and refrains that have been played before (Joyce, 1978–1979).

Because you are not an experienced teacher, learning how to write and use behavioral objectives can be one of the fastest routes to becoming an effective teacher. If well written, objectives can give you those themes, rhythms, and refrains you will use time and again as an experienced teacher.

Practically speaking, objectives have two purposes. The first is to tie general aims and goals to specific classroom strategies by which those aims and goals can be achieved. The second is to express teaching strategies in a manner that allows their effects upon the learner to be measured. These two purposes, while simple and straightforward, carry several subtle assumptions.

One of these assumptions is communicated whenever the word *behavioral* precedes the word *objectives*. This means that learning is being defined as a change in the learner's *observable* behavior. Covert or mentalistic activities occurring in the seclusion of one's mind are not observable and, therefore, cannot be the focus of a behavioral objective. This is not to say that nonobservable activities, such as the creation of mental images or rehearsing a response subvocally, cannot precede learning, but that they *cannot constitute evidence that learning has occurred,* because they cannot be observed directly. Therefore, the writing of behavioral objectives assumes that the behavior being addressed can be observed in some form and measured with some type of measuring device (e.g., test, attitude survey, checklist).

Also, the behavior must not only be observable, but must be observable over a period of time in which specifiable content, teaching strategies, and instructional media (e.g., films, homework exercises, texts) have been used. This effectively limits a behavioral objective to a time frame consistent with logical divisions within the school curriculum, such as lessons, chapters, units, and grading periods. Feedback from behavioral objectives (e.g., tests, work samples, and student observation) provides data for monitoring the consequence of the instructional strategy chosen and for revising the goal–learning need–organization–method match.

Although the notion of objectives appears to be a relatively new phenomenon in education, historically its roots can be traced to 1934, when Tyler formulated the basic idea of an objective. He noticed that teachers tended to be concerned far more with the content of instruction (i.e., with what to teach) than with what the student should be able to do with the content (i.e., whether the student could apply what was taught) (Tyler, 1934). Tyler noticed what Fuller (1969) later conceptualized as levels or stages of concern through which teachers moved, starting with concerns for self (e.g., Can I make it through the day?) to concerns for task (e.g., What will I teach next?) and, finally, to concerns for students (e.g., Are they learning what I teach?). Recall that Fuller noted that beginning teachers, particularly those in their first weeks and months of teaching, tended to be preoccupied with concerns for self to the exclusion of concerns for their impact upon students. This has been borne out in more recent studies in which the average amount of planning time devoted to goals and objectives in four sep-

arate studies ranged from a low of 2.7% to a high of only 13.9% (Clark & Peterson, 1986), indicating relatively little attention was being focused on student outcomes. Tyler also noticed a preoccupation among teachers with concerns for self and task with little or no concern for the impact of their instruction on students. To help teachers shift to a concern for their impact on students, Tyler developed the idea of behavioral objectives which subsequently has been expanded on by a number of educators. Portions of the contributions of these educators to the concept and development of behavioral objectives will be reviewed in this chapter.

An inability to specify or even to conceptualize the learning outcomes resulting from instruction is perhaps the most important factor in the lack of clarity and task orientation among beginning teachers (Rosenshine, 1971b). If student outcomes are ignored, there can be no consistent structure for teaching and, in the absence of this structure, learning will either not occur or will occur in undesirable ways. The danger is twofold when planning does not go beyond a concern for self or for the teaching task. The first danger is that any and all organizational patterns and teaching methods become equally desirable to the teacher. The second danger is that any and all forms of learning outcomes become equally desirable to the students. The result may be a teacher who is teaching on one "frequency" and students who are listening on another. The teacher may, for example, be organizing the content and selecting teaching strategies to promote problem solving, but the students are receiving the instruction with the intent of parroting back names, dates, and lists of facts devoid of any problem-solving context. When objectives are left unspecified, students can easily become confused both about what is expected and about the extent to which they must be able to perform the behaviors taught. This is why a goal–learning need–organization–method match is important for planning instruction. Learning outcomes expressed in the form of specific objectives must be tightly coupled to specific learning needs, organizational patterns, and teaching methods to ensure that the most efficient and effective instruction takes place in the least amount of time. Needless to say, objectives expressing the desired outcomes provide a means both for evaluating the goal–learning need–organization–method match chosen and for revising it as needed. Aside from their role in directing instructional decisions during lesson planning, objectives may be the single best way of shifting from a concern for self and task to a concern for your impact on students and your focus on the learner, thereby reaching the highest and most mature level of concern.

The focus in this chapter will be to make the process of preparing objectives as painless and as useful to teachers as possible. To this end, a synthesis of the key concepts of other and more elaborate schemes and rules for the writing of objectives are presented to arrive at the most essential ingredients of this important topic.

Simply put, the use of behavioral objectives serves three purposes:

1. They focus the instruction on a specific goal which has outcomes that may actually be observed.
2. They identify the conditions under which the learning can be expected to occur (e.g., with what materials, texts, and facilities and in what period of time).
3. They specify the level or amount of behavior that can be expected from the instruction under the conditions specified.

Before consideration of the actual form of writing behavioral objectives, these three points will be examined in more detail.

Specifying the Learning Outcomes

The first purpose involves the identification of an observable learning outcome. Recall that for an objective to be behavioral it must be observable. That is to say, it must be measurable in some way that reliably reports whether the behavior is present or absent, or partially present or ab-

sent, at any given time. The key to achieving this purpose is the language or, more specifically, the words chosen to represent the goal to be taught. Word choice is a particularly troublesome aspect of any language because slightly different words can have vastly different connotations (such as when a foreign speaker makes what seems to be a perfectly logical word choice which happens to be different from our accustomed usage). Words, however, can represent not only right and wrong ways of expressing a concept, but also either specific or vague ways of saying something. It is this latter that gives the most trouble to the behavioral objective writer. This is because the specificity with which learning outcomes must be expressed in a behavioral objective must be more direct, concrete, and observable than the way behaviors are usually referred to in the popular press, television, and even some textbooks. If these sources are taken as a guide for the behavioral expressions needed in the classroom, one would quickly find that they could not be easily observed and, therefore, probably could not be measured. For example, we often hear or read the following expressions as desirable goals:

mentally healthy citizens

well-rounded individuals

self-actualized schoolchildren

informed adults

literate populace

But, what do *mentally healthy, well-rounded, self-actualized, informed,* and *literate* actually mean? If everyone were asked to provide simple definitions of these, it would not be surprising if quite an assortment of responses resulted, with widely divergent implications for how to achieve the desired behavior and for observing its attainment. The reason for this, of course, is that the words themselves are vague and, therefore, open to many different interpretations. Imagine the confusion such vagueness could cause in a classroom if, for example, the objective for the first grading period were simply to make the class *informed* about the content of the lesson or to make them *high achievers* in that content. Johnny's parents may have one interpretation about what being informed is, but Betty's parents may have quite another. One hopes they both do not show up on parent-teacher night! Also, a teacher may mean one thing by *high achievers*, but the principal may mean another which the teacher hopes will not imply a higher level of achievement than his or her own definition. The point is, vague behavioral language can quickly become a problem for the ones who are accountable for bringing about the behavior in question. This is why vague language can be heard and seen so often in the press and everyday conversation—those who write or speak it are, unlike teachers, seldom accountable for having to produce it. Needless to say, school boards, school administrators, parents, and taxpayers may call to account those who use vague or general language to describe the behavioral outcomes for which they are responsible.

To solve this dilemma, state the behavioral outcome in language that makes observation and measurement more specific and, therefore, less controversial. This is done by exchanging such popular but vague expressions as *mentally healthy, well-rounded, self-actualized, informed,* and *literate* with expressions that show *what specifically the individual will have to do* to show mental health, well-roundedness, self-actualization, and so on. Even here the task is not easy, because these example expressions are so broad that the activities that might be needed to show the attribute of mental health, for example, could be quite extensive (ranging from staying out of a mental institution, to passing psychological tests, to getting along with family and friends). This is one reason that such expressions generally are not suited for behavioral objectives, because the behavior indicated could be expected only after a long period of time unrelated to any specific curriculum, instructional strategy, or media. A solution to this is to choose behavioral expressions from a list of action verbs that have generally accepted meanings. These action verbs also allow easy identification of the operations necessary for displaying the behavior.

For example, instead of simply expecting students to be informed or literate in a certain subject, a teacher expects them to

> differentiate between . . .
>
> identify outcomes of . . .
>
> solve a problem in . . .
>
> compare and contrast . . .

These action verbs can help operationalize the goal of being informed or literate by specifying what specific behaviors represent the general intent. While nothing has yet been said about grading or determining the acceptability of the differentiation, identification, problem solving, and comparing and contrasting that has gone on, this is a lot closer to specifying the type of evidence that can be used to determine whether or not the objective has been achieved.

Although a behavioral objective should include an action verb that specifies a learning outcome, not all action verbs specify learning outcomes, which often are confused with learning activities. For example, which of the following examples represents learning outcomes and which represents learning activities?

1. The child will identify pictures of words that sound alike.
2. The child will demonstrate an appreciation of poetry.
3. The student will subtract one-digit numbers.
4. The student will show a knowledge of punctuation.
5. The student will practice the multiplication tables.
6. The student will sing the "Star-Spangled Banner."

In the first four objectives, the action words *identify, demonstrate, subtract,* and *show* all point to outcomes—end products of units of instruction. However, *practice,* the action word in the fifth example, implies only an activity that may lead to a learning outcome; thus, it has no learning outcome. It is a learning activity; a means rather than an end is identified. The sixth objective is troublesome, too. Is *sing* an outcome or an activity? It is hard to say without more information. If the goal is to have a stage-frightened student sing in public, this may be a learning outcome. However, if singing is only practice for a later performance, it is a learning activity. The following examples differentiate between learning outcomes and learning activities:

Learning Outcomes (Ends)	Learning Activities (Means)
identify	study
recall	watch
list	listen
write	read

Behavioral objectives should include the end product, since it is on the basis of this end product that the teacher will choose instructional procedures and evaluate the goal–learning need–organization–method match.

Identifying the Conditions

The second purpose for writing behavioral objectives is to identify the conditions under which learning can be expected to occur. Along with identifying the precise behavior to be attained through the use of action verbs (e.g., to be able to differentiate between . . . , identify outcomes of . . . , solve a problem in . . . , compare and contrast . . .), a behavioral objective describes any special condition under which the learning will take place. If the observable learning outcome is to take place using particular materials, equipment, tools, or other resources, then the conditions must be stated explicitly in the objective, as the following examples indicate:

- Using examples from short stories by John Steinbeck and Mark Twain, differentiate between naturalism and realism in American literature.
- Using the map of strategic resources handed out in class, identify the economic conditions in the South resulting from the Civil War.
- Using an electronic calculator, solve problems involving the addition of two-digit signed numbers.

- Using pictures of 14th-to-18th-century Gothic and Baroque European cathedrals, compare and contrast the styles of architecture.

When the conditions are obvious they need not be made explicit, because to do so would add nothing new. On the other hand, when conditions can focus learning in specific ways, eliminating some areas of study and including others, the statement of conditions can become critical to the attainment of the objective and therefore must be included. For example, imagine that a student will be tested on the behaviors indicated in each of the four objectives above *but* for which no conditions were indicated. Differentiating naturalism and realism without reference to concrete examples in the writings of specific authors representing these styles would no doubt result in a more general and perhaps less structured response than with reference to the conditions. Also, studying with a knowledge of the conditions would focus more tightly on the precise behavior being called for which, in this instance, would be the ability to apply already learned definitions of the naturalistic and realistic styles of writing to specific examples as opposed to parroting back general distinctions between them. Note also that without a statement of conditions to focus instruction, different students might easily assume different conditions: Some students might prepare by studying the *philosophical differences* between the two styles of writing in the absence of any concrete examples; other students might focus their study on being able to *apply their knowledge* to examples in the literature. Since objectives form the basis for tests, the tests might be more fair to some students than to others simply on the basis of the assumptions students will make in the absence of any stated conditions.

Notice that in the other preceding examples learning can take on quite a different meaning depending on whether students study and practice with or without the use of a map, with or without the use of a calculator, and with or without the use of pictures of particular cathedrals from a particular period. As should now be obvious, teaching and learning become more structured and the resources with which learning occurs become more organized when conditions are stated as part of the objectives. Also, perhaps most important for good relations with students, tests will be seen as more fair when the conditions of learning are kept clearly in mind. The proper statement of the conditions of learning is one of the most important ingredients for achieving the key behaviors of clarity and a moderate-to-high rate of success.

Conditional statements within a behavioral objective can be singular or multiple. It would be possible, and is sometimes necessary, to have two or even three conditional statements in an objective in order to suitably focus the learning. Although too many conditions attached to an objective could narrow the learning to irrelevant details, multiple conditions are often important adjuncts to improving both the clarity of the behavior desired and also the organization and preparation of needed instructional resources. The following are some examples of multiple conditions, which are indicated by italics:

- Using a centigrade *thermometer,* measure the temperature of two liters of *water* at a depth of 25 centimeters.
- Using a *compass, ruler,* and *protractor,* draw three conic sections of different sizes and three triangles of different types.
- Using four grams of *sodium carbonate* and four grams of *sodium bicarbonate,* indicate their different reactions in H_2O.
- *Within 15 minutes* and using the *reference books* provided, find the formuli for wattage, voltage, amperage, and resistance.
- Using a *microcomputer* with word processing capability, correct the spelling and punctuation errors on a *two-page manuscript* in 20 minutes or less.

It is important not to add so many conditions that learning is reduced to some trivial detail. However, it is also important to choose conditions that are realistic. Setting extremely short time periods in which a behavior is to be acquired or requiring the use either of complicated equipment or of resources not generally available in the setting in which the behavior is to be

used would not only place unrealistic restrictions on the learning but also would promote learning that would not be generalizable to the real world. The idea behind stating conditions, and especially multiple conditions, is to make the behavior not more complicated but rather more natural and *close to the conditions under which the behavior will have to be performed in the real world* and in subsequent instructional settings. The conditions specified should be checked to see if they are those under which the behavior is *most likely to be performed outside the classroom or in subsequent instructional settings.*

Now that the usefulness of stating conditions of learning has been discussed, the third and final ingredient of a well-written objective will be addressed.

Stating Criterion Levels

The third purpose of a behavioral objective is to state the level of performance that must be attained in order for the objective to be met. Recall that one of the most important reasons for translating goals into objectives was to provide some way of determining if the behavior implied by the goal was attained. Part of this purpose was accomplished by becoming more specific about the exact nature of the behavior intended (e.g., to "differentiate between . . ." instead of to "inform," or "to identify outcomes of . . ." rather than to "educate") and by stating the conditions under which the learning could be expected to take place. These procedures helped to operationalize the behavior, that is, to reveal the procedures actually needed to be performed in order for the behavior to be observed. There is, however, one important element missing. It is necessary to know *how much* of the behavior is required for the objective to have been attained. This element of objective writing is referred to as the **criterion level**. It represents the level or degree of performance desired or the level of proficiency which will satisfy the teacher that the objective has been met.

The setting of criterion levels is perhaps one of the most misunderstood aspects of objective writing. At the root of this misunderstanding is the lack of recognition that criterion or proficiency levels represent value judgments, or educated guesses, as to what level of performance is required for adequately performing the behavior in some later setting. The mistaken assumption is often made that a single "correct" level of proficiency exists that, once established, must forever remain in its original form. Criterion levels should be viewed as educated guesses about the degree of proficiency needed to adequately perform the behavior in the next grade, another instructional setting, or the world outside the context of the immediate classroom. Most important to the setting of criterion levels, then, is their periodic adjustment upward or downward to conform with knowledge of how well the students are able to perform the behavior in contexts other than the one in which the behavior was originally taught. This means that observing your students in other subjects and class periods as well as observing students in other grades and classes is a necessary part of establishing nonarbitrary criterion levels. Often criterion levels are set for the purpose of establishing some benchmark for testing whether the objective has been met but without recognizing that the level at which the criterion was set may be irrelevant for any subsequent learning task or instructional setting. To avoid this, criterion levels should always be considered to be in a state of adjustment and dependent on continual evaluation of how well students can *adequately use the behavior in contexts different than the one in which it was taught.*

Proficiency levels come in many sizes and shapes. For example, they can be stated as

number of items correct on a test

number of consecutive items correct (or consecutive errorless performances)

essential features included (as in an essay question or paper)

completion within a prescribed time limit (where speed of performance is important)

completion with a certain degree of accuracy

Several objectives were shown earlier in this chapter to illustrate the notion of criterion levels. Recall that the first objective was: Using short stories by John Steinbeck and Mark Twain, differentiate between naturalism and realism in American literature. Has a criterion level been stated? Remember, a criterion level sets the level of behavior required for the objective to be met. This level is the *minimum proficiency that must be exhibited.* How would the teacher know if a minimum level of differentiation has been demonstrated by a student's written response to this objective? With only the previous information it would be difficult and perhaps quite arbitrary, because no criterion level of performance has been stated. Now a criterion is added to this objective as follows:

■ Using short stories by John Steinbeck and Mark Twain, differentiate between naturalism and realism by selecting four passages from each author that illustrate differences in these writing styles.

Now there is a basis for evaluating the objective. The newly added criterion level includes the identification of differences illustrated over a total of four passages. This particular way of expressing a criterion level is fairly complex; it requires considerable skill in applying learned information in different contexts and allows for flexibility in the range of responses that are acceptable. This type of objective is sometimes referred to as an expressive or **expressive-type objective** (Eisner, 1969) because it allows for a variety of correct responses or for the student to express himself or herself in a variety of forms for which there is not any *single* correct answer. The amount of expressiveness in a response allowed by an objective is always a matter of degree. In other words, objectives can have either more or less rigid criterion levels.

Consider another example:

■ Using an electronic calculator, the student will solve problems involving the addition of two-digit signed numbers.

Is there a stated criterion level for this objective? No; there is no unambiguous basis for deciding whether Mary met the objective and Bobby did not. Now a criterion level is added in the following:

- Using an electronic calculator, the student will correctly solve 8 out of 10 problems involving the addition of two-digit signed numbers.

This objective now precisely identifies the minimum level of proficiency that must be shown in order to conclude that the desired behavior has been attained. Unlike the first objective, little flexibility is allowed in the response required (except that *more* than 8 out of 10 could be solved correctly). Notice that far less expression is possible in answering a question about mathematics than about literature; the former is more highly structured and more rigid in terms of the responses permitted. Notice also that this more structured approach to an acceptable response seems to fit well with the nature of this particular objective, while the less structured approach seems to fit well with the previous objective requiring the differentiation of naturalism and realism. While neither of these objectives represents a possible extreme, both of them illustrate that the expressiveness of an objective is established by the manner in which an acceptable criterion is stated. Also, the level of expressiveness that fits best often is a function of the objective itself: for example, whether a right answer or only one answer is possible. Different types of criterion behaviors will be discussed shortly, but for now keep in mind that along with the level of proficiency that is set for an objective, the degree of expressiveness allowed as evidence that the behavior has been attained is established by the teacher and is alterable at any time. These two considerations—level of proficiency and expressiveness—are under the teacher's control and should be continually reevaluated and adjusted as experience is gained regarding the level and quality of the students' responses.

Here are some of the earlier objectives with criterion levels added in brackets where needed or italicized where a criterion was already contained in the original expression:

- Using a centigrade thermometer, measure the temperature of two liters of water at a depth of 24 centimeters [accurate to within one degree].
- Using a compass, ruler, and protractor, draw *three* conic sections *of different sizes* and *three* triangles of *different types*.
- Using four grams of sodium carbonate and four grams of sodium bicarbonate, indicate their different reactions with H_2O [by testing the alkalinity of the H_2O and reporting results in parts per million (PPM)].
- Within 15 minutes and using the reference books provided, find [and write correctly] the formuli for wattage, voltage, amperage, and resistance.
- Using a microcomputer with word processing capability, correct the spelling and punctuation errors for a two-page manuscript in *20 minutes* [with 100% accuracy].

These examples give some idea of what is necessary for a well-written behavioral objective. It has now been demonstrated how to specify the learning outcomes, state conditions for learning, and establish criterion levels. These are the three most important ingredients to well-written behavioral objectives. Before moving to the next topic, there is one more issue related to preparing well-written objectives.

Keeping It Simple

Teachers often make the mistake of being too sophisticated in measuring learning outcomes. As a result, they resort to indirect or unnecessarily complex methods to measure learning outcomes. If one wants to know whether Johnny can write his name, ask him to write his name—but not while blindfolded! Resist the temptation to be tricky. Consider the following examples:

- The student will show his or her ability to recall characters of the book Tom Sawyer by painting a picture of each.
- Discriminate between a telephone and television by drawing an electrical diagram of each.

- Demonstrate that you understand how to use an encyclopedia index by listing the page a given subject can be found on in the Encyclopædia Britannica.

In the first example, painting a picture might allow the teacher to determine whether the students could recall the characters in Tom Sawyer, but is there an easier (and less time-consuming) way to measure recall? How about asking the students to simply list the characters? If the objective is to determine recall, listing is sufficient.

For the second example, another unnecessarily complex task is suggested. Instead, how about presenting students with two illustrations, one of a telephone, the other of a television, and simply ask them to tell (verbally or in writing) which is which?

Finally, the third example is on target. The task required is a simple and efficient way of measuring whether someone can use an encyclopedia index.

Teachers must practice writing objectives on their own. Return to these examples when there is a question, and be sure to include the three components in each objective. Remember, the three components are (a) observable learning outcome, (b) conditions, and (c) criterion level. Once a behavioral objective has been written, it is always a good idea to analyze it to make sure that these three necessary components are included.

Introduction to the Cognitive, Affective, and Psychomotor Domains

Without drawing attention to it at the time, some of the example objectives shown in previous pages of this chapter have illustrated vastly different types of behavior. For example, compare the behavior being called for in this objective:

- Using short stories by John Steinbeck and Mark Twain, differentiate between naturalism and realism by selecting four passages from each author that illustrate differences in these writing styles

with the behavior being called for in another objective:

- Using a centigrade thermometer, measure the temperature of two liters of water at a depth of 24 centimeters accurate to within one degree.

Intuition tells one that the behaviors being called for in each of these objectives require quite different preparation and study if they are to be attained. Common sense suggests that the study and preparation to achieve each of these objectives would take the student in different directions.

In the case of the former objective, the study and practice would focus on analysis—identifying the key aspects of naturalism and realism and explaining relationships among them, noting their similarities and differences and the application of these ideas to actual examples of the writings of a known naturalist and a realist. Contrast this rather complicated process with how one might go about studying to acquire the behavior in the second objective. In that case, the study and practice might consist simply of learning to accurately perceive distances between the markings on a centigrade scale. Such practice might be limited to training one's eyes to count spaces between the gradations and then to assign the appropriate number representing temperature in degrees centigrade. Note also the difference in study and preparation time it might take to achieve these two different objectives: the second could be learned in a matter of minutes, the other might take hours, days, or even weeks. These different objectives represent only two examples of the variety in behavioral outcomes that is possible in a classroom.

Not only can objectives require vastly different levels of cognitive complexity, as shown by these preceding examples, but of affective and psychomotor complexity as well. The following section is devoted to the introduction of behaviors at different levels of complexity for which behavioral objectives can be prepared. For convenience, these will be organized into cognitive behaviors, which are devoted to the development of intellectual abilities and skills; affective behaviors, which are devoted to the development of attitudes, beliefs, and values; and psychomotor behaviors, which are devoted to the coordination of physical movements and bodily performances.

Some Misunderstandings About Behavioral Objectives

Before turning to these three areas, however, several key points and some possible misunderstandings need to be mentioned. Every teacher should be aware of several misconceptions that unfortunately have grown up around behaviors associated with the cognitive, affective, and psychomotor domains. These misconceptions are understandable results of attempts to develop and describe in great detail a system of categorizing behaviors that is useful and appealing to teachers, but which make it more difficult to "see the forest for the trees." In other words, when behavior is divided into such appealing bits and chunks, it is easy to lose sight of the larger concepts that give the pieces their meaning.

One misconception that often results from study of the cognitive, affective, and psychomotor domains is that the simple-to-complex ordering of behavior within each of these domains also represents an ordering from least desirable to most desirable. That is, it is sometimes believed that simple behaviors involving, for example, the recall of facts and dates are less desirable than more complex behaviors requiring the cognitive operations of, for example, analysis, synthesis, and decision making. The behaviors within the cognitive, affective, and psychomotor domains, however, do not imply behaviors that are more or less desirable in your classroom, since obviously many lower order behaviors such as those involving the memorizing of facts must be learned before higher order behaviors can even be attempted. Some teachers pride themselves on preparing objectives almost exclusively at the highest levels of cognitive complexity; they do not recognize that objectives at a lower order of complexity will always be required for some stu-

dents to stay actively engaged in the learning process with moderate-to-high rates of success. Without adequate instruction in the simplest behaviors, students will not be actively engaged when behaviors of greater complexity are taught. In this case, neither task-relevant prior knowledge nor skills necessary for acquiring more complex behaviors will have been taught, which may result in high failure rates and predictably less active engagement in the learning process. One of the most important uses of the taxonomies of behavior to be presented is to provide the teacher with a menu of behaviors at different levels of complexity from which to choose. As with any good diet, variety and proper proportion are the keys to good results.

Another misconception about behaviors in the cognitive, affective, and psychomotor domains is that behaviors of less complexity (e.g., the recall of facts) are easier to teach than behaviors of greater complexity (e.g., problem solving). This is an appealing argument because intuition and common sense indicate that this should be so. After all, complexity, especially cognitive complexity, has often been associated with greater difficulty, greater amounts of study time, and more extensive instructional resources. Although this may be true some of the time, it would be misleading to assume this will be true all of the time. For example, it would not be difficult to point to the elaborate study card and mnemonic system that might be needed to recall the periodic table of chemical elements as opposed to the simple visual demonstration of an experiment that might suffice to promote problem-solving activity. In this case, both time and instructional resources might be greater for the so-called less complex behavior. Also, of course, whether a behavior is easier or more difficult to teach will always depend on the ability level, motivation, discipline, and prior achievement of the students. It is quite possible that the teaching of dull but important facts to less able, poorly motivated students will be considerably more difficult than demonstrating the practical application of those facts to the same students. These examples serve to point out that errors of judgment can easily be made by automatically assuming that lower order, less complex behaviors necessarily require little preparation on the teacher's part, fewer instructional resources, and less teaching time than do higher order, more complex behaviors. The ease with which a behavior can be taught should not be construed to be synonymous with the level of the behavior (e.g., lower or higher) in the taxonomy. These designations refer to the *operations required of the student to produce the behavior and not the complexity of the teaching activities required,* that is, the level of preparation, instructional resources, and teaching time needed to invoke the necessary cognitive operation in the students.

Finally, it is important to note that categorizing behaviors into cognitive, affective, and psychomotor domains does not mean that the behaviors listed in one domain are mutually exclusive of behaviors listed in other domains. For example, it would be inconceivable that we could think without at the same time having some feeling about or reaction to what we are thinking, or that we could feel or have a reaction devoid of any cognition. Also, much thinking (e.g., conducting a laboratory experiment) requires physical movements and bodily performances (e.g., pouring from one test tube to another, safely igniting a Bunsen burner, adjusting a microscope correctly) that require psychomotor skills and abilities. It is usually convenient for objectives to contain behaviors from only one of the three domains at a time, but it should always be kept in mind that one or more behaviors from the other domains may also be required for the behavior to occur; for example, a good attitude is required for the memorization of facts to occur. This is one of the best reasons for preparing objectives in all three domains: it is evidence of the awareness of the close and necessary relationship among cognitive, affective, and psychomotor behaviors.

Now that precautions have been given for the proper use and understanding of the cognitive, affective, and psychomotor domains, it is time to present the categories or levels of behavior within each domain. The rest of this chapter will be concerned with the different levels of complexity at which objectives can be written and, not coincidently, the levels of behavior at which test items can be written.

To sum up, keep in mind the following cautions when using and writing behavioral objectives:

- Behaviors listed within the cognitive, affective, and psychomotor domains do not imply that some behaviors will be more or less desirable in your classroom than others.
- Less complex behaviors within the cognitive, affective, and psychomotor domains do not imply that less teacher preparation, fewer instructional resources, or less teaching time will be required than for more complex behaviors.
- Although objectives usually contain behaviors from only one of the three domains, one or more behaviors from the other domains may also be required for the behavior to occur.

The Cognitive Domain

A method for categorizing objectives according to cognitive complexity was devised by Bloom, Englehart, Hill, Furst, and Krathwohl (1956). It is a taxonomy of educational objectives for the cognitive domain that delineates six levels of cognitive complexity ranging from the knowledge level (least complex) to the evaluation level (most complex). As illustrated in Figure 4.1, the levels are presumed to be hierarchical. That is, higher level objectives are assumed to include, and to be dependent on, lower level cognitive skills. Each level of the taxonomy has different characteristics. Each of these is described in the following sections with examples of action verbs representing the different levels.

Knowledge
Objectives at the knowledge level require the students to remember or recall information such as facts, terminology, problem-solving strategies, and rules. Some action verbs that describe learning outcomes at the knowledge level are:

FIGURE 4.1
Taxonomy of
educational objectives:
Cognitive domain

Highest
Level

Lowest
Level

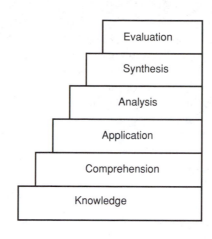

| Evaluation |
| Synthesis |
| Analysis |
| Application |
| Comprehension |
| Knowledge |

Least
Common

Most
Common

define	list	recall
describe	match	recite
identify	name	select
label	outline	state

Some example objectives are:

- The student will recall the four major food groups, without error, by Friday.
- From memory, the student will match each United States general with his most famous battle, with 80% accuracy

Comprehension

Objectives at this level require some level of understanding. Students are expected to be able to change the form of a communication, translate, restate what has been read, see connections or relationships among parts of a communication (interpretation), or draw conclusions or consequences from information (inference). Some action verbs that describe learning outcomes at the comprehension level are:

convert	estimate	summarize
defend	explain	infer
distinguish	extend	paraphrase
discriminate	generalize	predict

Some example objectives are:

- By the end of the semester, the student will summarize the main events of a story in grammatically correct English.
- The student will discriminate between the *realists* and the *naturalists,* citing examples from the readings.

Application

Objectives written at this level require the student to use previously acquired information in a setting other than the one in which it was learned. Application objectives differ from comprehension objectives in that application requires the presentation of a problem in a different and often applied context. Thus, the student can rely on neither the *content* nor the *context* in which the original learning occurred to solve the problem. Some action verbs that describe learning outcomes at the application level are:

change	modify	relate
compute	operate	solve
demonstrate	organize	transfer
develop	prepare	use

Some example objectives are:

- On Monday, the student will demonstrate for the class an application to real life of the law of conservation.
- Given fractions not covered in class, the student will multiply them on paper with 85% accuracy.

Analysis

Objectives written at the analysis level require the student to identify logical errors (e.g., point out a contradiction or an erroneous inference) or to differentiate among facts, opinions, assumptions, hypotheses, and conclusions. At the analysis level students are expected to draw relationships among ideas and to compare and contrast. Some action verbs that describe learning outcomes at the analysis level are:

break down	distinguish	point out
deduce	illustrate	relate
diagram	infer	separate out
differentiate	outline	subdivide

Some example objectives are:

- Given a presidential speech, the student will be able to point out the positions that attack an individual rather than his or her program.
- Given absurd statements (e.g., A man had flu twice. The first time it killed him. The second time he got well quickly.), the student will be able to point out the contradiction.

Synthesis

Objectives written at the synthesis level require the student to produce something unique or original. At the synthesis level students are expected to solve some unfamiliar problem in a unique way or to combine parts to form a unique or novel solution. Some action verbs that describe learning outcomes at the synthesis level are:

categorize	create	formulate
compile	design	predict
compose	devise	produce

Some example objectives at the synthesis level are:

- Given a short story, the student will write a different but plausible ending.

- Given a problem to be solved, the student will design on paper a scientific experiment to address the problem.

Evaluation

Objectives written at this level require the student to form judgments and make decisions about the value or worth of methods, ideas, people, or products that have a specific purpose. Students are expected to state the bases for their judgments (e.g., the external criteria or principles that were drawn upon to reach a conclusion). Some action verbs that describe learning outcomes at the evaluation level are:

appraise	criticize	support
compare	defend	validate
contrast	justify	judge

Some example objectives at the evaluation level are:

- Given a previously unread paragraph, the student will judge its value according to the five criteria discussed in class.
- Given a description of a country's economic system, the student will defend it, basing arguments on principles of democracy.

The Affective Domain

Another method of categorizing objectives was devised by Krathwohl, Bloom, and Masia, 1964. This taxonomy delineates five levels of affective complexity ranging from the receiving level (least complex) to the characterization level (most complex). As illustrated in Figure 4.2, these levels are presumed to be hierarchical just as in the cognitive domain. That is, higher level objectives are assumed to include and be dependent on lower level affective skills. As one moves up the hierarchy, more involvement, commitment, and reliance on one's self as to what to feel occurs as opposed to having one's feelings, attitudes, and values dictated by outside sources. The fol-

FIGURE 4.2
Taxonomy of
educational objectives:
Affective domain

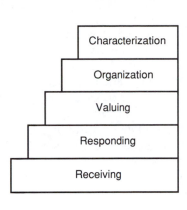

lowing sections contain some examples of action verbs indicating each of the levels of the affective domain.

Receiving

Objectives at the receiving level require the student to be aware of or to passively attend to certain phenomena and stimuli. At this level students simply are expected to listen or to be attentive. Some action verbs that describe outcomes at the receiving level are:

listen	notice	look
attend	be aware	hear
share	control	discern

Some example objectives are:

- The student will be able to notice a change from small-group discussion to large-group lecture by following the lead of others in the class.
- The student will be able to listen to all of a Mozart concerto without leaving his or her seat.

Responding

Objectives at the responding level require the student to comply with given expectations by attending or reacting to certain stimuli. Students are expected to obey, participate, or respond willingly when asked or directed to do something. Some action verbs that describe outcomes at the responding level are:

comply	discuss	applaud
follow	practice	participate
volunteer	play	obey

Some example objectives are:

- The student will follow the directions given in the book without argument when asked to do so.
- The student will show an interest in music by practicing a musical instrument when directed to do so.

Valuing

Objectives at the valuing level require the student to display behavior consistent with a single belief or attitude in situations where he or she is not forced or asked to comply. Students are expected to demonstrate a preference or display a high degree of certainty and conviction. Some action verbs that describe outcomes at the valuing level are:

help	act	prefer
debate	express	convince
argue	organize	display

Some example objectives are:

- The student will express an opinion about nuclear disarmament whenever national events raise the issue.
- The student will display an opinion about the elimination of pornography whenever discussing social issues.

Organization

Objectives at the organization level require a commitment to a set of values. This level of the affective domain involves both forming a reason for why one values certain things and not others and also making appropriate choices among things that are and are not valued. Students are expected to organize their likings and preferences into a value system and determine their interrelationships, and then to decide which ones will be dominant. Some action verbs that describe outcomes at the organization level are:

select	compare	systematize
decide	define	theorize
balance	formulate	abstract

Some example objectives are:

- The student will be able to compare the alternatives to the death penalty and decide which ones are compatible with his or her beliefs.
- The student will be able to formulate the reasons why she or he supports civil rights legislation and will be able to identify the legislation that does not support her or his beliefs.

Characterization

Objectives at the characterization level require that all the behavior displayed by the student be consistent with his or her values. At this level the student has not only acquired the behaviors at all previous levels but, in addition, has integrated his or her values into a system representing a complete and persuasive philosophy which never allows expressions that are out of character with these values. Evaluations of this level of behavior involve the extent to which the student has developed a consistent philosophy of life (e.g., exhibits respect for the worth and dignity of human beings in any and all situations). Some action verbs that describe outcomes at this level are:

display	avoid	resist
require	manage	internalize
revise	resolve	exhibit

Some example objectives are:

- The student will exhibit a helping and caring attitude toward handicapped students by assisting with their mobility both in and out of classrooms.
- The student will display a scientific attitude by stating and then testing hypotheses whenever the choice of alternatives is unclear.

The Psychomotor Domain

A third method of categorizing objectives has been devised by Harrow (1969). This taxonomy delineates five levels of psychomotor complexity ranging from the imitation level (least complex) to the naturalization level (most complex). Figure 4.3 illustrates the hierarchical arrangement

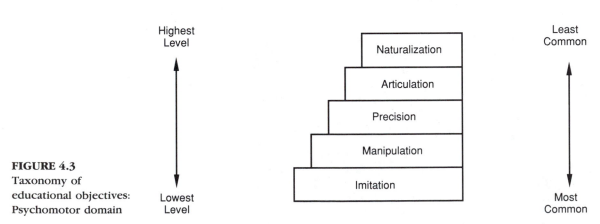

FIGURE 4.3
Taxonomy of educational objectives: Psychomotor domain

of the levels of the psychomotor domain. These behaviors place primary emphasis on neuro-muscular skills involving various degrees of physical dexterity. As behaviors in the taxonomy move from least to most complex, behavior changes from gross to fine motor skills.

Imitation

Objectives at this level require that the student be exposed to an observable action and then overtly imitate that action, such as when an instructor demonstrates use of the microscope by placing a slide on the specimen tray. Performance at this level, however, usually lacks neuromuscular coordination (e.g., the slide may hit the side of the tray or be improperly aligned beneath the lens) and, therefore, the behavior is generally crude and imperfect. At this level students are expected to observe and be able to repeat (although imperfectly) the action being visually demonstrated. Some action verbs that describe outcomes at this level are:

repeat	align	hold
place	rest (on)	grasp
step (here)	follow	balance

Some example objectives are:

- After being shown a safe method for heating a beaker of water to boiling temperature, the student will be able to repeat the action.
- After being shown a freehand drawing of a parallelogram, the student will be able to reproduce the drawing.

Manipulation

Objectives at this level require the student to perform selected actions from written or verbal directions, without the aid of a visual model or direct observation as in the previous level. Students are expected to complete the action from reading or listening to instructions, although the behavior may still be performed crudely and without neuromuscular coordination. Useful expressions to describe outcomes at the manip-

ulation level are the same as at the imitation level except that they are performed from spoken or written instructions.

Some example objectives are:

- Based on the picture provided in the textbook, type a salutation to a prospective employer using the format shown.
- With the instructions on the handout in front of you, practice focusing your microscope until the outline of the specimen can be seen.

Precision

Objectives at this level require the student to perform an action independent of either a visual model or a written set of directions. Proficiency in reproducing the action at this level reaches a higher level of refinement than at the previous levels. Accuracy, proportion, balance, and exactness in performance accompany the action. Students are expected to reproduce the action with control and to reduce errors to a minimum. Expressions that describe outcomes at this level include performing the behavior:

accurately	with control	proficiently
independently	errorlessly	with balance

Some example objectives are:

- The student will be able to accurately place the specimen on the microscope tray and use the high-power focus with proficiency as determined by the correct identification of three out of four easily recognizable objects.
- The student will be able to balance a light pen sufficiently to place it against the computer screen to identify misspelled words.

Articulation

Objectives at this level require the student to display the coordination of a series of related acts by establishing the appropriate sequence and by performing the acts accurately, with control as well as with speed and timing. Expressions that describe outcomes at this level include performing the behaviors with:

harmony	speed	confidence
coordination	timing	stability
integration	smoothness	proportion

Some example objectives are:

- Students will be able to write all the letters of the alphabet, displaying the appropriate proportion between upper and lower case, in 10 minutes.
- Students will be able to accurately complete 10 simple arithmetic problems on a hand-held electronic calculator quickly and smoothly within 90 seconds.

Naturalization

Objectives at this level require a high level of proficiency in the skill or performance being taught. At this level the behavior is performed with the least expenditure of energy and becomes routine, automatic, and spontaneous. Students are expected to repeat the behavior naturally and effortlessly time and again. Some expressions that describe this level of behavior are:

naturally	effortlessly	professionally
with ease	automatically	with poise
routinely	spontaneously	with perfection

Some example objectives are:

- At the end of the semester, students will be able to write routinely all the letters of the alphabet and all the numbers up to 100 each time requested.
- After the first grading period, students will be able to automatically draw correct isosceles, equilateral, and right triangles, without the aid of a template, for each homework assignment that requires this task.

Creating a Content-by-Behavior Blueprint with Teaching Objectives

Thus far a good deal of time has been devoted to writing and analyzing objectives. It is also necessary to spend some time discussing a technique to help the teacher remember to write objectives at different levels. This technique is referred to as a **content-by-behavior blueprint**. Much like a blueprint used to guide the construction of a new building, the content-by-behavior blueprint is used to guide unit and lesson planning.

The blueprint for a building ensures that the builder will not overlook essential details. Similarly, the content-by-behavior blueprint ensures that the teacher will not overlook details considered essential to good teaching. More specifically, it ensures that the lessons will address both all the content areas covered in the curriculum guide and text, and also all the behaviors considered to represent important learning needs.

A content-by-behavior blueprint is also essential to good test construction, ensuring that tests include a variety of items that tap different levels of behavioral complexity. The blueprint should be assembled before the teacher actually begins teaching a unit. Table 4.1 illustrates a content-by-behavior blueprint for a unit in secondary school mathematics.

Consider each component of the blueprint. Once one understands how the components are interrelated, the significance of a content-by-behavior blueprint will become clear.

Content Outline

The content outline lists the topic areas to be taught; these are usually found in the curriculum guide and adopted text. It is for these topical areas that the teacher will write objectives and test items. Generally, one objective is written for each topic area. Keep the number of topic areas to a manageable number within any single blueprint—otherwise, the number of objectives for unit plans, lesson plans, and tests will be too large.

TABLE 4.1
Context by behavior blueprint for secondary school mathematics

Behavior Categories

CONTENT OUTLINE	A.O. Knowledge			B.O. Comprehension					C.O. Application				D.O. Analysis				
	A.1 Ability to list specific facts	A.2 Ability to define terminology	A.3 Ability to state algorithms	B.1 Ability to summarize	B.2 Ability to distinguish principles, rules, and generalizations	B.3 Ability to infer mathematical structure	B.4 Ability to extend problem elements from one mode to another	B.5 Ability to defend a line of reasoning	C.1 Ability to solve routine problems	C.2 Ability to develop comparisons	C.3 Ability to operate on data	C.4 Ability to organize patterns, isomorphisms, and symmetries	D.1 Ability to separate out nonroutine problems	D.2 Ability to decide relationships	D.3 Ability to illustrate proofs	D.4 Ability to break down proofs	D.5 Ability to outline generalizations
Number systems																	
1.1 Whole numbers																	
1.2 Integers																	
1.3 Rational numbers																	
1.4 Real numbers																	
1.5 Complex numbers																	
1.6 Finite number systems																	
1.7 Matrices and determinants																	
1.8 Probability																	
1.9 Numeration systems																	
Algebra																	
2.1 Algebraic expressions																	

TABLE 4.1
Concluded

Behavior Categories

CONTENT OUTLINE	A.O. Knowledge			B.O. Comprehension					C.O. Application				D.O. Analysis				
	A.1 Ability to list specific facts	A.2 Ability to define terminology	A.3 Ability to state algorithms	B.1 Ability to summarize	B.2 Ability to distinguish principles, rules, and generalizations	B.3 Ability to infer mathematical structure	B.4 Ability to extend problem elements from one mode to another	B.5 Ability to defend a line of reasoning	C.1 Ability to solve routine problems	C.2 Ability to develop comparisons	C.3 Ability to operate on data	C.4 Ability to organize patterns, isomorphisms, and symmetries	D.1 Ability to separate out nonroutine problems	D.2 Ability to decide relationships	D.3 Ability to illustrate proofs	D.4 Ability to break down proofs	D.5 Ability to outline generalizations
2.2 Algebraic sentence																	
2.3 Relations and functions																	
Geometry																	
3.1 Measurement																	
3.2 Geometric phenomena																	
3.3 Formal reasoning																	
3.4 Coordinate systems and graphs																	

Behavioral Categories

These categories serve as a reminder or a check on the behavioral complexity of your instruction. In the cells under each category in Table 4.1, the teacher can report the number of test items that will be needed to cover a particular area. Obviously, some units will contain objectives that do not go beyond the comprehension or application level. However, depending on the content outline, one might want to incorporate behaviors at higher (or lower) levels into the instruction and tests. In summary, the information in Table 4.1 is intended to indicate:

The content and behaviors for which objectives are to be written;

Whether the instruction reflects a balanced picture of what is to be taught; and

Whether instruction will be planned for all topics and objectives specified in the curriculum and text.

Seldom can a perfectly balanced blueprint that incorporates all levels of behavior for each content area be attained—nor is such a balance always desirable. However, the little extra time required to construct such a blueprint for instruction often will be repaid; it can suggest levels of behavioral complexity that were not originally planned but which can and should be incorporated into the unit and lesson plan. With a content-by-behavior blueprint one will avoid not only spotty instruction but also the necessity of going back to teach concepts needed for subsequent learning—but which were neglected in previous lesson plans. One will also have a sense of satisfaction from constructing a framework from which fair and representative tests can be formulated when the time comes to test the objectives that have been taught.

The Cultural Roots of Objectives

Before leaving the topic of behavioral objectives, it will be useful to review and expand upon a few of the key points presented in this chapter.

Recall that the three ingredients to a well-written objective are:

1. specification of the learning outcome using observable actions,
2. statement of conditions under which the learning is to occur, and
3. identification of the level of proficiency required for the behavior to be demonstrated.

Behavioral objectives incorporating these key ingredients can be written for the cognitive, affective, and psychomotor domains, but one must keep in mind that these three domains are not exclusive of one another.

In addition to these important points, questions are frequently raised by parents, community members, and students about the source of the objectives. As noted earlier, the technical process of writing objectives can sometimes obscure seeing the forest because of the trees: that is, prevent recognition of what otherwise might be obvious had one not worked so hard to produce objectives of the correct technical form. Therefore, typical responses by teachers about where their objectives come from include "from textbooks," "from curriculum guides," or "from department policies." These answers are technically correct but miss the fundamental point, which is that objectives have roots that lie much deeper than any single text, curriculum guide, or set of policies. These roots lie in the educational values we espouse as a nation. While parents, students, and other teachers may argue with the text used, the curriculum guide followed, or the department policies accepted, it is quite another thing to take exception to the values we share as a nation and that were created by many different interest groups over many years of thoughtful deliberation. *Texts, curricula, and policies are interpretations of these values* shared at the broadest national level and translated into practice through goals and objectives. Texts, curriculum guides, and school district policies can no more create objectives than they can create values. Goals and their operationalizations in the form of objectives are carefully, in ways that reflect our values, created from sources such as curriculum reform committees, state and national legislative mandates, and national educational policies. This is why without a knowledge of these sources from which your objectives derive you may continually be caught in the position of justifying a particular text, curriculum, or policy to parents, students, and peers—some of whom will always disagree with you. Reference to any one text, curriculum, or policy can never prove that Johnny should appreciate art or that Mary should know how to solve an equation. On the other hand, our values, as indicated by curriculum reform committees, state and national mandates, and national educational policies, can provide appropriate and adequate justification for intended learning outcomes. Attention to these values as reported by the press, professional papers and books, curriculum committees, and national teacher groups is as important to teaching as are the objectives that are written.

Summing Up

This chapter introduced instructional objectives. Its main points were:

1. Objectives have two purposes: (a) to tie general aims and goals to specific classroom strategies by which the aims and goals can be achieved and (b) to express teaching strategies that serve stated goals in a manner that allows their effects upon the learner to be measured.
2. When the word *behavioral* precedes the word *objective,* the learning is being defined as a change in *observable* behavior that can be *measured* within a *specified period of time.*
3. The need for behavioral objectives stems from a natural preoccupation with concerns for self and task, sometimes to the exclusion of concerns for the impact on students.
4. Objectives expressing the desired outcomes provide the means for evaluating the goal-learning need-organization-method match chosen.

5. Simply put, behavioral objectives

   - focus instruction on a specific goal whose outcomes can be observed,
   - identify the conditions under which learning can be expected to occur, and
   - specify the level or amount of behavior that can be expected from the instruction under the conditions specified.

6. Action verbs help operationalize the learning outcome expected from an objective and identify exactly what the learner must do to achieve the outcome.
7. The outcome specified in a behavioral objective should be expressed as an end (e.g., to identify, recall, list) and not as a means (e.g., to study, watch, listen).
8. If the observable learning outcome is to take place with particular materials, equipment, tools, or other resources, the conditions must be stated explicitly in the objective.
9. Conditional statements within a behavioral objective can be singular (one condition) or multiple (more than one condition).
10. Conditions should match those under which the behavior will have to be performed in the real world.
11. A proficiency level is the minimum degree of performance which will satisfy the teacher that the objective has been met.
12. Proficiency levels represent value judgments, or educated guesses, as to what level of performance will be required for adequately performing the behavior in some later setting.
13. The expressiveness of an objective refers to the amount of flexibility in a response that is allowed the learner. More expressive objectives allow for less structured and less rigid responses than do less expressive objectives, which may call for only a single right answer. The expressiveness in response allowed by an objective is always a matter of degree.
14. Three important cautions in using the taxonomies of behavioral objectives are:

- no behavior specified is necessarily more or less desirable than any other,
- less complex behaviors are not necessarily easier, less time consuming, or dependent on fewer resources to teach than are more complex behaviors, and
- behavior in one domain may require one or more behaviors in other domains in order to be achieved.

15. The complexity of a behavior in the cognitive, affective, or psychomotor domain pertains to the operations required of the student to produce the behavior and not the complexity of the teaching activities required.
16. Behaviors in the cognitive domain from least to most complex are: knowledge, comprehension, application, analysis, synthesis, and evaluation.
17. Behaviors in the affective domain from least to most complex are receiving, responding, valuing, organization, and characterization.
18. Behaviors in the psychomotor domain from least to most complex are imitation, manipulation, precision, articulation, and naturalization.
19. A content-by-behavior blueprint is a graphic device for ensuring that the lesson and tests adequately address and provide a balanced coverage of (a) all the content areas identified in the curriculum guide and (b) all the cognitive, affective, and psychomotor behaviors considered important.
20. Behavioral objectives have their roots in the educational values we espouse as a nation. Texts, curricula, and department and school policies are interpretations of these values shared at the broadest national level and translated into practice through behavioral objectives.

For Discussion and Practice

*1. Identify the two purposes for preparing behavioral objectives. If you could choose only one of these purposes, which would be the more important to you and why?
*2. Explain why the formal preparation of behavioral objectives is often a necessity for the beginning teacher but less necessary for the experienced teacher. In what ways is the experienced teacher like the experienced musician?
*3. Explain what three things the word *behavioral* implies when it appears before the word *objectives.*
*4. Identify the three components of a well-written behavioral objective and give one example of each component.
*5. Historically, what was the reason the concept of behavioral objectives emerged?
*6. Why are action verbs necessary in translating goals such as *mentally healthy citizens, well-rounded individuals* and *self-actualized schoolchildren* into behavioral outcomes?
*7. Distinguish learning outcomes (ends) from learning activities (means) by placing an *O* or *A* beside the following expressions:

_____ working on a car radio
_____ adding signed numbers correctly
_____ practicing the violin
_____ playing basketball
_____ using a microscope
_____ identifying an amoeba
_____ naming the seven parts of speech
_____ punctuating an essay correctly

*8. What is the definition of a *condition* in a behavioral objective? Give three examples.
*9. How can the specification of conditions help students study and prepare for tests?
*10. In trying to decide upon what condition(s) to include in a behavioral objective, what single most important consideration should guide your selection?
*11. What is the definition of *criterion level* in a behavioral objective? Give three examples.
12. Provide examples of two behavioral objectives that differ in the degree of expressiveness they allow.
*13. Identify three cautions in using the taxonomies of behavioral objectives.
*14. Column A contains objectives. Column B contains levels of cognitive behavior. Match the levels in Column B with the most appropriate objective in Column A. Column B levels can be used more than once.

Column A	Column B

_____1. Given a two-page essay, the student can distinguish the assumptions basic to the author's position.

_____2. The student will correctly spell the word *mountain*.

_____3. The student will convert the following English passage into Spanish.

_____4. The student will compose new pieces of prose and poetry according to the classification system emphasized in lecture.

_____5. Given a sinking passenger ship with 19 of its 20 lifeboats destroyed, the captain will decide, based on his perceptions of their potential worth to society, who is to be placed on the last lifeboat.

Column B
a. knowledge
b. comprehension
c. application
d. analysis
e. synthesis
f. evaluation

15. Make up two objectives for each of the knowledge, comprehension, application, analysis, synthesis, and evaluation levels of the taxonomy of cognitive objectives. Select verbs for each level from the lists provided. Try to make your objectives cover the same subject.

16. Exchange the objectives you have just written with a classmate. Have the classmate check each objective for (a) an observable behavior, (b) any special conditions under which the behavior must be displayed, and (c) a performance level considered sufficient to demonstrate mastery. Revise your objectives if necessary.

17. A parent calls to tell you that, after a long talk with her son, she disapproves of the objectives you have written for health education—particularly those referring to the anatomy of the human body—but which you have taken almost verbatim from the teachers' guide to the adopted textbook. Compose a response to this parent that shows your understanding of the roots of objectives and justifies your decision to teach these objectives.

Suggested Readings

Deno, S. & Jenkins, J. (1969). On the "behaviorality" of behavioral objectives. Psychology in the Schools, 6, 18–24.
A thorough accounting of what the behavioral *in* behavioral objectives *really means.*

Duchastel, P. & Merrill, P. (1973). The effects of behavioral objectives on learning: A review of empirical studies. Review of Educational Research, 43, 53–69.
A comprehensive piece that traces the research evidence both supporting and failing to support effects of objectives on student learning.

Gagné, R. (1972). Behavioral objectives? Yes! Educational Leadership, 29, 304–306.
The case for behavioral objectives articulately expressed by an eminent scholar who has contributed much to the concept.

Gagné, R. Analysis of objectives. (1977). In L. J. Briggs (Ed.), Instructional design: Principles and application. Englewood Cliffs, NJ: Educational Technology Publications.
A closer look at objectives from the field of psychology—an alternative to the taxonomic approach provided in this chapter.

Grondlund, N. (1985). Measurement and evaluation in teaching. New York: Macmillan.
This text contains several excellent chapters on the many possible types of objectives and how to put them to use in your classroom.

Kneller, G. (1972). Behavioral objectives? No! Educational Leadership, 29 397–400.
The case against behavioral objectives, expressing the pitfalls and problems with their indiscriminate use.

Kubiszyn, T. & Borich, G. (1987). Educational testing and measurement: Classroom application and practice (2nd edition). Glenview, IL: Scott, Foresman.
A practical text including chapters on instructional goals and objectives, measuring learning outcomes, and writing essay and objective test items.

Mager, R. (1975). Preparing instructional objectives (2nd edition). Palo Alto, CA: Fearon Publishers.
The first and most popular book on how to write

objectives; written for the teacher and school administrator.

Melton, R. (1978). Resolution of conflicting claims concerning the effect of behavioral objectives on student learning. Review of Educational Research, 48, 291–302.

An attempt to resolve the dilemma of why some researchers have found positive effects on student learning with the use of objectives while others have not.

Popham, W. (1981). Modern educational measurement. Englewood Cliffs, NJ: Prentice-Hall.

Contains several chapters that cogently state the case for the use of objectives in the schools—widely read and often referenced.

5
Unit and Lesson Planning

In chapter 3 it was noted that before a lesson plan can be prepared decisions must be made about instructional goals, learning needs, content, and methods. These prelesson planning decisions are crucial for developing effective lesson plans, because they give structure to lesson planning and tie it to important sources of societal and professional values. In this chapter, unit and lesson plans will be presented as tools for tying these societal and professional values to the learning needs in the classroom and to the school curriculum. Before discussing how to prepare unit and lesson plans, however, it is useful to review all of the inputs to the planning process that were covered in chapter 3 and are represented in Figure 5.1.

These inputs represent the first of a three-stage process which includes (a) prelesson planning (Figure 5.1), (b) the actual preparation of lesson plans, and (c) the evaluation of lesson plans. In the prelesson planning stage covered in chapter 3, you learned of an approach for

organizing your instructional planning according to the inputs shown in Figure 5.1. In this chapter you will learn specific ways to use these inputs to build unit and lesson plans.

Unit and Lesson Plans

The important process of unit and lesson planning begins with implementing the five inputs to the planning process in Figure 5.1. This stage of the planning process will take a **system perspective**. This means that the lessons that are prepared will always be part of something greater. This is the unit, which will be composed of a system of interrelated lessons.

Although the words *system* and *systematic* are often used interchangeably, the notion of a system has a far more powerful meaning than that implied by the more simple notion of being systematic. The strength of a system may best be

FIGURE 5.1
Inputs to the planning process

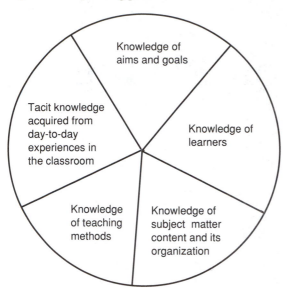

explained by the common adage, "the whole is greater than the sum of its parts." How can anything be more than the sum of its parts? Can a unit of instruction comprised of individual lessons, for example, ever add up to anything more than the sum of the individual lessons? Getting something for nothing is not a concept that rings true. And, if the sum of a system of individual lessons will produce outcomes in learners that are greater than the sum of the outcomes of all of the lessons taken individually, then surely something is missing from the description of an educational system. What is this missing ingredient?

The missing ingredient is *the relationship between the individual lessons.* This relationship must be such that it allows the outcome of one lesson to build upon the outcomes of other lessons that preceded it; knowledge, skills, and understanding evolve gradually through the joint contribution of many lessons arranged sequentially to build to more and more complex outcomes. It is this invisible but all-important relationship among the parts of a system, or instructional unit, that will allow the unit out-

comes to be greater than the sum of the lesson outcomes.

This does not mean, of course, that anything called a system or an instructional unit will achieve outcomes greater than the sum of its parts. If the relationship among parts of the system or instructional unit are not painstakingly planned to ensure that lessons taught earlier become building blocks for more complex lessons taught later, a true system has not been created. Instead, only a mixture of bits and pieces bound together by some common unit title may exist—like the accumulation of junk in the attic or in the glove compartment of a car; nothing works in harmony with anything else to produce a coherent whole or a single unified concept. One of the goals of this chapter will be to provide some concepts and tools that increase the likelihood that the individual lessons will add up to more than the sum total of their individual outcomes.

The word *system* frequently brings to mind phrases like *school system, mental health system,* and *legal system.* Schools, mental health agencies, and the courts are supposed to work as systems—that is, with their component parts, departments, and branches interrelating to each other and building to some unified concept: an educated adult, a mentally healthy individual, a rehabilitated offender. In a school system, for example, discrete facts, skills, and understandings learned by the completion of the sixth grade are not only important in themselves but are also important for the successful completion of the seventh grade. This, in turn, is important for completion of the eighth grade, and so on through the educational system until the high-school graduate has many of the facts, skills, and understandings necessary for adult living. Notice that these skills, facts, and understandings were not acquired from twelfth-grade instruction alone but rather were *accumulated* through the entire process of schooling, a sequence of many different learning activities. At no one point or at no one time could it be said that Johnny's education was complete (not even at grade twelve); nor could Mary's facts at grade seven, Bobby's skills at grade ten, and Betty Jo's understandings at grade twelve be added together to define an educated adult. This illustrates not only how dependent a system outcome is upon the outcomes of all its individual component parts, but also the importance of the relationship among its parts.

In chapter 2 the phrase *task-relevant prior knowledge* was used to refer to those previously acquired facts, skills, and undertandings needed by learners in order for them to benefit from instruction. Planning instruction first in units and *then* in lessons helps us to see the task-relevant prior knowledge assumed to be present at each step in the instructional process. By mapping out an instructional unit in a way that allows all of the component lessons to be seen at once, the teacher will also see all of the ways previously acquired learning can influence, or constrain, future learning. This understanding of the whole system or unit will help prevent teaching over or under the heads of learners by sequencing instruction so that the prerequisite knowledge required by each lesson has been taught. Failure to plan lessons in a proper sequence will make it less likely that the unit outcomes will be achieved.

Units consist of a series of lessons placed in a certain order so that the outcomes of each individual lesson can build upon one another to achieve the unit outcome. This same idea can be extended to units; they, too, comprise still larger domains of content and must be placed in proper sequence to attain the outcomes expected at the subject or grade level. Because such content generally includes entire prepackaged instructional goals, media, and materials in the form of adopted textbooks, workbooks, and curricula, preparing plans at this comprehensive of a level of instruction will not be discussed except to note that adopted texts, curriculum materials, and curriculum guides will provide much of the content for unit and lesson plans. The focus instead will be at the unit and lesson plan level, which will afford the greatest opportunity of selecting and rearranging instructional goals, media, and materials to meet the unique needs of the learners. Before moving to this focus, however, it is important to note how curriculum content formu-

lated at the state level in the form of laws, policies, and administrative codes gets translated into content taught in the classroom. Figure 5.2 illustrates the important stages in this process.

Of considerable importance is the relationship between a district's curriculum guide and the teacher's unit and lesson plans. Units generally extend over an instructional time period of from two to six weeks and usually correspond to a set of well-defined topics on the curriculum guide. Lessons, on the other hand, are considerably shorter, spanning a single class period or occasionally extending across two or three class periods. Lessons, because they are of relatively short duration, are more difficult to associate with a bounded segment of a curriculum guide. This means that the teacher can expect to find that unit content is fairly well structured and defined but lesson content is spelled out in much less detail. This is as it should be, since the arrangement of day-to-day content in the classroom must be flexible in order to meet individual student needs, the teacher's instructional preferences, and special priorities and initiatives in the school and school district. Therefore, although the overall picture at the unit level may be communicated through a district's curriculum guide, considerable independent thought, organization, and judgment will be required at the lesson level.

Making Planning Decisions

Unit planning begins with an understanding of the alternative goals, learning needs, content, and methods which are involved in writing lesson plans. These inputs to the learning process result from the prelesson planning activity, in which sources of societal and professional values are consulted and certain goals, learning needs, content, and methods are selected as relevant. This selection will in part be made by the curriculum adopted by the school district, since both societal and professional values were instrumental in the selection of a particular curriculum. However, this is not to say the entire job of determining goals, learning needs, and content is likely to be

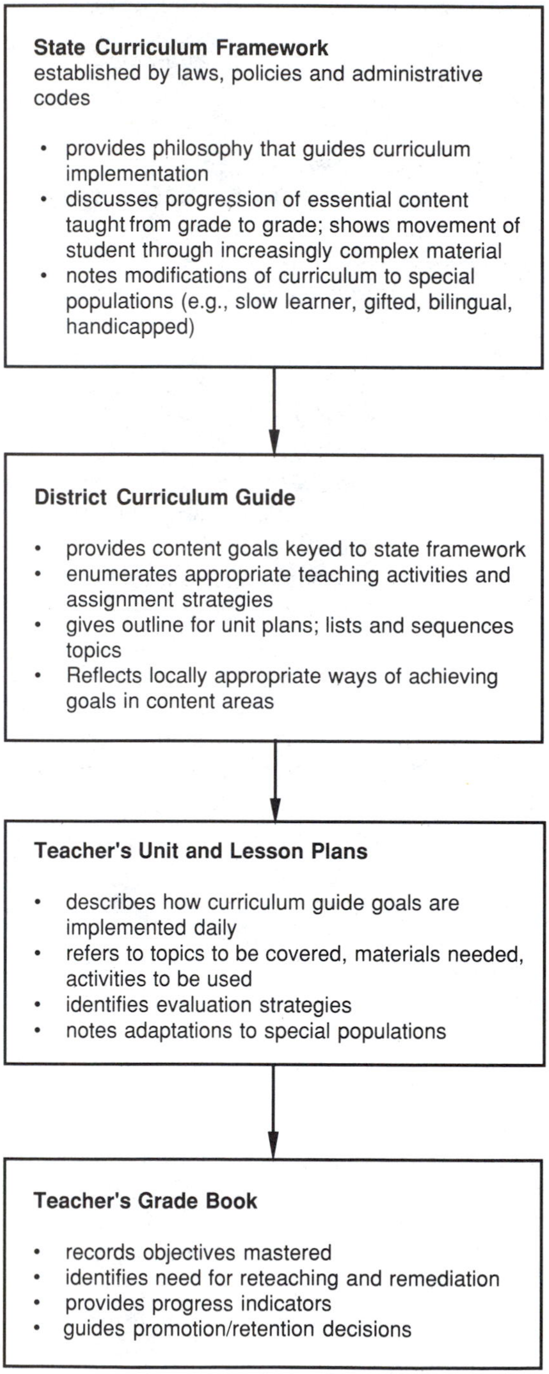

FIGURE 5.2

Flow of teaching content from the state level to the classroom level

```
┌─────────────────────────────────────────────┐
│ State Curriculum Framework                   │
│ established by laws, policies and            │
│ administrative codes                         │
│                                              │
│ • provides philosophy that guides curriculum │
│   implementation                             │
│ • discusses progression of essential content │
│   taught from grade to grade; shows movement │
│   of student through increasingly complex    │
│   material                                   │
│ • notes modifications of curriculum to       │
│   special populations (e.g., slow learner,   │
│   gifted, bilingual, handicapped)            │
└─────────────────────────────────────────────┘
                      │
                      ▼
┌─────────────────────────────────────────────┐
│ District Curriculum Guide                    │
│                                              │
│ • provides content goals keyed to state      │
│   framework                                  │
│ • enumerates appropriate teaching activities │
│   and assignment strategies                  │
│ • gives outline for unit plans; lists and    │
│   sequences topics                           │
│ • Reflects locally appropriate ways of       │
│   achieving goals in content areas           │
└─────────────────────────────────────────────┘
                      │
                      ▼
┌─────────────────────────────────────────────┐
│ Teacher's Unit and Lesson Plans              │
│                                              │
│ • describes how curriculum guide goals are   │
│   implemented daily                          │
│ • refers to topics to be covered, materials  │
│   needed, activities to be used              │
│ • identifies evaluation strategies           │
│ • notes adaptations to special populations   │
└─────────────────────────────────────────────┘
                      │
                      ▼
┌─────────────────────────────────────────────┐
│ Teacher's Grade Book                         │
│                                              │
│ • records objectives mastered                │
│ • identifies need for reteaching and         │
│   remediation                                │
│ • provides progress indicators               │
│ • guides promotion/retention decisions       │
└─────────────────────────────────────────────┘
```

done by this selection process. Many decisions must be made about the relative degree of emphasis the teacher will place upon these goals, and to what learning needs, using what area of content, they will be directed. Look in more detail at several different types of decisions a teacher will probably have to make pertaining to goals, learners, and content.

Goals

While curriculum guides at the department and school district level usually are clear about specifying what content must be covered in what periods of time, they may be far less clear about the specific behaviors that students are expected to acquire. For example, an excerpt from a curriculum guide for English language instruction might take the following form:

I. Writing concepts and skills. The student shall be provided opportunities to learn:
   A. the composing process
   B. descriptive, narrative, and expository paragraphs
   C. multiple paragraph compositions
   D. persuasive discourse
   E. meanings and uses of colloquialism, slang, idiom, and jargon

Or, for a Life Science curriculum:

I. Life Science. The student shall be provided the opportunity to learn:
   A. skills in acquiring data through the senses
   B. classification skills in ordering and sequencing data
   C. oral and written communication of data in appropriate form
   D. concepts and skills of measurement using relationships and standards
   E. drawing logical inferences, predicting outcomes, and forming generalized statements

Notice from these excerpts the specificity at which the content to be taught is identified (e.g., the composing process; descriptive, narrative, and expository paragraphs; multiple paragraph composition) but the lack of clarity concerning the *level of behavioral complexity* to which the instruction should be directed. This is typical of many curriculum guides. Recalling the taxonomy of behavior in the cognitive domain presented in the previous chapter, the teacher may ask, "For which of these content areas will the simple recall of facts be sufficient . . . for which areas will a comprehension of those facts be required . . . for which areas will an application of what is comprehended be expected . . . and for which areas will higher level outcomes involving analysis, synthesis, and decision-making skills be desired?" The decisions made about goals often involve selecting the level of behavioral complexity for which teachers will prepare an instructional unit or lesson and the level at which they will expect and test for student outcomes. The flexibility afforded by most curriculum guides in selecting the behavioral level to which instruction can be directed is often both purposeful and advantageous for the teacher. In order for the curriculum guide to be adapted to the realities of the classroom, a wide latitude of expected outcomes must be possible; these depend upon the unique behavioral characteristics of the students, the time that can be devoted to a specific topic, and the overall behavioral outcomes desired at the unit level.

Learners

The primary reason that curriculum guides, textbooks, and even some workbooks are flexible in terms of their behavioral complexity—or allow for different activities at different levels of behavioral complexity—is so that the teacher's behavioral expectations for the learners can be adapted to their learning needs. In chapter 2 several categories of individual differences were presented that may be characteristic of the students in a classroom. These include differences in intelligence, prior achievement, anxiety, self-concept, motivation, and the degree of disadvantageness of your learners, all of which can reflect entire classrooms as well as individuals. Other

categories of learners to be discussed in chapter 11 include slow learners, bilingual learners, gifted learners, and handicapped learners; these can add even greater diversity to a classroom as well as create the need for subgroups of students that may have to be instructed either individually or in special-ability groups. Therefore, teachers must remain flexible when deciding about the behavioral complexity of goals, regardless of how rigidly they may be expected to follow an adopted text or curriculum guide. This flexibility should be maintained both across classes, since the behavioral characteristics of classes may differ even at the same grade level, and also within classes, because the success of efforts at one level of behavioral complexity may require either shifting expected outcomes within a single unit or lesson or adapting instruction to different sets of learners. For this area of decision making, test results, classroom performance, and homework and workbook exercises can provide the basis for adapting the behavioral complexity of the instruction to the needs of the learners.

Content

Perhaps foremost in the mind of the beginning teacher is the content to be taught. At first glance decisions concerning content appear easy inasmuch as textbooks, workbooks, and curriculum guides will have been selected long before the first day in the classroom. Indeed, as can be noted from the excerpts from the curriculum guide presented previously, the content to be taught is often designated in great detail. Textbooks and workbooks carry this detail one step further by offering various activities and exercises that further define and expand content in the curriculum guide. From this perspective it appears that all of the content has been handed to the teacher, if not on a silver platter, then surely in readily accessible and highly organized tests, workbooks, and curriculum materials.

Although at some time or other every teacher wishes this were true, most quickly realize that as many decisions must be made about content, or what to teach, as about behavioral goals and learning needs. As one quickly comes to realize, adopted texts, workbooks, and even detailed curriculum guides identify the content but do not select, organize, and sequence that content *according to the needs of the learners in the classroom*. For this task the classroom teacher must be capable of selecting from among textbook and curriculum guide content and, where necessary, of expanding upon it in ways that strengthen the relationship among the desired behavioral goals, the prospective learners, and the required content. This matching process converts the textbook and curriculum guide into a menu and content organizer delineating all the various facets of the curriculum that could be covered. This is not to say that the school district, principal, and department chairperson do not take seriously the important role of textbooks and curriculum guides in determining what should be taught, but curriculum guides specifying content are only one source of input to the planning process, which must be designed with specific behavioral goals and learners in mind. Content cannot be decided upon without recognizing the level of complexity of the desired behavioral outcome (e.g., knowledge, comprehension, application), and the learning characteristics of the students (e.g., low achieving, poorly motivated). Therefore, while textbook and curriculum guides represent the content coverage to strive for, the effective teacher knows that this content must be *selected from* for some behavioral goals and learners and *added to* for other goals and learners. This does not mean that wholesale changes and the deletion of content from a curriculum guide can be made, but rather that a legitimate interpretation as to the *most appropriate level of behavioral complexity* is often possible and sometimes necessary in order to teach prescribed lesson content to a certain type of learner with moderate-to-high rates of success.

Organization

Chapter 3 provided some brief examples of organization. These examples explained how content can be sequenced or ordered (e.g., simple-to-complex, abstract-to-concrete, or general-to-detailed). These are only a few of the many ways content can be arranged, which, however arranged, must contribute to goals for learners. Establishing content sequence represents one of the most troublesome planning decisions for beginning teachers because the sequence of lessons will be largely responsible for achieving unit outcomes. In other words, how the lessons are interrelated is important to the achievement of higher levels of cognitive, affective, and psychomotor complexity at the unit level. Because these higher levels of behavior (i.e., analysis, synthesis, evaluation; value, organization, characterization; precision, articulation, naturalization) can rarely if ever be achieved in a single lesson, lessons must be placed within a unit—or system—in which the individual lessons successively build upon previously taught behaviors to achieve these higher order behaviors. This is why the sequence, or organization, of content is so important to unit planning: Without attention to it, it is unlikely that behavioral outcomes at the unit's end will be any different than the outcomes achieved at the completion of each single lesson. Unlike junk in the attic or the glove compartment, units must have a coherent, unified theme that rises above the cognitive, affective, and psychomotor complexity of any single lesson.

The organization and sequencing of content has been spoken of thus far as though it is only a matter of personal preference, perhaps when one's teaching style dictates a simple-to-complex ordering as a matter of habit or tradition. As was noted earlier, however, the organization of content cannot be selected without regard to decisions about goals and learners. Content organization decisions are heavily dependent on the decisions made about the complexity of unit level goals and the types of learners addressed. For example, one reason for choosing an abstract-to-concrete content organization is the desire to achieve outcomes at a high level of behavioral complexity (e.g., application, analysis, and synthesis) with less able learners. The reasoning behind this choice might be that, since more difficult behaviors will be expected toward the end of the unit, the most concrete content should be presented last to maintain the motivation and interest level of learners who might otherwise "tune out." In this case, the unit goal and the learner each played a role in the selection of a particular organization. Of course, one might well make the opposite decision—to present the most concrete content first and most abstract last—if one thinks the greater problem is getting the learners' attention at the beginning of the unit. This illustrates how decisions about the behavioral complexity of goals and learners are dependent upon the knowledge teachers have about their own classrooms.

As noted in Figure 5.1, choosing a teaching method is yet another important decision area in the planning process. Chapters 6–11 will be devoted exclusively to this area, however, so the discussion of teaching methods in this chapter will be limited to examples included in lesson plans.

Making Unit Plans

A Chinese proverb says that "a picture is worth a thousand words." In this section we will apply this idea to the process of unit planning by learning how to create a diagram, or blueprint, of a unit. While this diagram or visual blueprint will not substitute entirely for a written description or outline of what one plans to teach, it can serve as an effective means for organizing one's thinking—that is, for planning. Scientists, administrators, engineers, and business executives have long known the value of pictures in the form of flow charts, organization charts, blueprints, technical diagrams, and even "doodles" to convey the essence, if not the details, of a concept. Teachers can borrow the basic notion; pictures in one form or another not only can communicate the results of the planning process but also can be a useful aid during that process, helping to select, organize, order, evaluate, and revise the substance of unit plans.

Although teaching parallels many other professions that use visual devices in the plan-

ning process, in many ways teaching is a unique profession. It does not have a product that rolls off an assembly line, as many businesses do, and it does not build its product using the mathematical laws and physical substances used by the scientist and engineer. Consequently, a teacher's visual blueprints must differ from those of others in many important ways but at the same time must reflect the qualities that have made pictures so important to planning in these other professions. You have already been introduced to two of these qualities: the concept of hierarchy, showing the relationship of parts to whole (lessons to unit), and the concept of constraint, showing the necessity for a certain order of events (lesson sequence). These two concepts will be put to work in creating a visual picture of a unit; such a picture can both stimulate and organize thoughts and communicate the results of these thoughts to others in an easy-to-follow graphic format.

There are two simple rules for drawing a picture of a planned unit. The first rule is that any teaching goal can be divided into specific instructional activities. A teaching activity is usually described by indicating the content to be taught and the outcome that is expected to result. General teaching activities and outcomes tend to serve as unit objectives, while specific teaching activities and outcomes tend to serve as lesson objectives. General teaching activities and outcomes always require the identification of more specific activities and outcomes to show *how the more generally stated activities and outcomes will be achieved.* In other words, any goal at the unit level can be broken into its component parts at the lesson level, with those component parts representing everything that is important for attaining the goal. This point is illustrated in Figure 5.3.

Notice that Figure 5.3 has three levels; for the moment, focus on the top and bottom levels. The top represents the unit's general intent that is derived from the curriculum guide and adopted textbook, which are based upon societal, state, or locally stated goals. The bottom represents content expressed at a level of specificity suitable for preparing individual lessons. Notice that, in

FIGURE 5.3
Example of a hierarchy of reading content at different levels of specificity

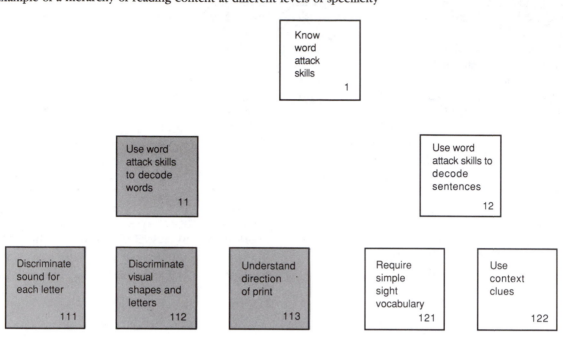

the judgment of this unit planner, ending the plan at a more detailed level would result in content sized for less than one lesson; beginning the plan with content at a more general level would result in content sized too big for one unit. This unit plan ends with bite-sized chunks which together exhaust the content specified at the higher levels. Just like in the story of Goldilocks and the three bears, the bottom of the unit plan hierarchy must end with the portion of content being served up as "not too big and not too small, but just right." Experience and judgment are the best guides for deciding what can be accomplished in a single lesson, although logical divisions within the curriculum guide and text will be helpful too.

By now it is obvious that the second level of Figure 5.3 is nothing more than a logical means of getting from some general goal to specific lesson content. It is an intermediate thinking process resulting in bite-sized pieces of just the right size. There is no magic number for determining the number of intermediate levels that will be needed; this will depend on how broadly the

initial goal is stated and the number of steps needed to produce content in just the right amounts for lesson planning. In some cases the route from unit to lesson content can be direct (two levels), while in other instances several additional levels may have to be worked through before arriving at lesson-sized chunks. If difficulty arises in getting sufficiently specific for lesson-sized content, the teacher may revise the goal, dividing it into two or more subgoals and beginning a new hierarchy from each subgoal. This was the way the bottom level of Figure 5.3 was created, in which each lesson at this third level fits concisely into one box at the next higher level. Starting at such a high level of generality, the unit planner has devised two units of instruction. This is the same way that an outline is created, beginning with Roman numerals (I, II, III, etc.); their subdivisions (A, B, C, etc.), might be subdivided still further. The initial statement of unit content (top box) often turns out to be more comprehensive than expected, representing a whole domain or cluster of units (which was the case in Figure 5.3); what initially was conceived of as an individual lesson sometimes turns out to be a whole unit. Flexibility in choosing which part of the hierarchy constitutes the right-sized chunks for unit and lesson content is the key to its use. In Figure 5.3 this is indicated by the shaded portion (representing word-specific content), with another possible unit indicated by the unshaded portion (representing sentence-specific content). The process of building a content hierarchy will guide you in making the important distinction between unit and lesson content; this can prevent many false starts in lesson planning.

Thus far the first of two rules to be used in completing a unit plan has been discussed. The first rule simply entailed the use of boxes to illustrate or picture areas of content—or instructional goals—at various levels of generality. The second rule, equally simple, will pertain to how we show sequence among lessons and how outcomes of lessons can build upon one another to achieve a unit goal. First, the intended outcome

of the unit will be indicated with an arrow on the top box as shown in Figure 5.4.

The unit could have been either of the two boxes representing the second level of the hierarchy in Figure 5.3. The first of these was chosen arbitrarily for our illustration. Next, intended outcomes at the lesson level are identified as shown in Figure 5.4, but in a way that implies a certain order if that is important. The second rule, then, is to connect the content of the lessons using the behavioral outcomes implied for each lesson; the outcome of all the lessons taken together must be the same as the unit outcome. This is necessary to show what must be taught at the lesson level and what behaviors must be acquired to achieve the stated unit outcome. This will always be true whether or not the sequence is important. In some, but probably not many, instances the sequence of lessons can be arbitrary, while for others only a partial sequence need be maintained. These two alternatives are shown in Figures 5.5a and 5.5b.

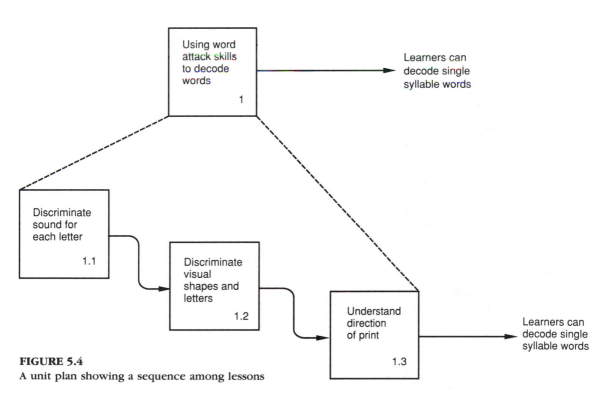

FIGURE 5.4
A unit plan showing a sequence among lessons

FIGURE 5.5 (a)
A unit plan without
lesson sequence
(Lesson 1.1, 1.2, and 1.3
can occur in any order)

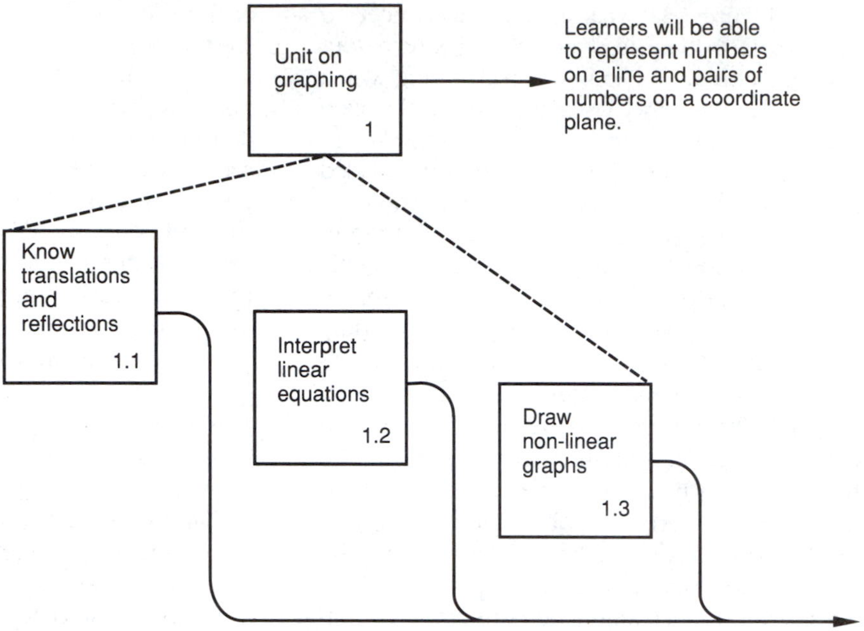

Unit on
graphing

1

Learners will be able
to represent numbers
on a line and pairs of
numbers on a coordinate
plane.

Know
translations
and
reflections

1.1

Interpret
linear
equations

1.2

Draw
non-linear
graphs

1.3

FIGURE 5.5 (b)
A unit plan with partial
lesson sequence
(Lesson 1.1 must
precede Lesson 1.2)

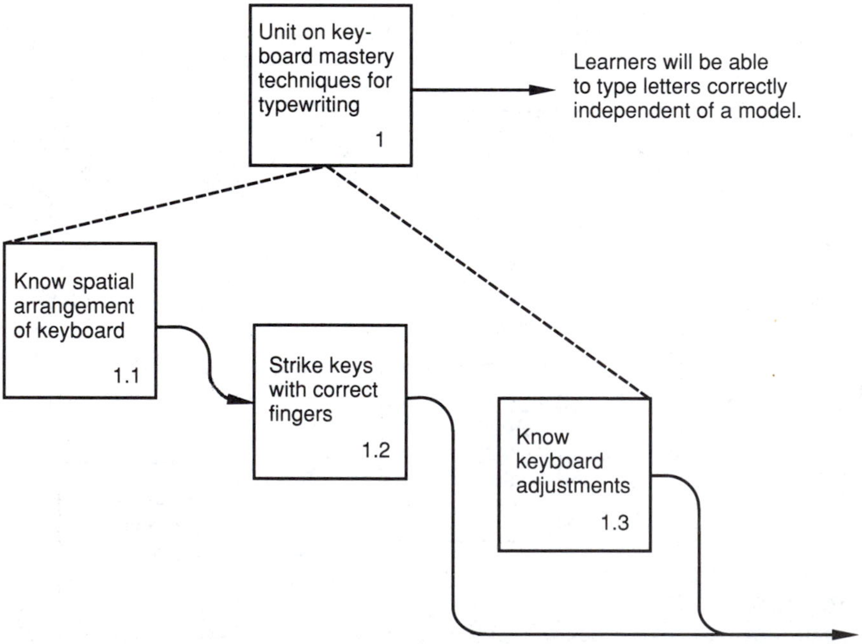

Unit on key-
board mastery
techniques for
typewriting

1

Learners will be able
to type letters correctly
independent of a model.

Know spatial
arrangement
of keyboard

1.1

Strike keys
with correct
fingers

1.2

Know
keyboard
adjustments

1.3

116 CHAPTER 5

The second rule recognizes how previous lessons can constrain or modify the outcomes of subsequent lessons and encourages the teacher to utilize sequence, building upon previously taught learning to produce more behaviorally complex outcomes at the unit level. If lesson outcomes are not connected in any way, it is unlikely that the unit outcome will be at any higher level of cognitive, affective, or psychomotor complexity than are the individual lessons. This was the earlier point about the whole being "greater than the sum of its parts." The *whole* is the unit, and the *parts* are the lessons. An effective unit, therefore, is one that uses the relationship between lessons and their cumulative effect to achieve unit outcomes at the analysis, synthesis, or evaluation levels of complexity, if cognitive objectives are being sought; at the value, organization, and characterization level, if affective objectives are being sought; or, at the precision, articulation, and naturalization level, if psychomotor objectives are being sought. Behaviors at these higher levels of complexity represent the learning of concepts, the application of facts and understandings to real world problem solving, and the ability to make value judgments—these are among the most sought after and most frequently used behaviors in adult life. The effective teacher plans the interrelationships among lessons in a way that not only allows but also encourages these behaviors to emerge at the unit level.

Seeing whole units visually in this manner has several advantages. For example, seeing a lesson in the context of other lessons sharing the same purpose at the unit level brings to one's attention the importance of task-relevant prior knowledge to the success of the lessons. Recall that if prerequisite knowledge and skills relevant to the lesson have not been acquired or inadequately acquired, the lesson objective cannot be obtained. Some prior lessons, then, may be expressly planned to bring subsequent lessons to the learner's current level of functioning. One purpose of seeing lessons within the bounded context of a unit plan is to determine if all necessary task-relevant prior knowledge required by each lesson has been provided by the unit plan. Since unit plans precede lesson plans, overlooked lessons and objectives prerequisite to later lessons can be added easily to the unit plan. A more painful and unnecessary way to arrive at the same understanding is teaching a lesson that students are unprepared for and only afterward learning that they lack the necessary prior knowledge or skills relevant to the tasks they are expected to perform.

Unit plans can take various forms. One such is the visual blueprint introduced previously in this chapter. Although such a blueprint is helpful in organizing, sequencing, and arriving at bite-sized pieces of content suitable for presentation at the lesson level, a written description will be necessary for communicating the details of the unit to others and to yourself at a later time. Therefore, when the organizing, sequencing, and sizing is completed graphically, the teacher will want to write down all the details needed for presenting it to students at a later time. One possible format for preparing a written version of a unit plan appears in Figure 5.6. This format, suggested by Kim and Kellough (1978), divides a written unit plan into its (a) main purpose, (b) behavioral objectives, (c) content, (d) procedures and activities, (e) instructional aids or resources, and (f) evaluation methods. To this written plan can be attached the visual blueprint which indicates at a glance the organization, sequence, and sizing of the unit and provides both an introduction to and overview of the written details that follow. Finally, in this unit plan both objectives and individual learners progress from the lower levels (comprehension, application, imitation) to the higher levels (analysis, synthesis, precision) of cognitive and psychomotor complexity, thereby illustrating that early lessons in the unit can be used as building blocks for higher levels of behavioral complexity at the end of the unit.

Making Lesson Plans

Up to this point emphasis has been given to:

1. classifying unit outcomes at a higher level of behavioral complexity than lesson outcomes

FIGURE 5.6
Example unit plan (Zenger & Zenger, 1982)

Grade: 10
Unit Topic: Pizza with Yeast Dough Crust
Course/Subject: Contemporary Home Economics
Approximate Time Required: One week

1. Main Purpose of the Unit: The purpose of this unit is to acquaint the students with the principles of making yeast dough by making pizza. The historical background, nutritional value, and variations of pizza will also be covered.
2. Behavioral Objectives
   The student will be able to:
   1. Describe the functions of each of the ingredients in yeast dough. (Cognitive-knowledge)
   2. Explain the steps in preparing yeast dough. (Cognitive-comprehension)
   3. Make a yeast dough for a pizza crust. (Cognitive-application and psychomotor-imitation)
   4. State briefly the history of pizza. (Cognitive-knowledge)
   5. Match the ingredients in pizza to the food groups they represent. (Cognitive-knowledge)
   6. Classify and give examples of different types of pizza. (Cognitive-analysis)
   7. Create and bake a pizza of their choice. (Cognitive-synthesis and psychomotor-precision)
3. Content Outline
   A. Essential ingredients in yeast dough
      (1) Flour
      (2) Yeast
      (3) Liquid
      (4) Sugar
      (5) Salt
   B. Non-essential ingredients
      (1) Fats
      (2) Eggs
      (3) Other, such as fruit and nuts
   C. Preparing yeast dough
      (1) Mixing
      (2) Kneading
      (3) Rising (fermenting)
      (4) Punching down
      (5) Shaping
      (6) Baking

   D. History of pizza
      (1) First pizza was from Naples.
      (2) Pizza is an Italian word meaning pie.
      (3) Originally eaten by the poor, pizza was also enjoyed by royalty.
      (4) Italian immigrants brought pizza to the United States in the late 1800s.
   E. Types of pizza
      (1) Neapolitan
      (2) Sicilian
      (3) Pizza Rustica
      (4) Pizza de Polenta
   F. Nutritional value of pizza
      (1) Nutritious meal or snack
      (2) Can contain all four food groups
      (3) One serving of cheese pizza contains:
         (a) Protein
         (b) Vitamins
         (c) Minerals
   G. Making a pizza
      (1) Prepare dough
      (2) Roll out dough
      (3) Transfer to pan
      (4) Spread sauce
      (5) Top as desired
      (6) Bake
4. Procedures and Activities
   A. Informal lecture
   B. Discussion
   C. Demonstration of mixing and kneading dough
   D. Filmstrip on pizza
   E. Education game (Pizzeria): Each time a student answers correctly a question about yeast dough or pizza, he gets a part of a paper pizza. The first to collect a complete pizza wins.
   F. Cooking lab
5. Instructional Aids or Resources
   A. Test: *Guide to Modern Meals* (Webster, McGraw-Hill, 1970)
   B. Filmstrip: *Pizza, Pizza* 10 minutes
   C. *Pizza, Pizza* booklets by Chef Boyardee
   D. Eduational game (Pizzeria)
   E. *Bake-it-easy Yeast Book* by Fleischmann's Yeast
   F. Poster (showing different kinds of pizza from Pizza Hut)
6. Evaluation
   A. Unit test
   B. Lab performance

by using one of the three taxonomies presented in chapter 4;

2. deriving lesson content from unit outcomes in bite-sized chunks suitable for presentation in one or two instructional periods;

3. planning these bite-sized pieces sequentially so that outcomes of previously taught lessons are instrumental in achieving the outcomes of subsequent lessons, and

4. rearranging or adding lesson content where necessary to provide the task-relevant prior knowledge required for subsequent learning.

The visual scheme for unit planning forces a systematic consideration of these processes, but the real work of lesson planning has yet to be done.

Writing the lesson plans will become easier and the lessons more effective to the extent that unit plans precede lesson plans and that the preceding four processes are used to guide the construction of a unit plan. Without these four steps as a guide, unit outcomes can never be greater than the sum of the outcomes of the individual lessons. When lessons are planned without any conception of a higher level unit outcome, attention falls exclusively on each individual lesson without consideration of the relationship between the lessons. This relationship will appear deceptively unimportant until it becomes apparent (often too late) that the lessons seem to pull students first in one direction (e.g., knowledge acquisition) and then abruptly in another (e.g., problem solving) without any intermediate instruction to guide them in the transition. The end result of such a conglomeration of isolated lesson outcomes might well be confusion, anxiety, and distrust on the part of the students, regardless of how meticulously the lessons were prepared and how effective they were in accomplishing their stated, but isolated, outcomes. Since outcomes at higher levels of behavioral complexity can rarely be attained within the time frame of a single lesson, they must be achieved in the context of unit plans. Before actually writing out a lesson plan, three preliminary considerations need to be mentioned in order for the task to flow smoothly.

Determining Where to Start

Perhaps most perplexing to new teachers is deciding at which level of behavioral complexity a lesson should begin. Does one always begin by teaching facts (i.e., to instill knowledge), or can one begin with activities at the application or even synthesis and decision-making level? Both of these alternatives are possible, but each makes different assumptions about the behavioral characteristics of the students and the sequence of lessons that has gone before. Beginning a lesson or a sequence of lessons at the knowledge level (e.g., to list, to recall, to recite, etc.) assumes that the topic of the lesson is mostly new material. Such a lesson usually occurs at the beginning of a sequence of lessons which will progressively use this knowledge to build toward more complex behaviors—perhaps ending at the application, synthesis, or evaluation level. When no task-relevant prior knowledge is required, the starting point for the lesson is often at the knowledge or comprehension level. Lessons that begin at higher levels of behavioral complexity will require some task-relevant prior knowledge. Notice from the list of objectives in the example unit plan in Figure 5.6 that each lesson having an outcome at a higher level of behavioral complexity was preceded by a lesson at some lower level of complexity: The proper level of behavioral complexity with which the lesson starts depends upon where the lesson falls in the sequence of lessons.

Typically, unit plans should attempt to instill a range of behaviors and to end with a higher level of behavioral complexity than they were begun. Some units might begin at the application level and end at a higher level if a previous unit has provided the task-relevant prior knowledge and understandings required. It is also possible, and probable in some content areas, to progress from one behavioral level to another within a single lesson. While this becomes increasingly difficult when the lessons start at the higher levels of behavioral complexity, it is possible and often desirable to move from knowledge to comprehension and even to application activities within a single lesson. This is illustrated in the flow of objectives for the following third-grade social studies lesson.

Unit Title: Local, State, and National Geography
Lesson Title: Local Geography
Objectives:

- Know geographical location of community relative to state and nation (knowledge)
- Describe physical features of one's community (comprehension)
- Locate community on map and globe (application)
- Discuss how one's community is similar to and different from other communities (analysis)

In this lesson a comprehensive span of behaviors is being required in a relatively brief span of time by using objects already known to the students (one's own community, maps) and by dovetailing one objective into another so that each new activity is seen as a continuation of the preceding one. When a transition across behavioral levels is planned within a single lesson, the necessary question before each new level of complexity is taught is "Has all the task-relevant prior knowledge required been provided?" Only when the answer is yes will the lesson be directed at the students' current level of functioning, and only then will it be possible to attain the unit objective.

Provisions for Individual Learning.

A second consideration before beginning to write a lesson plan is the extent to which the lesson is intended to provide opportunities for individual learning. Thus far all the students within a class have been considered identical, sharing the same behavioral characteristics and task-relevant prior knowledge. Chapter 2 presented some of the varieties of students that are likely to be in a classroom. Regardless of where the entry level of the lesson is positioned, some students will be above it while other students will be below it. Much of the work of unit and lesson planning is playing a game of averages in which the teacher attempts to provide *most* of the instruction at the

current level of functioning of *most* of the learners. Unless an entire course of study is individualized, as is sometimes done in programmed and computer-assisted instruction curricula, most instruction will have to be directed at the "average" learner in your classroom. There are, however, some procedures that can supplement the game of averages and allow for more individualized learning for the students who may need it the most. One must decide before beginning the lesson plan, however, the extent to which the diversity of students in the class requires one or more of these alternatives. These and other alternatives for individualizing instruction will be described in subsequent chapters. For now, the following entries will serve to present some of the options for individualizing instruction.

Ability Grouping. A class can be subdivided according to the intellectual skills required for grasping the subsequent content. More able students can read ahead and work independently on advanced exercises while the lesson is directed to the average and less able learner. Lesson plans, objectives, activities, instructional materials, and tests could be split into two (or more) appropriate parts.

Peer Tutoring. The lesson plan can contain a minimum of classroom discourse by the teacher and a maximum of independent work by students. In this case each more able student would be assigned to help a less able student who had not acquired task-relevant prior knowledge. Since each student in need would require different amounts and levels of remediation, the peer tutor would begin at the student's current level of functioning and bring it to the level required for the next lesson.

Learning Centers. Some types of students profit more from working at learning centers tucked away in a classroom than from listening to a lecture. When a learning center contains media, supplemental resources, and exercises directly related to your lesson content, these should be included as an integral part of your lesson plan. These centers can help individualize a lesson for those students who lack the prerequisite knowledge or skills required by the lesson entry level.

Review and Follow-up Materials. The lesson may begin with a review of the task-relevant prior knowledge required. A quick summary, together with supplementary handouts in which the required information can be looked up as needed, may be sufficient to bring some students up to the required level while not boring others for whom the review may be redundant. The key to this technique is the preparation of a handout covering the most critically needed prerequisite knowledge. This will allow you to limit your review to the barest essentials involving the least amount of time.

The splitting of lesson objectives into higher and lower levels of complexity; the use of remedial resources, supplemental media, learning centers, and special handouts; and even the physical arrangement of your room should be included in the lesson plan when one of the previous forms or other forms of individualization are to be implemented.

Mastery Learning and Relearning

The third consideration concerns the level of proficiency expected of all of the students at the end of the lesson. This consideration is related to alternatives for individualized instruction, because those alternatives are often implemented to foster what has come to be called *mastery learning* (Block, 1987). **Mastery learning** requires that each student display a high level, if not complete proficiency, of each intended outcome before he or she can receive instruction at the next higher level. If mastery learning is desired, each lesson would have to be designed with that end in mind. Notice that a sequence of lessons in a least-to-most complex or concrete-to-abstract ordering requires proficiency at some lower level before an outcome at a higher level of complexity could be attained. If such a sequence comprised a unit plan, some lessons

would provide the task-relevant prior knowledge that would be needed in order to attain the outcomes of subsequent lessons. When units are planned in such a manner, mastery learning becomes an indispensable concept. This is why some provision for mastery learning must be made for every lesson that provides critical task-relevant prior knowledge. Most frequently, this provision for mastery learning will take the form of techniques for individualizing instruction. This provision need not appear in every lesson, because not all lessons will provide critical task-relevant information for subsequent learning, but it may be expected in many of the lessons. In both the following chapter and chapter 11 other alternatives related to individualizing instruction will be addressed.

Events of Instruction

After determining where to start the lesson, the extent to which it will be individualized, and if and where mastery learning may be required, one is ready to start planning a lesson. This is the process of specification of the key events that will take place during the lesson and for which the teacher alone will be responsible. By placing the responsibility on the teacher for providing these events, one makes a distinction between the often-used words *teaching* and *learning*. Learning refers to the internal events which go on in the heads of your learners; it is the end product of the external events provided by a teacher. It is hoped that the external event of teaching causes the internal event of learning. The sequence of steps in the description of lesson planning takes into consideration that whatever instructional events one plans, they must influence events in the heads of the learners. It is not unusual to have teaching unrelated to learning, as when teachers teach and students listen without anything sinking in. The process of getting the instructional events to sink in is one of planning a sequence of instruction that fosters a close relationship between the external events of instruction and the internal events of learning, *actively engaging the learners in the learning process*. One can achieve this tightly knit relationship between teaching and learning by following the sequence of seven instructional events suggested by Gagné and Briggs (1979). Although not all of these events may be applicable to every lesson, they can provide a basis—or menu—from which many different lesson plans can be formulated. These events are:

1. Gaining attention
2. Informing the learner of the objective
3. Stimulating recall of prerequisite learning
4. Presenting the stimulus material
5. Eliciting the desired behavior
6. Providing feedback
7. Assessing the behavior

Describing the instructional events provided in each of these seven areas is the heart of the lesson-writing process. Now consider the types of instructional events each entails and how each can be related to the internal processes of learning to promote active engagement in the learning process.

Gaining Attention

Without the students' attention nothing in the lesson will be heard, let alone actively engage them in the learning process. Each lesson plan, therefore, begins with a description of an instructional event to engage the students' interest, curiosity, and attention. In some classes this will mean raising their attention from an almost totally uninvolved stage to one where their vision and hearing is at a receptive level. In other instances this will mean raising their attention from an already receptive mode to a higher level of curiosity, interest, and attention. The intensity of the attention-gaining event will depend upon the starting point of the learners. A less able 5th-period class that meets after lunch may require a more dramatic attention-gaining event than will a bright and eager 1st-period class. Therefore, conscious awareness of students' characteristics

in this regard is important for finding the right event for gaining their attention.

One of the most common attention-gaining devices is to relate the content to be covered to the students' interests or to arouse their curiosity. Often this can be accomplished by asking a question, such as "Have you ever wondered how we got the word 'horsepower'? Who would like to guess?" (from a lesson on methods of measurement), "Can anyone think of a popular automobile with the name of a Greek god?" (from an introductory lesson on mythology), or, "Have you ever wondered how some creatures can live both in the water and on land?" (from a lesson on amphibious animals). These questions are called *openers* and are designed not to have any single correct answer or even to accurately reflect the fine details of what is to follow, but to amuse, stimulate, and sometimes even bewilder students so that they will be receptive to the more detailed content and questions that follow. Some other questions used as openers might be:

Why do some scientists think that traveling to the planets will make the space traveler younger? (from a lesson in physics)

Why do we have a word "its" and another word "it's"? (from a lesson in punctuation)

Why do you think the Greek empire collapsed when it was at its strongest? (from a lesson in world history)

Why is the dollar worth more today in Mexico than in Switzerland? (from a lesson in economics)

Why do you think some eloquently speaking lawyers become disliked by the juries they speak to? (from a lesson in public speaking)

Another useful technique for gaining students' attention is the presentation of an apparent contradiction (e.g., Why do we illustrate water using the color blue when water is really clear?), a seeming inconsistency in real life (e.g., Why do some lower forms of animal life live longer than human beings?), or something that appears at first glance to be illogical (e.g., Why must something go backward every time something else goes forward?) For example, introducing a lesson in signed numbers by informing your learners that the multiplication of two negative numbers always results in a positive product may be a bit alarming, but it could raise their curiosity about how two negatives can ever result in something that is positive. The lesson might continue by explaining the mathematical rules behind the apparent contradiction. Some other opening questions designed to make learners curious and, therefore, more ready to learn are:

> Who thinks he or she, with just the eyes, can see an amoeba? (from a biology lesson)
>
> How do you think the Grand Canyon was formed? (from a lesson in physical geography)
>
> What occupations use numbers instead of words? (from a math lesson)
>
> On the average, how many spelling mistakes do you think occur each day in a large metropolitan newspaper? (from a spelling lesson)
>
> When is the value of paper greater than its own worth? (from a lesson in economics)

Diagrams, pictures, illustrations, scale models, and films are other types of attention-getting aids. These devices can be used to appeal to the students' sense of vision while the oral presentation is appealing to their sense of hearing. Graphics or visuals of almost any kind can be a particularly effective opener with less able students who are known to be more oriented and responsive to visual than to auditory presentations. This type of opener can include both samples of materials to be used in the day's lesson so students can touch and feel before the lesson actually gets started and also various pieces of equipment (e.g., scales, buttons, meters) to be used so students can actually try them out before the start of the lesson.

Informing the Learner of the Objective

Once the learner's attention has been gained through one or more of the attention-getting aids suggested previously, the internal processes of learning must be activated in ways that correspond to the content to be presented. Just because the learners have been turned on with some attention-getting device, it does not mean they will be tuned in to the wavelength at which the lesson will be presented; they will need to be given the channel on which the lesson will be transmitted. The most effective way of focusing learners' receptivity is to inform them of the complexity of the behavioral outcome they are expected to attain by the end of the lesson. This can be done by telling them early in the lesson or unit how they will be examined or expected to show competence over the subject matter being taught. For example, such expectations may include the following:

- remember the four definitions of *power* that will be presented (science)
- be able to express ownership orally in a sentence to the class (English)
- identify correctly a mystery specimen of lower animal life using the microscope (life science)
- state their true feelings about the laws dealing with pornography (social studies)

Such statements allow the learner to know when he or she has attained the level of behavior that is expected and to become selective in how the lesson information should be used and remembered. If the students know that they are expected to be able to recall four definitions of *power* at the end of your lesson on energy, they know to focus their search, retrieval, and retention processes *during the lesson* on the various definitions or categories of *power* presented. Informing the learner of an objective helps the student organize his or her thinking in advance of the lesson by providing mental "hooks" on which to hang the key aspects of your lesson. This activates the learning process and focuses it in the direction that is most efficient and conducive to obtaining the required behavioral outcome.

The key to the success of this instructional event is the communication of the objective in a manner that can be readily understood by the learners. The taxonomies of cognitive, affective, and psychomotor behavior were presented in the previous chapter, but students will not have had the opportunity to be acquainted with them, nor need they be. Therefore, the language used to convey behavioral expectations to students should be chosen with their vocabulary and language level in mind and recorded as a reminder in this second part of your lesson plan. This is most easily accomplished by providing some examples of the tasks that the students will be expected to perform after the lesson, thus effectively translating the action verb associated with a level of behavioral complexity to some possible ways this behavior might be measured on tests, in class discussions, and in question-and-answer sessions. For example, a teacher might write the following examples of expected behavior on the blackboard at the beginning of a unit on lower forms of animal life and then place a check beside the ones that most apply at the start of that day's lesson:

Give a definition of an amoeba.

Draw the cellular structure of an amoeba.

Explain the reproduction cycle of an amoeba.

Using a microscrope, properly identify an amoeba from other single-celled animals.

Notice that these behavioral outcomes range from recounting a fact to making decisions and judgments in a real biological environment. Without knowing at which of these levels they are expected to perform that day, the students will have no way of selecting and focusing their attention on those parts of the instruction leading to the desired behavior. This is not to say that other aspects of the presentation should be ignored; they can now be seen as tools or means for gaining the highest level of behavior required and not as ends in themselves.

Stimulating Recall of Prerequisite Learning

Before the actual presentation of new lesson content can proceed, one final preliminary instructional event is needed. Since learning cannot occur in a vacuum, the necessary task-relevant prior information must be retrieved and made ready for use. This calls for some method of reviewing, summarizing, restating, or otherwise stimulating the key concepts acquired in previous lessons; this is information instrumental for achieving the level of behavioral complexity intended in the present lesson. If a goal is to have learners use a microscope to properly identify an amoeba from other single-celled animals, it is clear that facts, concepts, and skills acquired previously would be relevant to this new task. Definitions of single-celled animals, unique characteristics of an amoeba that make it distinguishable from other one-celled animals, and skill in using the microscope are among some of the task-relevant prior knowledge that could greatly influence the attainment of the outcome. One of the purposes of a unit plan is to provide a sequence of instruction in which lessons are explicitly planned to provide all the relevant prerequisite information necessary to attain outcomes at higher levels of behavioral complexity. This, however, will not be sufficient when key prerequisite lessons are separated from subsequent ones by intervening lessons or when the content of these earlier lessons is to be used in new and unique ways. Stimulating the recall of task-relevant prior information at the beginning of the lesson will bring this needed information to the immediate attention of the learners and make the instructional context more conducive to the combining of old and new facts, concepts, and skills. It is this mixing of previous learning with new learning that leads to a higher level of behavioral complexity.

Helping students to retrieve previously acquired information requires the condensing of the key aspects of this prior learning into a brief and easily understood form. Obviously, not all of what has gone on before can be summarized in a few brief minutes of preparatory comments, so thought-provoking and stimulating techniques are needed to bring back into focus sizable amounts of prior learning. Do not attempt to recall all the content that was covered or that may be needed for the new learning, but only the most significant parts of this content; call the learners' attention to key events of a previous lesson. For example, questions might help students recall memorable episodes in earlier lessons: "Do you remember why Johnny couldn't see the amoeba in the microscope?" (it was on low magnification instead of high); "Do you remember Betty Jo's humorous attempt to relate the reproduction cycle of an amoeba to that of human beings?" (she had equated cell division with waking up one morning to find a new baby in the family); "Do you remember the three-color picture Bobby drew of the cellular structure of an amoeba?" (everyone had commented on how lifelike the picture was). Such questions help students retrieve task-relevant prior learning not by summarizing that learning, but by tapping into a single *mental image* that could bring forth that learning. Once the image is retrieved, students can turn it on and off at will to search for the details that may be nested within it and bring forth still greater recall. Describing how to stimulate the recall of prerequisite learning, then, will be the third entry in the lesson plan.

Presenting the Stimulus Material

This is the heart of the lesson plan. Although this component seems to require little explanation, there are several considerations important to the presentation of lesson content that often go unnoticed.

One of these considerations is the presentation of lesson content in the form and mode that is expected to be displayed by learners on tests, in class assignments, and in the real world. This means, for example, that if the intention is for students to have a complete understanding of signed numbers, they must be given examples using both single and multiple digit numbers in various formats. The *irrelevant* aspects of the learning stimulus should be changed as often as possible and in as many different ways as possible (e.g., using both whole numbers and decimals, showing $\begin{array}{r} -2 \\ +5 \\ \hline \end{array}$ *as well as* $-2 + 5 =$) so that students can learn which dimensions of the problem are irrelevant. This will protect them from learning an objective under one condition but not under any other that may be encountered in subsequent lessons, grades, and courses. Some other examples of changing the irrelevant aspects of a learning stimulus include:

- Introducing learners to examples of proper punctuation by using popular magazines and newspapers as well as the text and workbook (English or a foreign language)
- Showing how the laws of electricity apply to lightning during a thunderstorm as well as to electrical circuitry in the laboratory (science)
- Relating rules of social behavior found among humans to those that often can be found among animals (social studies)
- Comparing the central processing unit in a microcomputer to the executive processes in the human brain (computer science)
- Showing how the reasons for a particular war also can be applied to other conflicts hundreds of years earlier (history)

In each of these examples the lesson designer is changing the irrelevant dimensions of the objective by applying key lesson ideas in new and different contexts. As a result, the learners are more likely to (a) notice improper punctuation when it appears in a slick and important publication, (b) understand the universality of the physical laws governing electricity, (c) not think social behavior is a uniquely human phenomenon, (d) not confuse the wonders of data processing with the hardware and equipment that is only sometimes needed to do it, and (e) understand that some reasons for conflict, war, and hostility are general as well as specific.

A second consideration in the presentation of content is the presentation of instructional stimuli in a manner that fosters the selective perception of the content presented. Not everything in a text, workbook, film, lecture, or on the chalkboard will be of equal importance to the day's objective. Consequently, highlighting the key aspects of the text and workbook provides important guidance for helping students selectively perceive and retain the main parts of your lesson. Examples of such highlighting include verbally emphasizing importance, telling students what to look for in a film (even stopping it to reinforce an idea if need be), underlining, circling, or otherwise emphasizing key words on the chalkboard and using verbal markers ("This is important...", "Notice the relevance of this...", "This information will be needed later...").

One of the key behaviors of the effective teacher described in chapter 1 was the ability to teach with variety. Gaining students' attention at the start of the lesson is one thing, but keeping their attention throughout your lesson is quite another. Variety with respect to the modalities in which instruction is presented (e.g., visual, oral, tactile) or some combination of instructional procedures (large group lecture, question and answer, small group discussion, etc.) can add a dimension to the lesson, stimulating the thinking and the interest of the students. The value of shifting from visually dominated instruction to orally dominated instruction (or using both simultaneously) and breaking a lesson into several instructional arrangements (e.g., a lecture followed by question and answer) cannot be overemphasized. The importance of planning occasional changes in modality and procedure is that they present the lesson in a variety of contexts, giving learners an opportunity to grasp the material in several different ways according to their individual learning styles and personal differences. These changes also provide students with the opportunity to see previously learned material used in different ways; this reinforces learned material better than simply restating it in the same mode and form. It also encourages the learner to extend or expand material according to the new mode or procedure being used. For example, material learned in a lecture may be pushed to its limit in a question-and-answer period when the learner answers a question and finds out that previous understandings were partly incorrect due to the limited context in which they were learned. Quite apart from the well-known fact that variety helps to keep students awake and actively engaged in the learning process, it also can offer them an individualized learning experience and test their previous learnings.

The preparation of a lesson plan can divide presentation of content into three parts representing (a) the content to be taught, (b) the modalities through which content will be transmitted (e.g., oral, visual, tactile), and (c) the procedures which will be used to convey the content (e.g., lecture, small group, question and answer).

Eliciting the Desired Behavior

At or near the end of the presentation of the stimulus material, the learners should be provided with an opportunity to show whether or not they can perform the behaviors at the intended level of complexity. Learning cannot occur effectively in a passive environment—one in which activities are not provided to actively engage the learner in the learning process at moderate-to-high rates of success. Active engagement in the learning process at an appropriate level of difficulty should be a goal of every lesson, because without it little or no learning can occur. Such engagement can be accomplished in many ways. It may even occur spontaneously because of getting the students' attention, informing them of the objectives, stimulating the recall of prerequisite learning, and presenting the stimulus material—but a teacher cannot count on it! Active engagement, especially at an appropriate level of difficulty, is a slippery concept, and if it is left to chance it will rarely occur to the extent required for significant learning to take place. While all of the instructional events that have been presented thus far are required for the active engagement of learners, these events do not guarantee that engagement will occur. Therefore, a fifth instructional event is needed; when added to a lesson plan it encourages and guides learners through a process that can be expected to produce the behavior intended.

This fifth event differs from the four preceding ones in that it is the individual's covert and personal engagement in the learning process that is desired. Each learner must be placed in a position of grappling in a trial-and-error fashion with summarizing, paraphrasing, applying, or solving a problem involving the lesson content. It is not important that the behavior ever be produced at this stage in a recognizable form, as long as the activity provided stimulates an *attempt to produce the intended behavior*. This activity is intended to encourage the learner to *organize a response* that corresponds to the level of behavioral complexity stated when the student is informed of the objective.

The primary ways of staging this instructional event include workbooks, handouts, textbook study questions, verbal and written exercises, and questions in which students are asked to apply what was learned, if only in the privacy of their own minds. The idea is to pose a classroom activity as close in time as possible to the presentation of new material, an activity that encourages students, in a nonevaluative atmosphere, to use the material presented. Sometimes these activities can be inserted throughout the lesson at the end of each new chunk of information; this also adds variety to the lesson. In other instances, these activities occur toward or at the end of the presentation of all the new material. In either case the eliciting activity is brief, nonevaluative, and focused exclusively on posing a condition (such as a question, problem, or exercise) for which the learner must organize a response. This response may be written, oral, or subvocal (as when the teacher poses a question and the students answer in the privacy of their own minds). Eliciting activities can be as simple as a question posed by the teacher at any point in a lesson or as complex as a problem exercise completed in a workbook at the end of

the lesson. It is important, however, that these activities be *nonevaluative* to encourage a response unhampered by the anxiety and conservative response patterns that generally occur in a test-taking situation. Rosenshine and Stevens (1986) have suggested several additional ways of eliciting the desired behavior which include:

- Preparing a large number of oral questions beforehand
- Asking many brief questions on main points, on supplementary points, and on the process being taught
- Calling on students whose hands are not raised in addition to calling on those who volunteer
- Asking students to summarize a rule or process in their own words
- Having all students write their answers (on paper or the chalkboard) while the teacher circulates
- Having all students write their answers and check them with a neighbor (frequently used with older students)
- At the end of a lecture/discussion (especially with older students), writing the main points on the chalkboard and then having the class meet in groups to summarize the main points to each other

Providing Feedback

The sixth instructional event is closely connected in time and substance to the eliciting activity previously described. An eliciting activity will promote learning to the extent that the learner can determine the correctness of the attempted response, whether oral, written, or subvocal. Although the response itself must be an individual's attempt to recall, summarize, paraphrase, apply, or problem solve with the new learning, the feedback that should immediately follow can be directed to the entire class. For example, the teacher may want either to reveal his or her answer to the question or to hold up to the class another student's answer for comparison. A wrong answer by a student, however, would be responded to encouragingly in order to maintain the nonevaluative flavor of the eliciting activity. Responses such as "That's a good try," or "That's not quite what I'm looking for," or "Keep thinking" can switch the focus to more useful responses without penalizing students for attempting to respond. Other ways of confirming a correct response would be to read aloud the correct answers in a workbook or to provide a handout with the correct answers or a copy of the exercise with the correct answers penciled in. A transparency could be used to pose the eliciting activity and then volunteered answers could be recorded. Also, if students are working silently at their seats, the teacher may want to walk about the room, using a simple nod and smile to indicate the correctness of an individual performance or to encourage the revision of a wrong response. This part of the lesson plan, then, should include the means by which information will be provided to the learners about the correctness of their responses. These and some additional ways of providing feedback are summarized in Table 5.1.

Assessing the Behavior

It is important to note that not all eliciting activities and related feedback must be provided within the context of a single instructional period. Tests and homework problems that are returned the next day in class, or extended assignments such as essays and research papers that are returned days or even weeks after the pertinent instruction has been given, can also engage the student in the learning process, encourage the creation of a product, and organize a response. Tests, essays, term papers, and projects, however, result from several individual lessons and therefore are considerably larger in scope and effort than the type of elicitation activities discussed thus far. These larger eliciting activities are particularly valuable both for eliciting behavior at higher levels of complexity than could be expected at the end of any single lesson and also for evaluating the degree to which intended behaviors can be performed.

This final instructional event specifies the activity by which the intended behavior will be evaluated. As we have seen, eliciting activities can be immediate (e.g., a question stated orally) or delayed (e.g., a research paper or test) and evaluative or nonevaluative. The fifth event described an eliciting activity that was immediate and nonevaluative. For this instructional event the teacher will describe a delayed eliciting activity that is primarily evaluative in nature. Eliciting activities that are primarily evaluative, such as tests, research papers, and graded homework, sometimes are disadvantageous in limiting freedom to make mistakes and in lacking immediacy of the feedback given—both of these can be counterproductive to learning. As a result they should

TABLE 5.1
Some methods of providing feedback

Individual students	Small Groups	Class
Nod while walking past	Sit with group and discuss answers	Place answers on a transparency
Point to correct answer in workbook or text	Have one group critique another group's answers	Provide answers on a handout
Show student the answer key	Give each group the answer key when finished	Read answers aloud
Place check alongside incorrect answers	Assign one group member the task of checking the answers of other group members	Place answers on the chalkboard
Have students grade each others' papers by using the text, or assign references as a guide		Have selected students read their answers aloud
		Have students grade each others' papers as you give answers

not be used to the exclusion of immediate and nonevaluative eliciting activities within or at the end of a lesson. On the other hand, these longer term activities are undeniably helpful for engaging students in the learning process by encouraging the creation of a product and the organization of a response to a real-life learning stimulus and evaluating the extent to which lesson and unit objectives have been met. Therefore, the seventh instructional event to be specified on the lesson plan will be the means by which you intend to elicit behavior for purposes of evaluation. These can include:

Tests and quizzes

Homework exercises

In-class workbook assignments

Performance evaluations

Lab assignments

Oral presentations

Extended essays

Research papers

Example Lesson Plans

We are now ready to place these seven instructional events, with appropriate elaboration, into the form of a brief but effective lesson plan. To be both practical and effective, lesson plans must be brief but also capable of providing—almost at a glance—all the necessary ingredients needed to deliver the lesson. Following are some example plans on a variety of subjects and grade levels showing how easy lesson planning can be when the task is organized by these seven critical events.

First, the lesson will be given both a title that indicates the content to be taught and also a number which references the lesson back to the unit plan of which it is a part. In Figure 5.3 there are numbers in the lower right corners of each box, or lesson, in the unit blueprint; these numbers tie each lesson at the lower portion of the unit blueprint to the larger content domain from which the more specific lesson content was derived. As multiple lessons are developed for a single unit, these numbers will become a ready reference to how the lessons contribute to a unit outcome at a higher level of complexity. The following shows the format of a typical lesson for beginning readers.

Unit Title: Reading: Word Attack Skills
Lesson Title: Sound Discrimination, Letters of the Alphabet   Lesson: 2.1

This indicates the general content of the lesson and its placement in a unit on word attack skills. The lesson identifier, 2.1, indicates that this lesson is the first lesson in Unit 2. It would appear on the graphic unit plan as indicated in Figure 5.7

Now there is the elaboration of each of the seven instructional events for delivering this lesson to students.

1. Gaining attention   Play an audiotape of a voice articulating the sounds.

This instructional event will gain the attention of your students and focus them on what is about to be presented. Whatever device or procedure is used, it should not only gain the attention of the learners but also motivate them to continue concentrating well into the lesson. Keep in mind that students, especially young students, have trouble picking up subtle transitions in classroom activities. Often their attention is steadfastly on what has immediately preceded the lesson, and they are reluctant to change focus unless something new, interesting, or exciting is on the horizon. Visual or audio stimuli are often effective as attention getters, because their ability to penetrate the senses exceeds the more neutrally oriented stimuli, such as written words, verbal expressions, or pronouncements. Changing sensory modalities, for example, from listening to looking (or from looking to listening) often can provide the incentive necessary to more selectively perceive and receive the message about to be communicated.

FIGURE 5.7
The relationship between lessons, units, and a
course or domain

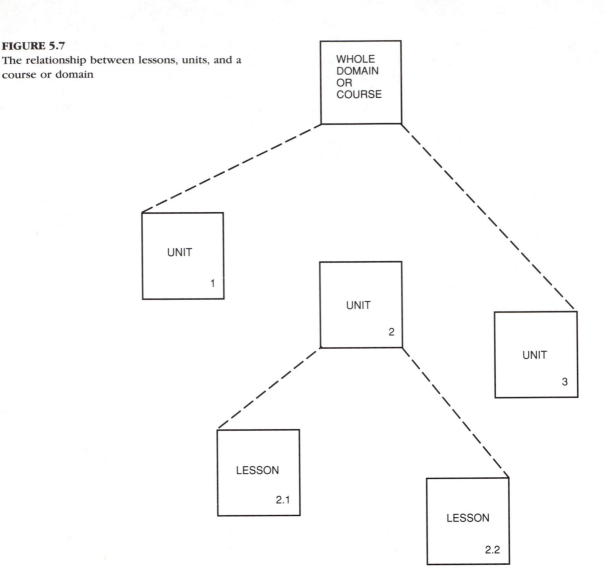

2. Informing the learner of the objective — When the tape is finished, indicate that by the end of the lesson students will be expected to repeat the vowel sounds out loud, independently of the tape.

This instructional event translates the behavioral objective for the lesson into a form that is meaningful to students. In this example, the transfer of information from one modality (listening) to another (speaking) is being sought, indicating that the objective for this lesson has been written at the comprehension level of the taxonomy of the cognitive domain. The attention-getting device should be chosen to lead into the objective for the lesson. Simply clapping one's hands to gain attention, followed by conveying the objective of the lesson, will not be as effective as when the objective is actually *contained within* or *reflected by* the attention-getting procedure.

In this case, the audiotape was directly related to the lesson's content, allowing these two instructional events to work together to produce a single unified theme with the effect of enhancing the learners' attention. A picture or chart, a question on the chalkboard, or a demonstration derived directly from lesson content often are simple but effective attention getters that can easily be made to reflect the lesson objective.

3. Stimulating recall of prerequisite learning — Show how each vowel sound is produced by the correct positioning of the mouth and lips.

The ability to identify and successfully communicate task-relevant prior knowledge to students is critical to attainment of the lesson objective. Without paraphrasing, summarizing, or otherwise reviewing this information, at least some of the students will be unable to comprehend the information to be conveyed. Among the most frequent reasons that learners are unable to attain lesson outcomes is that they lack the outcomes of previously taught lessons that are necessary for subsequent learning. Although prerequisite content that was never learned cannot be retaught in the context of subsequent lessons, it must be recalled or stimulated into action in order for it to play a meaningful role in the acquisition of new learning. Most lessons require some previous facts, understandings, or skills, and these should be recalled and identified at this step of the lesson plan. This can be achieved by touching on the high points or more significant aspects of this prior learning for the present lesson.

4. Presenting the stimulus material — Say each vowel sound and then have the class repeat it twice, pointing to a chart of the position of the mouth and lips during the articulation of each vowel sound. Do the most commonly used vowels first.

One may feel that this is the heart of the lesson. This is correct, except that there are six other hearts, each of which could entail as much effort in planning and instructional time as this event does. The tendency is for beginning teachers to pack their lessons almost entirely with the presentation of new stimulus material and to devote far less effort to gaining attention, to informing the learner of the objective, to recalling prerequisite learning, and to other instructional events that must follow the presentation of new material. Obviously the presentation of new material will be indispensable to most lessons, but it need not always encompass most (or even a large portion) of the lesson; this is a mistake that is often made. The result of devoting a large portion of the lesson to new material, exclusively of the other instructional events, is that the lesson is likely to present content in pieces too big for the learners to grasp. This often results in considerable reteaching during subsequent lessons and ultimately less content coverage at the end of a unit. Although the presentation of new stimulus material will be an important part of most lessons, it does not always have to comprise the majority of instructional time. Just as the first three instructional events must come before the presentation of new material for this material to be meaningful, the next three instructional events will make clear that this new stimulus material must indeed be a stimulus for something more to come.

5. Eliciting the desired behavior — Have students silently practice forming correct mouth and lip positions for each vowel sound, following the pictures in their workbooks.

For this instructional event the learner is given both guidance in how to perform the intended behavior and an opportunity to practice the behavior. These two activities must go hand in hand. Eliciting the desired behavior without providing an opportunity to practice can cancel out whatever positive effect this instructional event might have on the lesson outcome. Here, the new stimulus material described in the previous event can be presented in some different form with an opportunity to practice the behavior in as nonthreatening, nonevaluative an atmosphere as possible. Grading or performance evaluations should not be part of the performance being elicited in this instructional event, because spontaneity, freedom to make mistakes, and an opportunity for immediate feedback are the goal of this activity. An opportunity should be provided for independently practicing or applying the new stimulus material presented in the previous event along with any graphic or verbal aids that contain key portions of the stimulus material.

6. Providing feedback	Randomly choose students to recite the vowel sounds; correct their errors to demonstrate to the class the desired sound.

Feedback should be integrally related to the eliciting activity. A short time between performance and feedback has long been thought to be an essential element of learning; the closer the correspondence between a performance and feedback, the more quickly learning will occur.

Feedback either can be integrated with eliciting the desired behavior, or it can be a subsequent separate activity. In the previous example of an eliciting activity (i.e., the sixth instructional event), feedback was not provided; learners had no way of knowing the correctness of their behavior (mouth and lip movements). Pictures in the text guided the behavior, but because students could not see themselves, they could not determine the accuracy of their responses. In such a case, feedback would have to follow the eliciting activity. The eliciting activity, however, easily could have included feedback—for example, having the student recite a vowel sound and the teacher immediately report its accuracy. The correspondence of an eliciting activity and feedback is always a matter of degree, but these two events should take place as closely in time as possible.

7. Assessing the behavior	This lesson objective will be assessed as part of the unit test on word attack skills and from exercises completed in the workbook.

Few lesson objectives will be assessed by individual lesson tests. Amounts of content larger than contained in a single lesson usually are necessary to make tests efficient and practical. However, it will be important to indicate on what unit or subunit tests the lesson content will be covered and what individual means other than formal tests will be used to grade the correctness of the behaviors that are taught. This entry on the lesson plan will serve as a reminder to either include the lesson's content on subsequent tests or to find other means of checking learners' attainment of it. Some method of assessment (tests, workbook exercises, homework, handouts, worksheets, oral responses, etc.) should always be designed into a lesson plan. This information will provide important feedback about both students' readiness for new stimulus material and also possible reasons for poor performance in later lessons for which the current material is prerequisite content.

Table 5.2 presents the *approximate* amount of time during a hypothetical 50-minute period that might be devoted to each instructional event. Some periods could differ considerably from the suggested amounts of time, such as when the entire lesson is devoted to a review or when recall of prior learning and assessing behavior is not relevant to the day's lesson. Keep in mind that experience, familiarity with content, and common sense will always be the best guides for the percentage of time that should be devoted to each of these instructional events. From Table 5.2 it is apparent that when one instructional event is emphasized another must be deemphasized and, hence, tradeoffs will always be necessary. Although every teacher would like at some

TABLE 5.2

Approximate distribution of instructional time across instructional events for a hypothetical 50-minute lesson

Instructional event	Ranges in minutes	Ranges in percentages of time
Gaining attention	1–5	2–10
Informing learners of the objective	1–3	2–6
Stimulating recall of prerequisite learning	5–10	10–20
Presenting the stimulus material	10–20	20–40
Eliciting the desired behavior	10–20	20–40
Providing feedback	5–10	10–20
Assessing behavior	0–10	0–20

time to have more (or less) time than is allotted for an instructional period, decisions must be made that fit a lesson into the available time frame. Table 5.2 indicates some of the ways this might be done for starting to plan a typical lesson.

This chapter concludes with several additional lesson plans illustrating the seven instructional events in other content areas and grade levels.

Unit Title: United States History (Early Beginning through Reconstruction)
Lesson Title: Causes of the Civil War   Lesson 2.3

1. Gaining attention

Show the following list of wars on a transparency:
French and Indian War
   1754–1769
Revolutionary War
   1775–1781
Civil War   1861–1865
World War I   1914–1918
World War II   1941–1945
Korean War   1950–1953
Vietnam War   1965–1975

2. Informing the learner of the objective

Learners will be expected to know the causes of the Civil War and to show that those causes also can apply to at least one of the wars shown on the transparency.

3. Stimulating recall of prerequisite learning

Briefly review the causes of both the French and Indian War and the Revolutionary War as covered in Lessons 2.1 and 2.2.

4. Presenting the stimulus material

(a) Summarize major events leading to the Civil War:
—rise of sectionalism,
—labor-intensive economy,
—lack of diversification.
(b) Identify significant individuals during the Civil War and their roles:
—Lincoln,
—Lee,
—Davis,
—Grant.
(c) Describe four general causes of war and explain

which are most relevant to
the Civil War:
—economic (to profit),
—political (to control),
—social (to influence),
—military (to protect).

5. Eliciting the desired behavior

Ask the class to identify which of the four causes is most relevant to the major events leading up to the Civil War.

6. Providing feedback

Ask for student answers and indicate plausibility of the volunteered responses.

7. Assessing the behavior

Assign as homework a one-page essay assessing the relative importance of the four causes for one of the wars listed on the transparency.

Unit Title: Writing Concepts and Skills
Lesson Title: Descriptive, Narrative, and Expository Paragraphs   Lesson 1.3

1. Gaining attention

Read examples of short descriptive, narrative, and expository paragraphs from Sunday's newspaper.

2. Informing the learner of the objective

Students will be able to discriminate among descriptive, narrative, and expository paragraphs from a list of written examples in the popular press.

3. Stimulating recall of prerequisite learning

Review the meanings of the words *description, narration,* and *exposition* as they are used in everyday language.

4. Presenting the stimulus material

Using a headline from Sunday's newspaper, give examples of how this story could be reported by description, narration, and exposition.

5. Eliciting the desired behavior

Take another front-page story from Sunday's newspaper and ask students to write a paragraph relating the story in descriptive, narrative, or

expository form, whichever they prefer.

6. Providing feedback

Call on individuals to read their paragraphs, checking each against the type of paragraph he or she intended to write.

7. Assessing the behavior

Provide multiple choice examples of each form of writing on the unit test. Have students revise their paragraphs as needed and turn in as homework the following day.

Unit Title: Consumer Mathematics
Lesson Title: Operations and Properties of Ratio, Proportion, and Percentage   Lesson 3.3

1. Gaining attention

Display so all can see:
(a) can of diet soft drink
(b) one-pound package of spaghetti
(c) box of breakfast cereal

2. Informing the learner of the objective

Learners will be expected to know how to determine ratios, proportions, and percentages from the information on labels of popular food products.

3. Stimulating recall of prerequisite learning

Review the definitions of *ratio, proportion,* and *percentage* from the math workbook.

4. Presenting the stimulus material

Place the information from the soft-drink label on a transparency and ask students to identify the percentage of sodium.

5. Eliciting the desired behavior

Write on the board the list of ingredients given on the cereal box; ask students to determine (a) the percentage of daily allowance of protein, (b) the proportion of daily allowance of Vitamin A, and (c) the ratio of protein to carbohydrates.

6. Providing feedback	Using the information on the board, point to the correct answer for *a* and *b* and show how to find the appropriate numerator and denominator for *c* from the ingredients on the label.
7. Assessing the behavior	Provide on the weekly quiz five problems covering ratios (two problems), proportions (two problems), and percentages (one problem) using labels from other consumer products.

Unit Title: Manipulative Laboratory Skills
Lesson Title: Use of the Microscope   Lesson 1.1

1. Gaining attention	Show the first five minutes of a film about making a lens.
2. Informing the learner of the objective	Learners will be expected to be able to focus correctly a specimen of one-celled animal life, using both high and low magnification.
3. Stimulating recall of prerequisite learning	Review procedures for selecting a slide from the one-celled specimen collection and mounting it on the specimen tray of the microscope.
4. Presenting the stimulus material	Using a student in front of the class as a demonstrator, help position his or her posture and hands on the microscope. Gently bend body and hands until the correct posture results. Demonstrate the position of the eyes and show counter and counter-clockwise rotation of low and then high magnification adjustment.
5. Eliciting the desired behavior	Have each student obtain a specimen slide, mount it on a microscope and focus on low magnification. Randomly check microscopes, correcting slide positions and focus as needed with student observing. Repeat for high magnification.

6. Providing feedback	Feedback has been provided in the context of the eliciting activity (step 5) to increase immediacy of the feedback. Also, refer students to the text for examples of focused and unfocused specimens.
7. Assessing the behavior	At the completion of the unit, students will be assessed during a practical lab exam requiring the correct mounting and identification of three unknown specimens using the microscope.

Summing Up

This chapter introduced you to unit and lesson planning. Its main points were:

1. A unit of instruction may be thought of as a "system" and individual lessons within the unit its component parts.
2. The concept of *hierarchy* tells us the relationship of parts to whole (lessons to units) and the concept of *constraint* tells us what must come before what in a sequence of events (lesson sequence). Systems thinking draws our attention to the relationship among parts of varying sizes to see what lessons make up what units, what units make up what content domains, and what content domains make up what grades and subjects.
3. Establishing instructional goals, identifying the type of learner to which your instruction will be directed, and selecting and organizing content are three primary activities within the planning process.
4. Any goal at the unit level can be broken into its component parts at the lesson level—those parts representing everything that is important for attaining the goal.
5. The two purposes of unit planning are:
   (a) to convert generally stated activities and outcomes into specific objectives and lessons, and
   (b) to provide a picture of long-term goals.

6. Lesson outcomes are the means by which unit goals are achieved.

7. In the graphic approach to lesson planning, boxes illustrate areas of content, or instructional goals, at various levels of generality. Lines and arrows indicate sequences among lessons and how outcomes of lessons build upon one another to achieve a unit goal.

8. A graphic representation of a unit plan may specify that every lesson *must* be taught in a specific sequence or that lessons may be taught in any order. In some (but probably not many) unit plans, the ordering of lessons may be unimportant.

9. The bottom of a unit plan hierarchy represents content suitably sized for the preparation of individual lessons.

10. An effective unit uses the relationship between individual lessons and their cumulative effects to achieve outcomes at higher levels of behavioral complexity, which may include the learning of concepts, the application of facts and understandings to real world problem solving, and the ability to make value judgments.

11. One purpose of seeing a whole unit at a glance in a graphic format is to determine if all necessary task-relevant prior knowledge required by each lesson has been provided by the unit plan.

12. The three activities of unit planning are:

   - classifying unit outcomes at a higher level of behavioral complexity than lesson outcomes by using one or more taxonomies of behavior.
   - planning the chunks in a sequence in which the outcomes of previously taught lessons are instrumental in achieving the outcomes of subsequent lessons, and
   - rearranging or adding lesson content where necessary to provide task-relevant prior knowledge where needed.

13. Before the preparation of a lesson plan can begin, it must be determined at what level of behavioral complexity the lesson will begin (e.g., knowledge, application, evalua-

tion), to what extent opportunities for individualized learning will accompany the lesson plan (e.g., ability grouping, peer tutoring, learning centers, specialized handouts), and what level of proficiency will be expected of students at the end of the lesson (e.g., whether mastery learning will be required).

14. *Learning* refers to the internal events going on in the heads of the learners which result from the external events provided by a teacher. Hence, the words *teaching* and *learning* refer to two different but related sets of activities.

15. The external events that can be specified in a lesson plan are:

   - Gaining attention
   - Informing the learner of the objective
   - Stimulating recall of prerequisite learning
   - Presenting the stimulus material
   - Eliciting the desired behavior
   - Providing feedback
   - Assessing the behavior

16. Gaining attention involves gaining your students' interest in what you will present and getting them to switch to the appropriate modality for the coming lesson.

17. Informing learners of the objective involves also informing them of the complexity of the behavior expected at the end of the lesson.

18. Stimulating recall of prerequisite learning involves reviewing task-relevant prior information required by the lesson.

19. Presenting the stimulus material involves delivering the desired content in a manner conducive to the modality in which it is to be received, using procedures that stimulate thought processing and maintain interest.

20. Eliciting the desired behavior involves getting learners to attempt to produce the intended behavior by organizing a response corresponding with the level of complexity of the stated objective.

21. Providing feedback involves allowing the learner to know the accuracy of his or her elicited response in a nonthreatening, nonevaluative atmosphere.

22. Assessing the behavior involves evaluating the learner's performance with tests, homework, and extended assignments.

For Discussion and Practice

*1. Identify the five inputs to the planning process from which the preparation of lesson plans proceeds.

*2. Differentiate between the words *system* and *systematic*.

*3. How can a unit outcome be more than the sum of individual lesson outcomes?

*4. Explain in your own words how the concepts of hierarchy and constraint are used in unit planning.

*5. How are the concepts of *constraint* and *task-relevant prior learning* related to one another?

*6. Name the levels of behavioral complexity in each of the three domains (cognitive, affective, and psychomotor) that, generally, would be most suitable for a unit outcome.

*7. How are the boxes further down on a graphic unit plan different than the boxes higher up?

8. Graphically portray a three-lesson unit in which the sequence of lessons is critical to achieving the unit outcome. Then, portray another three-lesson unit in which the lesson sequence is unimportant. Be sure to draw the lesson outcomes for each unit to properly reflect the unit outcome.

*9. Explain why a graphic unit plan that began with a very broad and encompassing outcome (e.g., understanding poetry) would have more intermediate levels represented in it than a unit plan that began with a very narrow and specific outcome (e.g., understanding poetic meter).

*10. Identify some ways of providing opportunities for individual learning in the context of a lesson plan.

*11. Explain what is meant by mastery learning and what its relationship is to task-relevant prior knowledge.

*12. Name the seven events of instruction that can be described in a lesson plan. Give a specific example of how you would implement each one of these events in a lesson of your own choosing.

*13. Identify the instructional event(s) for which the key behavior of *variety* would be most important.

*14. Identify the instructional event(s) for which the key behavior of *high rate of success* would be most important.

*15. Identify the instructional event(s) for which the key behavior of *engagement in the learning process* would be most important.

*16. Indicate how the instructional events of (a) providing feedback and (b) assessing behavior differ according to the evaluative nature of the feedback provided and the immediacy with which the feedback is given.

17. Following the form of the examples provided in this chapter, prepare a lesson plan for a topic in your major or preferred teaching area and another in your minor teaching area. Include the approximate number of minutes you expect to devote to each event out of a 50-minute class period.

Suggested Readings

Block, J. (1987). Mastery Learning Models. In M. J. Dunkin (Ed.), *International encyclopedia of teaching and teaching education*. New York: Pergamon.
An excellent article on how to achieve mastery learning and what this important concept means for effective teaching.

Briggs, L. (Ed.). (1977). *Instructional design: Principles and applications*. Englewood Cliffs, NJ: Educational Technology Publications.
One of the most read and practical texts on how to plan, design, and implement instruction at the lesson and unit levels.

Clark, C. & Yinger, R. (1979). *Three studies of teacher planning*. East Lansing, MI: Michigan State University, Institute for Research on Teaching. (Available by writing the Institute for Research on Teaching, Michigan State University, East Lansing, MI.)
This informative report details the results of three research studies which related the planning activities of teachers to observable changes in teachers in the classroom.

Dunkin, M. J. (1987). Lesson formats. In M. J. Dunkin (Ed.), *International encyclopedia of teaching and teacher education*. New York: Pergamon.
A sampling of the many varieties of and ways to prepare lesson plans.

Gagné, R. & Briggs, L. (1979). *Principles of instructional design*. New York: Holt, Rinehart & Winston.
One of the most thorough and authoritative texts

on the design of instruction from a psychological perspective.

Kim, E. & Kellough, R. (1978). *A resource guide for secondary teaching* (2nd ed.). New York: Macmillan.

A useful, practical guide with models for writing unit and lesson plans at the secondary level.

Pratt, D. (1980). *Curriculum, design and development.* New York: Harcourt, Brace, Jovanovich.

An introductory text on how to design classroom instruction using many of the concepts presented in this chapter.

Saylor, G., Alexander, W., & Lewis, A. (1981). *A curriculum planning for better teaching and learning* (4th ed.). Chicago: Holt, Rinehart and Winston.

A companion volume to the previous one that relates lesson planning to unit planning to produce an integrated sequence of instruction.

6
Direct Instruction Strategies

The previous chapter presented seven instructional events as the skeletal structure of a lesson plan. These seven events were

gaining attention,

informing the learner of the objective,

stimulating recall of prerequisite learning,

presenting the stimulus material,

eliciting the desired behavior,

providing feedback, and

assessing the behavior.

To put some flesh on this skeleton, this chapter and the next present and illustrate different instructional strategies by which these seven events can be carried out with ease and perfection. This chapter will cover strategies for performing these seven events; it is a model of instruction that involves explanations, examples, review, practice, and feedback in the context of a lecture format. The next chapter will present performance strategies that use guided questions, inductive and deductive logic, student ideas, and group discussion in an inquiry format.

Have you ever wondered why some teachers are more interesting than others? This is an ageless phenomenon for anyone who has spent time in school. There are some teachers whose classes a student cannot wait to attend and others whose classes are dreaded. The first and perhaps most natural reaction of preferring one teacher over another is to describe the teacher with phrases such as "more intelligent," "has a better personality," and "is warmer and friendlier." Although these qualities may have been present in the teachers judged to be the most interesting, they are not the only reasons that a teacher can be interesting.

It may appear surprising that one of the most important factors associated with how interesting teachers are to their students is their use of the key behavior *variety*. In a research study by Emmer, Evertson, and Anderson (1980) involving experienced and inexperienced teachers, experienced teachers who were flexible and showed variety in their instructional strategies were found to be more interesting to their students than were inexperienced teachers who had no knowledge of alternative teaching strategies. Knowledge of a variety of instructional strategies and the flexibility to change instructional approaches both within and among lessons are two of the greatest assets a teacher can have (McNair, 1978–1979). Without variety and flexibility to capture the interest and attention of students, it is unlikely that any other key behavior, however well executed, will have an effect on them. This chapter will provide a variety of teaching strategies that can be used to compose lesson plans and to create and maintain an atmosphere of interest and variety in the classroom.

Categories of Teaching and Learning

Just as the carpenter, electrician, and plumber must select the proper tool for a specific task, the teacher must select the proper instructional strategy for a given type of learning outcome. Because a specific teaching strategy should always be selected with a given purpose in mind, this chapter will begin by identifying two broad classifications that can be used to determine your choice of teaching strategies. These two classifications of learning outcomes are

1. facts, rules, and action sequences, and
2. concepts, patterns, and abstractions.

Type 1 outcomes often represent behaviors at lower levels of complexity in the cognitive, affective, and psychomotor domains. These were discussed in chapter 4 and include the knowledge, comprehension, and application levels of the cognitive domain; the awareness, responding, and valuing levels of the affective domain; and the imitation, manipulation, and precision levels of the psychomotor domain.

Type 2 outcomes, on the other hand, frequently represent behaviors at the higher levels of complexity in these domains. They include objectives at the analysis, synthesis, and evaluation levels of the cognitive domain; the organization and characterization levels of the affective domain; and the articulation and naturalization levels of the psychomotor domain. Although these are fairly broad distinctions for which some overlap can occur, they are useful guides in selecting an instructional strategy that can maximize learning when the objectives include either the teaching of facts, rules, and action sequences or the teaching of concepts, patterns, and abstractions. Some of the important differences between instructional goals requiring these two types of learning are represented in Table 6.1.

Notice across the left and right columns of Table 6.1 that two different types of learning are being required. In the examples representing the left column, the tasks require combining facts and rules at the knowledge and comprehension level into a sequence of actions that could be learned by observation, rote repetition, and practice. The "right answers" can be learned by memorizing and practicing behaviors modeled by the teacher. Learning of a quite different type is being called for in the examples in the right column, however; the "right answers" are not so closely connected to facts, rules, or action sequences that can be memorized and practiced in some limited context. Something more is needed to help the learner go beyond the facts, rules, or sequences in order to create, synthesize, and, ultimately, identify and recognize an answer that cannot be easily modeled or memorized. The missing link involves learning an abstraction called a *concept*.

For example, to learn the *concept* of a frog involves learning the essential characteristics that make an organism a frog and not some other animal closely resembling it (e.g., a green chameleon). In other words, the learner needs to know not only what characteristics are in common among many different varieties of frogs (e.g., green color, four legs, eats insects, is amphibious) but also what characteristics distinguish frogs

TABLE 6.1
*Some instructional goals requiring Type 1 and Type 2 behaviors**

Type 1: Goals requiring facts, rules, and sequences	Type 2: Goals requiring concepts, patterns, and abstractions
1. IF	BUT IF

GOAL is to keep ANIMAL alive
    and ANIMAL has four legs
    and ANIMAL is green
    and ANIMAL is slimy
    and ANIMAL is size of fist
	GOAL is to recognize and
	    identify frogs
	    and ANIMAL has four legs
	    and ANIMAL is green
	    and ANIMAL is slimy
	    and ANIMAL is size of fist

THEN TEACH HOW TO
    Put ANIMAL near water, catch
    flies and feed ANIMAL flies
	THEN TEACH HOW TO
	    Classify ANIMAL as a frog

2. IF	BUT IF

GOAL is to combine two
    SENTENCES
    and there are two IDEAS in the
    SENTENCES
    and the IDEA in one
    SENTENCE is different from the
    IDEA in the other SENTENCE on
    one DIMENSION
	GOAL is to recognize and
	    identify contrasts
	    and there are two IDEAS
	    and one IDEA is different from
	    other IDEA on one DIMENSION

THEN TEACH HOW TO
    Remove period from end of first
    SENTENCE and put comma at
    end of first SENTENCE and write
    but after comma and write
    second SENTENCE after *but*
	THEN TEACH HOW TO
	    Classify pair of IDEAS as a
	    contrast

3. IF	BUT IF

GOAL is to plot a linear EQUATION
    and the EQUATION has the form
    $y = a + bX$
	GOAL is to recognize
	    and identify EQUATIONS of
	    the form $y = a + bX$

THEN TEACH HOW TO
    Put POINT 1 at *a* on *y* axis and
    count 1 to the right from POINT 1
    and go up whatever number *b* is
    and put POINT 2 there and draw
    LINE through POINT 1 and POINT 2
	THEN TEACH HOW TO
	    Classify EQUATIONS that
	    describe a straight line

*From *The Cognitive Psychology of School Learning* (p. 105) by E. Gagné, 1985. Boston: Little, Brown & Company. Adapted by permission.

from other animals. If only the facts that frogs are green, have four legs, eat insects, and are amphibious were used to classify frogs, some turtles might be mistakenly identified as frogs.

Another category of knowledge must be learned that represents characteristics separating frogs from animals that might be mistaken for them (e.g., frogs have soft bodies, moist skin, strong hind limbs, do not change color). Notice that to properly classify a frog, that is, to correctly pick it out from among other animals that may look like it, the nonessential as well as the essential attributes of a frog need to be learned. These nonessential attributes can only be learned by seeing nonexamples, thereby eliminating the characteristics of frogs that do not represent their essential features. Finally, as the learner gains more practice with both examples and nonexamples, the concept of a frog emerges as a tightly woven combination of many different characteristics. This is illustrated in Figure 6.1.

Now the learner is able to disregard superficial characteristics such as color and to focus on those characteristics that only frogs have and that many other animals with which it may be confused do not have. Given pictures of many different varieties of toads, chameleons, turtles, snakes, and so on, the learner learns to identify correctly those that are frogs.

At this point it can be said that the learner has discovered at least some of the essential attributes of a frog and has formed an initial concept of a frog. Notice how different this teaching/ learning process is from asking Johnny simply to repeat some recently memorized facts about frogs, to which he might well respond by saying, "Frogs are green, have four legs, eat insects, and can swim." This does not tell the teacher whether Johnny has the concept of a frog, or a pattern, (e.g., amphibian) of which frogs are a part, or even the most general and abstract characteristics of frogs (e.g., that they are classified under the category "water life"). Even if Johnny learns the considerably more complex task of how to care for frogs, Johnny still has not learned the *concept* of a frog but only how to arrange a constellation

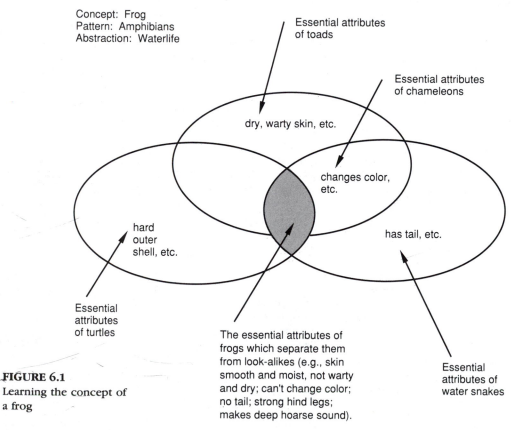

Concept: Frog
Pattern: Amphibians
Abstraction: Waterlife

Essential attributes of toads

Essential attributes of chameleons

dry, warty skin, etc.

changes color, etc.

hard outer shell, etc.

has tail, etc.

Essential attributes of turtles

The essential attributes of frogs which separate them from look-alikes (e.g., skin smooth and moist, not warty and dry; can't change color; no tail; strong hind legs; makes deep hoarse sound).

Essential attributes of water snakes

FIGURE 6.1
Learning the concept of a frog

of facts (and, perhaps, some other concepts) into an action sequence (Table 6.1). This preceding discussion illustrates that the processes used to learn facts, rules, and action sequences are different from those used to learn concepts, patterns, and abstractions.

Just as the processes involved in learning to recognize patterns and in learning to carry out sequences of action are different, so too are the instructional strategies used to teach these different outcomes. Various expressions have been used by different learning theorists to describe these two types of learning, but facts, rules, and action sequences are most commonly taught using instructional strategies that emphasize knowledge acquisition, and concepts, patterns, and abstractions are most commonly taught using instructional strategies that emphasize inquiry or problem solving. These follow distinctions suggested by R. M. Gagné (1977), J. R. Anderson (1980), and E. Gagné (1985), all of whose writings have highlighted the different instructional strategies required by these two types of learning.

Since knowledge acquisition and inquiry represent different types of learning outcomes, they must be linked up with the specific instructional strategies most likely to produce them. This chapter will present a group of instructional strategies for teaching knowledge acquisition involving facts, rules, and action sequences; the next chapter will present a group of instructional strategies for teaching inquiry and problem solving involving concepts, patterns, and abstractions. These two types of learning will be compared and contrasted to see how, together, they can be used to build higher level outcomes at the unit level.

Introduction to Direct Instruction Strategies

The teaching of facts, rules, and action sequences is most efficiently achieved through a process that has come to be known as the **direct instruction model**. Direct instruction, sometimes synonomous with expository or didactic teaching, is primarily a *teacher-centered* strategy in which the teacher is the major provider of information. In the direct instruction model, the teacher's role is to pass facts, rules, or action sequences on to students in the most direct way possible; this usually takes the form of a lecture consisting of explanations, examples, and opportunities for practice and feedback. The direct instruction lecture is a multifaceted presentation that involves not only large amounts of verbal lecture but also teacher-student interactions involving questions and answers, review and practice, and the correction of student errors. In this sense, the notion of a lecture in the direct instruction model as used in the elementary and secondary classroom differs considerably from the notion of a lecture that may be acquired from college experience. The typical one-hour college monologue will rarely be suitable for your classroom, because attention spans, interest levels, and the motivation of your learners cannot be expected to be the same as your own. Therefore, the lecture as presented here is neither a lengthy (and boring) diatribe by the teacher nor an open free-wheeling discussion of problems of interest to the student. Instead, it is a quickly paced, highly organized set of interchanges, controlled by the teacher and focusing exclusively on the acquisition of a limited set of predetermined facts, rules, or action sequences.

Rosenshine and Stevens (1986) have equated this type of lecture with that of an effective demonstration in which the teacher

1. is clear about goals and main points by
   a. stating the goals or objectives of the presentation beforehand
   b. focusing on one thought (point, direction) at a time
   c. avoiding digressions
   d. avoiding ambiguous phrases and pronouns
2. presents content sequentially by
   a. presenting material in small steps
   b. organizing and presenting the material so that one point is mastered before the next point is given

c. giving explicit, step-by-step directions (when possible)

d. presenting an outline when the material is complex

3. is specific and concrete by
   a. modeling the skill or process (when appropriate)
   b. giving detailed and redundant explanations for difficult points
   c. providing students with concrete and varied examples

4. checks for students' understanding by
   a. being sure that students understand one point before proceeding to the next
   b. asking students questions to monitor their comprehension of what has been presented
   c. having students summarize the main points in their own words
   d. reteaching, either by further teacher explanation or by students tutoring each other, the parts of the presentation that the students have difficulty comprehending

The examples ahead will illustrate this type of lecture. For now, note the following action verbs that correspond to the objectives most suited for direct instruction:

Cognitive objectives	Affective objectives	Psychomotor objectives
to recall	to listen	to repeat
to describe	to attend	to follow
to list	to be aware	to place
to summarize	to comply	to perform accurately
to paraphrase	to follow	to perform independently
to distinguish	to obey	to perform independently
to use	to display	
to organize	to express	to perform proficiently
to demonstrate	to prefer	to perform with speed
		to perform with coordination
		to perform with timing

These outcomes are intended to be learned through the application of facts, rules, and action sequences that usually can be taught within the context of a single lesson. They are most easily and directly tested by means of multiple choice, listing, matching, and fill-in types of test items that call for the listing of memorized names, dates, and other facts; the summarization or paraphrasing of learned facts, rules, or sequences; or the connecting together and application of learned facts, rules, and sequences in a context that is slightly different than the one in which it was learned. Both Rosenshine (1983) and Good (1979) have identified this type of learning as that which most often results from direct instruction, that is, "active teaching." This type of instruction is most often characterized by full-class (as opposed to small-group) instruction; the organization of learning around questions posed by the teacher; the provision of detailed and redundant practice; the presentation of material so that one new fact, rule, or sequence is mastered before the next fact, rule, or sequence is presented; and the formal arrangement of the classroom to maximize drill and practice. Table 6.2 presents some of the teacher behaviors most commonly associated with the direct instruction model.

The behaviors in Table 6.2 show that a large share of teaching time is likely to be devoted to direct instruction, that is, to providing information directly to students through the form of a lecture interspersed with explanations, examples, practice, and feedback. Whether lecturing, explaining, pointing out relationships, giving examples, or correcting errors, there is much to be said for the teacher's use of strategies that follow the direct instruction model. Research studies have indicated that the direct instruction functions illustrated in Table 6.2 and the teaching behaviors that comprise them (e.g., teacher reviews previous day's work, teacher provides feedback and corrections, teacher provides for student practice) are among the teaching functions that have the highest correlations with student achievement (Anderson, Evertson, & Brophy, 1982; Becker, 1977).

TABLE 6.2
*Some direct instruction functions**

1. Daily review, checking previous day's work, and reteaching (if necessary):
   Checking homework
   Reteaching areas where there were student errors
2. Presenting and structuring new content:
   Provide overview
   Proceed in small steps (if necessary), but at a rapid pace
   If necessary, give detailed or redundant instructions and explanations
   New skills are phased in while old skills are being measured
3. Guided student practice:
   High frequency of questions and overt student practice (from teacher and materials)
   Prompts are provided during initial learning (when appropriate)
   All students have a chance to respond and receive feedback
   Teacher *checks for understanding* by evaluating student responses
   Continue practice until students are firm
   Success rate of 80% or higher during initial learning
4. Feedback and correctives (and recycling of instruction, if necessary):
   Feedback to students, particularly when they are correct but hesitant
   Student errors provide feedback to the teacher that corrections and/or reteaching is necessary
   Corrections by simplifying question, giving clues, explaining or reviewing steps, or reteaching last steps
   When necessary, reteach using smaller steps
5. Independent practice so that student responses are firm and automatic:
   Seatwork
   Unitization and automaticity (practice to overlearning)
   Need for procedure to ensure student engagement during seatwork (i.e., teacher or aide monitoring)
   95% correct or higher
6. Weekly and monthly reviews:
   Reteaching, if necessary

*From "Teaching Functions in Instructional Programs" by B. Rosenshine, 1983, *Elementary School Journal,* 83, p. 338. Reprinted by permission.

When Is Direct Instruction Appropriate?

When direct instruction strategies are used for the proper purpose, with the appropriate content, and at the right time, they will be important adjuncts to a teaching strategy menu. Most of these strategies are at their best when the teacher's purpose is to disseminate information that is not readily available from texts or workbooks in appropriately sized pieces. If such information were available, then the students might well learn the material from these sources independently, with only introductory or structuring comments being provided by the teacher. However, when you must partition, subdivide, and translate textbook and workbook material into a more digestible form before it can be understood by your students, a direct instruction lecture is appropriate.

Another time for direct instruction strategies is when the teacher wishes to arouse or heighten student interest. Students often will fail to complete textbook readings and exercises in the mistaken belief that the chapter is boring, is not worth the effort, or represents material already learned. The teacher's active participation in the presentation of content can change such misperceptions by mixing interesting supplemental or introductory information with the "boring" facts, by showing their application to future schoolwork or world events, and by illustrating with questions and answers that the material is neither easy nor previously mastered. Direct involvement in the presentation of content can provide the human element that may be necessary for learning to occur in some or most of your students.

Finally, direct instruction strategies can be indispensable for achieving the mastery of content and the overlearning of fundamental facts, rules, and action sequences that may be essential to subsequent learning (Anderson & Block, 1987). The degree of learning that occurs will be directly related to the time a student is actively engaged in the learning process. Therefore, the efficient utilization of class time and the active involvement of the student in practicing the content learned are important ingredients of mastery learning. These two goals in the mastery learning concept are approached by an instructional sequence that involves review, presenting new content, practice, feedback, and reteaching; these repetitive cycles compose nearly all of the instructional time scheduled for a lesson. Many of the examples in this chapter will illustrate this type of instructional sequence. When the content to be taught represents task-relevant prior knowledge for subsequent learning, mastery learning is the best insurance that this knowledge will be remembered and available for later use.

There are also times in which direct instruction strategies are inappropriate. When objectives other than the acquisition of information pertaining to the learning of facts, rules, and sequences of behavior are desired, direct instruction strategies will be clumsy, less efficient, and often far less effective than the inquiry, or problem-solving, strategies discussed in the next chapter. Such teaching situations needing strategies other than direct instruction include presenting complex material involving objectives at the analysis, synthesis, and evaluation levels of the cognitive domain as well as presenting content that must be learned gradually over a long period of time. For such material, learner participation will be required to heighten a commitment to the learning process and to create the intellectual framework necessary for learning

concepts and recognizing patterns. Finally, when students are considerably above average in intelligence and achievement or are already well versed in the content to be taught, direct instruction strategies can be boring, inefficient, and ineffective forms of instruction.

An Example of Direct Instruction

To see what direct instruction looks like in the classroom, consider the following in which the teacher is beginning a direct instruction lecture to teach the acquisition of facts, rules, and action sequences for forming and punctuating possessives. The teacher begins with some attention-getting examples showing errors that have appeared in several past editions of the school newspaper. She begins by informing her students of the lesson's objective:

TEACHER: Today we will learn how to avoid embarrassing errors such as this (circles an incorrectly punctuated possessive in a newspaper headline) when forming and punctuating possessives. At the end of the period I will give each of you several additional examples of errors taken from my collection of mistakes found in other newspapers and magazines and will ask you to make the proper corrections and to report your changes to the class.

Who knows what a possessive is?

BOBBY: It means you own something.

TEACHER: Yes, a possessive is a way of indicating ownership. It comes from the word *possession,* which means *"something owned"* or *"something possessed."*

Forming possessives and punctuating them correctly can be difficult, as this newspaper example shows (points to paper again). Today I will give you two simple rules that will help you form possessives correctly.

But first, in order to show ownership or possession, we must know who or what is doing the possessing. Mary, can you recall the parts of speech from last week's lesson? (Mary hesitates, then nods.) What part of speech is most likely to own or possess something?

MARY: Well, umm . . . I think . . . I think a noun can own something.

TEACHER: Yes. A noun can own something. What is an example of a noun that owns something? Tommy.

TOMMY: I don't know.

TEACHER: Debbie.

DEBBIE: Not sure.

TEACHER: Ricky.

RICKY: A student can own a pencil. The word *student* is a noun.

TEACHER: Good. And who can remember our definition for a noun?

JIM: It's a person, place, or thing.

TEACHER: Good. Our first rule will be: Use the possessive form whenever an *of* phrase can be substituted for a noun (teacher points to this rule written on board). Let's look at some phrases on the board to see when to apply this rule. Johnny, what does the first one say?

JOHNNY: The daughter of the policeman.

TEACHER: How else could we express the same idea of ownership?

MARY: We could say "the policeman's daughter."

TEACHER: And, we could say "the policeman's daughter" because I can substitute a phrase starting with *of* and ending with policeman for the noun *policeman*. Notice how easily I could switch the placement of *policeman* and *daughter* by using the connective word *of*. Whenever this can be done you can form a possessive by adding an apostrophe s to the noun following *of*.
Now we have the phrase (writes on board) *policeman's daughter* (points to the apostrophe).
Betty, what about our next example, *holiday of three days* (pointing to board)?

BETTY: We could say "three days' holiday."

TEACHER: Come up and write that on the board just the way it should be printed in the school paper. (Mary writes *three day's holiday*.)
Would anyone want to change anything?

SUSAN: I'm not sure but I think I would put the apostrophe after the *s* in days.

TEACHER: You're right, which leads to our second rule: If the word for which we are denoting ownership already ends in an *s*, place the apostrophe after, not before, the *s*. This is an important rule to remember, because it accounts for many of the mistakes that are made in forming possessives.
As I write this rule on the board, copy down these two rules for use later. (Teacher finishes writing second rule on board.) Now let's take a moment to convert each of the phrases on the overhead to the possessive form. Write down your answer

to the first one. When I see all heads up again I will write the correct answer.
(All heads are up.) Good. Now watch how I change this first one to the possessive form; pay particular attention to where I place the apostrophe, then check your answer with mine. (Teacher converts *delay of a month* to *month's delay*.) Any problems? (Teacher pauses for any response.) OK, do the next one. (After all heads are up, teacher converts *home of Jenkins* to *Jenkins' home*.)
Any problems? (Johnny looks distressed.)

TEACHER: Johnny, what did you write?

JOHNNY: *J-E-N-K-I-N* apostrophe *S*.

TEACHER: What is the man's name, Johnny?

JOHNNY: Jenkins.

TEACHER: Look at what you wrote for the second rule. What does it say?

JOHNNY: Add the apostrophe after the *s* when the word already ends in an *s*. Oh, I get it. His name already has the *s*, so it would be *s* apostrophe. That's the mistake you showed us in the headline, isn't it?

TEACHER: Now you've got it. Let's continue. (Teacher proceeds with the following in the same manner: *speech of the President* to *President's speech, the television set of Mr. Burns* to *Mr. Burns' television set, pastimes of boys* to *boys' pastimes*.)
Now open your workbooks to the exercise on page 87.
Starting with the first row, let's go around the room and hear your possessives for each of the sentences listed. Spell aloud the word indicating ownership, so we can tell if you've placed the apostrophe in the right place. Debbie . . . (looking at "wings of geese")

DEBBIE: geeses wings . . . spelled *W-I-N-G-S* apostrophe.

TEACHER: That's not correct. What word is doing the possessing?

DEBBIE: The geese, so it must be *G-E-E-S-E* apostrophe *S*.

TEACHER: Good. Next.

Although this appears to be the kind of instructional sequence that is repeated thousands of times a day across our nation's classrooms, it has some very special qualities that did not happen by chance. This teacher planned this lesson with the direct instruction model firmly in mind, and she knew precisely how to use the model to maximize the learning of facts, rules, and action sequences. Look at this sequence in terms of each of the functions listed in Table 6.2 and see the extent to which this teacher's lesson actually followed the direct instruction model.

Daily Review and Checking the Previous Day's Work

The major purpose of daily review and checking is to emphasize the relationship between lessons so that students remember previous knowledge and see new knowledge as a logical extension of content already mastered. Notice that early in the example lesson the definition of a noun was brought into the presentation. This provided a review of the task-relevant prior knowledge needed for the day's lesson. It also provided students with a sense of wholeness and continuity, assuring them that what was to follow was not a bit of isolated knowledge unrelated to past lessons. This is particularly important for securing the engagement of less able students who often do not have appropriate levels of task-relevant prior knowledge or who may be overly anxious about having to master yet another piece of unfamiliar content. Review and checking at the beginning of a lesson also is the most efficient and timely way of finding out if the students have mastered task-relevant prior knowledge sufficiently to begin a new lesson; if not, the missing content can be retaught.

One might think that beginning a lesson by checking previously learned task-relevant knowledge is a common practice. Yet, in a study by Good and Grouws (1979) only 50% of experienced teachers began a lesson in this fashion. This is unfortunate, because daily review and checking at the beginning of a lesson can be accomplished in several simple ways. Among these are

1. having students correct each other's homework at the beginning of class,
2. having students identify especially difficult homework problems in a question-and-answer format,

3. sampling the understanding of a few students who probably are good indicators of the range of knowledge possessed by the entire class, and
4. explicitly reviewing the task-relevant information necessary for the day's lesson.

Dahllof and Lundgren (1970) have proposed the use of a steering group composed of low achievers as a particularly effective way of determining the extent to which review and reteaching may be needed. A somewhat expanded notion of the steering group is a small number of low, average, and high performers that can be queried at the start of class on the task-relevant prior knowledge that is needed for the day's lesson. When high performers miss a large proportion of answers, this is an indication that extensive reteaching for the entire class will be necessary. When high performers answer questions correctly but average performers do not, some reteaching should be undertaken before the start of the lesson. And, finally, if most of the high and average performers answer the questions correctly but most of the low performers do not, then individualized materials, extra reading and worksheets, or a tutorial arrangement should be used for these learners. This ensures that large amounts of class time are not devoted to review and reteaching, which may benefit only a small number of students.

Strategies such as these for daily review and checking, especially when used with a carefully selected steering group, will be indispensable for informing a teacher that previous instruction has been over the heads of some or most of the students and, therefore, that additional review and reteaching is necessary.

Presenting and Structuring New Content

One of the primary ingredients of the direct instruction model is the presentation of material in small steps. Recall from chapter 5 that lessons must be served up in small portions that are consistent with the previous knowledge, ability level, and interests of the students. Likewise, the content *within* the lessons must be partitioned and subdivided to organize the material into small bits. No portion can be too large; if it is, the students' attention will be lost, which possibly may lead to disruptive or distracted behaviors. The key is to focus the material on one idea at a time and to present it so that one point is mastered before the next point is introduced. This is most easily accomplished by dividing a lesson into easily recognizable subparts, rules, or categories. It is no coincidence that the strategy of "divide and conquer" is as appropriate in the classroom as it is in military battles. You, like any great warrior, can derive much benefit from it.

Remember that the subdivisions you use can be your own; they need not always follow those provided by the text, workbook, or curriculum guide you may be using. Content divisions in texts, workbooks, and curriculum guides generally are created for the purpose of communicating *content intended to be read,* not for the purpose of presenting *content that must be explained* orally to learners within the time frame of a specific lesson. Consequently, these published divisions in the form of chapter titles, subheadings, or Roman numerals in outlines are sometimes too broad to represent bite-sized pieces that students can easily digest within a single lesson. Unfortunately, many beginning teachers stick tenaciously to these formal headings without realizing either the volume of content that falls within them or the time it takes to orally explain, illustrate, and practice this content. The truth is that content is not being discarded by creating new organizational divisions; it is only being broken into smaller steps suitable for presentation in a single period. These subdivisions can consist of rules (e.g., here are some rules to follow), steps (e.g., we will do this, then that), or practices (e.g., here is the first of five things we will cover) that organize your instruction into bite-sized pieces in advance and, most importantly, that communicate this organization to your students.

In chapter 3 several suggestions were provided for organizing content in ways that are meaningful to students. Following is an elaboration of four suggestions that are particularly relevant to direct instruction. These are the part-whole, sequential, combinatorial, and comparative methods of structuring direct instruction content.

Part-whole relationships

A part-whole organizational format introduces the topic in its most general form (e.g., "What is a possessive?") and then divides the topic into easy-to-distinguish subdivisions (e.g., "Rule 1" and "Rule 2"). This creates subdivisions that are easily digested and presents them in ways that always relate back to the whole. Students should always be aware of the part being covered at any particular time ("This is Rule 2") and its relationship to the whole ("This leads to our second rule for denoting ownership.") Verbal markers (e.g., "This is Rule 1," "Here is the first part," "This is the last example of this type, now let's move to the next type") are important for alerting students that a transition is under way, because the divisions created may be arbitrary and, therefore, unfamiliar to the students. This type of organization is intended to create bite-sized chunks; it helps students organize and see what is being taught and also informs them of what piece they are on. Part-whole organization is illustrated in Figure 6.2a.

Sequential relationships

Another way of structuring content is by sequential ordering; the content is taught according to the way in which the facts, rules, or sequences to be learned occur in the real world. Students may already have a feel for sequential ordering because of practical experience, which can increase student attention and involvement in the learning task.

In algebra, for example, equations are solved by first multiplying, then dividing, then adding, and finally subtracting; this order of operations must occur for any solution to be correct. A lesson that is sequentially structured, therefore, might introduce the manipulation of signed numbers in a multiplication, division, addition, and subtraction order, which reinforces the way equations must actually be solved. In other words, all examples used in teaching signed-number multiplication would be completed before any examples about division would be introduced, thereby teaching the correct sequence as well as the intended content. Sequential ordering is illustrated in Figure 6.2b.

Combinatorial relationships

A third way of structuring lesson content is to bring together in a single format various elements or dimensions that influence the use of facts, rules, and sequences. This allows an overall framework to direct the order of content by showing the logic of some combinations of facts, rules, and sequences and the illogic of other combinations. For example, in teaching a direct instruction lesson in social studies, a scheme might be developed to reveal the relationship between marketable products and the various means of transporting them to market. An organizational chart such as that shown in Figure 6.2c might be developed to structure the instructional content. The chart could be shown to the students and then all the relevant facts (e.g., relative weights of products), rules (e.g., the heavier the product the more efficient the means of transportation must be), and action sequences (e.g., first analyze the product's size and weight, *then* choose the best location) could be taught. The shaded cells, then, identify the *combinations,* or dimensions of content, that are most relevant to the lesson objectives.

Comparative relationships

Comparative structuring of content places different pieces of content side by side to make comparisons and contrasts. This structuring places facts, rules, or sequences side by side across two or more categories so that the similarities and differences can be noted. For example, a government teacher may wish to compare and contrast several aspects of the United States and the Soviet Union; the instruction could be ordered according to the format shown in Figure 6.2d. Teaching of the relevant facts (e.g., definitions of democracy and communism), rules (e.g., democratic "rights" versus totalitarian "privileges"), and sequences (e.g., democratic principles tend to create laws to protect; communistic principles tend to create laws to control) could then be accomplished by moving first across the chart and then down. The chart structures content in advance, and students can easily see the structure and content to be covered.

Whether you use one structuring method or a combination of them to organize a lesson, remember to divide the content into bite-sized pieces. To the extent that these structuring techniques divide larger divisions of content into smaller and more meaningful units, they will have served an important purpose.

Finally, note how this teacher combined rules and examples in organizing and presenting the content. The rule was always presented first and then followed by one or more examples. Note also that after some examples illustrating the rule, the rule itself was repeated—either by having students write the rule after having seen it on the board or by having a student orally repeat the rule to the class. Learning a rule in one sensory modality (e.g., seeing it on the board) and then recreating it in a sensory modality different than the one with which it was learned (e.g., writing or speaking it) generally promotes a greater level of learning and retention than does either seeing the rule only once or producing it in the same modality in which it was learned (e.g., repeating the rule *orally* after having *heard* it from the teacher). In addition, giving a rule, then an example of the rule, followed by repetition of the rule (rule-example-rule order) generally will be more productive (Hermann, 1971; Tomlinson & Hunt, 1971) than will simply giving the rule and then an example (rule-example order) or giving an example followed by the rule (example-rule order).

FIGURE 6.2a
Structuring a lesson by identifying part-whole relationships

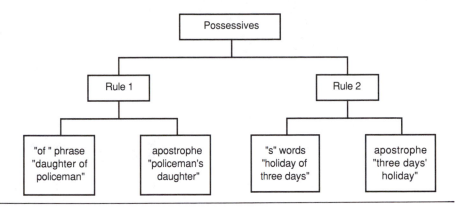

```
                        ┌─────────────┐
                        │ Possessives │
                        └─────────────┘
              ┌─────────────────┴─────────────────┐
          ┌────────┐                          ┌────────┐
          │ Rule 1 │                          │ Rule 2 │
          └────────┘                          └────────┘
        ┌─────┴─────┐                       ┌─────┴─────┐
```

| "of " phrase "daughter of policeman" | apostrophe "policeman's daughter" | "s" words "holiday of three days" | apostrophe "three days' holiday" |

FIGURE 6.2b
Structuring a lesson by identifying sequential relationships

$$y = a - b + \frac{cd}{e}$$

1. First, let's determine cd when

   c = -1, d = 2

   c = 0, d = -4

   c = 2, d = -3

2. Next, let's determine $\frac{cd}{e}$ when

   cd = -2, e = -2

   cd = 0, e = 1

   cd = -6, e = 4

3. Now, let's determine $b + \frac{cd}{e}$ when

   $b = 1, \frac{cd}{e} = 1$

   $b = -3, \frac{cd}{e} = 0$

   $b = 2, \frac{cd}{e} = -1.5$

4. Finally, let's determine $a - b + \frac{cd}{e}$ when

   $a = 10, b + \frac{cd}{e} = 2$

   $a = 7, b + \frac{cd}{e} = -3$

   $a = 5, b + \frac{cd}{e} = .5$

FIGURE 6.2c
Structuring a lesson by identifying combinatorial relationships

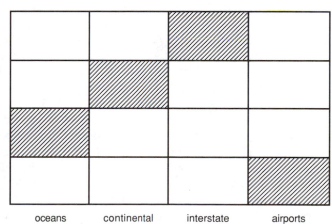

P R O D U C T S	oceans	continental rivers	interstate highways	airports
Food for regional use			▨	
Raw materials for domestic production		▨		
Heavy machinery for export	▨			
Magazine for international readership				▨

TRANSPORTATION SYSTEMS

FIGURE 6.2d
Structuring a lesson by
identifying comparative
relationships

Points of Comparison	U.S.	SOVIETS
Economics	capitalism	communism
Politics	democracy	totalitarianism
Source of laws	constitution	Marxist-Leninist doctrine
Purpose of laws	to protect	to control
Governing body	elected	mostly appointed

Guided Student Practice

Recall from the structure of a lesson plan that the presentation of stimulus material is followed by the need to elicit practice in the desired behavior. In this section are given several ways of accomplishing this in the context of the direct instruction model. The elicitations discussed in this chapter are teacher guided; that is, they provide students with guided practice that is organized and directed by the teacher.

Recall that chapter 5 gives several important ingredients to elicit behavior. One ingredient is that the behavior should be elicited in as non-evaluative an atmosphere as possible; this will help students feel free to risk creating responses of which they may be unsure but from which they can begin to build a correct response. Any response, however crude or incorrect, can be the basis for learning if it is properly followed by feedback and correctives.

Recall that the second ingredient for eliciting student behavior was the use of covert responses. This helps ensure a nonthreatening environment, but it also encourages student engagement in the learning task with the least amount of expenditure of time and effort on the teacher's part. In the example, by having all the students write down their responses privately prior to seeing the correct answers on the overhead, the teacher guided each student to formulate a response; it was not necessary to call on each and every one of them. The teacher guided the students into responding by encouraging, and later rewarding, their covert responses.

An equally important aspect of eliciting the desired behavior is checking for the students' understanding of this behavior and, when necessary, prompting them to convert wrong answers to right ones. In the example, the teacher stopped after every item to see if there were any problems and prompted students to create correct answers when necessary. Prompting is an important part of eliciting the desired behavior, because it strengthens and builds the learners' confidence by encouraging them to use some aspects of the answer that have already been given in formulating the correct response (E. Gagné, 1985). In the example Johnny was encouraged to *rethink* his response, to *focus* consciously on the specific part of the problem causing the error, and to *remember* the rule that will prevent such errors in the future.

Checking for understanding and prompting a correct response can be accomplished in several ways. One approach was illustrated in a previous example: All the students were asked to respond privately at the same time and then were encouraged to ask for individual help ("Any problems?"). Another approach is to call on students whether or not their hands are raised, thereby seeking out opportunities to prompt and correct wrong answers. A version of this approach is referred to as *ordered turns,* in which the teacher systematically goes through the class and expects students to respond when their turn arrives. This approach has been found to be more effective in producing gains in student achievement than has randomly calling on students when groups are small (Brophy & Evertson, 1976; Anderson, 1979), but, generally, is less efficient than selecting students to respond during full-class instruction (Anderson et al., 1982). Yet another approach is to have students write out answers to be checked and, if need be, corrected by a classmate. Finally, the teacher can prepare a number of questions beforehand to test for the most frequently occurring errors. Students would then be asked to provide responses which the teacher checks for accuracy and prompts when necessary. This approach has the advantage of assuming that not everyone understands or has the correct answer when no responses are heard following a call for questions. It has been found to be particularly effective in increasing student achievement (Singer & Donlon, 1982; McKenzie, 1979).

Feedback and Correctives

The next ingredient in the direct instruction model pertains to the provision of feedback and correctives. Simply put, it involves strategies for handling right and wrong answers. Based upon the findings of several research studies, Rosenshine (1983) identified four broad categories of student response and some direct instruction strategies for handling these responses.

A category of student response that most teachers hope to inspire is one that is **correct, quick, and firm**. Although such a response most frequently occurs during the latter stages of a lesson or unit, it can occur at almost anytime during a lesson or unit if content has been divided into bite-sized portions. A moderate-to-high percentage of correct, quick, and firm responses is important if students are to become actively engaged in the learning process. Not every response from every student must be a correct one,

but *for most learning that involves knowledge acquisition, the steps between successive portions of your lesson should be made small enough to produce approximately 60–80% correct answers in a practice and feedback session* (Bennett et al., 1981; Brophy & Evertson, 1976). This research suggests that the best teacher response to a correct, quick, and firm student response is to ask another question of the same student. This increases the potential for feedback or, if time does not permit, to move on quickly to another question and student. The teacher should keep the lesson moving at a quick pace, involving as many students as possible in the practice exercise, and covering as many stimulus problems as possible. Once 60–80% right answers are produced, a rhythm and momentum will have been created that heightens student attention and engagement and provides for a high level of task orientation. The brisk pace of right answers also will help ensure that irrelevant student responses and classroom distractions are kept to a minimum.

A second category of student response is one that is **correct but hesitant**, which frequently occurs in a practice and feedback session at the beginning or middle of a lesson. It is important to provide positive feedback to the student who supplies a correct but hesitant response. The first feedback that should be provided in this instance is a positive, reinforcing statement, such as "good," or "that's correct," because the correct but hesitant response is likely to be remembered more easily when it has been linked to a warm and acknowledging reply. This will help make the student's next response to the same type of problem correct, quick, and firm.

Affirmative replies, however, are rarely sufficient in themselves to effect significant change on a subsequent problem of the same type unless the reasons behind the hesitant response are addressed. Although discovering the precise reason for a student's hesitant response is desirable, a quick restatement of the facts, rules, or steps needed to obtain the right answer often can accomplish the same end more efficiently. This restatement will not only aid the student giving the correct but hesitant response, it will also help reduce subsequent wrong answers or hesitant responses among other students who listen to the restatement.

A third category of student response is one that is **incorrect but careless**. Sometimes as many as 20% of student responses can fall into this category, depending on the time of day and the students' level of fatigue and inattentiveness. When this occurs, you may be tempted to scold, admonish, or even verbally punish the student for responding thoughtlessly when you feel that she or he does know the correct response. However, it is important that you resist this temptation, no matter how justified you feel it to be. Nothing is more frustrating than to repress genuine emotions, but researchers and experienced teachers agree that more harm than good often results from attempting to deal emotionally with this type of problem (e.g., "I'm ashamed of you," "That's a dumb mistake," "I thought you were brighter than that"). Verbal punishment rarely teaches one to avoid careless mistakes. Experience has shown that the rhythm and momentum built and maintained through a brisk and lively pace can easily be broken by off-task attention to an individual student. Emotional reaction rarely has a positive effect, so the best procedure is to acknowledge that the answer is wrong and to move immediately to the next student for the correct response. You have made a point to the careless student by immediately passing the opportunity to respond correctly to the next student.

Perhaps the most challenging category of responses is that of **incorrect because of a lack of knowledge**. Such errors typically occur, sometimes in large numbers, during the initial stages of a lesson or unit. Providing hints, probing, or changing the question or stimulus to a simpler one which engages the student in finding the correct response is more desirable than giving the student the correct response. The goal is not to get the correct answer out of the student, but to engage the learner in the process by which the right answer can be found. In a previous example, the teacher tried to focus Johnny on the *s* he had missed at the end of the proper noun *Jenkins* and to restate the rule concerning forma-

tion of possessives in words ending in *s*. Likewise, the teacher probed Debbie after her wrong answer by asking, "What word is doing the possessing?" Each of these instances led to the right answer without actually telling the student what the right answer was. Any time an instructional strategy can channel a student's thoughts in ways that result in the right answer without actually giving that answer, a framework is provided for producing a correct response in all subsequent problems of a similar nature.

The most common strategies for responding to an incorrect answer are

1. reviewing key facts or rules needed for a correct solution,
2. explaining the steps used to reach a correct solution,
3. prompting with clues or hints representing a partially correct answer, and
4. taking a different but similar problem and guiding the student to the correct solution.

Such strategies, when used with a specific student, benefit all the students by clarifying information that they may have learned only partially. Because this type of corrective feedback is used with individual students, its effects on the entire class will be seen by an increase in the overall percentage of correct responses. Reviewing, reexplaining, and prompting will be effective until approximately 80% of the students respond correctly. After that point the correctives should be made briefer, eventually guiding students with incorrect responses to helpful exercises in the text or to specially prepared remedial exercises (Bennett et al., 1981).

Finally, it should be noted that when using the direct instruction model for the teaching of facts, rules, and sequences, an incorrect answer should never go undetected or uncorrected. Every wrong answer should be responded to with one or more of the strategies noted previously, because leaving an answer uncorrected due to inattentiveness or distraction provides a signal to those who do know the answer that paying attention, responding correctly, and mastering the subject are not to be taken seriously.

Independent Practice

The next ingredient in direct instruction is the opportunity for independent practice. When the behavior has been successfully elicited and some feedback and correctives administered, then an opportunity for practicing the behavior independently should be provided. This is often the time in which facts and rules are put together to form action sequences. For example, learning to drive a car requires a knowledge of terminology (e.g., gear shift, ignition, accelerator) and of rules (e.g., signalling for turns, knowing what to do at stoplights, parking on hills). But until this knowledge and these rules are put together, meaningful learning cannot occur. Independent practice provides the opportunity, in a carefully controlled and organized environment, to make a meaningful whole out of the bits and pieces. Facts and rules must come together under the teacher's guidance and example in ways that (a) force the simultaneous consideration of all the individual units of a problem and (b) connect the units into a single harmonious sequence of action. These two processes are referred to by learning theorists as **unitization** and **automaticity** (La Berge & Samuels, 1974).

Notice the manner in which these two processes were required in the example lesson. The individual "units" consisted of the definition of a possessive (a fact) and two statements concerning the forming of possessives (Rules 1 and 2). The lesson connected these units into a single harmonious sequence of action in two ways. First there was the exercise with which the example ends. For this exercise, the teacher directed students to a workbook, providing opportunities for independent practice. Presumably, the sentences with which the students would be working are similar to sentences containing possessives found in any newspaper, magazine, or school essay. Therefore, we may assume that they contain opportunities to apply either one or both rules. Table 6.3 traces the steps a student might take in combining the facts and rules into a sequence of action for one sentence in the workbook.

In this exercise the bits and pieces of the lesson have been put together in a meaningful sequence of learning. This is not to say that a lesson focusing on the bits and pieces is not a valuable one; without well-taught bits and pieces no other advanced form of learning is possible. Thus, the meaningful application of knowledge requires that there be some knowledge that is both highly familiar to the learner and also rich in examples and associations (e.g, month's delay, Jenkins' home) learned from detailed and redundant practice. In this sense, less complex levels of behavior are almost always required in order for more complex forms of learning to occur.

TABLE 6.3

Steps involved in translating the sentence, "In Mrs. Jones paper there was an article about a friend of Robert" into correct possessive form

Step 1	Is ownership indicated in this sentence?
Step 2	If yes, where?
	the paper belongs to Mrs. Jones
	the friend belongs to Robert
Step 3	Has an *of* phrase been substituted for a noun (Rule 1)?
	If yes, where?
	friend of Robert has been substituted for Robert's friend
Step 4	Does any word denoting ownership end in *s*? (Rule 2)
	If yes, where?
	Jones paper should be written *Jones' paper*
Step 5	Therefore, the correct possessive form of this sentence is
	"In Mrs. Jones' paper there was an article about Robert's friend."

It is important that these facts and rules not be left dangling but be practiced with detailed and redundant examples that create and reinforce action sequences. Assembling facts and rules into action sequences through detailed and redundant practice is one of the most effective procedures that can be employed to ensure that the task-relevant information required for future lessons will be learned. The outcome of this lesson will provide task-relevant prior information for future lessons on sentence punctuation, paragraph writing, and composition.

So far there has been no mention of one other opportunity for independent practice that was incorporated into this teacher's lesson about possessives. Recall that at the beginning of the lesson the teacher told her students that they would be given other examples of errors from newspapers and magazines. Presumably, this exercise also would provide students with the opportunity to form action sequences out of the facts and rules they have learned. These real-life examples could be expected to increase still further the meaningfulness of what has been learned. Opportunities for practice should increasingly resemble applications in the real world, until the examples and exercises provided are indistinguishable from those found outside the classroom. Using clippings from actual newspapers and magazines was this teacher's way of providing practice indistinguishable from the contexts in which the desired learning is likely to be applied outside of the classroom.

The purpose of providing opportunities for all types of independent practice is to develop automatic responses in students—they no longer need to recall each individual unit of content but can use all the units simultaneously. The goal of the example lesson, then, is "to write a correct sentence using possessives," and not "to use Rule 1 and Rule 2." As we have seen, "automaticity" is reached through mastery of the units comprising a complete response and sufficient practice in composing these pieces into a complete action sequence. Your goal should be to schedule suf-ficient opportunities for independent practice to allow individual responses to become "composed" and automatic (Samuels, 1981).

Following are several recommendations to ensure that your students become actively engaged in the seatwork you provide. One of these is that you direct the class through the first independent practice item. In this manner the scheduled seatwork has a definite beginning, and students who are unclear about the assignment can ask questions without distracting other students. Another suggestion is to schedule seatwork as soon as possible after both the exercises designed to elicit the desired behavior and the exercises that provide feedback and correctives. This will help the students understand that independent practice is relevant to the guided practice provided earlier in the lesson. For example, opportunities for independent practice provided on a later day are likely to be met with a high number of requests for information; this will lead you inefficiently to repeat key portions of the previous day's lesson. As with all forms of learning, *practice should follow the time of learning as soon as possible* for maximum recall and understanding.

Finally, Fisher et al. (1978) recommend that teachers circulate around the classroom while students are engaged in independent practice, to provide feedback, ask questions, and give brief explanations. However, circulation time should be spent equally across most of your students and not concentrated on a small number of students. Scanning written responses, prompting for alternative answers when they are incorrect, or reminding students of necessary facts or rules should be kept to a minimum (on the average of 30 seconds or less per student) in order not to reduce the time available for monitoring the work of other students (Fisher et al., 1978; Scott and Bushell, 1974). Monitoring student responses during independent seatwork can be an important direct instruction function, but contacts should be kept short and focused on specific issues for which a brief explanation is adequate.

Weekly and Monthly Reviews

The last direct instruction function involves conducting weekly and monthly reviews. The primary purpose of periodic review is to ensure that all task-relevant information for future lessons has been taught and to identify areas for which re-teaching of key facts, rules, and sequences may be necessary. Without periodic review there is no way of knowing whether direct instruction has been successful in teaching the required facts, rules, and sequences.

Periodic review has long been a part of almost every instructional strategy. In the context of direct instruction, however, periodic review and the recycling of instruction take on added importance because of the brisk pace at which direct instruction is conducted. The teacher usually establishes the proper pace by noting the approximate percentage of errors occurring during guided practice and feedback; 60–80% correct responses indicates a satisfactory pace. Weekly and monthly reviews provide other opportunities to determine if the pace is appropriate and to make adjustments upward or downward before too much content has been covered. When student responses to questions posed in weekly and monthly review sessions are correct, quick, and firm about 95% of the time, the pace is adequate (Bennett et. al., 1981). Independent practice and homework should raise the percentage of correct responses from approximately 60–80% during guided practice and feedback to approximately 95% on weekly and monthly reviews. When results are below these levels, and especially when they are substantially below, the pace has been too fast. Some recycling of facts, rules, and sequences will be necessary, especially when they are prerequisites to later learning.

Another obvious advantage of weekly and monthly review sessions is that they strengthen correct but hesitant responses. Providing a review of facts, rules, and sequences that will form the basis of task-relevant prior understandings for later lessons will give some learners a second chance to grasp material that was either missed or only partially learned the first time around. These sessions are often welcomed by students; it is a chance to go over material that may have been missed, that was difficult to learn the first time through, and that may be covered on unit tests.

Finally, it can be noted that a regular weekly review, not just a review every so often, is the key to performing this direct instruction function. The weekly review is intended to build momentum. Momentum is the result of gradually increasing the coverage and depth of the weekly reviews until time for a comprehensive monthly review arrives (Posner, 1987). The objective is to create a review cycle that rises and falls in about one-month cycles. The low point of this cycle occurs at the start of a direct instruction unit, when only one week's material need be reviewed. The weekly reviews then become increasingly comprehensive until a major, monthly review restates and checks for understanding of all of the previous month's learning. Momentum is built by targeting greater and greater amounts of instruction for review, but in gradual stages so that students do not become overwhelmed with unfamiliar review content and that they always know what will be covered in the next review.

Table 6.4 presents the lesson plan for direct instruction based on the dialogue about possessives presented in this chapter.

Other Forms of Direct Instruction

So far direct instruction has been discussed as though it occurs only in a lecture format; this is perhaps the most popular, but by no means the only, format for direct instruction. Other ways of executing the direct instruction model (either independent of the lecture format or in association with it) include programmed instruction, computer-assisted instruction, peer and cross-age tutoring, various kinds of audiolingual devices (such as "speaking machines" for learning to read in the early grades), and single-concept films.

TABLE 6.4
Lesson Plan: Direct Instruction

Unit Title: Punctuation
Lesson Title: Forming and punctuating possessives

1. Gaining attention	Display October school newspaper with punctuation error in headline. Point to error.
2. Informing the learner of the objective	At the end of the period students will be able to find mistakes in the newspapers (on file under "Punctuation") and make the necessary changes.
3. Stimulating recall of prerequisite learning	Review part of speech most likely to own or possess something by asking for the definition of a noun.
4. Presenting the stimulus material	Present two rules of possession: Rule 1. Use the possessive form whenever an *of* phrase can be substituted for a noun. Rule 2. For words ending in *s,* place the apostrophe after, not before, the *s.* Write rules on board.
5. Eliciting the desired behavior	Display the following examples on a transparency and ask students to convert them to the possessive form one at a time. On transparency: delay of a month home of Jenkins speech of the President the television set of Mr. Burns (See Smith, G. [1985]. *Understanding Grammar.* New York: City Press, pp. 101–103 for other examples.)
6 Providing feedback	Write the correct possessive form on the transparency as students finish each example. Wait for students to finish (all heads up) before providing the answer for the next example. Probe for complete understanding by asking for the rule.
7. Assessing the behavior	Use the exercise on page 87 of the workbook to assess student understanding and to provide additional practice. Use ordered recitation until about 90% correct responses are attained. Place 10 possessives on the unit test requiring the application of Rule 1 and Rule 2. Use examples in Smith (1985), pp. 101–103.

Some of these approaches have been creatively programmed to include all, or almost all, of the six direct instruction functions identified previously (daily review, new content, guided practice, feedback and correctives, independent practice, and periodic review). There is little question that some of these approaches to direct instruction have been successful with certain types of content and with certain types of students (Slavin, Leavey & Madden, 1982). However, since they are much less under the control of the teacher than is the lecture format, their applicability to specific instructional goals and students should be considered carefully.

As was noted previously, direct instruction works most effectively when objectives are at the lower levels of the cognitive, affective, and psychomotor domains. Because the content presented in programmed texts and computer-assisted instruction software, single-concept films, and audiolingual devices will not have been chosen or organized by the teacher, he or she will need to preview the instructional content for its applicability to curriculum objectives. In other words, simply choosing a programmed learning text from the apparent relevance of its title to the curriculum objectives is no guarantee the resulting instruction will be either relevant or following the direct instruction model. Although such devices as programmed texts, computer-assisted instructional software, and various forms of drill and practice media often have been associated with the direct instruction model, their treatment of the intended content may be far from direct. Therefore, whenever using these formats and associated "courseware" the teacher will need to preview both method and content for their close adherence to the six functions of the direct instruction model described previously.

Finally, it can be noted that programmed texts, computer-assisted instruction software, specialized media, and audiolingual devices tend to follow a direct instruction model most closely when they are programmed for remedial learning. This is where the formats, including peer and cross-age tutoring, will also be most effective in increasing student achievement (Slavin, 1980); at the same time they can relieve the classroom teacher of the sometimes arduous chore of providing individualized remedial instruction to a small number of students. Courseware to fit these formats tends to be most plentiful and direct in the area of remedial instruction. Building a library of remedial courseware is necessary in classes with less able learners who can be served part of the time through individualized remedial instruction.

A Final Word

This chapter has emphasized some of the direct, or more didactic, functions of teaching. As you have seen, these functions are particularly useful for the teaching of facts, rules, and action sequences, which tend to correspond to objectives at lower levels of behavioral complexity. When used in the proper sequence and with the types of behavioral objectives for which they are best suited, these teaching functions can make teaching easier, more efficient, and more effective.

The following chapter discusses another and equally valuable model of instruction, emphasizing still other teaching strategies. This model will not only complement a menu of direct instructional strategies with still other varieties of instruction, but will also represent an approach to teaching that will enable you to move your teaching to higher levels of behavioral complexity. As noted in chapter 5, behaviors at these higher levels should comprise a significant portion of the outcomes planned at the unit level. Because these behaviors are among those most frequently required outside of the classroom, techniques through which your students can acquire them will be indispensable additions to your teaching strategy menu.

Summing Up

This chapter introduced you to direct instruction strategies. Its main points were:

1. Two broad classifications of learning are facts, rules, and action sequences (Type 1) and concepts, patterns, and abstractions (Type 2).

2. Type 1 outcomes generally represent behaviors at the lower levels of complexity in the cognitive, affective, and psychomotor domains; Type 2 outcomes frequently represent behaviors at the higher levels of complexity in these domains.

3. Type 1 teaching activities require combining facts and rules at the knowledge and comprehension level into a sequence of actions that can be learned through observation, rote repetition, and practice. Type 1 outcomes have "right answers" that can be learned by memorization and practice.

4. Type 2 teaching activities go beyond facts, rules, and sequences to help the learner create, synthesize, identify, and recognize an answer that cannot be easily modeled or memorized. Type 2 outcomes may have many right answers that contain criterial attributes forming a concept or pattern.

5. The learning of facts, rules, and action sequences are most commonly taught with teaching strategies that emphasize knowledge acquisition; the learning of concepts, patterns, and abstractions are most commonly taught with teaching strategies that emphasize inquiry or problem solving.

6. The acquisition of facts, rules, and action sequences is most efficiently achieved through a process known as the *direct instruction model*. This model is primarily teacher-centered; facts, rules, and action sequences are passed on to students in a lecture format involving large amounts of teacher talk, questions and answers, review and practice, and the immediate correction of student errors.

7. The direct instruction model is characterized by full-class (as opposed to small-group) instruction; by the organization of learning based on questions posed by the teacher; by the provision of detailed and redundant practice; by the presentation of material so that one new fact, rule, or sequence is mastered before the next is presented; and by the formal arrangement of the classroom to maximize drill and practice.

8. Direct instruction is most appropriate when content in texts and workbooks does not appear in appropriately sized pieces, when your active involvement in the teaching process is necessary to arouse or heighten student interest, and when the content to be taught represents task-relevant prior knowledge for subsequent learning.

9. Some techniques for daily review and checking include:

   ■ having students identify difficult homework problems in a question-and-answer format,

   ■ sampling the understanding of a few students who are likely to represent the class, and

   ■ explicitly reviewing task-relevant prior learning required for the day's lesson.

10. Some techniques for presenting and structuring new content include:

   ■ establishing part-whole relationships,

   ■ identifying sequential relationships,

   ■ finding combinatorial relationships, and

   ■ drawing comparative relationships.

11. Some techniques for guiding student practice include:

   ■ asking students to respond privately and then be singled out for help,

   ■ calling on students to respond whether or not their hands are raised, and

   ■ preparing questions beforehand and randomly asking students to respond.

12. Providing appropriate feedback and correctives involves knowing how to respond to answers that are (a) correct, quick, and firm, (b) correct but hesitant, (c) incorrect but careless, and (d) incorrect.

13. For a correct, quick, and firm response, you should acknowledge the correct response and either ask another question of the same student or move on quickly to another student.

14. For a correct but hesitant response, you should provide a reinforcing statement and quickly restate the facts, rules, or steps needed for the right answer.

15. For a correct but careless response, you should indicate that the response is incorrect and quickly move to the next student without further comment.

16. For an incorrect response that is not due to carelessness, you should engage the student in finding the correct response with hints, probes, or a related but simpler question.

17. For most learning involving knowledge acquisition, the steps between successive portions of your lesson should be made small enough to produce approximately 60–80% correct answers in a practice and feedback session.

18. Reviewing, reexplaining, and prompting will be effective until approximately 80% of your students respond correctly after which correctives should be made briefer or students should be guided to individualized learning materials.

19. Independent practice should be designed so that the learner puts together facts and rules to form action sequences that increasingly resemble applications in the real world. Any opportunities for independent practice should be made as soon after the time of learning as possible.

20. Instruction should be paced so that student responses to questions posed in weekly and monthly reviews are correct, quick, and firm about 95% of the time.

21. Independent practice and homework should be used to raise the percentage of correct responses from approximately 60–80% during guided practice and feedback to approximately 95% on weekly and monthly reviews.

22. Other forms of direct instruction may include programmed texts, computer-assisted instruction software, peer and cross-age tutoring, audiolingual devices, and specialized media, such as single-concept films.

For Discussion and Practice

*1. Identify the learning outcomes associated with Type 1 and Type 2 teaching strategies. To what levels of behavior in the cognitive domain does each type of learning apply?

*2. What type of learning outcomes are most commonly produced by instructional strategies that emphasize knowledge acquisition? What type of learning outcomes are most commonly produced by instructional strategies that emphasize inquiry or problem solving?

*3. Describe five instructional characteristics that define the direct instruction model.

*4. Give examples of action verbs that describe the type of outcomes expected by using the direct instruction model. Provide three examples each in the cognitive, affective, and psychomotor domains.

*5. Identify three areas of content in your teaching in which the use of the direct instruction model would be especially appropriate.

*6. Identify four techniques for reviewing and checking the previous day's work.

*7. Identify and provide one original example of each of the four techniques for structuring content and presenting it in bite-sized portions.

*8. Identify the order in which rules and examples of them should be given in order to promote the greatest amount of comprehension and retention of content. Provide a real-life example of such a sequence.

*9. Explain why providing guided student practice in a nonevaluative atmosphere is important for learning to occur.

*10. How is prompting used to provide guided student practice, and for what purpose is it used?

*11. Name four different types of student responses that vary in their correctness and describe how you would respond to each.

12. The following second-grade student responses were received by a teacher after asking the question, "What does five plus three equal?"

MARY: I think it's eight.
TOMMY: Nine.
BOB: Fifty three.
BETTY: Eight.

Role-play an appropriate teacher response to each of the answers.

13. The following tenth-grade student responses were received by a teacher to the question, "What was one of the underlying reasons for the Civil War?"

TIM: The South wanted the land owned by the North.

ROBERT: Religious persecution.

KEN: Well, let me think . . . it had something to do with slavery.

TRACY: The economic dependency of the South on slavery.

Role-play an appropriate teacher response to each of these answers.

*14. Identify four different strategies for responding to an incorrect response and give a real-life example of each.

*15. What approximate percentage of correct answers should you work toward in a practice and feedback session? Identify how you would change your instructional approach if only 30% of your student responses were correct in a practice and feedback session.

*16. What is the primary purpose of independent practice? How should the exercises used for independent practice change as additional time for practice becomes available?

*17. Identify two recommendations for being more effective in monitoring student work while you circulate around the classroom during independent practice.

*18. Approximately what percentage of student responses during weekly and monthly review sessions should be correct, quick, and firm?

*19. Explain how a review cycle could be planned so as to rise and fall in one-month cycles.

*20. What caution might you observe in choosing programmed texts, computer-assisted software, films, and other special types of media to provide direct instruction?

Suggested Readings

Bennett, D. (1982). Should teachers be expected to learn and use direct instruction? *Association for Supervision and Curriculum Development Update,* 24(4), 5.
A statement on some of the uses of direct instruction and when it is most likely to be effective.

Berliner, D. (1982). Should teachers be expected to learn and use direct instruction? *Association for Supervision and Curriculum Development Update,* 24(4), 5.
A critical statement on when and where direct instruction is most applicable.

Brophy, J. (1982). Successful teaching strategies for the inner-city child. *Phi Delta Kappan, 63,* 527–30.
A case for direct instruction employing recent research results confirming its positive effects on the achievement of inner-city students.

Fielding, G., Kameenui, E., & Gerstein, R. (1983). A comparison of an inquiry and a direct instruction approach to teach legal concepts and applications to secondary school students. *Journal of Educational Research, 76,* 243–50.
A description of a research study investigating the pros and cons of the direct instruction model compared with an alternative approach (to be presented in Chapter 7).

Good, T., Grouws, D., & Ebmeier, H. (1983). *Active mathematics teaching.* New York: Longman.
A thorough explanation of how to best apply direct instruction in the field of mathematics.

Hunger, M. & Russel, D. (1981). Planning for effective instruction: Lesson design. In *Increasing your teaching effectiveness.* Palo Alto, CA: The Learning Institute.
A very useful summary of how teachers can use the direct instruction model in preparing lesson plans.

Rosenshine, B. (1983). Teaching functions in instructional programs. *The Elementary School Journal, 4,* 335–351.
An often-cited article that describes all of the functions of the direct instruction model as described in this chapter.

7

Indirect Instruction
Strategies

Now that the topic of direct instruction has been discussed, it is appropriate to consider strategies of **indirect instruction** involving the teaching of concepts, patterns, and abstractions. These behaviors are most often associated with the words *inquiry, problem solving,* or *discovery learning.*

Perhaps no terms have been more misused or abused in recent times than the words *inquiry, problem solving,* and *discovery learning.* Although initially brought to the attention of educators through the writings of John Dewey (1938) and Jerome Bruner (1966), these terms have been redefined and expanded since then to mean many different things to many different individuals. Fortunately, all of the many forms of indirect instruction which may be labeled with these terms have far more in common than they have differences, and these similarities will be the primary focus of this chapter.

One popular misconception often associated with inquiry, problem solving, and discovery learning is the failure to understand that each of

them represents a different form of the more general concept of indirect instruction. Indirect instruction is an approach to teaching and learning in which the process of learning is *inquiry,* the result is *discovery,* and the learning context is a *problem.* These three ideas—inquiry, discovery, and problem solving—are brought together in special ways in the indirect model of teaching and learning. This chapter will present some instructional strategies that can be used to compose your own indirect teaching approach involving these three concepts.

An Introduction to Indirect Instruction

Recall that in the previous chapter a distinction was made between strategies for teaching facts, rules, and action sequences and those for teaching concepts, patterns, and abstractions. Table 6.1 (p. 141) illustrated some examples of the types of learning possible in each of these categories. These examples showed how the learning of facts, rules, and action sequences differs from the learning of concepts, patterns, and abstractions and how instructional strategies must differ accordingly. Because the previous chapter explained why direct instruction strategies were best suited for the teaching of facts, rules, and action sequences, it should be no surprise to learn that indirect instruction strategies are best suited for teaching concepts, patterns, and abstractions.

When sets of stimuli are presented to learners and they are asked to go beyond the data given (to make conclusions and generalizations or to find a pattern of relationships), the indirect model of instruction is being employed. The word *indirect* reflects the fact that the learner acquires a behavior indirectly by transforming stimulus material (such as rules and examples) into a response or behavior that differs from both (a) the stimulus used to present the learning and (b) any previous response given by the student. Because the stimulus material can be added to and rearranged by the learner during this process in order to make it more meaningful, the elicited response or behavior can take many different forms. In contrast to direct instruction outcomes, there is rarely a single, best answer when the indirect model of instruction is being used. Instead, the learner is guided to an answer that goes beyond the problem or stimulus material presented.

Indirect instruction would be inefficient and even ineffective for teaching many types of facts, rules, or action sequences for which the desired response is almost identical to the presented learning stimulus. Rules for forming and punctuating possessives, for example, would be most efficiently taught by giving students the rules and asking them to practice applying them, as was done in a previous example. In that example, knowledge acquisition and application were taught with a direct instruction strategy, because the stimulus material (e.g, written rules and examples) already contained the correct answers in the form most desired, and the purpose of the lesson was to apply the rules—not to discover them or to invent new ones.

One may wonder why, if direct instruction is so effective in these instances, it is not used all the time. It would be tempting were it not for an important complication: Not all the outcomes to be achieved will call for responses that look like the stimulus material being presented. Under the direct instruction model, the amount of conversion or change in the stimulus material required by the learner was minimal, limited to (a) learning units of the stimulus material in some meaningful way so that they could be remembered and (b) composing parts of the stimulus material into a whole, so a rapid and automatic response could occur. In the previous chapter these two cognitive processes were called unitization and automaticity. Learning at the lower levels of the cognitive, affective, and psychomotor domains places heavy reliance on these two processes, both of which can be placed efficiently into action by stimulus material closely resembling the desired response (e.g., "Look at this word and then say it"; "Watch me form a possessive and then you do the next one"; "Read the instructions, then focus the microscope.") The desired response does not need to go much beyond what is provided. The task for the learner is simply to produce a response that resembles, as closely as possible, the form and content of the stimulus. A great deal of instruction involves behaviors at the lower levels of complexity and, therefore, requires unitization and automaticity; for this, the direct instruction model is most efficient and most effective.

Not all learning is limited to the lower levels of behavioral complexity or requires only unitization and automaticity. In fact, if all (or even most) lessons required only these two processes, students would be unlikely to function successfully in subsequent grades or in the world outside of the classroom. This is because most of the jobs, responsibilities, and activities performed outside school require responses at higher levels of behavioral complexity; they often involve analysis, synthesis, and decision-making behaviors in the cognitive domain, organization and characterization behaviors in the affective domain, and articulation and naturalization behaviors in the psychomotor domain. This complicates the direct instruction model because these behaviors are not learned in the same way as behaviors at lower levels of complexity. To be sure, many behaviors at the lower levels of complexity will be required to attain more complex behaviors, but much more will be needed by both teacher and learners before these higher level behaviors can be learned. As you will see in this chapter, the teaching of the higher level behaviors requires a different set of instructional strategies.

Some Examples of Concepts, Patterns, and Abstractions

What is required in order for your learners to acquire these higher level behaviors? To begin to answer this question, consider some topics whose mastery could require behavior at higher levels of complexity. The following set of topics requires more than the acquisition of facts, rules, and action sequences:

> concept of a quadratic equation (algebra)
>
> process of acculturation (social studies)
>
> meaning of *contact sports* (physical education)
>
> workings of a democracy (government)
>
> playing of a concerto (music)
>
> demonstration of photosynthesis (biology)
>
> understanding of the law of conservation (general science)

These topics represent not only bodies of facts, rules, and action sequences, but also something more: *concepts, processes, meanings,* and *understandings*. It would be possible to teach facts, rules, and action sequences associated with these topics without ever knowing the concept that binds the facts, rules, or the action sequence together (e.g., "Here is the *definition* of a quadratic equation," "Here are the *rules* for solving a quadratic equation," "Follow this *sequence* of steps to solve this quadratic equation"). On the other hand, it would *not* be possible to teach the concept of a quadratic equation by introducing only facts, rules, and action sequences. This is because understanding concepts, and the patterns and abstractions they represent, requires cognitive processes as well as unitization (units of the stimulus material in some meaningful form) and automaticity (being able to rapidly compose the units into a whole). Further, the learning of concepts involves **generalization** and **discrimination**, processes which require the learner to rearrange and elaborate on the stimulus material. Consider how these two new processes help a learner to acquire concepts.

Recall from Table 6.1 the distinction between Type 1 and Type 2 behaviors. Type 1 behaviors became Type 2 behaviors by using facts, rules, and sequences to form concepts. Notice what would be required if students were to try, for example, to learn the concept of a frog in the same way they acquired facts, rules, and action sequences about a frog. First, they would have to commit to memory all possible instances of frogs (of which there may be hundreds). Memories, trying to retain hundreds of images of frogs *in the same form they were presented,* would quickly become overburdened. Second, even after committing many different types of frogs to memory, they could confuse frogs with animals that look in some ways like frogs; because the memorization process does not include the characteristics that exclude an animal from being a frog (e.g., a hard shell, dry skin, changes color, has a tail), even though these animals share some characteristics of frogs (e.g., have four legs, are amphibious, eat insects).

The processes of generalization and discrimination, if planned for in the presentation of stimulus material, can help students to overcome both of these problems. The process of *generalization* helps them respond in a similar manner to stimuli that differ, thereby increasing the range of instances (e.g., to all types of frogs) to which particular facts, rules, and sequences apply. In addition, the process of *discrimination* selectively restricts this range by eliminating things that appear to match the student's concept (e.g., a chameleon) but that differ from it in critical dimensions (e.g., has a tail). Generalization and discrimination help students classify visually different stimuli into the same category on the basis of *criterial attributes*. These criterial attributes act as magnets, drawing together all instances of the same type without requiring the learner to memorize, or even to see, all possible instances. As a concept (e.g., a frog) becomes combined with other concepts to form larger patterns (e.g., amphibians), patterns of increasing complexity are produced. An example of a hierarchy of concepts, patterns, and abstractions typically found in a science curriculum is represented in Figure 7.1.

It is apparent that both the role of the teacher and the organization of stimulus material need to be different for learning concepts, patterns, and abstractions than for learning facts, rules, and action sequences. It seems reasonable that for outcomes at higher levels of behavioral com-

plexity the stimulus material cannot contain all possible instances of the concept being learned. It must, however, provide the appropriate associations or generalizations necessary to distinguish the most important dimensions—the criterial attributes—of the concept being learned. In this sense, there is less similarity between the stimulus and the response in the teaching of concepts, patterns, and abstractions than there is in the teaching of facts, rules, and sequences.

The indirect instruction model is represented by instructional strategies that encourage the cognitive processes required to form concepts and to combine concepts into larger patterns and abstractions. This model represents a general approach consisting of many different but related strategies that can be used either individually or in combination with other strategies, including those of the direct instruction model. Table 7.1 represents some of the teaching functions most commonly associated with the indirect instruction model.

Table 7.1 illustrates that greater complexity in both teacher and student behavior is associated with indirect instruction than with direct instruction. Classroom activities are less teacher-

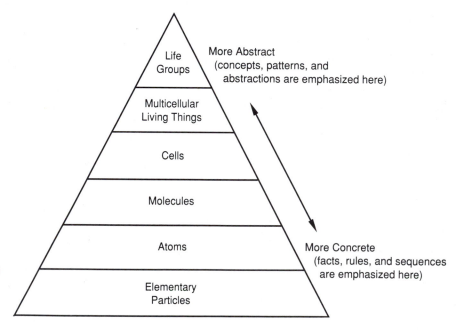

FIGURE 7.1
A hierarchy of abstraction representing possible units of instruction in a science curriculum

TABLE 7.1
Some indirect instruction functions

1. Provides a means of organizing content in advance
   Provides advance organizers and conceptual frameworks, which
       serve as "pegs" on which to hang key points that guide and channel thinking to the most
       productive areas
   Allows for concept expansion to higher levels of abstraction
2. Provides conceptual movement using inductive and deductive methods
   Focuses generalization to higher levels of abstraction by:
       Inductive methods (selected events used to establish concepts or patterns)
       Deductive methods (principles or generalizations applied to specific instances)
3. Uses examples and nonexamples:
   To define criterial attributes and promote accurate generalizations
   To gradually expand set of examples to reflect real world
   To enrich concept with noncriterial attributes
4. Uses questions to guide the search and discovery process
   Uses questions to: raise contradictions
                     probe for deeper level responses
                     extend the discussion
                     pass responsibility to the class
5. Encourages students to use examples and references from their own experience, to seek clarification, and to
   draw parallels and associations that aid understanding and retention
       Relates ideas to past learning and to students' own sphere of interests, concerns, and problems
6. Allows students to evaluate the appropriateness of their own responses and then provides guidance as
   necessary
       Provides cues, questions, or hints as needed to call attention to inappropriate responses
7. Uses discussion to encourage critical thinking and help students to:
   Examine alternatives, judge solutions, make predictions, and discover generalizations
   Orient, provide new content, review and summarize, alter flow of information, and combine areas to
   promote the most productive discussion

centered, bringing student ideas and experiences into the lesson and allowing students to evaluate their own responses to some extent. Because the behaviors are more complex, so too are the teaching strategies designed to produce them. Extended forms of reasoning and questioning are required to build toward outcomes that may require either advance forms of organization or inductive and/or deductive reasoning; a variety of examples and group discussions are used. Research studies have indicated that the indirect instruction functions represented in Table 7.1 and the teaching behaviors that comprise them (e.g., "Teacher gives students advance organizers," "Teacher uses examples from students' own experiences," "Teacher gets students to evaluate their own responses," and "Teacher

allows for group discussion") are among the teaching functions having the highest correlations with positive student attitudes (Fielding, Kameenui, & Gerstein, 1983; Rosenshine, 1970b). These also are those teaching functions that are thought to be most useful in providing the behaviors that students are most likely to use in their adult lives (Morine & Morine, 1973).

An Example of Indirect Instruction

It is useful to consider an example of indirect instruction so that it can be compared to the earlier example of direct instruction and to the functions listed in Table 7.1. Since the objective this time will be Type 2 and not Type 1 outcomes, a topic was chosen for which some facts, rules, and sequences have been taught previously, but for which the ultimate goal is the formation of concepts, patterns, and abstractions. This is a glimpse into a classroom where a government lesson on different economic systems is in progress. The teacher gets the students' attention by asking if anyone knows where the phrase "government of the people, by the people, for the people" comes from. Marty raises his hand.

TEACHER: Marty.

MARTY: From Lincoln's Gettysburg Address . . . I think near the end.

TEACHER: That's right. Most nations have similar statements that express the basic principles on which their laws, customs, and economics are based. Today we will study three systems by which individual nations can guide, control, and operate their economies. The three terms describing the systems are *capitalism, socialism,* and *communism,* terms which are often confused with the political systems that tend to be associated with them. A political system not only influences the economic system of a country but also guides the behavior of individuals in many other areas, such as what is taught in schools, what the relationship between church and state is, how people get chosen for or elected to political office, what jobs people can have, what newspapers can print, and so on. For example, in the United States we have an economic system that is based on the principles of capitalism—or private ownership of capital, but a political system that is based on the principle of democracy—or rule by the people. These two sets of principles are not the same, and in the next few days you will see how they sometimes work in harmony and sometimes create contradictions. Today we will cover only systems dealing with the ownership of goods and services in different countries—that is, only the economic systems. Later you will be asked to distinguish these from political systems.

Who would like to start by telling us what the word *capitalism* means?

ROBERT: It means making money.

TEACHER: What else, Robert?

ROBERT: Owning land . . . I think.

TEACHER: Not only land, but . . .

ROBERT: Owning anything.

TEACHER: The word *capital* means tangible goods or possessions. Is a house tangible?

BETTY: Yes.

TEACHER: Is a friendship tangible?

BETTY: Yes.

TEACHER: What about that, Mark?

MARK: I don't think so.

TEACHER: Why?

MARK: You can't touch it.

TEACHER: Right. You can touch a person who is a friend but not the friendship. Besides, you can't own or possess a person. . . . So, what would be a good definition of *tangible goods?*

BETTY: Something you own and can touch or see.

TEACHER: Not bad. Let me list some things on the board and you tell me whether they could be called capital. (Teacher writes the following:
car
stocks and bonds
religion
information
clothes
vacation)
OK. Who would like to say which of these are *capital?* (Ricky raises his hand.)

RICKY: Car and clothes are the only two I see.

BARBARA: I'd add stocks and bonds. They say you own a piece of something, although maybe not the whole thing.

TEACHER: Could you see or touch it?

BARBARA: Yes, if you went to see the place or thing you owned a part of.

TEACHER: Good. What about a vacation? Did that give anyone trouble?

MICKY: Well, you can own it . . . I mean you pay for it, and you can see yourself having a good time. (The class laughs.)

TEACHER: That may be true, so let's add one last condition to our definition of capital. You must be able to own it, see or touch it, and it must be durable—or last for a reasonable period of time. So now how would you define *capitalism?*

SUE: An economic system that allowed you to have capital—or to own tangible goods that last for a reasonable period of time. And, I suppose, sell the goods, if you wanted.

TEACHER: Very good. Many different countries across the world have this form of economic system. Just to see if you've got the idea, who can name three countries, besides our own, that allow the ownership of tangible goods?

JOE: Japan, West Germany, and Canada.

TEACHER: Good. In all these countries capital, in the form of tangible goods, can be owned by individuals.

Now that we know a little about capitalism, let's look at another system by which a nation can manage its economy. Ralph, what does the word *socialism* mean to you?

RALPH: Well, it probably comes from the word *social*.

TEACHER: And what does the word *social* mean?

RALPH: People coming together, like at a party—or maybe a meeting.

TEACHER: And why do people usually come together at a party or a meeting?

RALPH: To have fun. (laughter)

TEACHER: And what about at a meeting?

RALPH: To conduct some business or make some decisions, maybe.

TEACHER: Yes, they come together for some common purpose and benefits; for example, they make decisions about the things they need to live and prosper. Does that sound like a basis for a kind of economic system? (no response from class) Suppose that a large number of individuals came together to decide on what they needed to live and prosper? What types of things do you think they would consider?

BILLY: You mean like a car or a home of your own?

TEACHER: Yes, but let's say that the need for a car or a home of your own among individuals of the group is so very different that this group could never agree on the importance of these for everyone. What types of things could a group of people, perhaps the size of a nation, agree on that would be absolutely essential for everyone's existence?

RONNIE: Food.

TEACHER: Good. What else?

BILLY: A hospital.

TEACHER: Very good.

SUE: Highways.

TEACHER: OK. Any others?

RICKY: If they couldn't agree on the importance of cars for everyone, then they would have to agree on some other form of transportation, like buses, trains, or planes.

TEACHER: Yes; they would, wouldn't they? These examples show one of the purposes of a socialist economic system—that is, to control and make available to everyone as many things as possible that (a) everyone values equally and (b) everyone needs for everyday existence.

SUE: You mean free, without paying?

TEACHER: Yes, or paying very little. In that way both rich and poor can use these services about equally.

SUE: But who pays?

Teacher: Good question. Who pays for the services provided under a socialist system?

MARK: The government.

TEACHER: And who is the government?

MARK: Oh, I get it. The people pay taxes, just like us, and the government uses the taxes to provide the essential services.

SUE: So, how is that different from America?

TEACHER: Good question. Who can answer that one?

ROBERT: It's the same.

MARK: No, it's not. Our government doesn't own hospitals, farms, trains, and that kind of stuff.

TEACHER: Who owns Amtrak?

ROBERT: I think our government does.

TEACHER: It also, believe it or not, owns some hospitals; and at least some local governments, like ours, own their own bus lines. (The class looks bewildered.) So, if you looked at our country's economic system and compared it to that of a socialist country, you might not see such a big difference. But there *is* a difference. What might that difference be? Ralph, you began this discussion.

RALPH: I think it's a matter of degree. Almost all of the major things like hospitals and transportation systems that everyone needs are owned and run by the government under a socialist system, but only a few of these things are owned by the government in a capitalist system. On the other hand, there are things like highways, rivers, forests, and so on that are owned by the government under both systems.

TEACHER: And how would the amount of taxes you pay differ in these two systems?

RALPH: You'd pay more taxes under a socialist economy then under a capitalist economy, but some services would be free—or almost—in a socialist system. We'd pay more for these services but we'd also have more money to spend for them after taxes.

TEACHER: That was a nice way of putting it. Now, what about our third economic system? What's a word similar to communism?

BILLY: Oh, (hesitating) *community?*

TEACHER: Yes. And who has ownership under communism?

ROBERT: The community.

TEACHER: . . . which is represented by?

ROBERT: The government.

TEACHER: Yes. Just a moment ago we discovered that much of the difference between capitalism and socialism, as economic systems, was a matter of degree. If this were also true of the difference between socialism and communism, how might you describe ownership under the communist economic system?

SUE: More is owned by the community—I mean by the government.

TEACHER: Ronnie, you mentioned food before. Do you think food—or the farms on which the food is grown—is owned by the government under communism?

RONNIE: I guess so.

TEACHER: Billy, you mentioned hospitals; Sue, you mentioned highways; and Ricky, you mentioned planes. Who owns these in a communist economic system?

CLASS: The government.

TEACHER: OK. Now let's create a chart that shows some examples of things likely to be owned by the governments under all three of our economic systems, so that we can see them side by side and compare them.

(Teacher writes the following on board.)

Capitalism	Socialism	Communism
highways	highways	highways
rivers	rivers	rivers
forests	forests	forests
	hospitals	hospitals
	planes	planes
	buses	buses
	trains	trains
		food supply
		housing
		industries

Now, what kinds of things *don't* we find up here?

RICHARD: Personal things, like clothes, watches, and television sets.

TEACHER: Good. Ownership of these items can never be used to distinguish economic systems. What can distinguish economic systems, however, is the *degree* to which the goods and services that affect large numbers of individuals are owned by the government: The most is owned by the government under communism, and the least is owned by the government under capitalism. Now, how do you think the amount of taxes paid by individuals living under these three systems would differ?

CLASS: Communism would have the highest, then socialism, then capitalism.

TEACHER: Good. Tomorrow we will follow this point up and then compare each of these three economic systems with the political systems that represent them. For tomorrow, look up in the encyclopedia the words *democracy* and *totalitarianism* and bring with you a one-page description of the major differences between these two political systems. Be prepared to know the differences between economic and political systems. Then, choose two countries that you think represent these different political systems, and we will discuss and study them further.

This dialogue illustrates one variation of the indirect model of instruction as it might be implemented in a high-school government class. Table 7.1 provided a summary of some of the functions, which can be found in varying degrees in indirect instruction. Remembering these functions, consider the extent to which this example contains some of the key aspects of indirect instruction.

Advance Organizers

The first difference you may have noticed between the example dialogues for direct and indirect instruction is that they differ in length and in complexity. This did not occur by chance, because the teaching of behaviors at higher levels of complexity generally takes more time and planning. The amount of planning and effort needed to set up this higher order learning can be considerable, and this is one of the most overlooked aspects of indirect instruction. Because the range of content is more expansive and complex, the lesson must be introduced with an overall framework or structure that organizes the content into meaningful parts, *even before the content is presented*. This is the first element of planning for indirect instruction.

One way of providing this framework is to use advance organizers (Luiten, Ames, Aerson, 1980;

Ausubel, 1968). An advance organizer gives the learner a *conceptual preview* of what is to come and helps prepare the learner to store, label, and package the content for retention and later use. In a sense, an advance organizer is a tree-like structure with main limbs that act as pegs, or place holders, for the branches that are yet to come. Without these limbs on which to hang content, important distinctions can easily become blurred or lost. For example, the lesson dialogue began with an introduction about what would be covered in the day's lesson. Here, two abstractions (i.e., economic systems and political systems) each comprised of a complex network of concepts (e.g., taxes, ownership, goods, services, etc.) were introduced to set the stage for this lesson. At the beginning of the lesson students were alerted to the reason for drawing such an early distinction between a political and an economic system (e.g, "these terms . . . are often confused," "Today we will cover only . . . *economic* systems. Later you will be asked to distinguish these from political systems.") The overall ideas for which students will be responsible on homework assignments and in the following day's lesson will require them to distinguish between these systems. The important role of advance organization was to channel or focus student thinking for today's lesson onto the economic system branch of the overall organizer, while putting in place another branch on which additional content (i.e., political systems) will soon be placed.

Advance organizers, especially at the higher levels of behavioral complexity, are rarely single words or phrases that when merely uttered enlighten students. Instead, they are concepts, presented orally or in the form of charts and diagrams, that are woven into the fabric of the lesson to provide an overview of the day's work *and of all topics to which it will subsequently relate.* Examples of advance organizing activities provided at the beginning of a lesson are the following:

Showing a chart illustrating the skeletal evolution of man prior to explaining the skeletal relationships between forms of animal life (biology)

Drawing examples of right, equilateral, and isosceles triangles before introducing the concept of a right triangle (plane geometry)

Discussing origins of the Civil War before describing its first and major battles (American history)

Describing what is meant by a *figure of speech* before introducing the concepts of *metaphor* and *simile* (English)

Listening to examples of both vowels and consonants before teaching the vowel sounds (reading)

Showing and explaining the origins of the periodic table of elements before introducing any of the individual elements (chemistry)

Notice that each of these examples presents a general concept into which fits the specific concept that is the subject of the day's lesson. This is not accomplished by reviewing content taught at some earlier time—which is often confused with the idea of an advance organizer—but by creating a conceptual structure (e.g., evolutionary man, triangular shapes, battles of the Civil War, figures of speech, the alphabet, an organized system of atomic weights) into which can be placed not only the content to be taught but also the content for related lessons. Therefore, these advance organizers set the groundwork for expanding the present lesson topic, preventing every lesson from being seen as something entirely new and integrating related concepts into larger and larger patterns and abstractions that later become unit outcomes (e.g., evolution of skeletal forms, triangular shapes, major battles of the Civil War, figures of speech). An advance organizer identifies the highest level of behavior resulting from a sequence of lessons and to which the outcome of the present day's lesson is to contribute. In the example, this higher level outcome was to distinguish between economic and political systems, a distinction organized in advance by the teacher's introductory remarks.

In chapter 6 there were several suggestions for organizing content in ways that were particularly suited to direct instruction. You may recall that these were the part-whole, sequential, combinatorial, and comparative methods. This chapter adds several additional methods that are particularly suited for organizing content for indirect instruction. These methods are problem-centered, decision-making, and network approaches to structuring lesson content—and to composing advance organizers.

Problem-centered

A problem-centered approach identifies and provides students, in advance, with all the steps required to solve a particular problem. This approach begins with the observation of a specific event and ends with a conclusion about how or why the event took place. For example, a teacher might begin a lesson in general science by demonstrating that liquid cannot be removed through a straw from a tightly sealed bottle. The question, "Why does this happen?" establishes the problem. The teacher then might provide the students with a problem-solving sequence similar to the one in Figure 7.2a. Such a chart and the sequence of events it identifies become the advance organizer for the lesson. Each of these steps pro-

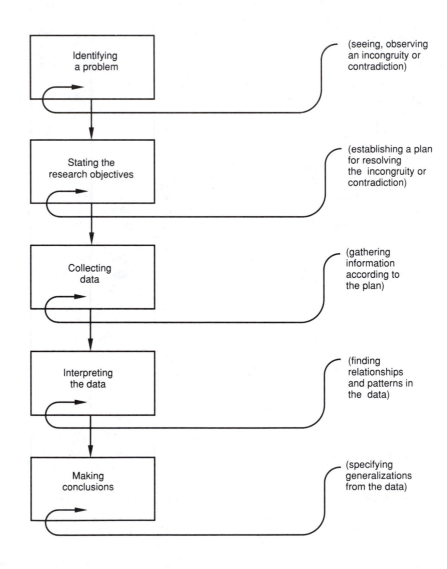

FIGURE 7.2a
Structuring a lesson using a problem-centered approach

vides an organizational branch for a particular part of the lesson.

Decision-making

This same problem can also be organized hierarchically by showing the internal branching, or steps, that must be followed to arrive at a final conclusion. While the problem-centered approach establishes the steps to be followed, the decision-making approach focuses on the *alternative paths* that might be followed—or decisions that will have to be made—in exploring and discovering new information about a topic. Figure 7.2b shows how this can be applied to the science question posed in the preceding paragraph. Although the students would not know at what level of the hierarchy the experiment will end, they could be shown the entire list of possible alternatives. This form of advance organizer can be a particularly effective attention-gaining device when students are asked to contribute branches to the hierarchy and are allowed to trace the results of their inquiry as each decision point is reached (as indicated by the solid lines).

Network

Networking is a third type of organization often helpful for organizing and communicating the

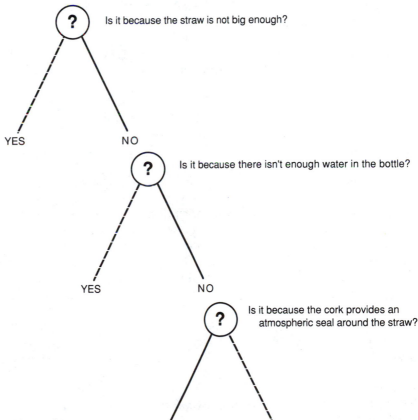

FIGURE 7.2b
Structuring a lesson using a decision-making approach

FIGURE 7.2c
Structuring a lesson using a network approach

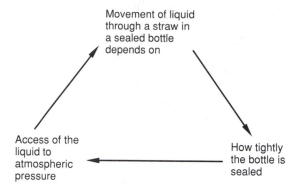

Movement of liquid
through a straw in
a sealed bottle
depends on

Access of the
liquid to
atmospheric
pressure

How tightly
the bottle is
sealed

structure of a lesson in advance. It involves building a pictorial representation of the relationships among the data, materials, objects, events, and so forth that must be considered in the solution of a problem. When different aspects of a problem are to be considered in relation to each other, as indicated in Figure 7.2c, a visual display of the network of relationships becomes the advance organizer. The triangular network indicated in Figure 7.2c would be of particular importance to the goals of this lesson, because it is the *relationship between several events* that may provide the best solution to this problem.

Each of these structuring methods is useful as an advance organizer when it is communicated to students in advance and when key steps, decisions, or relationships are tied back to the advance organizer as they occur in the lesson. To the extent these structuring devices can provide the branches on which subsequent content can be placed, they will serve a useful purpose as advance organizers.

Conceptual Movement—Inductive and Deductive

The words *inductive* and *deductive* refer to the way in which ideas flow. *Inductive reasoning* is a process of thinking used when a set of data is presented and students are asked to draw a con-

clusion, make a generalization, or develop a pattern of relationships from the data. It is a process in which students observe specific facts and then generalize to other circumstances to which the facts apply. Common sense tells us that much of our everyday thinking proceeds in this manner. For example:

1. We notice rain-slick roads are causing accidents on the way to school, so we reduce speed at all the remaining intersections.
2. We get an unsatisfactory grade on a chemistry exam, so we study six extra hours a week for the rest of the semester in all our subjects.
3. We see a close friend suffer from the effects of drug abuse, so we volunteer to disseminate information about substance abuse to all our acquaintances.
4. We get a math teacher who is cold and unfriendly, so we decide to never enroll in a math course again.

What these instances have in common is that they started with a specific observation of a limited set of data and ended with a generalization in a much broader context. Between the beginning and end of each sequence was an interpretation of observed events and the projection of this interpretation to all similar circumstances. Simply put, when we think inductively we believe that what happens in one place (e.g., at this intersection), can happen wherever or whenever circumstances are similar (e.g., at all other rain-slick intersections.)

Deductive thinking, on the other hand, proceeds from principles or generalizations to the application of these principles or generalizations to specific instances. It includes testing generalizations to see if they hold in specific instances. Typically, a laboratory experiment in most of the sciences (e.g., chemistry, physics, biology, psychology, mathematics) follows the deductive method. In these fields the experimenter often begins with a theory or hypothesis about what should happen and then conducts a test in the form of an experiment to see if the theory or hypothesis provides an accurate prediction. If it does, the generalization with which the experiment began is true at least some of the time. The steps in deductive thinking used in the laboratory frequently are:

1. Stating a theory or generalization to be tested,
2. Forming a hypothesis in the form of a prediction,
3. Observing or collecting data to test the hypothesis,
4. Analyzing and interpreting the data to determine if the prediction is true at least some of the time, and
5. Concluding whether or not the generalization held true in the specific context in which it was tested.

Deductive methods are familiar to us in everyday life. For example, consider the four examples of inductive thinking listed previously to see how much change is required for them to represent examples of deductive thinking. Here are the examples again—this time illustrating deduction:

1. We believe that rain-slick roads are the prime contributor to traffic accidents at intersections. We make observations one rainy morning on the way to school and find that, indeed, more accidents have occurred at intersections than usual—our prediction that wet roads cause accidents at intersections is confirmed.
2. We believe that studying six extra hours a week will *not* substantially raise our grades. We study six extra hours and find that our grades have gone up—our prediction that extra studying will not influence our grades is *not* confirmed.
3. We believe that drug abuse can be detrimental to one's physical and emotional well-being. We observe and find physical and emotional effects of drug use in everyone that has admitted to using them—our prediction that drug abuse and physical and emotional impairment are related has been confirmed.
4. We believe that we could never like a subject, regardless of how good we are in it, if it is taught by a cold and unfriendly teacher. We

think back and remember that we had just such a math teacher in high school and observe that we have always done everything possible never to take a math course—our prediction that the colder and more unfriendly the teacher, the less likely it is that we ever take a course like that again has been shown to be accurate, at least in one case.

These examples have in common the fact that they begin with a general statement of belief—called a theory or hypothesis—and end with some conclusion based upon a planned observation about the truth of the initial statement. Of course, we could be wrong even though in some instances the prediction *appeared* to be true (e.g., you might have no problem liking sports because you once had a cold and unfriendly gym teacher). As one might expect, deductive logic has been most closely associated with the scientific method. In the social, behavioral, and "hard" sciences, it is known as the **hypothetico-deductive** method (Kaplan, 1964) to emphasize the close connection between forming hypotheses and making predictions deduced or derived from general beliefs and theories.

Both induction and deduction are important methods for teaching concepts, patterns, and abstractions. One application for such teaching is to move into progressively deeper levels of subject complexity, using inductive and deductive methods and occasionally changing from one to the other. Greater levels of complexity are achieved using the *inductive* process when specific examples or events introduced earlier in the lesson are later linked to other examples or events creating concepts and generalizations. Greater levels of complexity are achieved using the *deductive* process when generalizations and patterns introduced earlier in the lesson are later applied to specific instances, testing the adequacy of the generalizations. Consider how this was done in the earlier example of the government lesson about economic systems.

Using the inductive method, the teacher built up a definition of *tangible goods* beginning with a specific example: "Is a house tangible?" Notice how the examples increased not only in number, but also in abstraction (e.g., stocks and bonds). Also, both examples and nonexamples were provided to round out the definition of tangible goods in a capitalist system and to fine tune the concept. In other words, tangible goods could exist at different levels of abstraction, but some abstractions (e.g., friendship, vacation) could not qualify as tangible goods. In this manner the inductive process, which began with the specific examples (making money and owning land) was increasingly broadened to form a generalization (tangible goods that last for a reasonable length of time).

Also notice that a brief venture into deduction ended the teacher's introduction to capitalism. By being asked to name three countries that fit the concept of capitalism, the students were being asked to find specific instances that fit the general concept. Students were being asked if the general notion of the ownership of tangible goods could be applied to the real world, and it could, of course, thereby providing a test of the credibility of the more general statement.

It is important to note, however, that although the concept of capitalism—as an economic system that allows the ownership of tangible goods that last—was understood by most students at the end of the first part of the lesson, it was a rather crude interpretation that would fail many subsequent tests. People in the Soviet Union own tangible goods that last a reasonable period of time (e.g., a wrist watch, a tie, a set of dinnerware), yet that country could hardly be considered capitalistic. Recall that this crude version of the concept of capitalism emerged even after providing carefully planned examples and nonexamples. This means that the teacher's job was far from over at the end of the first part of the lesson. Further *conceptual movement* would have to be made to fine tune this concept, producing finer and more accurate discriminations to be applied to the concept of capitalism.

This is precisely what occurs in subsequent portions of the lesson, in which the teacher can be seen moving students from the ownership of tangible goods as their working definition of an economic system to a definition that had the following five different elements:

> The degree to which
> goods and services
> that all value
> and see essential for daily living
> are owned by a government.

The teacher, using questions and examples, redefined the initial concept until it was expanded to include a greater number of attributes, thereby making it more accurate. The teaching of concepts, patterns, and abstractions with the indirect instructional model is patterned around the inductive and deductive movement of concepts wherein the teacher processes initially crude and overly restrictive concepts into more expansive and accurate abstractions. Table 7.2 illustrates the different steps involved in inductive versus deductive teaching.

Using Examples and Nonexamples

It has been demonstrated that both inductive and deductive methods help in the teaching of concepts and that both employ generalizations. Consider the previous examples of induction and deduction and see if they contain generalizations. Recall the generalization made after seeing many accidents that "accidents tend to occur at intersections on rainy days." Is there a concept, pattern, or abstraction here? Are there facts, rules, and sequences?

There is no question that facts, in the form of knowledge about cars, streets, rain, and intersections, had to be known for this generalization to be formed. Rules also had to be present, such as "don't accelerate quickly on wet pavement," "slow down at intersections," and "a red light means stop." And, of course, sequences of actions must be understood, such as "watch for intersections—look for signs—slow down—brake gently." However, the intended generalization cannot be derived from these facts, rules, and

TABLE 7.2
A comparison of steps in inductive versus deductive teaching

Teaching Inductively	Teaching Deductively
1. Teacher presents specific data from which a generalization is to be drawn.	1. Teacher introduces the generalization to be learned.
2. Each student is allowed uninterrupted time to observe or study the data that illustrates the generalization.	2. Teacher reviews the task-revelant prior facts, rules, and action sequences needed to form the generalization.
3. Students are shown additional examples and then nonexamples containing the generalization.	3. Students raise a question, pose an hypothesis, or make a prediction thought to be contained in the generalization.
4. Student attention is guided first to the criterial (relevant) aspects of the data containing the generalization and then to its noncriterial (irrelevant) aspects.	4. Data, events, materials, or objects are gathered and observed to test the prediction.
5. A generalization is made that can distinguish the examples from nonexamples.	5. Results of the test are analyzed and a conclusion is made as to whether the prediction is supported by the data, events, materials, or objects that were observed.
	6. The starting generalization is refined or revised in accordance with the observations.

sequences alone. Why? Because they are not sufficiently separated from specific examples to be applied appropriately in any and all circumstances. For example, you may learn the rule "stop at red lights" to perfection, but until you have seen examples of when to ignore the rule (e.g., when an emergency vehicle with flashing lights is behind you), you do not have the complete concept of a red light—only the rule. Likewise, without seeing examples and nonexamples of the rules we formulated previously (e.g., when six extra hours of study pays off and when it does not, when disseminating drug abuse literature is likely to pay off and when it is not, when a cold and unfriendly teacher is likely to adversely affect your performance in a subject and when not), you will have acquired facts, rules, and sequences—but not concepts. Therefore, the third element for the teaching of concepts, patterns, and abstractions is the use of both examples and nonexamples which define the **criterial** and **noncriterial attributes** of a concept that are needed for producing accurate generalizations.

As another example, consider the concept that private ownership of goods and services under socialism is more limited than under capitalism. How did this teacher develop this concept, moving from a definition of capitalism to a discussion of socialism? Recall that initially the concept was poorly understood by Billy, who concluded that "a car" and "a home of your own" were the types of capital that could become the basis for a socialist economic system. His response was reasonable, because both could be defined as tangible goods according to the discussion on capitalism. However, this teacher would be in trouble and the outcome of the lesson placed in jeopardy if further concept expansion did not occur. The abstraction of an economic system at this point in the lesson was limited to one in which nearly all tangible goods could be privately owned. The teacher's job was to fine tune this initial version of the abstraction so that it would include economic systems in which both goods and services are owned and that ownership extends to the government as well as to individuals.

Also, the teacher somehow had to make clear that ownership in the context of different economic systems is always a matter of degree. That is, the system determines not only *what* but also *how much* is owned by a government and, therefore, is unavailable for private ownership. Accordingly, the teacher set up the next set of interchanges to bring out these specific points. Recall this exchange:

TEACHER: . . . What types of things could a group of people, say the size of a nation, agree on that would be absolutely essential for everyone's existence?
RONNIE: Food.
TEACHER: Good. What else?
BILLY: A hospital.
TEACHER: Very good.
SUE: Highways.
TEACHER: OK. Any others?
RICKY: If they couldn't agree on the importance of cars for everyone, then they would have to agree on some other form of transportation, like buses, trains, or planes.
TEACHER: Yes; they would, wouldn't they? These examples show one of the purposes of a socialist economic system—that is, to control and make available to everyone as many things as possible that (a) everyone values equally, and (b) everyone needs for everyday existence.

The teacher redirected the discussion by asking students to think about the things that "a group of people, say the size of a nation, could agree on that would be absolutely essential for everyone's existence"—thereby encouraging them to broaden their earlier definitions. The question generates both examples that are useful in discriminating between capitalism and socialism (e.g., ownership of hospitals) and ones that are not (e.g., ownership of highways). However, since some hospitals are owned by capitalist governments, these examples could be confusing; but Ralph makes the clarifying statement:

RALPH: I think it's a matter of degree. Almost all of the major things like hospitals and transportation systems that everyone needs are owned and run by the government under a socialist system, but only a few of these things are owned by the government in a capitalist system. On the other hand, there are things like highways, rivers, forests, and so on that are owned by the government under both systems.

The nonexample of *highways* helps to further the notion that socialism and capitalism are not all-or-none propositions, mutually exclusive of each other. Some tangible things (e.g., highways and forests) are owned by capitalist as well as by socialist governments. Notice how, through the use of examples and nonexamples, this teacher was able to both expand the learners' concept of an economic system and also to provide for a fine degree of discrimination between capitalism and socialism.

These are not easy distinctions from a student's point of view. They were accomplished in this episode by

1. providing more than a single example,
2. using examples that vary in ways that are unimportant to the concept being defined (e.g., house is tangible, stocks and bonds are abstract, but both are instances of "tangible goods"),
3. including nonexamples of the concept that also include important dimensions of the concept (e.g., a vacation can be bought or "owned" but is not an example of a "tangible good"), and
4. explaining why nonexamples, which may have some of the same characteristics as examples, are not examples (e.g., a vacation is not durable).

The Use of Questions to Guide the Search and Discovery Process

One of the differences you may have noticed between the direct and indirect instruction dialogues concerns the way in which the teacher asked the questions. In the direct dialogue the questions were specific and to the point, aimed at eliciting a single right answer; whereas in the indirect dialogue they were intended to help the student search for and discover the answer with a minimum of assistance from the teacher. In direct instruction, answering questions is how students show what they know—or expose their level of understanding so that clues, hints, and probes may be provided. In indirect instruction, the teacher's questions guide students into discovering new dimensions of a problem or ways of resolving a dilemma.

The indirect instruction dialogue has several examples of questions used to guide the search and discovery process. Notice, for example, that several major twists and turns in the dialogue begin and end with questions for which there are no single right answers:

"Who would like to start by telling us what the word *capitalism* means to them . . . ?"

"What does the word *socialism* mean to you?"

"What's a word similar to *communism?*"

These questions did not ask for the definitions of capitalism, socialism, or communism; few students could be expected to know these with accuracy at the start of the lesson. Rather, they were asked in such a way that almost any student could search for and find an answer that would be at least partially correct. By inserting a phrase such as ". . . means to you" or ". . . similar to," this teacher encouraged a response from almost every student who has ever heard these words used in any context.

The purpose of the questions, therefore, was not to quiz or even to teach, but to focus students' attention and to promote the widest possible discussion of the topic. In this manner the class begins with almost everyone being equally able to participate, *regardless of their task-relevant prior knowledge.* By being able to accept almost any answer at the beginning, the teacher can use student responses to formulate subsequent questions, which will begin to shape more accurate responses. The point of using questioning strategies in indirect instruction, then, is not to arrive at the correct answer in the quickest and most efficient manner, but to *begin a process* whereby not only are successively more correct answers formed, but also that those answers are formed using a process of search and discovery. For example, the teacher follows up Robert's response that capitalism means "making money" with the phrase ". . . what else?" and, finally, follows Robert's next response, ("owning land") with a leading response (". . . not only land but . . .") in an effort to encourage Robert to broaden his answer.

By beginning with a broad question such as "What does the word capitalism mean to you?", this teacher could have been confronted just as easily with the task of narrowing, not broadening, Robert's first response. In the next interchange this problem actually occurs, because Robert replies that capitalism means "owning anything." Now the job is to narrow or limit his response, which is accomplished by presenting the first criterial attribute of the concept of capitalism, *tangible goods.* This illustrates that the use of a single guided question in the context of indirect instruction is rarely, if ever, useful in and of itself. The questions must dovetail into other questions that continue to focus the response (e.g., broaden, then narrow, then broaden slightly again) and keep the search going. The process is much like focusing a camera, because rarely is the camera initially set at the right focus for the subject; similarly, we could not expect Robert's first response to perfectly represent the concept of capitalism. Just as one begins focusing the camera in the appropriate direction, often passing the point at which the subject is in focus, so also the teacher's follow-up probe led Robert to overshoot the mark and respond with too broad a response (e.g., owning anything). The teacher acknowledged the error and slightly narrowed Robert's response by noting that "The word *capitalism* means tangible goods or possessions."

Questions also can be used in the search and discovery process to

Present contradictions to be resolved, such as:
   "Who owns Amtrak?"
   "But there is a difference. What might that difference be?"

Probe for deeper, more thorough responses, such as:
   "What does the word *social* mean?"
   "Why do people usually come together at a party or a meeting?"

Extend the discussion to new areas, such as:
  "What things could a group of people, say the size of a nation, agree are absolutely essential for everyone's existence?"
  "What types of things don't we find written here on the board?"
Pass responsibility back to the class, such as:
  "Good question. Who knows the answer to who pays for services provided under a socialist system?"
  "Good question. Who can answer that one?"

Questions like these guide students to increasingly better responses through a search and discovery process. This process is one of the most useful for forming concepts and abstractions and for recognizing patterns where the back-and-forth focusing of student responses is often required before the appropriate level of generalization is attained.

Use of Student Ideas

Until recently the use of student ideas was considered the centerpiece of indirect instruction. Using student ideas meant incorporating student experiences, points of view, feelings, and problems into the lesson by making the student the primary point of reference. A completely student-oriented lesson might be initiated by asking students what problems they were having with the content; these problems would become the focus of the lesson. This approach was intended to heighten student interest, to organize subject content around student problems, to tailor feedback to individual students, and to attempt to encourage positive attitudes and feelings toward the subject. When a lesson attempts to accomplish these objectives only, however, it runs the risk of failing to achieve the most important objective of all: teaching the content prescribed by the textbook and curriculum guide.

This is not to say that heightening student interest, focusing on student problems, giving specific feedback to individuals, and increasing positive attitudes are not laudable goals for every teacher, but these goals can and should be achieved *in the context of the prescribed curriculum.* This is where early attempts to use student ideas often went astray. The goals of incorporating student ideas, problems, feelings, and attitudes into the lesson in an open discussion format often became the end, rather than the means by which other significant forms of learning could be accomplished. Unfortunately, many forms of problem solving, inquiry, and discovery learning were thought to be synonymous with open, free-wheeling discussions that began and ended with student-determined ideas and content. Also, some advocates believed such goals and approaches could be executed solely as processes not requiring any of the formal structure or content of the traditional classroom. At least some of the curriculum reforms suggested by the national committees and reports reviewed in chapter 3 were a response to just such misguided notions.

The position taken in this text, as well as that of recent research, is that while the heightening of student interest, selection of content based on student problems, provision of individual feedback, and increased affect are desirable goals for every lesson, these goals cannot be achieved without an underlying organization and content determined by the curriculum and the teacher. As we have seen earlier in both the problem-centered, hierarchical, and network approaches and in our example dialogue, even content at a high level of abstraction both can be and should be structured. Therefore, even in the indirect instruction model which is designed to contribute to student-centered goals, these goals are only the means for achieving still more desirable outcomes in the form of concepts, patterns, and abstractions; they are not goals in themselves.

This leads to considering how student-centered ideas can be used productively in the context of indirect instruction. In such a context, the use of student ideas can take the form of

encouraging students to use *examples* and *references* from their own experience, asking students to seek clarification of and to draw *parallels* to and *associations* from things they already know, and

encouraging understanding and retention of ideas by relating them to the students' own sphere of *interests, concerns, and problems.*

For examples of these uses of student ideas, recall again the dialogue about economic systems. By asking the students to name three countries, besides their own, that followed a capitalistic economic system, or to name the things a nation could agree on that were absolutely essential for everyone's existence, the teacher elicited examples and references from the learners' own realm of experience. Perhaps more important than the questions themselves was the way in which the student responses were incorporated into the lesson. In one instance, the response even partially directed the content of the lesson. This followed a general question, "What things could a group of people . . . agree on that would be absolutely essential for everyone's existence?" Almost any equally general response could be used, as when students contributed the concepts of food, hospitals, and highways, all of which were within the overall framework of the lesson established by the teacher. This allowed students to contribute almost any response *without letting the choice itself alter the agenda for the lesson.*

Also, by asking what the word *capitalism* "means to you," this teacher was asking students to express themselves by using parallels and associations they already understood—perhaps by having a job, or by recalling a conversation about occupations, or by remembering television images of life in eastern Europe. Parallels and associations such as these are likely to be vastly different among students. This is desirable, both for heightening student interest and involvement and for exposing the students to a variety of responses, many of which may be appropriate instances of the concept to be learned.

A third way to incorporate student ideas into your lesson is to allow students to respond using their own interests, concerns, and problems. An instance of this occurred when the teacher asked students to name two countries having different political systems. Presumably these countries would be referred to in the future, perhaps in individual reports or research papers, perhaps in library reading or in a class discussion, in all of which cases the individuality of each student's choice could be examined. Student interests—and especially individual choices affecting future assignments—can be important motivators for ensuring active student involvement in subsequent assignments that may be lengthy and time consuming.

Finally, notice that even within the context of these examples the instruction remained *content centered;* that is, it allowed students to participate in determining the form in which the learning occurred but not the substance of what was learned. This substance usually will be determined by the curriculum guide and textbook. The example dialogue, therefore, contrasts with what is called *student-centered learning,* which allows for both the form and substance to be selected by the student. This is sometimes associated with *unguided discovery learning,* wherein the goal is to maintain high levels of student interest, accomplished largely by selecting content based on student problems or interests and by providing individually tailored feedback. However, even when unguided discovery learning is desired (e.g., in the context of independently conducted experiments, research projects, science fair projects, and demonstrations where the topic is independently decided upon by the student), the content still must fit comfortably within the confines of the prescribed curriculum. Therefore, whether your approach is the guided use of student ideas (as in this example) or unguided (as in research assignments) there will always be some preorganization and guidance necessary prior to your solicitation and use of student ideas.

Student Self-Evaluation

Another ingredient for indirect instruction is getting students to become engaged in the evaluation of their own responses. Since there will be many right answers in the teaching of concepts, patterns, and abstractions, it is virtually impossible for the teacher to pass judgment on all of them. In direct instruction nearly all instances of the learned facts, rules, or action sequences likely to be encountered can be learned during guided and independent practice. Since the specification of all possible instances of a concept would not be possible or efficient, indirect instruction must be used to get students to look critically at their own responses.

Self-evaluation of student responses in the indirect instruction model is usually encouraged by explicitly giving control of the evaluation function to students and by providing the opportunity for students to reason out their answers so that other students and the teacher can suggest needed changes. For example, early in the dialogue this teacher let it be known that at least part of the responsibility for determining appropriate answers will fall on the shoulders of the students. After making a list on the board, the teacher says "OK. Who would like to say which could be called *capital?*" The message is received when Ricky gives an answer and Barbara responds to the accuracy of Ricky's response.

RICKY: Car and clothes are the only two I see.
BARBARA: I'd add stocks and bonds. They say you own a piece of something, although maybe not the whole thing.

Even after Barbara's efforts to correct Ricky's response, the teacher still does not supply an answer, but instead keeps the evaluation of the previous responses going by responding with "Could you see or touch it?"

The goal in this instance was to create a student dialogue focused on the appropriateness of previous answers. The success of this self-evaluation strategy is most readily seen in the sequence of dialogue that occurs between students and teacher. This strategy tends to promote a student-to-student-back-to-teacher interchange as opposed to the more familiar teacher-to-student-back-to-teacher interchange. The role of

the teacher is to keep the momentum up by giving hints or focusing statements that can be used by the students to evaluate or reconsider their previous responses.

An example of a student-to-student-to-teacher interchange took place when Sue, hearing that people in socialist countries pay taxes, asks, "So how is that different from America?"

TEACHER: Good question. Who can answer that one?
ROBERT: It's the same.
MARK: No, it's not. Our government doesn't own hospitals, farms, trains, and that kind of stuff.
TEACHER: Who owns Amtrak?

The answer obviously needs some evaluation, so the teacher simply keeps the ball rolling by saying, "Good question. Who can answer that one?" Robert responds with an incomplete answer and Mark quickly informs the class not only that the answer is wrong, but also why he thinks it is wrong. At that point control is taken back by the teacher, who raises another question, suggesting that even Mark's response to Robert's answer is not completely accurate. In the process of these student-to-student-to-teacher exchanges, students are learning the reasons for their answers in slow, measured steps. By allowing partially correct answers to become the bases for more accurate ones, this teacher is allowing the class to see how both incorrect and partially correct answers are made into better ones. Especially for learning concepts, patterns, and abstractions that involve more than a single criterial attribute, these layers of refinement, gradually built up by student interchange, help the students develop a level of generalization.

Of course, there is no reason why such interchanges must be limited in size. Three, four, or even five successive exchanges among students before control returns to the teacher are both possible and desirable in circumstances when less guidance and structuring may be needed. Classes of more able students or classes who have considerable knowledge of the subject matter under discussion can sustain protracted exchanges without going so far astray that restructuring by the teacher is necessary.

Use of Group Discussion

When student-to-student-to-teacher exchanges grow into long interactions among large numbers of students, a group discussion has begun. For these discussions the teacher may intervene only occasionally to review and summarize the main points or may maintain a periodic schedule of interaction in which the group's progress is evaluated and, if need be, redirected.

Group discussion methods can be useful for encouraging critical thinking, for encouraging average and less able learners to become engaged in the learning process, and for promoting the ability to reason together that is necessary in a democratic society (Gall & Gall, 1976). Because group discussion can help students to think critically, that is, to examine alternatives, judge solutions, make predictions, and discover generalizations—it is yet another approach to teaching concepts, patterns, and abstractions.

There are times when group discussion involving extensive student interchange may be especially preferred over a lecture format. When the objective is to teach well-established concepts, patterns, or abstractions that have already been structured in the text and workbook, a lecture presentation will be more efficient and effective than a discussion format. In these cases, agreement among students on the important aspects of the topic may already be so high that little controversy or room for discussion exists; this might be the case with topics (e.g., photosynthesis, General McArthur, the legislative branch of government) which leave little or no room for personal opinion and judgment. On the other hand, when concepts, patterns, and abstractions have a less formal structure and are minimally treated in the text or workbook (e.g., Would photosynthesis be useful in space? How much aggression do you think it would take to start a war? In what ways can the legislative branch of government be influenced by the executive branch?), then the lack of consensus is likely to make a discussion rewarding and profitable. Simply put, topics that are not formally structured by the text and for which a high degree of consensus does not yet exist make good candidates for discussion sessions for building, expanding, and refining concepts, patterns, and abstractions.

The teacher's job during the discussion process is to perform a number of moderating functions, among which are

1. Orienting the students to the objective of the discussion:

   "Today we will discuss when a nation should decide to go to war. Specifically, we will discuss the meaning of the concept of aggression as it has occurred in history. In the context of wars between nations, your job at the end of the discussion will be to arrive at a generalization that could help a president decide if sufficient aggression has occurred to warrant going to war."

2. Providing new or more accurate information where it may be necessary:

   "It is not correct to assume that WW II started with the bombing of Pearl Harbor. Many events considered by some nations to be aggression occurred earlier on the European continent."

3. Reviewing, summarizing, or putting together opinions and facts into a meaningful relationship:

   "Bobby, Mary, and Billy, you seem to be arguing that the forcible entry of one nation into the territory of another nation constitutes aggression, while the rest of the class seems to be saying that undermining the economy of another nation can also constitute aggression."

4. Altering the flow of information and ideas to that which will be most productive to the goals of the lesson:

   "Mark, you seem to have extended our definition of aggression to include criticizing the government of another nation through political means, such as short-wave media broadcasts, speeches at the U.N., and so forth. But that fits better the idea of a cold war, and we are trying to study some of the instances of aggression that might have started WW II."

5. Combining ideas and promoting compromise to arrive at a final consensus:

> "We seem to have two definitions of aggression—one dealing with the forcible entry of one nation into the territory of another and another that has to do with undermining a nation's economy. Could we combine these two ideas by saying that anything that threatens either a nation's people or its prosperity, or both, could be considered aggression?"

Group discussion can take several different forms, the most familiar of which is the **large group discussion**, in which all members of the class participate as a single group. This group is perhaps the most difficult to handle, because discipline and management problems can occur easily when large numbers of students are interacting in student exchanges that are only occasionally interrupted by a teacher. The previously listed moderating functions will allow the teacher to control and, if need be, to redirect the discussion without overly restricting the flow of ideas. During a large group discussion, one or more of these functions should be frequently performed. The frequency with which these functions are employed can vary depending upon the topic and students; but the greater the consensus, the fewer the students, and the higher their ability to grasp the concepts and abstractions to be learned, *the more you can relinquish authority to the group* (Slavin, 1983).

Small group discussions of 5 to 10 students can also be useful for teaching concepts, patterns, and abstractions. Generally, when multiple topics must be discussed within the same lesson and time does not permit full class discussion of the topics in sequential order, two to four small groups can be used simultaneously. The task here is forming groups whose members can work together, spreading troublesome students across groups, and moving among the groups to perform the moderating functions described previously. Stopping the groups periodically, either to inform the entire class of important insights discovered by a single group or to apply moderating functions across groups, will help keep the groups reasonably close together and will aid the teacher's control and authority.

One additional group format for indirect instruction is students working in **pairs or teams**. This can be an effective format when the discussion entails writing (e.g., for a summary report), looking up information (e.g., in the text or an encyclopedia), or preparing materials (e.g., chart, diagram, graph, etc.) (Slavin, 1980, 1981). With this arrangement the teacher's role as moderator increases in proportion to the number of pairs or teams, so that only brief interchanges with each may be possible. The pair or team approach is best suited when the task is highly structured, when there is already a fair degree of consensus among pairs concerning the topic, and when the orienting instructions fully define the role of each member of the pair (e.g., student A searches for the information, student B writes a summary description of what is found, both students read summary for final agreement). Pairs frequently become highly task oriented under this arrangement, so it tends to be the most productive when the discussion objectives go beyond an oral report to include a product to be delivered to the class.

Table 7.3 presents the lesson plan for this indirect instruction lesson following the written format provided in chapter 5.

Some Comparisons of Direct and Indirect Instruction

As we come to the end of this two-chapter sequence on teaching strategies, it may be useful to place the direct and indirect models of instruction side by side. These two models have been presented in separate chapters, because each includes a considerable volume of strategies that could become blurred if not viewed within some overall model or framework. As you have seen, the models have two different purposes. The direct model was introduced for the purpose of providing six teaching functions—daily review and checking, presenting and struc-

TABLE 7.3
Lesson plan: Indirect instruction

Unit Plan: Economic Systems
Lesson Plan: Comparisons and contrasts among capitalist, socialist, and communist economies

1. Gaining attention	Ask if anyone knows where the phrase "government of the people, by the people, for the people" comes from, to establish the idea that the principles and rules by which a country is governed also influence its economic system.
2. Informing the learner of the objective	This session: To relate economic systems to the ownership of goods and services in different countries Next session: To be able to distinguish economic systems from political systems
3. Stimulating recall of prerequisite learning	Ask for a definition of capitalism and then refine with questioning and probing the definition given. Continue probing until a definition is arrived at that defines capitalism as "an economic system that allows the ownership of tangible goods that last for a reasonable period of time." Check understanding by asking for three countries (other than ours) that have capitalist economies.
4. Presenting the stimulus material	A. Ask what the word *socialism* means. Refine definition by questioning and probing until a definition is arrived at that defines socialism as "an economic system that allows the government to control and make available to everyone as many things as possible that (a) everyone values equally, and (b) are seen as essential for everyday existence." Have students compare capitalism and socialism by degree of ownership of public services and degree of taxes paid under each system. B. Ask what the word *communism* means and establish its relationship to the idea of *community*. Refine definition, using the concept of degree of ownership by questioning and probing until still more examples of things owned and controlled by the government under communism are arrived at by the students.
5. Eliciting the desired behavior	A. Use questions to encourage the identification of public services most commonly owned under socialism, for example, hospitals, trains, and communication systems. Some types of farms and industries will also be accepted when their relation to the public good is understood. B. Use questions to encourage the identification of those public services most commonly owned under communism, for example, food supply, housing, and industries. Emphasis will be placed on those services and goods that are different from those identified under socialism. C. Use questions to identify the amount and types of things owned by the government across the three systems, to establish the concept that differences among the systems are a matter of degree of ownership and degree of taxation.

TABLE 7.3
Continued

Unit Plan: Economic Systems
Lesson Plan: **Comparisons and contrasts among capitalist, socialist, and communist economies**

6. Providing feedback	Questions will be posed in a manner that encourages the student to evaluate his or her own response and those of other students. Probes will be given until student responses approximate an acceptable answer. Placed side by side on the board will be those goods and services the students have identified as likely to be owned by the government in all three systems and those likely to be owned uniquely by any one or combination of systems. A distinction may be made between these and the personal items that may have been mentioned, such as clothes or household goods, but which cannot be used to distinguish economies systems.
7. Evaluating the behavior	After completion of a research paper describing three countries of the students' own choosing each of which represents a different economic system, students will be graded on their comprehension of the concepts of (a) degree of ownership, and (b) degree of taxation as discussed by L. Rutherford, (1986) *Economics in a Modern World,* Columbus, OH: Intex.

turing new content, guided student practice, feedback and correctives, independent practice, and weekly and monthly reviews—most suited to the teaching of facts, rules, and action sequences. The indirect model was introduced for the purpose of providing a different set of teaching functions—advance organization of content, inductive and deductive conceptual movement, use of examples and nonexamples, use of questions to guide search and discovery, use of student ideas, student self-evaluation, and group discussion—best suited for the teaching of concepts, patterns, and abstractions. These two models rarely can, or should, be used to the exclusion of the other; neither will be found in any pure form. Table 7.4 summarizes some of the teaching events that can be employed by a teacher using these two different models.

As can be noted, these two teachers are proceeding along two different instructional paths. The first teacher's objective is the rapid attainment of facts, rules, and action sequences; the direct instruction model is used. This teacher divides the content into small, easily learned steps through a lecture format involving brief explanations, examples, practice, and feedback. Both guided and independent practice, under the tight control of the teacher, help to ensure that students are actively engaged in the learning process at high rates of success. Everything that is not learned is revealed on weekly and monthly reviews and, if need be, retaught.

The second teacher's objective is to engage students in a process of inquiry that will eventually lead to developing a concept or set of concepts in the form of a pattern or abstraction. Here the teacher prepares for the complexity of the lesson by providing an overall framework into which the day's lesson could be placed with room for expansion of concepts. Initially crude and inaccurate responses are gradually refined through inductive and deductive movement, which focuses the generalization at the most appropriate degree of accuracy. To do this, both examples and nonexamples, some of which are drawn from the students' own interests and

TABLE 7.4

Some example events under the direct and indirect models of instruction

Direct Instruction Objective: To teach facts, rules, and action sequences	Indirect Instruction Objective: To teach concepts, patterns, and abstractions
Teacher begins the lesson with a review of the previous day's work.	Teacher begins the lesson with advance organizers that provide an overall picture and that allow for concept expansion.
Teacher presents new content in small steps with explanations and examples.	Teacher focuses student responses using induction and/or deduction to refine and focus generalizations.
Teacher provides an opportunity for guided practice on a small number of sample problems. Prompts and models when necessary to attain 60–80% accuracy.	Teacher presents examples and nonexamples of the generalization identifying criterial and noncriterial attributes.
Teacher provides feedback and corrections according to whether the answer was correct, quick, and firm; correct but hesitant; careless; or incorrect.	Teacher draws additional examples from students' own experiences, interests, and problems.
Teacher provides an opportunity for independent practice with seatwork. Strives for automatic responses that are 95% correct or higher.	Teacher uses questions to guide discovery and articulation of the generalization.
Teacher provides weekly and monthly (accumulative) reviews and reteaches unlearned content.	Teacher involves students in evaluating their own responses.
	Teacher promotes and moderates discussion to firm up and extend generalizations when necessary.

experiences, are used to separate criterial from noncriterial attributes. Throughout the process the teacher uses questions to guide students into discovering the generalization and evaluating the correctness of their own responses. When concepts to be learned are relatively unstructured and have moderate-to-low degrees of consensus as to the correct or most appropriate generalization, large or small discussion groups may replace a more teacher-controlled format; in this case, the teacher becomes a moderator and has specific monitoring functions.

A Final Word

In this and the previous chapters, a variety of teaching strategies were presented that, when used with the appropriate content and purpose, can significantly improve your teaching effectiveness. Although both the direct and indirect models of instruction represent significant contributions, neither model should exclusively dominate your instructional style. It would be unfortunate, for example, to see a teacher who exemplified either the direct or indirect model of instruction and nothing else, because the original purpose of introducing these models was to increase the variety of instructional strategies at your disposal. The purpose was to create an extensive menu of teaching strategies. These models and the strategies they represent provide a variety of instructional tools that can be mixed in many combinations to match your particular objectives and your students. Just as different entrees have prominent and equal places on a menu, so, too, do the direct and indirect models have prominent and equal places in your classroom. The underlying point of these two chapters, then, is that the direct and indirect models of instruction should be employed alternately to create tantalizing combinations of "educational flavors" for your students. Your own objectives will be the best guide to what combination from the menu you will serve on any given day.

Now that the menu is in place, there is one detail that can appreciably add to its effectiveness in achieving your objectives. This detail involves one of the behaviors you will use the most frequently in making your menu irresistible to your students. Based on the example dialogues in this and the previous chapters, it should be no surprise that this behavior involves the art of asking questions. This important helping behavior will be discussed in the following chapter.

Summing Up

This chapter introduced you to indirect instruction strategies. Its main points were:

1. Indirect instruction is an approach to teaching and learning in which the process of learning is *inquiry,* the result is *discovery,* and the learning context is a *problem.*
2. In indirect instruction the learner acquires information by transforming stimulus material into a response that is different than (a) the stimulus used to present the learning and (b) any previous response emitted by the student.
3. Concepts, patterns, and abstractions are acquired during indirect instruction through the processes of generalization and discrimination, which require the learner to rearrange and elaborate on the stimulus material.
4. The process of generalization helps the learner respond in a similar manner to different stimuli, thereby increasing the range of instances to which particular facts, rules, and sequences apply.

5. The process of discrimination selectively restricts the acceptable range of instances by eliminating things that may look like the concept but that differ from it on critical dimensions.
6. The processes of generalization and discrimination together help students classify different-appearing stimuli into the same categories on the basis of criterial attributes. Criterial attributes act as magnets, drawing together all instances of a concept without the learner having to see or memorize all instances of it.
7. Instructional strategies that encourage the processes of generalization and discrimination for the purpose of forming concepts, patterns, and abstractions represent the indirect instruction model.
8. The instructional functions of the indirect model are

   - use of advance organizers
   - conceptual movement—inductive and deductive
   - use of examples and nonexamples
   - use of student ideas
   - student self-evaluation
   - use of group discussion

9. An advance organizer gives the learner a conceptual preview of what is to come and helps the learner store, label, and package content for retention and later use.
10. Three approaches to composing advance organizers are the problem-centered approach, the decision-making approach, and the networking approach.
11. Induction starts with a specific observation of a limited set of data and ends with a generalization about a much broader context.
12. Deduction proceeds from principles or generalizations to their application in specific contexts. The testing of a generalization to see if it holds in specific instances is sometimes referred to as the hypothetico—deductive method.

13. The provision of examples and nonexamples helps define the criterial and noncriterial attributes needed for making accurate generalizations.

14. Using examples and nonexamples correctly includes:

   - providing more than a single example
   - using examples that vary in ways that are irrelevant to the concept being defined
   - using nonexamples that also include relevant dimensions of the concept
   - explaining why nonexamples have some of the same characteristics as examples

15. In indirect instruction, the role of questions is to guide students into discovering new dimensions of a problem or new ways of resolving a dilemma.

16. Some uses of questions during indirect instruction include:

   - refocusing
   - presenting contradictions to be resolved
   - probing for deeper, more thorough responses
   - extending the discussion to new areas
   - passing responsibility to the class

17. Student ideas can be used to heighten student interest, organize subject content around student problems, tailor feedback to fit individual students, and encourage positive attitudes toward the subject. Moreover, because these goals should not be ends unto themselves, the use of student ideas must be planned and structured *in the context of the regularly prescribed curriculum.*

18. Student-centered learning, sometimes called unguided discovery learning, allows both the form and substance of the learning experience to be selected by the student; it is appropriate in the context of independently conducted experiments, research projects, science fair projects, and demonstrations. However, preorganization and guidance always will be necessary to ensure that the use of student ideas fits within the confines of the prescribed curriculum.

19. Self-evaluation of student responses occurs during indirect instruction when students are given the opportunity to reason out their answers so that other students and the teacher can suggest needed changes. Self-evaluation is most easily conducted in the context of student-to-student-to-teacher (or protracted) exchanges, wherein students are encouraged to comment on and consider the accuracy of their own and each others' responses.

20. A group discussion involves student exchanges with successive interactions among large numbers of students. During these exchanges, the teacher may intervene only occasionally to review and summarize or may maintain a periodic schedule of interaction in which each group's progress is evaluated and redirected when necessary.

21. The best topics for discussion include those that are not formally structured by texts and workbooks and for which a high degree of consensus among your students does not yet exist.

22. Some monitoring functions to be performed during discussion include:

   - orienting students to the objective of the discussion
   - providing new or more accurate information that may be needed
   - reviewing, summarizing, relating opinions and facts
   - redirecting the flow of information and ideas back to the objective of the discussion

23. The greater the group consensus, the fewer the students composing the group, and the higher their ability to grasp concepts and abstractions, then the more you can relinquish authority to the group.

24. Direct and indirect instruction rarely can be observed in any pure form, and one model should not be adopted to the exclusion of the other. However, each contains a set of functions that can compose an efficient and effective method for the teaching of facts, rules, and sequences or concepts, patterns, and abstractions.

For Discussion and Practice

*1. What three learning concepts are brought together in the indirect model of instruction?
*2. What types of behavioral outcomes are the direct and indirect instructional models most effective in achieving?
*3. Where does the word *indirect* come from in the *indirect instruction model?*
*4. Why can direct instruction not be used all the time?
*5. Explain in your own words what is meant by the words *unitization* and *automaticity* as applied to direct instruction. Give an example of a learning task in which only these two processes are required.
*6. Explain in your own words the meanings of *generalization* and *discrimination.* Give an example of a learning task in which both these processes are required.
*7. Identify which of the following learning tasks involve only facts, rules, or action sequences (Type 1) and which, in addition, involve concepts, patterns, and abstractions (Type 2).

naming the presidents

selecting the best speech

shifting a car

writing an essay

describing the main theme in George Orwell's *1984*

hitting a tennis ball

winning a tennis match

inventing a new soft drink

reciting the vowel sounds

becoming an effective teacher

*8. Describe two problems that would result if a concept or abstraction had to be learned using only the cognitive processes of unitization and automaticity by which facts, rules, and sequences are acquired.
9. Prepare a two-minute introduction to a lesson of your own choosing that provides your students with an advance organizer.
10. Provide one example of an advance organizer using the problem-centered, decision-making, and networking approaches.
*11. In your own words, define inductive and deductive reasoning. Give an example of each, using content from your preferred teaching area.
*12. Identify the five steps to deductive reasoning commonly applied in the laboratory.
13. For each of the following, show, with specific examples, how the concept might be taught both inductively and deductively. Pay particular attention to whether your instruction should begin or end with a generalization.

democracy

freedom

education

effective teaching

parenting

*14. For the concept of effective teaching, give five criterial attributes and five noncriterial attributes.
*15. Identify four ways in which examples and nonexamples should be used in the teaching of concepts.
*16. Distinguish the different purposes for asking questions in the direct and indirect models of instruction.
*17. Besides refocusing, what other types of questions can be used in the search and discovery process? Choose a lesson topic and provide an example of each of these.
*18. What type of learning might be represented by discussions that begin and end with student-determined ideas and content? How is this different from the use of student ideas in the context of the indirect instruction model?
*19. What are three ways student ideas might be incorporated into an indirect instruction lesson?
*20. Why is student self-evaluation more important in indirect model instruction than in direct model instruction?

*21. What are four monitoring responsibilities of the teacher during group discussion? In a normal discussion, approximately how often should one or more of these monitoring functions be employed?

22. For which of the following teaching objectives might you use the direct model of instruction, and for which might you use the indirect model?

Teaching your class to:

sing

use a microscope properly

appreciate Milton's *Paradise Lost*

become aware of the pollutants around us

solve an equation with two unknowns

read at grade level

type at the rate of 25 words per minute

write an original short story

build a winning science fair project

distinguish war from aggression

Are there any for which you might use both models?

Suggested Readings

Gagné, R. M. (1971). The learning of concepts. In M. David Merrill (Ed.), *Instructional design: Readings*. Englewood Cliffs, NJ: Prentice-Hall.
An excellent introduction to this important form of learning—with plenty of practical illustrations.

Gall, M. & Gall, J. (1976). The discussion method. In N. L. Gage (Ed.), *The psychology of teaching methods: The seventy-fifth yearbook of the national society for the study of education, part I*. Chicago: University of Chicago Press.
A comprehensive discussion of the research and logic that underlies this popular method.

Giaconia, R. (1987). Open versus formal methods. In M. J. Dunkin (Ed.), *International encyclopedia of teaching and teacher education*. New York: Pergamon.
A good introduction to some of the most important differences between the direct and indirect models.

Joyce, B. & Weils, M. (1986). *Models of teaching*. Englewood Cliffs, NJ: Prentice-Hall.
A review of many of our most popular styles of teaching—a good complement to the two models described in this chapter.

Maerhoff, G. (1983). Teaching to think: A new emphasis. *The New York Times*. January 9, Section 12, 1–37.
A current and thoughtful piece on how to teach thinking skills using many of the functions of the indirect model.

Morine, H. & Morine G. (1973). *Discovery: A challenge to teachers*. Englewood Cliffs, NJ: Prentice-Hall.
An informative and practical text about how to implement the indirect model in all of its many forms—with plenty of examples for lesson plans.

Shulman, L. & Keislar, E. (Eds.). (1966). *Learning by discovery: A critical appraisal*. Chicago: Rand McNally.
Still the most authoritative book on discovery learning which identifies its weaknesses as well as its strengths.

Slavin, R. (1983). *Cooperative learning*. New York: Longman.
An extensive presentation on how to form different kinds of groups and use them productively in the classroom.

Slavin, R. (1987). Small group methods. In M. J. Dunkin (Ed.), *International encyclopedia of teaching and teacher education*. New York: Pergamon.
An overview of some ideas on how to use small groups to promote a cooperative classroom environment.

Withall, J. (1987). Teacher-centered and learner-centered teaching. In M. J. Dunkin (Ed.), *International encyclopedia of teaching and teacher education*. New York: Pergamon.
An introduction to the direct and indirect models of instruction from the point of view of the teacher and learner.

8
Questioning Strategies

It was noticeable in the previous chapter's classroom dialogues that questions play an important role in the effective teacher's menu. This is no coincidence, because the majority of exchanges between teachers and students involve questions of one form or another. This chapter will explore the definition of a question, the many and varied ways questions can be asked, and the types of questions that should be asked more frequently than others. Also discussed is the closely related topic of **probes**, which, like questions, serve as effective catalysts for performing the five key behaviors of (a) clarity, (b) variety, (c) task-orientation, (d) engagement in the learning process at (e) moderate-to-high rates of success.

What Is a Question?

Although this may seem to be a simple question, it has no simple answer when asked in the context of a lively and fast-paced exchange in a class-room. As observed by Brown and Edmondson (1984), students routinely report that they have difficulty distinguishing some types of questions in the context of a classroom dialogue—and even whether or not a question has been asked! Imagine hearing, for example, the following two questions:

Raise your hand if you know the answer.

Aren't you going to answer the question?

The first is expressed in command form, yet it contains an implicit question; the second sounds like a question, yet contains an implicit command. Will both of these statements be perceived by your students as questions, and will they both evoke the same response?

Voice inflection may be another source of confusion; it can indicate a question even when sentence syntax does not. For example, imagine hearing the following two sentences spoken with the emphasis added:

You *said* the President can have two terms in office?

The President can have *two* terms in office?

The proper voice inflection can turn almost any sentence into a question, whether you intend it or not. In addition, a real question can be perceived as a rhetorical question because of inflection and word choice, such as: We all have done our homework today, *haven't we?* Whether this is intended to be a question or not, it is certain that all those who do not have their homework will assume that the question is rhetorical.

The previous examples show that *effective questions*—ones for which students actively compose a response and, thereby, become engaged in the learning process—depend on more than just words. Their effectiveness also depends on *voice inflection, word emphasis, word choice,* and the *context* in which the question is raised. Questions can be raised in many different ways, any one of which can determine whether and in what manner the question is perceived by your students. In this chapter any oral statement or gesture intended to evoke a response from a student is considered to be a question; and if it evokes a response that *actively engages a student in the learning process,* it is an effective question. With this distinction in mind you will now explore many ways of asking questions that actively engage students in the learning process.

In almost any classroom at any hour of the day one would be likely to observe a sequence of events in which the teacher structures the content to be discussed and solicits a student response, the student responds, and then the teacher reacts to this response. These activities performed in sequence are the four most commonly observed behaviors in any classroom. They were first described by Bellack, Kliebard, Hyman, and Smith (1966) as a chain of events in which

1. the teacher provides structure, briefly formulating the topic or issue to be discussed,
2. the teacher solicits a response or asks a question of one or more students,
3. the student responds or answers the question, and
4. the teacher reacts to the student's answer.

The teacher behaviors in this chain of events compose the activities of **structuring, soliciting,** and **reacting.** The previous two chapters discussed some of the strategies that can be used for structuring the topic or content to be presented. This chapter will focus on the soliciting and reacting elements in this chain of events.

At the heart of this chain is soliciting—or question-asking behavior. Questions are the tool for helping to bridge the gap between the teacher's presentation of content and the student's understanding of it. In the previous chapters were many different bridging strategies: advance organizers, guided practice, feedback and correctives, inductive and deductive logic, self-evaluation, discussion, and so on. These strategies have included all of the possible ingredients of both direct and indirect instruction, ingredients whose function is to promote and stimulate thinking. Just as these ingredients are intended to actively engage learners in the learning process, so also can questions perform this same function and add still more variety to a teaching menu. The point of using questions, therefore, should not be lost among the many different *forms* and *varieties* of questions to be presented in this chapter. Questions, like all the ingredients of direct and indirect instruction, must encourage students to think about and act upon the material structured by the teacher. Classrooms and content become boring, more often than not, because of a teacher's failure to devise ways of getting students to do something with the content being presented *as quickly as possible after it is presented.* This is why questions are so often interspersed throughout a lesson and wrapped around small bits of content—so that the content does not go too far or too long without actively engaging the student, or evoking a response (sometimes *any* response). Consequently, the cycle of structuring, soliciting, and reacting is the most frequently occurring chain of events that can be observed in any classroom.

The centerpiece of this chain—soliciting or questioning—is so prevalent that it has been estimated that, on the average, between 100 and 150 questions per class hour are asked in the typical elementary and secondary classroom (Brown & Edmondson, 1984) and that 80% of all school time is devoted to questions and answers (Gall, 1970). This enormous concentration on a single strategy must, in some sense, attest to both its convenience and its perceived effectiveness. But, as it has been noted, not all questions will be effective questions. That is, not all questions will engage students actively in the learning process where they act upon the content being presented.

Some research data show that this may indeed be the case. It has been estimated from several early research studies that 70–80% of all questions asked are ones requiring the simple recall of facts, while only 20–30% require clarifying, expanding, generalizing, and the making of inferences—behaviors requiring higher level thought processes (Haynes, 1935; Corey, 1940). Things may not have changed much since these early studies; recent work in both the United States and England tends to confirm that for about every five questions asked, three require data recall, one is managerial, and only one requires higher level thought processes (Brown & Edmondson, 1984). The disproportionate number of recall-versus-thought questions is somewhat alarming, because behaviors at the higher levels of cognitive complexity involving analysis, synthesis, and evaluation (that is, those behaviors most frequently required in adult life, at work, and in advanced training) seem to be those that are emphasized least in the classroom. There are, of course, reasons for asking questions at the knowledge, comprehension, and application level; but there seems to be little explanation for why such a large percentage of such questions should be asked to the exclusion of higher level thought questions, which are believed to more actively engage students in the learning process.

Purposes of Questions

Although it would be relatively easy to classify all questions as either lower order questions (requiring the recall of information) and higher order questions (requiring clarification, expansion, generalization, and inference), such a broad distinction would ignore the many specific purposes for which questions often are used. These purposes include:

To arouse interest and curiosity

To focus attention on an issue

To stimulate learners to ask questions

To diagnose specific learning difficulties

To encourage reflection and self-evaluation

To promote thought and the understanding of ideas

To review content already learned

To help recall specific information

To reinforce recently learned material

To manage or remind students of a procedure

To teach through student answers

To probe deeper after an answer is given

To redirect or structure the flow of ideas

To allow expressions of feelings

Although this is a substantial list, it probably does not represent all of the reasons why questions are asked. Nevertheless, most reasons for asking questions can be placed in the following general categories:

1. Interest- and attention-getting:
   "If you could go to the moon, what would be the first thing you would notice?"
2. Diagnosing and checking:
   "Does anyone know the meaning of the Latin word *via?*"
3. Recall of specific facts or information:
   "Who can name each of the main characters in *The Adventures of Huckleberry Finn?*"

4. Managerial:
   "Did you ask my permission?"
5. Encourage higher level thought processes:
   "Putting together all that we learned, what household products exhibit characteristics associated with the element sodium?"
6. Structure and redirect learning:
   "Now that we've covered the narrative form, who can tell me what an expository sentence is?"
7. Allow expression of affect:
   "What did you like about *Of Mice and Men?*"

Most of the questions in these categories have the purpose of shaping or setting up the learner's response. In this sense, a well-formulated question serves as an advance organizer, providing the framework into which must be placed the response which is to follow.

Types of Questions

These frameworks can be either narrow or broad, encouraging either a specific, limited response or a general, expansive one. A question that limits an answer to only a small number of responses or a single response is called a convergent, direct, or closed question. For such questions, the learner has previously read or heard the answer, which requires only the recall of facts. The question sets up the learner to respond in a limited, restrictive manner (e.g., "Does anyone know the meaning of the Latin word *via?*" "Who can name the main characters in *The Adventures of Huckleberry Finn?*"). The answers to these questions can be easily judged right or wrong. Many convergent, or closed, questions are used in direct instruction and, as was previously mentioned, as many as 80% of all questions may be of this type.

Another type of question is one that encourages a general, or open, response. This is the divergent, or indirect, question. It has no single best answer, but it can have wrong answers. This is perhaps the most misunderstood aspect of a divergent question: Not just any answer will be correct, even in the case of divergent

questions raised for the purpose of allowing students to express their feelings. If Johnny is asked what he liked about *Of Mice and Men* and says "Nothing" or "The happy ending," then either Johnny has not read the book or he needs help in better understanding the events that took place. A passive or accepting response on your part to answers like these would be inappropriate, regardless of your intent to allow an open response.

Convergent and divergent questions, therefore, both have right and wrong answers. It happens that divergent questions may have many right answers and, therefore, a much broader or expansive range of acceptable responses. This does not mean that misguided, meaningless, nonsensical, or nonresponses should be accepted without some suggestion that the response is inappropriate and should be rephrased; perhaps hints, encouragement, or further probing may be necessary (e.g., "Now, why would you say death and tragedy make a happy ending?"). This points up the fact that far more diversity in responses can be expected from divergent than from convergent questions—which may account for why only 20% of all questions are divergent. It always will be easier to determine whether the answer to a convergent question is right or wrong than it will be to sift through the range of responses that may be acceptable for a divergent question; even so, it will be your responsibility to identify inappropriate responses, to follow them up, and to bring them back into the range of acceptable answers. Divergent questions, therefore, often are followed by more detail, new information, or hints of encouragement; in this sense, they become a rich source of lively and spontaneous follow-up material that can make your teaching fresh and interesting.

It is important to point out that the same question can be convergent under one set of circumstances and divergent under another. For example, if the student is asked to *decide* or *evaluate,* according to a set of criteria, which household products exhibit characteristics associated with the element sodium, and the student only recalls products from a previously memorized list, then the question is convergent. If no such list has ever been seen, however, then the student must analyze the physical properties of certain products for the first time, and the question is divergent. Convergent questions also can inadvertently turn into divergent questions. When the answer to a question thought to involve simple recall (e.g., "Does anyone know the meaning of the Latin word *via?*") has never been seen before, and the student arrives at the right answer through generalization and inductive reasoning (e.g., by thinking about the meaning of the English word *viaduct* or the phrase "via route 35"), then the question is divergent.

To complicate matters further, a convergent question in one context may be a divergent question in another, and vice versa. The question "What do you think of disarmament?" may require the use of evaluation skills by eighth graders but only the recall of facts by twelfth graders who have just finished studying the details of the Strategic Arms Limitation Treaty. Also, keep in mind that both of the questions "What do you think about disarmament?" and "What do you think about the Dallas Cowboys?" may require some analysis, synthesis, or decision making, but for most of your students disarmament will require a higher level of thinking than will the Dallas Cowboys. As has been shown, effective questions depend on more than just words—they depend on the *context* of the discussion in which the question is raised, *voice inflection, word emphasis,* and *word choice.*

Classroom researchers have studied the effects on student achievement of teachers who have used convergent and divergent questions (Redfield & Rousseau, 1981; Winne, 1979; Gall et al., 1978). Remember that there were far more convergent questions raised in classrooms than there were divergent questions; the margin was almost 5 to 1. Interestingly, while most of the rationales given for using higher level, divergent-type questions included promotion of thinking; formation of concepts and abstractions; encouragement of analysis, synthesis, and evaluation; and so on, the research has not clearly substantiated that the use of higher order questions is related to gains in student achievement, at least not as measured by tests of *standardized* achievement.

Although some of these studies have reported modest improvements in achievement scores with the use of divergent questioning strategies, others have not, and some studies have reported larger achievement gains with convergent than with divergent questioning strategies. Although these studies found a large imbalance in favor of convergent questions, four important factors must be considered when looking at their results.

First, it should be noted that tests of achievement and particularly tests of *standardized* achievement, employ multiple choice items that generally test for behaviors at the lower levels of cognitive complexity. Therefore, the measures of achievement used in these studies may not have provided the opportunity to register increases in behaviors at the higher levels of cognitive complexity, increases that might have resulted from the use of divergent questions.

Second, the diversity of responses that normally can be expected to result from divergent questions, and the added time needed to build upon and follow up these responses, may prohibit large amounts of class time from being devoted to higher order questioning. Because the instructional time devoted to divergent questioning is often less than that devoted to convergent questioning, the results of some of the studies may have simply reflected the imbalance in instructional time, not in their relative effectiveness.

Third, content that is most suited for teaching behaviors at the higher levels of cognitive complexity may constitute only a small amount of the content identified in existing texts, workbooks, and curriculum guides. Much of the typical curricula in math, science, English, and even the social sciences, emphasizes facts and understandings at the knowledge and comprehension level. Perhaps this is both because such achievements are the most easily measured and also because needed improvements can be identified from standardized tests. But until larger portions of curricula are *written in ways that encourage or require higher level thought processes,* there probably will not be an increase in the amount of time teachers devote to these behaviors.

Fourth, thinking and problem-solving behaviors most closely associated with divergent questions may take much longer to accrue and become noticeable than will behaviors at lower levels of behavioral complexity. Behaviors at the lower levels of cognitive complexity (e.g., learning to form possessives, memorizing Latin roots, knowing the multiplication tables) can be both quickly elicited with convergent questioning strategies and also readily detected with fill-in, matching, or multiple-choice exams administered at the end of a lesson or unit. On the other hand, behaviors at the higher levels of cognitive complexity (e.g., learning to distinguish economic systems from political systems, knowing how to analyze household products for their chemical components, being able to recognize various forms of quadratic equations) may take a unit, a grading period, or even longer to build to a measurable outcome. This is a time span that is beyond that used in most, if not all, of the research studies comparing the effects of convergent and divergent strategies on school achievement.

There may be explanations for the seeming imbalance in the use and effectiveness of divergent and convergent questioning strategies, and they may not have much to do with the nature of the strategies themselves. Because the recall of facts will always be required for higher order thought processes, we can assume that a large number of convergent questions will always be a necessary precondition for achieving higher level behaviors. We might also conclude that because it may take more instructional time in narrowly defined content areas for the effects of higher order questioning to show up on tests of achievement, the consistent use of moderate amounts of divergent questions may be more important than brief intensive episodes of divergent questions. The most appropriate convergent to divergent question ratio may actually be about a 70:30 or 60:40 split.

It is important to note that many of the same research studies that have failed to link the use of higher order questions with increases in school achievement have indicated that higher order questioning tends to encourage students to use higher thought processes in composing a response. Research discussed by Dunkin and Biddle (1974) and Martin (1979) indicates that teachers who ask questions requiring analysis, synthesis, and evaluation elicit these behaviors from their students more frequently than do teachers who use fewer higher level questions. These process behaviors seem desirable regardless of whether or not their effects show up on immediate tests of student achievement. Therefore, the effects of higher level questioning on the process of thinking may be justification alone for applying higher level questions consistently at moderate rates over extended periods of time.

Targets of Questions

Research by Brown and Edmondson (1984) suggests that questions can be directed to individuals, to groups, or to the entire class, or to more able learners, average learners, less able learners, and learners of mixed ability. Figure 8.1 combines both of these dimensions to show some of the different targets at which your questions can be directed.

Although most questions are framed for a mixture of abilities and are directed to the entire class, not all questions need fit this format. The effective teacher varies not only the targets for whom questions are composed (individuals, groups of various sizes, or full class), but also the level of the question. Questions specifically "framed" for low ability and high ability learners targeted to individuals, "sprinkled" among questions framed for a mixture of abilities directed to the entire class, keep all students alert and engaged in the learning process. In a heterogeneous class with a mixture of abilities, occasionally posing questions over the heads of less able learners and under the heads of more able students may be a necessary precondition for engaging the entire class in considering and using the content being presented. For example, a general question can be composed in one way for less able learners and in another way for more able learners by varying the kind and amount of

FIGURE 8.1

Some possible targets and groups for framing questions

Groups for whom a question can be framed

Targets to which a question can be directed		less able learner	average learner	more able learner	mixed abilities
	full class				
	individuals				
	groups				

advance organization with which the question is framed, as illustrated in these examples:

For the Less Able
"Tell me, Johnny, if you sat down to breakfast, what things at the breakfast table would most likely contain the element sodium?"

For the More Able
"Mary, what are some forms of the element sodium in our universe?"

"After the death of Lenny in *Of Mice and Men,* what then happens to the other main character?"

"What would be an example of an anticlimax in *Of Mice and Men?*"

"After thinking about the words *photo* and *synthesis,* who wants to guess what *photosynthesis* means?"

"Who can tell me how photosynthesis supports plant life?"

"Ted, if we have the equation $10 = \dfrac{2}{x}$, do we find x by multiplying or dividing?"

"Rich, can you solve for x: $10 = \dfrac{2}{x}$?"

Notice that these examples vary not only in cognitive complexity but also in the way they are phrased. More advance organizers, hints, and clues are typical in questions specifically directed to less able learners—whether as individuals or in groups—than would be appropriate for average or more able learners.

Another way of framing questions for heterogeneous classes is to design the question so that different responses at various levels of complexity will be correct: Less complex responses received from less able learners are accepted as being just as correct as are more complex answers from more able learners. Although responses from less able learners may not be as complete as those received from more able learners, the response is evaluated in terms of the ability level of the student. This does not mean, however, that wrong answers or even only partially wrong answers need be accepted as correct answers. Rather, the elaboration given and the depth of understanding will be less for one type of learner than another. Chapter 11 will review specific instructional strategies for less able and more able learners. For now, however, it is important to keep in mind that while most of your questions will be aimed at the average ability level in your class—or targeted for a mixture of abilities—some questions should be specifically targeted to both the less able and the more able learners and should be varied among the full class, smaller groups, and individuals. Table 8.1 suggests some of the different questioning strategies that can be used with the less able and more able learner.

TABLE 8.1

Some different questioning strategies for the less and more able learner

More Able	Less Able
Use more open questions to make sure they can generalize the content to new problems.	Use more review questions to make sure they have not forgotten task-relevant prior content.
Ask some questions that stymie, mystify, and challenge that only the more able could be expected to answer.	Use questions with specific and concrete examples, settings, and objects with which your students are familiar.
Pose questions in the context of an investigation or problem that is broader than the question itself.	Use questions in a step-by-step approach, where each question is slightly broader or more complex than the preceding one.
Ask students to go deeper, clarify, and provide additional justification or reasons for the answers they provide.	Use questions that rephrase or reiterate the answers to previous questions.
Use more abstract concepts by asking students to see how their answers may apply across settings or objects.	Suggest one or two probable answers in your questions that lead students in the right direction.
Use sequences of questions to build to higher and more complex concepts, patterns, and abstractions.	Use questions and answers as a game (e.g., 20 questions) with points and scores.

Sequences of Questions

Questions also can vary according to the type of sequence in which they are used. Recall that the most basic sequence was one which involved structuring, soliciting, and reacting. However, many variations on this basic theme are possible. Studies by Brown and Edmondson (1984) and Smith and Meux (1970) have noted that employing divergent questions leading to convergent questions is one of the most popular sequences. They report that many teachers seem to prefer to begin structuring, soliciting, and reacting by beginning with an open question, which then leads to further structuring and subsequent questions involving recall or simple deduction. This general-to-specific approach can take several twists and turns; for example, a teacher begins by encouraging speculative responses and then narrows down to a question requiring simple deduction:

TEACHER: What do astronauts wear on the moon?
STUDENTS: Spacesuits.
TEACHER: So what element in our atmosphere must *not* be in the atmosphere on the moon?

It is the same approach when a teacher poses a problem, asks several simple recall questions, and then reformulates the question to narrow the problem still further:

TEACHER: If the Alaskan Eskimos originally came from Siberia on the Asian continent, how do you suppose they got to Alaska?
STUDENTS: No response
TEACHER: We studied the Bering Strait, which separates North America from Asia; how wide is the water between these two continents at their closest point?

STUDENT: About 60 miles, the Little and Big Diomede Islands are in between.

TEACHER: If this expanse of water were completely frozen, which some scientists believe it was years ago, how might Asians have come to the North American continent?

This type of funnelling, adding conditions of increasing specificity to a question, was frequently employed by teachers in many of the studies reviewed by Redfield and Rousseau (1981). There is, however, no evidence that one sequencing strategy is any more effective in promoting student achievement than any other. Because other sequences are possible and have been observed, the specific type of sequence chosen should depend on the behavioral objectives, the instructional content being taught, and the ability level of the students. Some other types of questioning sequences that can be implemented in a cycle of structuring, soliciting, and reacting have been suggested by Brown and Edmondson (1984) and are identified and illustrated in Table 8.2. With the appropriate objectives, content, and students, all of these offer useful additions to your teaching menu.

Levels of Questions

In addition to being able to formulate divergent and convergent questions, to target questions to specific types of learners, and to arrange questions in meaningful sequences, the effective teacher also must be able to formulate questions at different levels of cognitive complexity. There was a previous illustration of how important this is when classes are heterogeneously grouped with both less able and more able students.

One of the best known systems for classifying questions according to cognitive complexity is the taxonomy of objectives in the cognitive domain which was presented in chapter 4. This system has the advantage of going beyond the simple recall versus thought dichotomy frequently used in the research cited previously. A greater variation of complexity is employed; not all recall questions deal with the lowest and most

TABLE 8.2
Some sequences of questions

Type		Description
Extending		A string of questions of the same type and on the same topic
Extending and lifting		Initial questions request examples and instances of the same type, followed by a leap to a different type of question; a common sequence is likely to be recall, simple deduction and descriptions leading to reasons, hypothesis
Funnelling		Begins with open question and proceeds to narrow down to simple deductions and recall or to reasons and problem solving
Sowing and reaping		Problem posed, open questions asked, followed by more specific questions and restatement of initial problem
Step-by-step up		A sequence of questions moving systematically from recall to problem solving, evaluation or open ended
Step-by-step down		Begins with evaluation questions and moves systematically through problem solving towards direct recall
Nose-dive		Begins with evaluation and problem solving and then moves straight to simple recall

Adapted from Brown & Edmondson, 1984.

mundane forms of learning (e.g., recall of names, dates, facts), and not all thought questions deal with the highest and most superlative forms of learning (e.g., discovery, insight, judgment). Therefore, a continuum of question complexity that fills the space between the ends of this scale can be a useful addition to the art of asking questions. Recall that the taxonomy for the cognitive domain contains the following six levels of behavioral complexity:

Knowledge

Comprehension

Application

Analysis

Synthesis

Evaluation

Table 8.3 identifies the types of student behaviors that are associated with each of these levels. Look at each level to get a feel for the question-asking strategies that go along with them.

Knowledge

Recall from chapter 4 that knowledge objectives require the student to recall, describe, define, or recognize facts that already have been committed to memory. Some of the action verbs that can be used to formulate questions at the knowledge level are:

define	recite
describe	list
identify	name

Some example questions are:

What is the definition of capitalism?

How many elements are in the periodic table?

Can you recite the first rule for forming possessives?

Can you give the equation for a straight line?

Notice that each of these questions can be answered correctly only by recalling previously memorized facts. They do not require that the student understand what was memorized or be able to use the learned facts in a problem-solving context. Johnny could parrot back the definition of capitalism (as given in our dialogue in chapter 7) without having the slightest notion of the differences between capitalism and other economic systems—or even that he is living in a capitalist system.

It is not unusual for facts that have been meticulously committed to memory to be forgotten within days or weeks. When they are linked to other forms of knowledge, such as those in subsequent lessons and units, they become stepping stones for gradually increasing the behavioral complexity of teaching outcomes. Nearly everyone can cite a personal experience of doing well on individual fact-type quizzes during the semester only to do poorly on the end-of-semester exam. In these cases either the time spent memorizing the facts needed to do well on the quizzes was wasted or the instructor failed to relate those facts to the higher level behaviors tested at the end of the course. To avoid the overuse or disconnected use of questions at the knowledge level, ask yourself the question: Do the facts required by my questions represent task-relevant prior knowledge for subsequent lessons?

If your answer is "No," you might consider assigning text, workbook, or supplemental material which contains the facts instead of incorporating them into your question-asking behavior. If your answer is "Yes," then determine in what ways the facts will be used in subsequent lessons and raise questions that require answers that eventually will be helpful in forming more complex behaviors. Your students may *not* need to be able to recite the names of all the presidents, the Declaration of Independence, or all the elements in the periodic table, because these facts may not represent task-relevant prior knowledge for more complex behavioral outcomes. On the other hand, it is likely that your learners *will* need to recite the multiplication

TABLE 8.3
A question classification scheme

Level of Behavioral Complexity	Expected Student Behavior	Instructional Processes	Key Words
Knowledge (remembering)	Student is able to remember or recall information and recognize facts, terminology, and rules.	repetition memorization	define describe identify
Comprehension (understanding)	Student is able to change the form of a communication by translating and rephrasing what has been read or spoken.	explanation illustration	summarize paraphrase rephrase
Application (transferring)	Student is able to apply the information learned to a context different than the one in which it was learned.	practice transfer	apply use employ
Analysis (relating)	Student is able to break a problem down into its component parts and to draw relationships among the parts.	induction deduction	relate distinguish differentiate
Synthesis (creating)	Student is able to combine parts to form a unique or novel solution to a problem.	divergence generalization	formulate compose produce
Evaluation (judging)	Student is able to make decisions about the value or worth of methods, ideas, people, or products according to expressed criteria.	discrimination inference	appraise decide justify

tables, the parts of speech, and the rules for adding, subtracting, multiplying, and dividing signed numbers; these will be used countless other times in completing exercises and solving problems at more complex levels of behavioral complexity. Always take the time to think about whether the facts you are about to teach compose task-relevant prior knowledge for subsequent lessons, and you will avoid knowledge questions that may be trivial or irrelevant.

Comprehension

Comprehension questions require some level of understanding of facts that have been committed to memory. Responses to these questions should show that the learner can explain, summarize, or elaborate upon the facts that have been learned. Some of the action verbs that can be used in formulating questions at the comprehension level are:

summarize	convert
paraphrase	explain
rephrase	extend

Some example questions are:

Can you, in your own words, explain the concept of capitalism?

Who can summarize the main idea behind the periodic table of elements?

What would have to be rephrased so that the first rule applies in converting a possessive back to the nonpossessive form?

What steps are required for solving an equation for a straight line?

In each of the previous questions the student responds by first acting upon previously learned material by changing it in some respect from the form in which it was first learned. For example, the teacher asks a student not to give the definition of capitalism, but to explain "in your own words, the concept of capitalism." This requires the translation or conversion of one definition (the teacher's) into another (the student's).

There is an important step in moving from knowledge-level questions to comprehension-level questions. Knowledge level questions may be answered without any cognitive processing—or thinking—at the time a response is made, but comprehension-level questions require cognitive processing at the time of the response. In the former case the learner actually may think about the material only once, at the time it was originally learned; in the latter case the learner must actively think about the content twice: once when the facts are first memorized and again when these facts have to be composed into a response which is in a different form than that which was previously learned. Although fact

questions must logically precede comprehension questions, comprehension questions are superior to knowledge questions for arousing the cognitive processes of the learner and thereby encouraging long-term retention, understanding, and eventual use of the learned material.

Application

Application questions extend facts and understanding to the next level of behavioral complexity. They go beyond both the memorization of facts and the translation of these facts, and they require the student to use the previously acquired facts and understandings in a new and different environment. Application questions require the student to apply the facts learned to a problem, context, or environment that is different than the one in which the information was learned. Thus, the student can rely on neither the original context nor the original content to solve the problem. Some of the action verbs that can be used in formulating questions at the application level are:

use	demonstrate
apply	solve
employ	operate

Some example questions are:

What countries from among those listed do you believe have a capitalist economic system?

How is the periodic table of elements used to identify still-to-be-discovered elements?

Consider the first rule for forming possessives; who can apply it to the errors in the following newspaper article?

Who can solve for and plot the results of $Y = a + bX$, when $a = 1$, $b = 1.5$, $X_1 = 15$, $X_2 = 10$?

In these questions the learner is being asked to show an ability to use previously learned facts and understandings to solve a problem. The teacher's job in application questions, then, is to present the learner with a context or problem different than that in which the material was first learned, in which to apply previously learned facts and understandings. In this manner the question not only encourages the student to act upon the learned material, thereby increasing engagement in the learning process, but also encourages the transfer of newly learned material to a new and different environment.

Application questions require two related cognitive processes: (a) the simultaneous recall and consideration of all the individual units (facts) pertaining to the question, and (b) the composing of units into a single harmonious sequence wherein the response becomes rapid and automatic. Recall that these two cognitive processes were introduced in chapters 6 and 7 as unitization and automaticity. They are required for all Type 1 behaviors—that is, for acquiring facts, rules, and action sequences. It is through these two processes that action sequences are created out of the application of previously learned facts and rules. Application questions ask students to compose, or put together, previously learned responses under a condition that approximates some real-world problem, with the goal being that the correct response becomes rapid and automatic. Needless to say, without learned facts and understandings acquired by questions at the knowledge and comprehension levels, there could be no action sequences. However, without the opportunity to use and transfer previously learned facts and rules to new contexts, there also could be no action sequences. The number and quality of the application questions will determine the degree to which the learners' action sequences (e.g., facility in applying the concept of capitalism, use of the periodic table, application of the first rule, and solving a linear equation) will become rapid and automatic.

The **number** of application questions you ask, however, may be of lesser importance than is consistency in asking them. Many beginning teachers believe that application questions should be reserved for the end of a unit—or even worse, for the end of a grading period. But, as you have

seen, they are essential whenever a rapid and automatic response involving a set of facts or rules is required or whenever an action sequence is the goal of a lesson.

The **quality** of your application questions will be determined in large measure by the degree to which you change the problem, context, or environment in which the facts or rules were first learned. Too small a change, and the transfer of learning to an expanded context will not occur—only the parroting back of facts and rules from an earlier context. On the other hand, too large a change, and the new context will require a response that may be beyond the grasp of most of your learners. The key is to raise application questions requiring the transfer of learning to new problems or contexts only after all task-relevant facts and rules have been taught. The easiest way in which to accomplish this will be to change the context only to a small degree at first, and then gradually shift to more unfamiliar contexts.

Analysis

Questions asked at the analysis level require the student to break a problem down into its component parts and to draw relationships among the parts. Some of the purposes of asking questions at the analysis level are to identify logical errors; to differentiate among facts, opinions, and assumptions; to derive conclusions; to find inferences or generalizations—in short, to discover the reasons behind the information given. Some of the action verbs that can be used in formulating questions at the analysis level are:

support	relate
point out	distinguish
break down	differentiate

Some example questions are:

What factors distinguish capitalism from socialism?

Where on the periodic table are the next new elements likely to be found?

In what ways can you differentiate Rule 1 from Rule 2 possessive errors that occur in the following essay?

Where are the mistakes, if any, in the following graphs, given their respective linear equations?

Analysis questions tend to promote Type 2 behaviors in the form of concepts, patterns, and abstractions. They generally represent the most elementary form of the inquiry or problem-solving process, which is most closely associated with the functions of indirect instruction. In this respect, analysis questions represent a movement away from the teaching of facts, rules, and action sequences and toward more complex behavioral outcomes in the form of concepts, patterns, and abstractions. Analysis questions may be considered to be the start of the inquiry or problem-solving process and are the beginning of a change from a direct to an indirect instructional strategy.

Although not all Type 1 and Type 2 behaviors can be neatly divided between application and analysis in the taxonomy of behavior, there are several important changes that have occurred in the example questions at this level. One of these changes is that the majority of the questions do not have the single, best answer that is so common in the teaching of facts, rules, and action sequences. Consequently, the teacher must encounter and evaluate a much broader range of responses at the analysis level. Because there may be no efficient way to consciously identify all of the possible factors that distinguish, for example, capitalism from socialism, some student responses may be unusual and unexpected. If you cannot prepare all possible responses in advance (which will be increasingly unlikely at the higher levels of behavioral complexity) you can prepare yourself psychologically for the diversity of responses that frequently results from analysis questions. Preparing yourself psychologically may mean simply shifting your classroom to a less rigid, more deliberate, and slower paced climate to give yourself some time to evaluate responses on the spot. It may also help to admit to yourself that some of the responses you hear may never have been heard before.

Synthesis

Questions at the synthesis level ask the student to produce something unique or original. Such questions expect students to design a solution, compose a response, or predict an outcome to a problem for which the student has never before seen, read, or heard a response. This level of behavior often is associated with the word *creativity,* which may actually be broader than what is intended here; the creativity that is being sought at the synthesis level is *directed* creativity. Not all unique or original responses, regardless of how creative they may be, will be equally acceptable, however. The facts, rules, and action sequences that have gone before, as well as any analysis questions that may have been posed, will have set up or defined the limits and directions of the synthesis being called for. Therefore, the relationship of synthesis questions to the Type 1 behaviors they will need and the Type 2 behaviors you wish to create should always be obvious to your students. Some action verbs for formulating questions at the synthesis level are:

compare	formulate
create	produce
devise	predict

Some example questions are:

What would an economic system be like that combines the main features of capitalism and socialism?

Other than with the periodic table, how might we predict the missing elements?

How could a paragraph showing ownership be written without using any possessives?

Given a general equation for a curved line, what information would need to be added in order to graph the curve?

This illustrates that even more diversity can be expected with synthesis questions than with analysis questions. This is due to the divergent nature of the questions that are used to teach Type 2 behaviors. This openness is apparent at the analysis level, but it is even more pronounced at the synthesis level. Therefore, your preparation for diversity and your readiness to deal with it will play a predominant role in how your synthesis questions are received by your students. A question that asks for other ways to identify missing elements in the periodic table opens up many different possibilities. Some may not be acceptable (e.g., "consult an astrologer") but others will be (e.g., "analyze minerals from the moon and other planets"). Accept all answers within reason, even though your own solutions may be limited to one or two most efficient, practical, or accurate solutions. Recall that the question was sufficiently open that an acceptable answer need not be contingent on efficiency, practicality, or accuracy. Therefore, the notions of efficiency, practicality, and accuracy might be built up from initial student responses, but not initially expected of them.

Another characteristic of higher level questions is the multiple responses they are likely to generate. Multiple response questions are ones that actively encourage diverse, multiple responses and then use these responses to build increasingly more appropriate answers. Table 8.2 showed different types of questioning sequences, several of which were capable of molding student responses into a form either more expansive or more restrictive than the original point of origin. Diverse multiple responses to synthesis questions can be used to draw out and direct creativity in the direction deemed most profitable, without restricting or narrowing the question itself, as this dialogue illustrates:

TEACHER: In what ways other than from the periodic table might we predict the missing elements?

BOBBY: We could go to the moon and see if there are some elements there we don't have.

BETTY: We could dig down to the center of the earth and see if we find any of the missing elements.

RICKY: We could study debris from meteorites—if we can find any.

TEACHER: Those are all good answers, but what if those excursions to the moon, to the center of the earth, or to a meteor shower were too costly and time consuming? How might we take what elements we already have here on earth to find some new ones?

BETTY: Oh! Maybe we could try experimenting with the elements we do have to see if we can make new ones out of them.

This simple exchange illustrates a funnelling strategy; broad, expansive answers are accepted and then are followed up with a narrower question on the next round. In this manner, the diverse multiple responses that typically result from synthesis and other higher level questions can be used to direct creative responses into gradually more structured avenues of inquiry, thereby contributing to critical thinking.

Evaluation

Questions at this highest level of behavioral complexity require the student to form judgments and to make decisions using stated criteria. These criteria may be subjective (when a personal set of values is used in making a decision) or objective (when scientific evidence or procedures are used in evaluating something). In both cases, however, it is important that the criteria be expressed publicly, that is, articulated in ways that can be understood, although not necessarily valued, by others. Some action verbs that can be used in formulating questions at the evaluation level are:

appraise	assess
judge	defend
decide	justify

Some example questions are:

Using evidence of your own choosing, do capitalist or socialist countries have a higher standard of living?

If accuracy were your sole criterion, how would you compare laboratory analysis of known elements with interplanetary surveys for discovering the missing elements in the periodic table?

Using Rules 1 and 2 for forming possessives and assigning one point for each correct usage, what grade would you give the following student essay?

Given these graphed curved lines, how accurately have the four equations been plotted?

Evaluation questions have the distinct quality of confronting the learner with problems much as they appear in the real world. In this sense, evaluation questions link the classroom to the world outside. Because decisions and judgments are prime ingredients of adult life, it is essential that the experiences provided in the classroom start learners, regardless of their age or maturity level, toward the world in which they will live. Unfortunately, evaluation questions are often reserved for the end of a unit or, sometimes, of an even larger block of instruction. Even more misguided is the notion that evaluation questions are more suited to junior high and high school than to elementary grades. Both misconceptions have done much to reduce the potential impact of evaluation questions on learners and no doubt have contributed to the lower percentage of higher order questions observed in classrooms. If learners are to cope with real world problems, they must learn to do it at the earliest grades and throughout their schooling. Therefore, the ability to ask evaluation questions which can bring the world to your learners at their own level of knowledge and experience is one of the most valued abilities an effective teacher can have.

This ability, however, does not come easily. To be sure, all of the characteristics of the previously discussed higher order questions—diversity of responses, opportunities for open-ended or divergent questioning, and multiple responses—are present in evaluation questions. To these must be added a characteristic that requires the learner to apply a set of criteria in deciding upon the appropriateness of a solution. Notice in the preceding examples that the criteria (or the source from which criteria should come) is identified (e.g., "using evidence of your own choosing," "if accuracy were your sole criterion," "using Rules 1 and 2," "given the graphs"). The more specific these criteria are, and the more familiar your learners are with them, the more actively engaged they will become in answering the question.

It is important to note that evaluation questions can be both convergent or divergent. When you ask "Is the equation $2 + 2 = 4$ correct?", you are asking an evaluation question for which only a single, narrow, correct response is possible. Here, the student's engagement in the learning process may be limited to simply conjuring up a memorized portion of the multiplication table. This evaluation question has far fewer implications for training learners to judge, to make decisions, and to think critically than one that asks, "What kinds of goods and services would be owned by a government under a socialist economic system that would not be owned by a government under a capitalist economic system?" The first question is convergent, focusing on a single, best answer ("Yes, $2 + 2 = 4$ is correct."); the second question is divergent. It allows a range of responses, the acceptability of which could only be judged by applying a set of subjective or objective criteria. The criteria applied in determining the appropriateness of the first question allowed no room for judgment; the criteria used in the second question allowed a great deal of judgment. Decisions and judgments in the form they appear in the real world should guide questions at the evaluation level.

Summary of Question Types

You now are aware of the many levels of questions that can be asked of learners and some of the factors that must be considered in choosing a particular type of question. Much of the preceding portions of the chapter can be summarized by recalling that Type 1 behaviors (those calling for the acquisition of facts, rules, and action sequences) generally are most efficiently taught with the use of convergent questions that have a single best answer (or a small number of easily definable answers). Type 1 behaviors tend to be most effectively learned with a direct instruction model that focuses convergent questions at the knowledge, comprehension, and application levels of behavioral complexity. On the other hand, Type 2 behaviors (those calling for the acquisition of concepts, patterns, and abstractions) generally are most efficiently taught with the use of divergent questions, for which many different answers may be appropriate. Type 2 behaviors tend to be most effectively learned with an indirect instruction model that poses divergent questions at the analysis, synthesis, and evaluation levels of behavioral complexity. Now that you are acquainted with these broad distinctions among types of questions, we will turn to several specific techniques that can help you deliver these questions to your students with ease and perfection.

Using Probes

In chapter 1 you became acquainted with the concept of a probe as one of five catalytic, or helping, behaviors for performing the key behaviors (clarity, variety, task orientation, engagement in the learning process at moderate-to-high rates of success). In this section, we will look at probes in the context of a questioning strategy.

A probe is a question that immediately follows a student's response to a question provided for the purpose of

eliciting clarification of the student's response,

soliciting new information to extend or build upon the student's response, or

redirecting or restructuring the student's response in a more productive direction.

Probes that **elicit clarification** ask students to rephrase or reword a response so that a determination can be made about the appropriate-

ness or correctness of the response. These probes, such as "Could you say that in another way?" or "How would that answer apply in the case of _____?", are intended to get the learner to show more of what is known, thereby exposing the exact amount of understanding possessed by the student. Partially correct answers or correct answers for the wrong reason can be masked under the brief and vague responses often given in the context of a fast-paced and lively classroom discussion. When you are unsure of the amount of understanding that lies beneath a correct response, slow the pace with a probe for clarification.

Probes that **solicit new information** follow a response that is at least partially correct or that represents an acceptable level of understanding. This time, however, the probe pushes the learner's response to a new and more complex level of understanding (e.g., "Now that you've decided the laboratory is the best environment for discovering the missing elements, what kind of experiments would you conduct in this laboratory?" or "Now that you've taken the square root of that number, how could you use the same idea to take its cube root?"). This type of probe builds higher and higher plateaus of understanding by using the previous response as a stepping stone to greater expectations and more complete responses. This involves treating incomplete responses as part of the next higher level response—not as wrong answers. The key to probing for new information is to make your follow-up question only a small extension of your previous question; otherwise, the leap will be too great and the learner will become stymied by what appears to be an entirely new and different question. This type of probe, therefore, requires much of the same process for finding the right answer as does the previously correct question, only this time applied to a different and more complex problem.

Finally, probes can be posed for the purpose of **redirecting** the flow of ideas without the need for awkward and often punishing responses such as "You're on the wrong track," "That's not relevant," or "You're not getting the idea." Probes for redirecting responses into a more productive direction can accomplish the needed shift less abruptly and with less negativity, which can discourage some students from venturing another response. A probe that accomplishes this purpose moves the discussion sideways, setting up a new condition for a subsequent response that does not negate a previous response.

For example, recall that, in the context of our dialogue on socialism in chapter 7, the teacher asked the students for "the kinds of things individuals would likely need to live and prosper." Ricky responds, "You mean like a car or a home of your own." But, since all individuals in a socialist economy might not agree on the value of these for everyone, the teacher had to redirect the discussion to objects more consistent with a socialist economy, without negating the value of the earlier response. She does this by stepping sideways to impose two new conditions to get the discussion back on track: "What types of things could a *group of people,* say the size of a nation, agree on that would be *absolutely essential* for everyone's existence?" This probe successfully leaves behind objects such as cars and homes without ever having to negatively value these responses.

Probing to redirect or restructure a discussion can be a smooth and effortless way of getting learners back on track. Notice how the teacher in the following example blends the use of all three types of probes in the context of a single discussion:

TEACHER: What is the system of grids called by which we can identify the location of any object on the globe? (To begin the questioning)

BOBBY: Latitude and longitude.

TEACHER: Good. What does longitude mean? (To solicit new information)

BOBBY: It's the grids on the globe that . . . go up and down.

TEACHER: What do you mean by *up and down?* (To elicit clarification)

BOBBY: They extend north and south at equal intervals.

TEACHER: OK. Now tell me, where do they begin? (To solicit new information)

BOBBY: Well, I think they begin wherever it's midnight and end where it's almost midnight again.

TEACHER: Let's think about that for a minute. Wouldn't that mean the point of origin would always be changing according to where it happened to be midnight? (To redirect)

BOBBY: Yes, so the grids must start at some fixed point.

TEACHER: Anybody know where they begin? (To solicit new information)

SUE: Our book says the first one marked *0* starts at a place called Greenwich, England.

TEACHER: How can a grid that runs continuously north and south around the globe *start* anyplace, Sue? (To elicit clarification)

SUE: I meant to say that it *runs through* Greenwich, England.

TEACHER: Good. Now let's return to Bobby's point about time. If we have a fixed line of longitude, marked *0,* how might we use it to establish time? (To solicit new information)

BOBBY: Now I remember. Midnight at the *0* longitude—or in Greenwich, England—is called *0* hours. Starting from there, there are timelines drawn around the world, so that when it's midnight at the first timeline, it will be one o'clock back at Greenwich, England; and when it's midnight at the next timeline, it will be two o'clock back at Greenwich, England, and so on.

TEACHER: What does that mean? (To elicit clarification)

BOBBY: Each line equals one hour—so . . . so there must be 24 of them!

TEACHER: It should be no surprise to learn that time determined in reference to the *0* grid of longitude is called Greenwich Mean Time.

Use of Wait Time

An important consideration during questioning and probing is how long to wait before initiating another question. Sometimes a teacher's "wait time" can be as effective in contributing to the desired response as is the question or probe itself, especially when it gives students time to thoughtfully compose an answer of their own. Both too short and too long a wait time can be detrimental to a response—and in the latter case it also wastes valuable instructional time. Obviously, wait time must be longer when the students are expected to think about and to weigh alternative responses (which often occurs during indirect instruction) than it will be when the responses must be correct, quick, and firm (which often occurs during direct instruction). Generally, you should wait *at least three seconds* before either asking another question, repeating the previous question, or calling on another student. Teachers in a research study conducted by Rowe (1974), however, were observed to have waited an average of only about *one second* after having posed a question. Under conditions of indirect instruction where divergent questions are likely to require thinking through and weighing alternatives, up to *15 seconds* of wait time may be appropriate. Rowe (1980), Tobin (1980), and Tobin and Capie (1982) suggest that when wait time is increased to three seconds or longer,

> length of responses increases,
>
> number of voluntary (unsolicited) responses increases,
>
> level of behavioral complexity of responses increases,
>
> students ask more questions,
>
> students show more confidence in the responses, and
>
> students' failure to respond decreases.

These research findings provide impressive testimony to the important role that wait time can have on learners' responses. If only a single piece of advice were to be given to beginning teachers concerning wait time, it would be to *slow down and pause longer between questions and answers than what at first feels comfortable.*

Some Recommendations and Suggestions

The following recommendations and suggestions are based upon the classroom observations of the question-asking behavior of beginning teachers. Countless hours of observation and supervision have confirmed that there are problems in question-asking behavior at all grade levels and in all subject areas. Here are both some of the most frequently observed problems and some suggested remedies.

Raising overly complex, ambiguous, or "double" questions

One of the most frequently observed question-asking problems of beginning teachers is the use of the complex, ambiguous, or "double" question. This is a question that is so long and complicated that the students easily lose track of the main idea of the question by the time it is completed. Sometimes, although unknowingly, the teacher's question contains two (or even more) questions within its complicated structure. Since these questions are delivered orally and are not written, students have no way of rereading the question to gain its full intent. It is unfortunate that sometimes these questions are so complicated that even the teacher cannot repeat the question precisely when it is requested, providing different versions of the same question. Consider the following examples of needlessly complex questions alongside simpler but equally effective revisions.

Example 1

> *Complex Form:* "We all know what the three branches of government are, but where did they come from, how were they devised, and in what manner do they relate?"

This question is actually three questions in one, and requires too long a response if each point in the question were responded to individually. Besides, the first two questions may be redundant—or are they?—while the third is sufficiently vague to bewilder most students. Finally, what if some students do not know or cannot recall the three branches of government? For those students, everything that follows is irrelevant, opening the door to boredom and off-task behavior.

Simpler Form: Recall that there are three branches of government: the executive, judicial, and legislative. What governmental functions are assigned to each by the Constitution?

Example 2
Complex Form: How do single-celled animals propagate themselves and divide up to create similar animal life that look like themselves?

If you were to ask this question, you can be sure that some, if not many, of your students would ask you to repeat the question, in which case you might not remember your own complex wording. This question fails to get to the point quickly and appears to ask the same thing three times (e.g., how do single-celled animals propagate . . . divide up . . . create similar animal life?). This redundancy could easily be mistaken for three separate questions by students struggling to understand single-celled reproduction at an elementary level. State your questions only one way and rephrase later, if need be, when students know that it is the same question being rephrased.

Simpler Form: By what process do single-celled animals multiply?

Example 3
Complex Form: What do you think about the Civil War, or the Vietnam War, or war in general?

Depending on what part of this question a student wants to hear, you may get noticeably different answers. The intention was to raise a question that would provide enough options to get almost any student involved in composing a response; but, unless you intend only to start a controversy, the range of responses will probably be so broad that moving to the next substantive point may be almost impossible. This question may leave students arguing feverishly for the entire period without being able to focus on the real purpose for raising the question in the first

place (e.g., as an introduction to the Civil War, or to unpopular wars, or to the concept of war). In other words, this question is too broad, too open, and too divergent to be of practical value for framing a day's lesson.

Simpler Form: What are the factors that you believe would justify a war among groups within the same nation?

In summary, to avoid overly complex, ambiguous, or double questions:

1. focus your questions on only one idea at a time,
2. state the main idea only once,
3. use language as concrete as possible, and
4. state the question in as few words as possible.

Accepting only the answers you expect
Another common mistake made in posing a question for the first time is to rely almost exclusively on the answer you expect or think you have heard before. In chapter 3 was a discussion of the bias that teachers sometimes have regarding whom they call on, interact with, and otherwise talk to in classroom exchanges. (This is an important source of bias which you might want to review at this time.) However, biases can extend to certain favorite answers as well as to favorite students. When the content you are teaching is new, which is frequently the case during the first year of teaching, you naturally strive to become more secure and confident by raising questions and limiting answers to those with which you are most familiar. Your first reaction will be to discourage responses that are on the edge of the range that you think is appropriate for a given question. This range of responses will be directly related to the openness of the questions you ask. Open questions encourage diversity, and it is this diversity that often catches the beginning teacher off guard and forces an expansive question into a limited one. Note in the following dialogue how this teacher's posture is changed by the nature of the response.

TEACHER: OK, today we will study the early Americans and why they came to America. Why did they come to America?
STUDENT 1: To farm.
TEACHER: No, not to farm.
STUDENT 2: To build houses and churches.
TEACHER: No, that's not right either.

If this exchange were to continue for very long it would no doubt turn many students off, if only because they know that these responses cannot be entirely wrong even if they are not what the teacher wants. What does the teacher want? Probably, the desired answer is that the early Americans came because of religious persecution in their European communities. The last student's response, "to build houses and churches," would have been a perfect opportunity for a probe that simply asked "Why churches?"; unfortunately, this teacher missed that opportunity in favor of waiting for the exact response, being unable or unwilling to build upon existing responses. This teacher may have a long wait, in which case valuable instructional time will be lost by calling on student after student in the hope that the only acceptable answer will eventually emerge. Remember that while answers that are just what you are looking for are always desirable, partially correct answers and even unusual and unexpected answers can become effective additions to the discussion through the use of probes. The solution to this problem is to use probes to build gradually toward your targeted responses.

Not knowing why you are asking a question

Perhaps the most serious error of all in asking questions is either not knowing or forgetting why you are asking a question. Some time has been spent in detailing the types of questions that can be asked. These were convergent questions at the knowledge, comprehension, and application levels of behavioral complexity, and divergent questions at the analysis, synthesis, and evaluation levels. Your first decision is to determine if your lesson is primarily teaching facts, rules, and action sequences or concepts, patterns, and abstractions. If the former is your goal, convergent questions at the knowledge, comprehension, or application levels will probably represent the questions you will ask. If, however, the latter is your goal, divergent questions at the analysis, synthesis, or evaluation levels will usually represent the questions you will ask. This decision strategy is summarized in Figure 8.2.

If you have not determined where you are on Figure 8.2, you are likely to ask the wrong type of question and your questions will lack any logical sequence. They may jump from convergent to divergent and move back and forth from simple recall of facts to the acquisition of concepts and patterns. Your students will find your questions disconcerting, because your ideas will not be linked by any common thread—at least not by one that they can follow—and you will be seen as obscure, vague, remote, or lacking the ability to connect content in meaningful ways. Therefore, it is important that you decide in advance where your questioning strategy is going and then move toward this goal by choosing appropriate questions and levels of behavioral complexity.

Finally, it is important to note that just because your goal may be Type 1 or Type 2 behaviors, this does not mean that you should not vary your questioning strategy across the levels shown on Figure 8.2. Questions should vary within types of learning (e.g., from knowledge to application or from analysis to synthesis) and across types of learning (e.g., from application to analysis). It is important to keep in mind your ultimate goal for the lesson and to choose the best combination of questions to reach that goal.

Answering the question yourself

Another frequently observed problem occurs when a teacher poses a question and then answers his or her own question. Sometimes a student begins a response which the teacher knows is correct, and then is cut off only to hear the remainder of the response supplied by the teacher. Sometimes just the reverse occurs; a stu-

FIGURE 8.2
A decision tree for deciding on the types of questions to ask

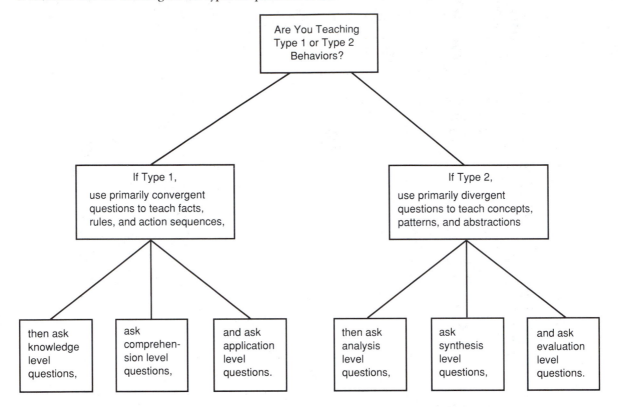

dent begins a response that the teacher knows is wrong and then is cut off by the teacher, who gives the correct response. Needless to say, both outcomes are demoralizing to the student, who either is deprived of the chance to give a right answer or is shown to have a response so incorrect that it is not even worth hearing in its entirety. Although neither of these outcomes may be intended, both are common perceptions on the part of students. Your job is to use student responses to build to other more complex outcomes. Probes that elicit new information, that go beyond that which has already been given by a right answer, or that provide hints and clues after a wrong answer are particularly useful for extending to your students the right to give a full and deliberate response, whether it is right or wrong. Teachers who frequently interrupt stu-

dent responses because of a desire for perfect answers, a dominant personality, or talkativeness, may ultimately produce frustrated learners who never learn to give full and thoughtful responses or to participate voluntarily.

Using questions as punishment

Our final problem, and perhaps the one most difficult to deal with, is the use of questions to punish or to put a student on the defensive. Being asked a question can be a punishment as well as a reward. For example, here are just some ways in which questions have been used as punishment:

1. A student who forgot to do the homework is asked a question from that homework.

2. A student who never volunteers is always asked a question.
3. A student gives a wrong response and then is asked an even harder question.
4. A student who disrupts the class is asked a question for which the answer cannot possibly be known.
5. A student who gives a careless response is asked four questions in a row.

Nearly every teacher has, at one time or another, used questions in one or more of these ways. Interestingly, some teachers do not always see these uses of questions as punishment. Regardless of intent, however, such questions are punishment in that they (a) are unlikely to engage the student actively in meaningful learning, and (b) leave the student with a poorer self-image, less confidence, and more anxiety (and perhaps anger) than was present before the question. These are behaviors that can only impede the learning process and which, therefore, have no place in your repertoire of questioning strategies. Each of the student-centered problems reflected in the examples above could have been handled more effectively, perhaps by

1. Making a list of students who don't do homework.
2. Giving example questions beforehand to students who never volunteer.
3. Giving another try and providing hints and clues to students who give wrong responses until partially correct answers are received.
4. Giving disciplinary sanctions or reprimands to students who disrupt class.
5. Passing quickly to another student after receiving a careless answer.

Ample means are available for dealing with misbehavior; such means are far more effective for correcting misbehavior than are questions. Questions are academic tools that should be prized and protected for their chosen purpose. To misuse them or to use them for any other purpose may affect how your questions will be perceived by your students (e.g., Did I get the hard question because she thinks I'm smart or because I'm being punished?). Such conflicts can drain students of the energy and concentration needed to answer your questions and may forever cast doubts on your motives.

The other side of questions is that they can be implicit rewards when they are used correctly. The opportunity to shine, to know and display the correct answer in front of others, and to be tested and get an approving grade are rewarding experiences for any learner. Consequently, every learner, regardless of ability level or knowledge of a correct response, should periodically experience these emotions. Rather than either ignoring students incapable of responding or considering wrong answers acceptable, a broader criteria than correct/incorrect may occasionally help in getting all students to share in the emotional rewards of answering questions. The most novel, most futuristic, most practical, and most thought-provoking answer may occasionally be rewarded along with the most factually accurate response.

A Final Word

This chapter has included many different aspects of the art of questioning. However, the most important lesson in this chapter is that questioning is a tool for actively engaging your learners in the learning process. All your teaching efforts will meet an untimely end unless you can get your learners to act upon, think about, or work on the content you present in ways that evoke the cognitive processes required by Type 1 and Type 2 learning. Guided practice, review, feedback and correctives, independent study, advance organizers, discussion, and so on are some approaches for setting in motion the cognitive processes necessary for meaningful learning to occur. Questions are another tool to add to your teaching menu. Because of their almost endless variety they may well be the most flexible tool on your menu.

Summing Up

This chapter introduced you to questioning strategies. Its main points were:

1. An effective question is one that evokes a response that actively engages a learner in the learning process.
2. An effective question depends on voice inflection, word emphasis, word choice, and the context in which it is raised.
3. The three most commonly observed teacher behaviors in the classroom are structuring, soliciting, and reacting.
4. Soliciting—or question-asking behavior—encourages students to act upon and think about the structured material as quickly as possible after it has been presented.
5. It has been estimated that from 70–80% of all questions require the simple recall of facts, and from 20–30% require clarifying, expanding, generalizing, and the making of inferences. In other words, as few as only one out of every five questions may require higher level thought processes, even though behaviors at the higher levels of cognitive complexity are among those most frequently required in adult life, at work, and in advanced training.
6. Some of the most common purposes for asking questions include:

   - getting interest and attention
   - diagnosing and checking
   - recalling specific facts or information
   - managerial
   - encouraging higher level thought processes
   - structuring and redirecting learning
   - allowing expression of affect

7. A question that limits a response to a small number of responses or to a single response is called a convergent, direct, or closed question. This type of question teaches the learner to respond in a limited, restrictive manner.

8. A question that has many right answers or a broad range of acceptable responses is called a divergent question. Divergent questions, however, can have wrong answers.
9. The same question can be convergent under one set of circumstances and divergent under another, as when so-called creative answers to a divergent question have been memorized from a list.
10. Research has not established that the use of higher order questions is related to improved performance on standardized achievement tests. However, higher order questions have been found to elicit analysis, synthesis, and evaluation skills, which are among the most sought-after skills in adult life.
11. Questions can be specifically worded for low-ability and mixed-ability learners as well as directed to individuals, groups, or the entire class.
12. Questions may be used in the context of many different sequences, such as funnelling, where increasingly specific conditions are added to an original question, narrowing it to one requiring simple deduction.
13. In addition to being divergent, convergent, and targeted to specific types of learners, questions can be formulated at different levels of cognitive complexity that comprise the knowledge, comprehension, application, analysis, synthesis, and evaluation levels of the cognitive domain.
14. Knowledge questions ask the learner to recall, describe, define, or recognize facts that already have been committed to memory.
15. Comprehension questions ask the learner to explain, summarize, or elaborate upon facts that have been learned.
16. Application questions ask the learner to go beyond the memorization of facts and their translation and to use previously acquired facts and understandings in a new and different environment.
17. Analysis questions ask the learner to break a problem down into its component parts and to draw relationships among the parts.

18. Synthesis questions ask the learner to design or produce a unique or unusual response to an unfamiliar problem.

19. Evaluation questions ask the learner to form judgments and make decisions, using stated criteria for determining the adequacy of the response.

20. A probe is a question that immediately follows a student's response to a question; its purpose is eliciting clarification, soliciting new information, and redirecting or restructuring a student's response.

21. The key to probing for new information is to make the follow-up question only a small extension of the previous question.

22. The time you wait before initiating another question or turning to another student may be as important in actively engaging the learner in the learning process as the question itself. A wait time of at least three seconds should be observed before asking another question, repeating the previous question, or calling on another student.

23. Longer wait times have been associated with longer responses, greater number of voluntary responses, greater behavioral complexity of the response, greater frequency of student questions, and increased confidence in responding.

24. To avoid problems commonly observed in the question-asking behavior of beginning teachers:

  ■ Do not raise overly complex or ambiguous questions that may require several different answers.

  ■ Be prepared to expect correct but unusual answers that may never have been heard before, especially when raising divergent questions.

  ■ Always establish beforehand why you are asking a particular question. Know the complexity of behavior you may expect as a result of the question.

  ■ Never supply the correct answer to your own questions without first probing or prevent a student from completing a response to a question. Use partially correct or wrong answers as a platform for eliciting clarification, soliciting new information, or redirecting.

  ■ Never use questions as a form of embarrassment or punishment. Their use rarely changes misbehavior.

For Discussion and Practice

*1. What is the definition of an effective question as it is used in this chapter?

*2. Identify the chain of events that forms the most frequently observed cycle of teacher-student interaction.

*3. Approximately what percentage of all school time may be devoted to questions and answers?

*4. Approximately what percentage of questions asked require simple recall of facts, and approximately what percentage require clarifying, expanding, generalizing, and the making of inferences?

*5. Identify seven specific purposes for asking questions and give an example of each.

*6. In your own words, what is a divergent question and what is a convergent question? How do they differ with respect to right answers? How are they the same with respect to wrong answers?

7. Using the same question content, give an example of both a convergent and a divergent question.

*8. Explain under what circumstances a divergent question such as, "What propulsion systems might airplanes use in the year 2050?" might actually function as a convergent question.

*9. Explain under what circumstances a convergent question such as, "What is 2 multiplied by 4?" might actually function as a divergent question.

*10. What is the relationship between asking higher order questions to a learner's (a) standardized achievement score, and (b) use of analysis, synthesis, and evaluation skills in thinking through a problem?

11. Using the same question content, compose a question to be directed to a less able learner and another to be directed to a more able learner. How do these two questions differ?

12. Using content familiar to you, compose a sequence of related questions that attempts to funnel student responses. Identify student responses to your questions that make the dialogue "real."

13. Using content familiar to you and Table 8.2 as your guide, compose a sequence of related questions that attempts to extend and lift student responses. Again, identify questions that make the dialogue real.

14. Using the same content area, prepare one question that elicits the appropriate level of behavioral complexity at each of the knowledge, comprehension, application, analysis, synthesis, and evaluation levels of the cognitive domain.

15. In the context of a hypothetical classroom dialogue, provide one example each of a question that attempts to (a) elicit clarification, (b) solicit new information, and (c) redirect or restructure a student's response.

*16. What is meant by the phrase *wait time?* Generally speaking, should beginning teachers work to increase or decrease their wait time?

*17. Identify and give an example of the five most troublesome question-asking problems for the beginning teacher.

Suggested Readings

Doneau, S. (1987). Soliciting. In M. J. Dunkin (Ed.), *International encyclopedia of teaching and teacher education.* New York: Pergamon.
An overview of the many ways teachers can solicit responses from their students during a lesson.

Gall, M. D., Ward, B., Berliner, D., Cahen, I., Winne, P., Elashoff, J., & Stanton, G. (1978). Effects of questioning techniques and recitation on student learning. *American Educational Research Journal, 15,* 175–199.
Results of a research study on the effects of various styles and types of questioning on student behavior.

Hunkins, F. (1976). *Involving students in questioning.* Boston: Allyn & Bacon.
Covers the important aspects of how to get students to ask questions and how to integrate student questions into the instructional dialogue of the classroom.

Martin, J. (1979). Effects of higher order questions on student process and product variables in a single-classroom study. *Journal of Educational Research, 72,* 183–187.
An interesting study that confirms the value of asking higher order (divergent) questions for engaging students in the learning process.

Redfield, D. & Rousseau, E. (1981). A meta-analysis of experimental research of teacher questioning behavior. *Review of Educational Research, 51,* 237–245.
A comprehensive review of research summarizing the most consistent findings on teacher questioning behavior.

Riegle, R. P. (1976). Classifying classroom questions. *Journal of Teacher Education, 27,* 156–161.
Reviews the many ways questions can be classified and shows examples of some important but less often used types of questions.

Ross, H. S. & Killey, J. C. (1977). The effect of questioning on retention. *Child Development, 48,* 312–314.
Results of a research study confirming the close connection between questioning strategies and their effects on what is remembered.

Servey, R. (1974). *Teacher talk: The knack of asking questions.* Belmont, CA: Fearon.
A brief how-to-do-it book on asking different types of questions—has long been popular with teachers.

Tobin, K. (1980). The effect of an extended teacher wait time on science achievement. *Journal of Research in Science Teaching, 17,* 469–475.
An interesting report of research that shows the influence wait time can have on your students' behavior.

9
Motivation and Classroom Management

For most teachers, confronting some sort of discipline problem is a daily occurrence. These problems may include simple infractions of school or classroom rules, or they can involve far more serious events, including disrespect, cheating, obscene words and gestures, and the open display of hostility. This chapter and the next will explore the important related topics of classroom management and discipline. This chapter will present strategies for motivating students and managing the classroom. These strategies assist in *preventing* classroom discipline problems from occurring and in *anticipating* problems that are about to occur. The following chapter will present strategies for maintaining classroom order and discipline, strategies that assist in *altering* or *stopping* disruptive behavior if it occurs.

The best way to deal with classroom discipline problems is to prevent them. The adage "An ounce of prevention is worth a pound of cure" applies to your classroom as well as to your health. The "ounce of prevention" is pre-sented in this chapter in the hope that you will never need the "pound of cure" to be presented in the next.

Motivating Students

The first step in preventing classroom discipline problems is to keep students motivated and, thereby, engaged in the learning process. Motivation is a word used to describe what energizes or directs a learner's attention, emotions, and activity. It often can account for why one student uses free time to complete homework, while another plays baseball; or why one student spends class time writing a "love note," while another eagerly attends to the lesson; or why one student wants to "pick a fight" with another, but the second student declines the invitation. Sports, affections toward the opposite sex, or aggressive needs are just three of the many motivators that can energize and direct students away from the learning process. This chapter shows that other types of motivators, when properly applied, can just as easily energize and direct students toward the learning process.

Motivators are things that influence learners to choose one activity over another (e.g., homework v. baseball, a love note v. paying attention, fighting v. studying). Motivators can be *internal,* or coming from within the individual, such as a natural tendency to be aggressive, as well as *external,* or coming from the environment, such as a need for a boyfriend or girlfriend. Behavior is often the result of the complex blending of these two sources of motivation. When both internal and external sources motivate in the same direction, they have a powerful influence in determining a learner's behavior both in and out of the classroom.

To motivate learners in positive ways, a teacher needs to know some things about them that can represent internal sources of motivation, such as their interests, attitudes, and aspirations. A teacher will also need to know some things about the classroom that can represent external sources of motivation, such as peer-group influences, the physical arrangement of the classroom, and classroom rules. The key to motivating students is bringing these internal and external sources of motivation together in ways that actively engage the students in the learning process. This chapter will explore some of the many ways effective teachers use internal and external sources of motivation to energize and engage their students in the learning process.

Interests, Needs, and Aspirations

Among the most important personal characteristics that can be known about students are their interests, needs, and aspirations. When it comes to motivating learners, these internal sources of motivation must somehow be linked to classroom activities: lessons must be directed at the learners' current level of experience and familiarity with the world around them.

Although it is not often recognized, textbooks and workbooks are written for the hypothetical average student who has no specific interests, needs, and aspirations. Therefore, such books seldom are motivators, in and of themselves, for energizing learners and engaging them in the learning process. What is known about the learners' interests, needs, and aspirations must be blended with the knowledge and facts found in textbooks to produce a sufficient level of motivation. Take a closer look at interests, needs, and aspirations and how they might be put to work in the classroom:

Interest: A focusing of attention on an object, event, or idea that is enjoyable (e.g., cars, football, the opposite sex—but also computers, "live" demonstrations, science fiction)

Need: A perceived lack of something that is important to one's well-being (e.g., a ride to the game, to be seen and noticed, a date for the dance—but also a good grade, recognition from adults, being liked by others)

Aspiration: A wish or longing for a certain kind of achievement (e.g., to be class president, an athlete, a fashion model—but also to be a good student, a scientist, a National Honor Society member)

These three characteristics can account for a learner's classroom performance when differences in intellectual ability seem inadequate to explain this performance (e.g., when an *A* student fails the test while a less able learner does unexpectedly well). Regardless of learners' intellectual abilities, their interests, needs, and aspirations can either accentuate or dampen the effects of their abilities on tests of school achievement. This is never more obvious than when the terms *underachiever* and *overachiever* are used.

The terms *underachiever* and *overachiever* are sometimes used when ability level alone cannot account for a learner's performance on tests of achievement. A designation of *overachiever* may be given to an individual whose school achievement is greater than that predicted by tests of intelligence or scholastic aptitude; the designation of *underachiever* may be given to an individual whose achievement in school is less than that predicted. Although there are no strict rules about when these terms are used, and even the use of the terms is sometimes controversial, it is generally believed that interests, needs, and aspirations (or their lack) can be responsible for individuals performing above or below the level that might be expected from their intelligence or aptitude test scores. If interests, needs, and aspirations can have that powerful an effect on something as important as school achievement, it is worthwhile to take note of them and, whenever possible, plan classroom instruction around them. This process begins by actively soliciting learners' interests, needs, and aspirations at the start of the school year.

At the start of the school year the teacher should convey to the students that they are not destined to be passive participants in the classroom, but that their interests, needs, and aspirations will be the origin of at least some of the things that will be presented during the year. A feeling among your students that their interests, needs, and aspirations will have some influence in the classroom, which is both theirs and yours, will be an important step toward activating their internal sources of motivation. It also is important that students feel that they can make some choices or contributions concerning instructional materials (e.g., contributing readings to a class library), topics to be covered (e.g., choosing some special areas of interest to be covered), and methods of learning (e.g., arranging for special investigations or independent projects), even

if these are conditional upon good behavior and satisfactory achievement in the regular curriculum. Students should not decide for you what and how to teach; but these things should, in part, be influenced by the interests, needs, and aspirations of your learners. There is no better way to find out learners' interests, needs, and aspirations than to ask them. Figure 9.1 suggests some typical questions that can be used as the basis of a class discussion or given in the form of a brief questionnaire at the beginning of the school year.

Some Techniques for Motivating Learners

Some of the ways that instruction can be organized to motivate learners to become actively engaged in the learning process include the use of

contracts,

games and simulations,

self-paced, programmed texts,

grouping,

volunteering, and

grades and tests.

Consider each of these to see how they might be used in the classroom.

Contracts

Contracts can apply to portions of the standard curriculum, or they can apply to special interest areas that are explored in addition to the prescribed curriculum. In either case, work is completed in anticipation of an agreed-upon reward. Contracts exchange work for a grade or some other type of reward (e.g., extra credit, dropping the lowest test score, skipping an assignment). They may involve additional reading, writing, or research, or they may simply state that the reward will be given when performance on regularly scheduled assignments is greater than what is expected based upon past performance. In order

FIGURE 9.1

Some questions for
determining the
interests, needs, and
aspirations of learners

Name _____   Class _____

1. What was the most interesting or exciting thing that you did this past
   summer?
   _____
   _____

2. What job would you like to have when you finish school?
   _____

3. What hobbies or interests do you like to spend time on after school?
   _____

4a. How difficult do you find   4b. How much do you enjoy
    school work?   coming to school?

    _____ very difficult   _____ very much
    _____ fairly difficult   _____ some
    _____ a little difficult   _____ a little
    _____ not difficult   _____ not at all

5. Name something you look forward to about this coming school year.
   _____

6. What worries you the most about this coming school year?
   _____

7a. What subjects do you like   7b. What subjects do you like
    the most?   the least?

    _____   _____
    _____   _____
    _____   _____
    _____   _____

to tap students' interests, needs, and aspirations, the teacher can give them some flexibility in writing their own contracts—for example, they may suggest what additional reading they would like to complete, or what will be written in what style or format, or what type of experiment or research would be undertaken. Students may also be allowed to negotiate how high a level of achievement they must attain, and thereby be awarded points or a grade both for the quantity and for the quality of work completed. Contracts have been especially useful in encouraging less able learners to review fundamental concepts by allowing them to use materials and methods of their own choosing (e.g., reading popular magazines they find particularly interesting) and in stimulating more able learners to go beyond the standard curriculum to acquire inquiry and problem-solving behaviors independently (e.g., conducting an experiment on their own for extra credit) (O'Banion & Whaley, 1981). Most importantly, contracts allow students to match their interests, needs, and aspirations to their own learning styles.

Games and Simulations

Games and simulations are other ways of capturing the attention of learners. With the large-scale availability of computers in schools, games and simulations have taken on added importance as an instructional technique. Because games and simulations usually allow a great deal of independent choice and judgment about how they are carried out, they can become excellent motivators in the classroom. They typically provide pictures of real-life situations that promote the direct involvement of learners in the learning process. Economic theories, forms of government, scientific experiments, and even musical scores have been simulated by computer software in gamelike settings. In addition, spelling, punctuation, and word choice games are available at different grade levels; they motivate learners during traditionally boring and repetitive tasks. Although games and simulations will make up only a small portion of your total instructional time, they are valuable assets when they can be matched to your learners' interests, needs, and aspirations.

Self-paced, Programmed Texts

These are perhaps the most popular motivators used in classrooms today. Programmed texts break content into small pieces and present the learner with immediate feedback about the correctness of the response to each piece, which is called a frame. Although more able students typically find them boring due to their slow and repetitive pace, programmed texts often are successful in getting less able learners to master basic facts and understandings that would not have been acquired through full-class instruction (Bunderson & Faust, 1976). As an extra bonus, less able learners sometimes can be given an assignment in a self-paced text while average and above-average students complete more advanced assignments. Self-paced materials can contribute to a high level of motivation by providing a non-threatening, individualized context in which learning can take place.

Grouping

Another motivator is the ability or interest group. When students are assigned to groups containing members much like themselves, generally they will work harder and be more attentive to the learning task (Sharan, 1980). One of the most frequent comments of poorly motivated learners is "I can't do the work." Whether or not they can do the work may be less important than *why* they do not try to do the work. Many times, fear of failure is the reason. To avoid the embarrassment of failure, the student avoids even starting to work, sometimes in favor of off-task or disruptive behavior. Grouping by abilities (e.g., less able, average, more able), interests (e.g., practical, academic), needs (e.g., facts, problem-solving skills) can break down a fear of failure and get the learner to begin to sample the learning task. If the groups have been properly composed of similar students and if the materials are appropriate to the group, the student is likely to continue sampling until the task is completed.

Volunteering

The use of volunteers has not always been recognized as a motivational strategy, but it sometimes works when nothing else does. As simple as this strategy seems, it has been known to energize even the most reluctant of learners. The secret to this strategy lies not in a simple call for volunteers but in the design of the task for which students are asked to volunteer. By creating an appealing but instructive task at the current level of functioning of poorly motivated learners and asking for their assistance, the teacher can provide a sense of pride and accomplishment that can pique a student's interest in a topic. For example, volunteers can be asked to search for elementary spelling and punctuation errors in other students' papers, to prepare a practical demonstration about something with which they are especially familiar, or to serve as tutors to those who know less; these tasks can provide a sense of immediacy and accomplishment which may motivate some learners, who might otherwise be disinterested and inattentive, to become engaged in the learning process.

Grades and Tests

Finally, note the role of grades and tests in motivating learners. Grades and tests are included as motivators with the understanding that, when used for motivating learners, they be used selectively. As you have seen, grades and tests can be used for many different purposes, such as to check progress, to diagnose weaknesses, to evaluate performance, and to review content. To these can be added *to motivate*, a use which is not entirely independent of these other purposes. Tests become motivators, however, only when their difficulty level allows for moderate-to-high rates of success. In other words, tests specifically prepared and administered to raise the motivation level of learners should be of minimal difficulty. Grades and tests can be incentives to work harder as well as to stop working altogether. Difficult tests, although sometimes needed and inevitable, may act as a disincentive for some types of learners.

Students associate grades with reinforcement, both internal (e.g., a sense of accomplishment) and external (e.g., praise from parents). But a poor test grade can have a double edge. For some students it may be all the reason that they need for giving up, while for others it may be all the reason that they need for studying harder. Frequent tests whose difficulty level allows for moderate-to-high success rates have been associated with more frequent attendance in class, greater amounts of work being completed outside of class, and higher achievement on school tests (Fitch, Drucker, & Norton, 1957). However, the frequent use of difficult tests that result in low success rates have been associated with high levels of student anxiety, more self-doubt, and greater uncertainty (Dowaliby & Schumer, 1973). Tests that work best as motivators tend to cover recently learned material for which most students have an adequate grasp. These progress checks or review quizzes provide a timely reward for staying on top of homework and class

exercises as well as an incentive to continue to work hard to maintain an impressive string of good marks.

Less Formal Ways of Motivating Learners

In addition to using contracts, games and simulations, self-paced texts, grouping, volunteering, and grades and tests to increase the attention and motivation of your learners, there are many less formal means of accomplishing this same end. Here are some other ways of motivating learners that have proven to be effective.

Using Praise and Encouragement

The most efficient means for motivating and engaging students in the learning process is the use of praise and encouragement. Surprisingly, the use of praise occupies relatively little class time of most teachers (Brophy & Good, 1986). Wragg and Wood (1984) report that, on the average, only about 2% of a teacher's day is devoted to any kind of praise. A simple reply, such as "Well done," "That was good," or "Good work; keep it up," can be a particularly effective motivator when it is applied *consistently* and represents an *honest appraisal* of the learner's true achievement. These simple verbal responses tell the student that the reward is contingent upon appropriate performance. More importantly, it tells the learner that by producing the correct response, he or she can control the flow of reward. When consistently applied, the link between the performance and the reward can become strong enough that a need to achieve is created; this occurs when the link becomes so internalized that much of the behavior of the learner is directed by the expectation of the next reward that comes from a correct or acceptable response. There is little doubt among behavioral psychologists that a reward that is contingent upon an appropriate behavior increases the frequency of that behavior. Since praise is a strategy that is always available to the teacher, it can be one of the most effective means of motivating learners—when it is applied consistently and immediately after an acceptable response.

Providing Explanations

Another effective device for motivating learners is to explain why a certain request or assignment is being given. Learners who know the reasons behind a request, even if they may not fully understand it or agree with it, are more likely to work on the assignment earnestly and to complete it. In a study reported by Wragg and Wood (1984), relatively few teachers were observed providing any kind of explanation for why a particular work assignment was given, but students appreciated the explanations when they were given and responded with renewed motivation. When assignments are lengthy or particularly difficult, placing them in perspective (e.g., "This assignment will help prepare you for the end of the chapter test," or "We are doing this exercise to check on our basic skills so that we will not have difficulty with our next topic") can be an important external source of motivation. As simple and as brief as these explanations are, they inform your learners that you think highly of their abilities to reason and that they naturally want to know the reasons behind what you are doing. These explanations also loosen up the sometimes rigid teacher-student authority structure against which some students naturally rebel. By treating your students much like you would treat any adult, they will come to see your assignments as a means to an end and not as arbitrary orders, which too often are misconstrued as an effort to punish and control. When punishment or control is perceived to be the motivation, it is likely that learners will respond begrudgingly and with a lack of motivation.

Offering to Help

Another way to motivate learners is through frequent offers of help. Not all students may require individual assistance, but all students will appreciate knowing that assistance is available if it is needed. Some students fail to start assignments or to take them seriously because they fear being unable to complete them. For these students, off-task or disruptive behavior may be far safer than possibly losing self-respect or being ridiculed because they are not able to understand an assignment or to complete it correctly. Even when these students do begin the activity, their anxiety and self-doubts usually bring their engagement in the learning process to a halt at the slightest difficulty. Whether many or only a few of your learners will actually need your assistance, the warmth and support that is implied by your offer to help goes a long way toward getting all of your learners to start an assignment with equal and sufficient motivation. The assistance given to individual students, however, should be brief and focused directly on the problem so that instruction time is not monopolized by any one student or set of students. Not only must an offer of assistance be genuine, but it must be given so that students feel that help will be available when a problem arises.

Accepting Diversity

The classroom is likely to be a microcosm of the world outside; the variety of people, ideas, needs, habits, and cultures that can be found in a community will probably not stop at the classroom door. Although students may have similar ability levels, they are likely to be vastly different in many other ways. Perhaps more devastating to students' motivation than anything else is a teacher's unwillingness to accept and be tolerant of the natural diversity in interests, needs, and aspirations that exist in the classroom. Because teachers often come from a narrower social stratum than do their students, teachers will be confronted with values, habits, dress, and life-styles that are different than those to which they are accustomed. Infractions of school rules and unacceptable dress and personal habits that impede the learning process should not be tolerated, regardless of their origins. However, the teacher's ability to accept the learners for who and what they are, regardless of how different that may be from the teacher's own experience, can be an important motivating factor for at least some of the students. An intolerant attitude, however subtle and hidden the teacher may think it is, will create an almost immediate sense of isolation among some of your learners; this will extend to their reluctance, resistance, and even refusal to complete the assignments given. Once an "I'm different from you" attitude prevails in a classroom, experience reveals that almost any overture on a teacher's part to break the ice probably will not be successful. If students feel a sense of futility in being able to gain your unconditional acceptance, they are unlikely to give you the respect you will need to conduct your classroom in an orderly and efficient manner. Tolerance for the diversity of life-styles, attitudes, and values that are likely to exist among your learners can be an important motivating force in your classroom as well as an example of how your students, who must one day live and work in a diverse democratic society, should behave toward others.

Emphasizing Reward, Not Punishment

Finally, it is important to note the difference between the use of reinforcement, or incentives, and the use of punishment, or aversives, in motivating your learners. It is often natural in a school setting to set an aversive tone—to say why we *should not* do something rather than why we *should* do something. Recall how frequently you have heard phrases similar to:

If you don't study, you'll flunk the course.

Failure to do the homework will mean 5 points off.

Do it right the first time, or you'll have to do it over.

If you fail to understand it today, you'll have to get it on your own later on.

If it's too difficult, you shouldn't be here.

If you think I'm going too fast, you must not have studied.

If you don't get it, we will drill and practice it until you do get it.

It is natural in a superordinate-subordinate environment such as school for those in authority to reinforce the existing structure with penalties for failing to comply with it. However, when this is the only form of incentive for good conduct, it can be detrimental to the motivation of learners. Learners generally will be far more responsive to rewards for producing acceptable behavior than to punishment for not producing it. Although a penalty-oriented structure may work well in the military, it is unlikely to be as effective as a reward-oriented structure in the classroom.

Unless special circumstances prevail (e.g., in times of crisis), rewards are more effective than punishments in getting individuals to behave appropriately. Television advertisers learned this lesson early when they discovered, to their surprise, that the rewards of having fresh, clean teeth were more persuasive in getting people to change brands of toothpaste than were the negative consequences of ugly tooth decay. When negative consequences in the form of penalties provoke high levels of anxiety and fear of the consequences, they become dysfunctional in motivating behavior. The implications of research in the world of advertising should not be lost on educators: It is more effective to inform learners of the consequences of engaging in appropriate behavior than it will be to enumerate and dwell upon the consequences of misbehavior. Although both rewards and penalties are necessary, the emphasis placed on rewards (or on the positive consequences of performing the right behavior) should always outweigh the emphasis placed on enumerating penalties for misbehavior. Consider the restatement of the preceding phrases to emphasize reward and not punishment:

Let's not forget to do the studying. It will make the lectures a lot more meaningful.

If you do all the homework, the tests will be easy. There will be a 5-point penalty, however, for homework not turned in.

Be careful to follow the directions carefully. Otherwise, you may have to do it over.

Listen carefully today, because it will be easier to understand my explanation now than if you have to get it on your own.

Tell me if this assignment is too difficult. That will help us decide on what to do next.

I may be going too fast for some of you. If so, you may want to reexamine how much study time you should be devoting to this subject.

Listen and study hard so that you know the material well. That way, we will not have to practice any more.

Table 9.1 summarizes the five informal motivational devices and provides some suggestions for their use.

Establishing an Effective Classroom Climate

Classroom climate is the atmosphere or mood in which interactions between teacher and students take place. Classroom climate, for example, will determine the manner and degree to which a teacher will exercise authority, show warmth and support, encourage competitiveness, and allow for independent judgment and choice. Although seldom recognized, the climate or atmosphere of the classroom is a matter of choice just as instructional methods are a matter of choice.

It is unfortunate that in many classrooms the climate is determined haphazardly, allowed to develop randomly, depending on what is occurring at the moment. This is not the case in a well-managed classroom. This section will discuss two

TABLE 9.1
Some motivators and their appropriate uses

Motivator	Use phrases such as . . .	Avoid phrases such as . . .
Using praise and encouragement	You've got it.	That's a dumb answer.
	Good work.	You're being lazy again.
	Good try.	I can see you never study.
	That was quick.	You can never pay attention, can you?
Providing explanations	The reason this is so important is . . .	Today you will have to learn this, or else . . .
	We are doing this assignment because . . .	Complete this excercise; otherwise, there'll be trouble.
	This will be difficult, but it fits in with . . .	This is a long assignment, but you'll just have to do it.
	Experience has shown that without these facts the next unit will be very difficult.	We must cover this material, so let's get going.

TABLE 9.1
(*Concluded*)

Motivator	Use phrases such as . . .	Avoid phrases such as . . .
Offering to help	Should you need help, I'll be here.	You should be able to do this on your own.
	Ask if you need help.	If you have to ask for help, you must not have studied.
	I'll be walking around; catch me if you have a problem.	Please don't ask a dumb question.
	Don't be afraid to ask a question if you're having trouble.	Raise your hand only if you're stuck on a difficult problem.
Accepting diversity	That's not the answer I expected, but I can see your point.	That's not the kind of answer we can accept around here.
	That's not how I see it, but I can understand how others might see it differently.	I've never heard that expression before—so let's not start something new.
	This is not something I'm familiar with. Where did you get that idea?	Please use ideas that fit in with what I say in class.
	That is not a word I've heard before. Tell us what it means.	Don't ever use foreign words I haven't heard before.
Emphasizing reinforcement and reward	All homework completed means five extra points.	Five points off for missing homework.
	If you get a *C* or better on all the tests, I'll drop the lowest grade.	If you have less than a *C* average on all your tests, you'll have to take an extra test.
	Those who complete all the exercises on time can go to the learning center.	If you don't complete the exercise on time, there can be no use of the learning center.
	If you have a *C* average, you get to choose any topic for your term paper.	If you don't have a *C* average, you must choose your term paper topic from a resticted list of difficult topics.

related aspects of an effective classroom climate: The **social environment** pertaining to the patterns of interaction to be promoted in the classroom and the **organizational environment** pertaining to the physical or visual arrangement of the classroom. Both of these aspects are a matter of choice; they can be altered to create just the right climate for the proper objective.

The Social Environment

The social environment that is created may vary from authoritarian, in which the teacher is the primary provider of information, opinions, and instruction, to laissez-faire, in which the students become the primary providers of information, opinions, and instruction. Between these extremes lies the middle ground in which teacher and students share responsibilities; students are given freedom of choice and judgment under the direction of the teacher. Although many variations on these themes are possible, the variation chosen will have pronounced effects on what can and cannot take place in the classroom. For example, a group discussion might be a colossal failure in a rigid authoritarian climate, because students will have been given clues that their opinions are less important than the teacher's, that teacher talk and not student talk should take up most of the instructional time, and that the freedom to express oneself spontaneously is the right of the teacher but not of students. In a more open atmosphere this same attempt at discussion might well be a smashing success, because all the ingredients of a good discussion—freedom to express one's opinion, high degree of student talk, and spontaneity—have been provided by the classroom climate.

The social atmosphere you create, whether authoritarian, laissez-faire, or somewhere between these extremes, will determine the extent to which you see yourself as (a) a commander-in-chief who carefully controls and hones student behavior by organizing and providing all of the learning stimuli, (b) a translator or summarizer of the ideas provided by students, or (c) an equal partner with students in creating ideas and problem solutions. Consider the effects of each climate and how it can be created.

The effective teacher not only can use a variety of teaching strategies, but also can create a variety of classroom climates. However, the ability to create a certain climate will always be less important than the ability to change the climate when the objectives and the situation demand. Although early research in the field of social psychology tried to identify the type of climate most conducive to individual behavior (Lewin, Lippitt, & White, 1939), the results suggest that each distinctive climate has its advantages as well as disadvantages, depending on the intended goals. Because goals will change from lesson to lesson and from week to week, so too must the classroom climate that supports the goals. When goals have changed but the classroom climate has not, the stage has been set for off-task, disruptive, and even antagonistic behavior among students.

Several ways have already been suggested which you can use to vary your authority—and that of your students—in accordance with your objectives. These variations correspond not only with how much or how little you wish to relinquish your authority and, therefore, your control of the learning process, but also how competitive, cooperative, or individualistic you wish the interactions among members of your class to be. These three conditions are illustrated in Table 9.2.

As a teacher moves from a competitive to a cooperative and, finally, to an individualistic setting, greater amounts of authority and control over the learning process will be relinquished until, in the individualistic mode, the student has almost sole responsibility for judging her or his own work. Note also that an individualistic mode all but eliminates student expressions of opinion, student talk, and spontaneity of responses, all of which are encouraged and promoted in a cooperative climate. Detailed seatwork assignments in which students practice independently are representative of the individualistic mode, group discussion in which both students and teacher pose questions and answers is representative of the cooperative mode, and drill and practice in which students respond to the teach-

TABLE 9.2
Three types of classroom climate

Social climate	Definition	Example activity	Authority vested in students	Authority vested in teacher
Competitive	Students compete for right answers among themselves or with a standard established by the teacher. The teacher is the sole judge of the appropriateness of a response.	Drill and practice	None	To organize the instruction, present the stimulus material, and evaluate correctness of responses
Cooperative	Students engage in dialogue that is monitored by the teacher. The teacher systematically intervenes in the discussion to sharpen ideas and move the discussion to a higher level.	Small and large group discussion	To present opinions, to provide ideas, and to speak and discuss freely and spontaneously	To stimulate the discussion, arbitrate differences, organize and summarize student contributions
Individualistic	Students complete assignments monitored by the teacher. Students are encouraged to complete the assignment with the answers they think are best. Emphasis is on getting through and testing one's self.	Independent seatwork	To complete the assignment with the best possible responses	To assign the work and see that orderly progress is made toward its completion

er's questions are representative of the competitive mode. Your control and authority and the behaviors you can expect from your students will differ among these social climates in ways indicated in Table 9.2.

In addition to encouraging the proper climate for a given instructional activity (e.g., drill and practice, group discussion, or seatwork), the teacher must decide to which segments of the class each of these climates will apply. Figure 9.2 suggests that each climate can be applied to the full class, to groups, and to individuals with equal effectiveness. For example, it is not necessary that all group discussions be conducted in a cooperative climate. Subgroups can be formed to compete against each other in a gamelike atmosphere (see Cell 21 of Figure 9.2), or individuals can work in a cooperative arrangement by exchanging papers and correcting each other's errors (Cell 32). Likewise, the entire class can be asked to perform seatwork in lock-step fashion as though the class were a single individual (Cell 13), subgroups can be asked to work as independently functioning teams (Cell 23), and different individuals can be teamed in pairs to compete with each other (Cell 31). Although some cells in Figure 9.2 may be more popular than others, many different arrangements of students and climates are possible, depending on the instructional goals. Your job is to ensure that the degree of authority you impose (e.g., the expression of student opinion you allow, the amount of time you devote to student talk, and the spontaneity with which you want your students to respond) matches your instructional goal.

The Organizational Environment

In addition to arranging the social climate in the classroom, the teacher must also arrange the

FIGURE 9.2
Targets for three types of classroom climates

	Competitive	Cooperative	Individualistic
Full Class	Students compete with other students by having the correct answer when it's their turn. 11	Students are allowed to call out hints or clues when a student is having difficulty finding the right 12	The entire class recites answers in unison. 13
Groups	Subgroups compete against each other as opposing teams. 21	Subgroups work on different but related aspects of a topic combining their results into a final report to the class. 22	Each subgroup completes its own assigned topic which is independent of the topics assigned the other supgroups. No shared report is given to the class. 23
Individual	Individuals compete with each other by having to respond to the same question. The quickest most accurate response "wins." 31	Pairs of individuals cooperate by exchanging papers, sharing responses, or correcting each other's errors. 32	Individuals complete seat work on their own without direct teacher involvement. 33

physical climate of the classroom. It goes without saying that a classroom should be attractive, well-lighted, comfortable, and colorful, but, aside from a colorful bulletin board and a neat and clean appearance, you may have very little influence over the external features of your classroom (e.g., paint, lighting, windows, and even such things as the availability of bookshelves and file cabinets). Attempts to improve these external conditions are always worth a try, but do not be surprised if repeated calls to the custodian are in vain. It is not unusual for a teacher to bring essential items, such as a clock, bookcase, file cabinet, rug, or pedestal stool to the classroom at the beginning of the year and take them home again for the summer. What may be more important than these items, however, is the way the internal features (the desks, chairs, and other items available) of the classroom are arranged. Students quickly get used to and accept the external features of a classroom, regardless of their limitations, but the internal arrangement of the classroom will affect your students every day of the school year.

The most flexible arrangement of the furniture in a classroom is one in which the teacher's desk is at the front of the room and the student desks are aligned in rows. Although it may seem strange to associate this traditional format with flexibility, it is the most flexible arrangement; it can be used to create either competitive, cooperative, or individualistic environments, although not always with equal effectiveness. This fact, plus the difficulty of rearranging classroom furniture every time a change in social climate is desired, makes the traditional classroom arrangement almost as popular today as it was 50 years ago.

There are times, however, when the arrangement is changed to encourage a more cooperative, interactive, and group sharing climate. Such a classroom arrangement has many variations that depend on the external features of the classroom and available furniture, but one such model is shown in Figure 9.3.

The important feature to note in this arrangement is the deliberate attempt to get people together. The barriers to interpersonal sharing and communication that sometimes result from the rigid alignment of desks are avoided in this setting by the more informal, but still systematic, arrangement of classroom furniture. As the internal features of the classroom turn from traditional to this less formal arrangement, so too will the social climate of the classroom change. Since the arrangement of desks, tables, and chairs shown in this arrangement suggests that interpersonal communication and sharing is permitted, increased interpersonal communication and sharing will undoubtedly occur—whether this is desirable or not.

From such an arrangement one can expect more expression of student opinion, increased student talk, and greater spontaneity in student responses. This emphasizes the important notion that *the social climate created by words and deeds should always match the organizational climate created by the physical arrangement of the classroom*. It also explains why the traditional or formal classroom has remained so popular. A cooperative climate (e.g., for conducting a group discussion) can always occur in a formal classroom, but a competitive climate (e.g., for drill and practice) becomes exceedingly difficult in a less formal arrangement. This is not a reason to abandon the appeal of a less rigid classroom arrangement, but only to use it with a firm grasp of the student behavior it is likely to promote and accentuate. It is, of course, always refreshing to change the internal arrangement of a classroom from time to time for the sake of variety; this can be an effective psychological boost for both teacher and students in the midst of a long and arduous school year. Keep in mind, however, that time and effort allow for only so much back-and-forth switching. A compromise might be struck by maintaining the basic nature of the formal classroom but, space permitting, setting aside one or two less formal areas (e.g., a learning center or group discussion table) for times when the instructional goals call for interpersonal communication and sharing.

FIGURE 9.3

A classroom arrangement conducive to group work

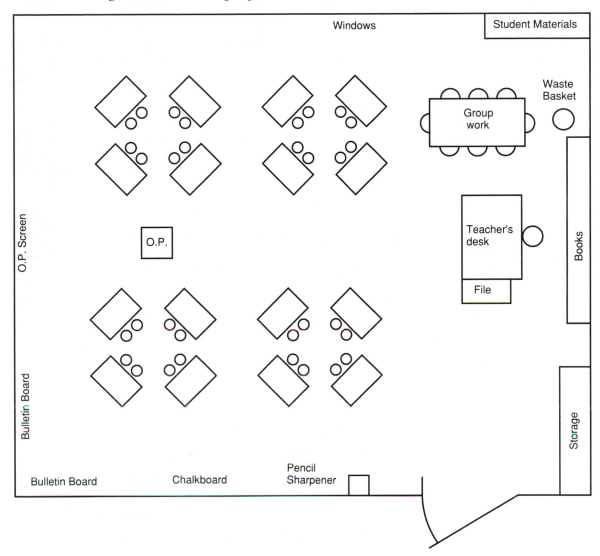

Establishing Rules and Procedures

Establishing rules and procedures to reduce the occurrence of classroom discipline problems is one of the most important classroom management activities. These rules and procedures, which should be formulated prior to the first school day, are a commitment to providing the ounce of prevention in order to avoid having to provide a pound of cure. Because different types of rules and procedures are needed for effectively managing a classroom, the rules you will need have been divided into four different categories. These are

Rules related to academic work

Rules related to classroom conduct

Rules that must be communicated your first teaching day

Rules that can be communicated later

Rules pertaining to 27 different areas of classroom management are shown in Figure 9.4.

Figure 9.4 indicates many of the areas for which you will need to communicate rules either on the first day of class or shortly thereafter. The rules in each of these categories need not be communicated to the students all at the same time or in the same way. For example, some rules are best held until just the right opportunity presents itself to reinforce the rule (e.g., when a visitor comes to the door); others should be communicated the first day of class (e.g., how to respond or speak out) or shortly thereafter (e.g., when to complete make-up work). Rules can be communicated orally in the form of a handout, placed on the bulletin board, or shown on an overhead projector. Regardless of how or when a rule may be communicated, however, you will need to consider the problem area and compose a rule for it prior to the first day of school.

Not all rules must or even should be communicated to your learners the first day of class, but some must be. In the top half of Figure 9.4 are identified those areas for which rules are most commonly needed the very first day of class, either because students will ask about them or because incidents are likely to arise requiring their use. Notice that these rules are divided into conduct and work rules. For the elementary grades rules pertaining to most of these two areas should be presented orally, provided in the form of a handout, and posted for later reference by the students. In these grades they can forget oral messages quickly—or choose to ignore them if there is no physical representation of the rule as a constant reminder. In the later elementary grades and junior high grades, the teacher's re-

FIGURE 9.4
Classroom rules related to conduct and work

	Rules related to classroom conduct	Rules related to academic work
Rules that need to be communicated first day	1. where to sit 2. how seats are assigned 3. what to do before the bell rings 4. responding, speaking out 5. leaving at the bell 6. drinks, food and gum 7. washroom and drinking privileges	8. materials required for class 9. homework completion 10. make-up work 11. incomplete work 12. missed quizzes and examinations 13. determining grades 14. violation of rules
Rules that can be communicated later	15. tardiness/absences 16. coming up to desk 17. when a visitor comes to the door 18. leaving the classroom 19. consequences of rule violation	20. notebook completion 21. obtaining help 22. notetaking 23. sharing work with others 24. use of learning center and/or reference works 25. communication during group work 26. neatness 27. lab safety

citation of the rules while students copy them into their notebooks may be sufficient; for high-school students simply hearing the rules may be sufficient, as long as they are posted for later reference.

Although not all "first day" rules will be equally important, and other rules may have to be added as special circumstances require, rules pertaining to responding and speaking out, making up work, determining grades, and violation of due dates are among the most important. It is in these areas that confusion often occurs on the very first day. For example, some of the issues you will need to consider in these four rule areas are

Rule Area	Issues
Responding, speaking out	■ Must hands be raised? ■ Are other forms of acknowledgment possible (e.g., head nod)? ■ What will happen if a student speaks when others are speaking? ■ What will the teacher do about shouting or using a loud voice?
Make-up work	■ Will make-up work be allowed? ■ Will there be penalties for not completing it? ■ Will it be graded? ■ Whose responsibility is it to know the work is missing?
Determining grades	■ What percentage will quizzes and tests contribute to the total grade? ■ What percentage will class participation count? ■ When will notification be given of failing performance? ■ How much will home-work count?
Violation of due dates	■ What happens when repeated violations occur? ■ Where can a student learn the due dates if she or he was absent? ■ What penalties will there be for copying another's assignment? ■ Will make-up work be required when a due date is missed?

A few moments of thought before these issues are raised in class can avoid embarrassing pauses and an uncertain response when a student asks a question. You may want to identify alternative issues for the remaining rule areas in Figure 9.4 and to extend those just listed.

The bottom half of Figure 9.4 identifies rule areas for which rules can be communicated as the situation arises. Some of these are specific to a particular situation (e.g., safety during a lab experiment, notebook completion, obtaining help) and are best presented in the context to which they apply. They will be more meaningful and more easily remembered *when there is a circumstance or incident which applies to the rule and aids in its retention*. Many other rules in these areas, however, are likely to be needed in the first few days or weeks of school (e.g., tardiness, absences; leaving at the bell; notetaking). Even though these rules may not be communicated during the first day of school, they are usually required so soon afterward that you must compose a procedure for them prior to your first class day.

Some of the most troublesome behaviors in this category include a student getting out of his or her seat, communicating during group work, completing in-class assignments early, and violating rules. Some issues to be considered for these behaviors are

Behavior	Issues
Getting out of seat	■ When is out-of-seat movement permissible? ■ When can a student come to the teacher's desk?

Communicating during group work	■ When can reference books or learning centers be visited?
	■ What if a student visits another?
	■ Can a student leave an assigned seat?
	■ How loud should a student speak?
	■ Who determines who can talk next?
	■ Will there be a group leader?
Early completion of in-class assignments	■ Can work for other classes or subjects be done?
	■ Can a newspaper or magazine be read?
	■ Can the next exercise or assignment be worked on?
	■ Can a student rest her or his head on the desk?
Rule violation	■ Will names be written on the board?
	■ Will extra work penalties be assigned?
	■ Will you have after-class detention?
	■ When will a disciplinary referral be made?

It is always a secure feeling to know that you have created procedures for dealing with many possible rule areas, but unless the rules you create are communicated clearly and applied consistently, all your work in making them will be meaningless. Consistency is one of the most important reasons why some rules are effective in controlling and directing the behavior of learners while others are not. Rules, once formulated, actually can become a double-edged sword: They can at one moment work to control and manage your classroom and at another show you in the poorest light. No one likes a rule that is not en-

forced or one that is not applied evenly and consistently over time; this results in a loss of prestige and respect for the person who has created the rule and has the responsibility for carrying it out.

There can be many reasons why a particular rule is not applied consistently. However, Emmer, Evertson, Sanford, Clements, & Worsham (1984) suggest that among the most frequent of these are the following:

1. The rule is not workable or appropriate. It does not fit a particular context or is not reasonable, given the nature of the individuals to whom it applies.
2. The teacher fails to monitor students closely enough so that some individuals violating the rule are caught while others are not.
3. The teacher does not feel strongly enough about the rule to be persistent about its implementation, and thus makes many exceptions to the rule.

When a teacher realizes that any of the preceding conditions apply, he or she should begin to think about changing the rule. One cannot state flatly that rules are made to be broken, but it is true that even good rules should be altered, changed, or even abandoned when circumstances change. To allow a rule to be repeatedly ignored or broken will have the worst possible effect on your ability to manage your classroom effectively; on the other hand, to rigidly cling to a rule that obviously is not working or is not needed will have an equally detrimental effect. When a rule is unworkable or inappropriate for particular students or a particular classroom situation, modify the rule. Be sure, however, to give the rule a chance by keeping it in effect for a while after you first suspect it may not be working. Keep in mind that no one likes rules and that almost all of your students would prefer not having any, but that does not mean the rule is not working or needed. *The inability to enforce the rule over a reasonable period of time is the best sign a change may be needed.*

When a teacher cannot monitor a situation

closely enough to enforce a rule, another kind of change may be necessary. Of course, not every infraction of a rule can be observed, but when a sufficient number of infractions are overlooked so that the response to the rule is inconsistent, some changes may be in order. If you find yourself being inconsistent about a rule, be fair when you finally discover an infraction. Sometimes it is all too easy to purge your guilt for not catching past infractions by overreacting to the person finally caught disobeying a rule. Overreacting in such cases can be as damaging to your respect as is missing the prior infractions. Keep in mind that minor deviations in a rule may not be worth the effort to respond when (a) it would interrupt the lesson and possibly cause even a greater violation to the rule or (b) it is only momentary and not likely to recur. However, when problems in applying a rule persist over time, either your viligance in looking for infractions of the rule should be stepped up or you should adjust the rule to allow for more flexibility in how you respond to it (e.g., coming up to the desk without permission for help may be acceptable, but coming up just to talk is not).

Problem Areas in Classroom Management

One of the purposes of effective classroom management is to keep learners actively engaged in the learning process. Active engagement means getting the learners to work with and act upon the material presented to them as evidenced by, for example, carefully attending to the material, progressing through seatwork at a steady pace, participating in class discussions, and being attentive when called upon. This section will describe four events that are particularly crucial for keeping students actively engaged in the learning process: *monitoring students, making transitions, giving assignments,* and *bringing closure* to lessons. Following are some effective classroom management practices in each of these areas.

Monitoring Students

Monitoring is the process of observing, mentally recording, and, when necessary, redirecting or correcting students' behaviors. Monitoring occurs when you look for active, alert eyes during discussion sessions, faces down and directed at the book or assignment during seatwork, raised hands during a question-and-answer period, and, in general, signs that indicate the learner is participating in what is going on. These signs of engagement (or their absence) can indicate when changes may be needed in the pace with which you are delivering the content, in the difficulty of the material, or even in the activity itself.

Kounin (1970) used the word *withitness* to refer to a teacher's ability to keep track of many different signs of engagement at the same time. One of the most important distinctions between effective and ineffective classroom managers as observed by Kounin was the degree to which they exhibited withitness. Effective classroom managers who exhibited withitness were aware of what was happening in all parts of the classroom and were able to see different things happening in different parts of the room at the same time. Furthermore, these effective classroom managers were able to *communicate this awareness to their students.*

Although few of us are blessed with eyes in the backs of our heads—or are capable of detecting many different types of behaviors, even when they occur in front of our heads—there are several simple ways of increasing withitness and the extent to which students are kept actively engaged in the learning process.

One such way is for a teacher to increase his or her physical presence through the use of eye contact. When eye contact is limited to only a portion of the classroom, withitness with all the remaining parts of the classroom is effectively lost. It is surprising to note that a great many beginning teachers consistently

    talk only to the middle-front rows,

    talk with their backs to the class when writing on the chalkboard, talk while looking toward the windows or ceiling, or

talk while not being able to see all students due to some students blocking their view.

In each of these instances the teacher sees only a portion of the classroom, and the students *know only a portion of the classroom is seen.* Eye contact that moves across all portions of the classroom is one of the most important ingredients in conveying a sense of withitness.

A second ingredient for improving withitness is learning to monitor more than one activity at a time. Here, the key is not only to change eye contact to different parts of the room, but also to change the focus of attention as well. For example, progress on assigned seatwork might be the focus of a teacher's observations when scanning students in the front of the class, but potential disciplinary problems might be the focus of observations when scanning students in the back of the class. The teacher should switch back and forth from conduct-related observations to work-related observations at the same time as changing eye contact. One of the greatest impediments to making this switch, however, is a tendency to focus exclusively on one student who may be having either conduct or work-related problems. Once students become aware that the teacher is preoccupied with a single student, problems with other students in other parts of the classroom may be inevitable.

Making Transitions

Another problem area is transitions. It is difficult to keep students' attention during a transition from one instructional activity to another. Switching from lecture to seatwork, from discussion to lecture, or from seatwork to discussion is a time for some students to misbehave. Moving the entire class from one activity to another in a timely and orderly manner can be a major undertaking. Problems in making these transitions often occur for two reasons: a lack of readiness on the part of the learners to perform the next activity (or even not knowing what it is), and unclear expectations about appropriate behavior during the transition.

When students are uncertain about or unaware of what is to come next, they naturally become anxious about their ability to perform and make the change. This is the time that transitions can get noisy, with some individuals feeling more comfortable clinging to the previous activity than making the change to the next. At the beginning of the school year, transitions sometimes are noisy as students fumble to find the proper materials (or guess which ones will be needed) and to figure out what will be expected of them next; they are not prone to rush headlong into a new activity for fear it may not be something they will like or will be able to do well in. In this sense, transitions are as much psychological barriers as they are actual divisions in time between activities. Students may need some help because they must adjust their psychology for the next activity just as they must adjust their books and papers. It will help in the adjustment if they know the daily routine that is expected of them. This may be second nature after a few weeks of the semester, but it deserves special mention during the first days of school—at which time you should describe the typical classroom activities you will perform most days and the order in which they can be expected to occur (e.g., a 10-minute lecture, 15 minutes of questions and answers, 15 minutes of seatwork, and 10 minutes of checking and correcting).

Following are several suggestions that address these and other problems:

Problems	*Solutions*
Students talk loudly at the beginning of transitions.	Establish a rule that no talking is allowed between transitions. It is difficult to *allow* a small amount of talking and obtain a small amount.
Students socialize during the transition, delaying the start of the next activity.	Allow no more time than is absolutely necessary between activities (e.g., to

Students complete assignments before the scheduled time for an activity to end.

Students continue to work on the preceding activity after a change.

Some students lag behind others in completing the previous activity.

close books, gather up materials, select new materials). Make assignments according to the time which is to be filled, not to exercises to be completed. Always assign more than enough exercises to fill the alloted time.

Give five-minute and two-minute warnings before the end of any activity and use verbal markers such as "Shortly we will end this work" and "Let's finish this up so that we can begin . . ." Create definite beginning and end points to each activity, such as "OK, that's the end of this activity; now we will start . . ." or "Put your papers away and turn to . . ."

Don't wait for stragglers. Begin new activities on time. When a natural break occurs, visit privately with students still working on previous tasks to tell them that they must stop and change. Be sure to note the reason they have not finished (e.g., material too hard, lack of motivation, off-task behavior).

The teacher delays the beginning of the activity to find something (e.g., file-cabinet keys, materials, roster, references).

Always be prepared—pure and simple!

Giving Assignments

Another crucial time for effective classroom management is when the teacher is giving or explaining assignments. This can be a particularly troublesome time because it often means assigning work that at least some students will not be eager to complete. Grunts and groans are not uncommon ways for students to communicate their distaste for homework or other assignments that must be completed outside of the regular school day. At times like these outbursts of misbehavior are most likely to occur.

One of the differences found between effective and ineffective classroom managers in a study by Evertson and Emmer (1982) was the manner in which these teachers handled giving assignments, particularly homework. The handling of assignments appeared almost effortless for the effective managers, while for the ineffective managers the normal classroom routine sometimes came to an abrupt halt, noise level went up, and much commotion and fuss could be noted. The noticeable difference between these classrooms could be attributed to several simple procedures that were commonplace among experienced teachers but that were not observed among inexperienced teachers.

One of these procedures was attaching assignments directly to the end of an in-class activity, by which the teacher avoided an awkward pause and even the need for a transition, because the assignment was seen as a logical extension of what already was taking place. The practice of giving the assignment immediately after the activity to which it most closely relates, as opposed to at the end of class or the school day, may be much like getting an injection while the physician is engaging you in a friendly conversation and looking down with a smile: If the conversation is engaging enough, you might not feel the pain. Imagine how you might feel being given an assignment under the following conditions:

TEACHER A: I guess I'll have to assign some homework now, so do problems 1 through 10 on page 61.

TEACHER B: For homework do the problems under Exercise A and Exercise B—and be sure all of them are finished by tomorrow.

TEACHER C: We're out of time, so you'll have to finish these problems on your own.

In each of these expressions, there is the subtle question of whether the homework is really needed or whether it is being given mechanically or as some sort of punishment. Why this homework is being assigned may be a complete mystery to most students, because not one of the requests made any mention either of the in-class activities to which the homework presumably relates or of the future benefits that may accrue from completing the assignment. These explanations are important if anything other than a mechanical or begrudging response is expected. Students expect and appreciate knowing why an assignment is made before they are expected to do it. Consider these assignments again, this time with some explanations added:

TEACHER A: Today we have talked a lot about the origins of the Civil War and some of the economic unrest that preceded it. But some other types of unrest were also responsible for the Civil War. These will be important for understanding the real causes behind this war. Problems 1 through 10 on page 61 will help you understand some of these other causes.

TEACHER B: We have all had a chance now to try our skill at forming possessives. As most of you have found out, it's a little harder than it looks. So let's try Exercises A and B for tonight, which should give you just the right amount of practice in forming possessives.

TEACHER C: Well, it looks like time has run out before we could complete all the problems. The next set of problems we will study requires a lot of what we have learned here today. Let's complete the rest of these for tonight to see if you've got the

concept. This should make the next lesson go a lot smoother.

Keep in mind that effective classroom managers give assignments that (a) immediately follow the lesson or activities to which they relate, (b) provide reasons explaining to which in-class lessons the assignment relates, and (c) avoid any unnecessary negative connotations (e.g., "finish them all," "be sure they are correct," "complete it on time"), which may make your assignment look more like a punishment than an instructional activity.

Finally, it is always a good idea to display prior assignments somewhere in your classroom so that students who have missed an assignment can conveniently look it up without requiring the teacher to take the time to remember or to find an assignment that may be days or weeks old. A simple 2-foot square sheet of art board, divided into days of the month and covered with plastic to write on, can be a convenient and reusable way of communicating past assignments on a monthly basis.

Bringing Closure

Another time for effective classroom management is when the lesson is being brought to an end. The closure of a lesson will be as important as the attention-getting device with which it began. Typically, beginning teachers pay relatively little attention to closure, coming to abrupt endings such as:

Oops, there's the bell!

I guess we're out of time, so we'll have to stop.

That's all for today.

We'll have to finish tomorrow.

Our time is gone; let's move on.

Although phrases such as these do the job of ending the lesson, they do little else. Recall that in chapter 5 the attention-getting event could serve the double purpose of both gaining students' attention and also providing an advance organizer to mentally prepare students for the ensuing lesson. Closing comments also should serve a double purpose, by not only ending the lesson but also by reviewing, summarizing, or highlighting its most important points. If good attention-getting devices help organize a lesson in advance, then good closing comments help organize it in retrospect and provide students a mirror through which they can see the preceding events.

Closure, therefore, is more than simply calling attention to the end of a lesson. It means reorganizing the bits and pieces of what has gone before into some unified body of knowledge that can help students remember what has been taught. One way of accomplishing this is by combining or consolidating key points into a single overall conclusion, such as the following:

TEACHER: Today we have studied the economic systems of capitalism, socialism, and communism. We have found each of these to be similar in that some of the same goods and services are owned by the government. We have, however, found them different with respect to the *degree* to which various goods and services are owned by the government; the least number of goods and services are owned by a government under capitalism and the most goods and services are owned by a government under communism.

This teacher is attempting to draw together or highlight the single most important conclusion from the day's lesson. To do this, the highest level generalization or conclusion that can be made from the lesson is expressed without reference to any of the details that were necessary to arrive at it. This teacher consolidated many different bits and pieces by going to the broadest, most sweeping conclusion that could be made, capturing the meaning and essence of all that has gone before.

Another procedure for bringing closure to a lesson is by summarizing or reviewing the key content that has been presented. Here the teacher reviews the most important content to be sure everyone understands it. Obviously, not all of the content can be repeated in this manner, so some selecting is in order, as is illustrated by the following:

TEACHER: Before we end, let's look at our two rules once again. Rule 1: Use the possessive form whenever an *of* phrase can be substituted for a noun. Rule 2: If the word for which we are denoting ownership already ends in an *s*, place the apostrophe after, **not** before, the *s*. Remember, both these rules make use of the apostrophe.

Now the teacher is consolidating by summarizing—or touching on each of the key features of the lesson. The teacher's review is rapid and to the point, providing students with an opportunity to fill in any gaps about the main features of the lesson.

Still another method for closing consists of providing learners with a structure by which key facts and ideas can be remembered without an actual review of them. With this procedure, facts and ideas are reorganized into a framework for easy recall, as indicated in this example:

TEACHER: Today we studied the formulation and punctuation of possessives. Recall that we used two rules—one for forming possessives wherever an *of* phrase can be substituted for a noun and another for forming possessives for words ending in *s*. From now on, let's call these rules the *of rule* and the *s rule,* keeping in mind that both make use of the apostrophe.

By giving the students a framework for remembering the rules (the *of rule* and *s rule*), the teacher organizes the content and indicates how it should be stored and remembered. The key to this procedure is to give a code or symbol system whereby the contents of the lesson can be more easily stored and recalled for later use.

Notice that in each of the previous dialogues closure has been accomplished by looking back at the lesson and reinforcing its key components. In the first instance this was accomplished by restating the highest level generalization that could be made; in the second by summarizing the content at the level at which it was taught;

and in the third by helping students to remember each of the important categories of information by providing some codes or symbols. The most important point to these dialogues is that closure means more than just calling attention to the end of a lesson. Endings to good lessons are like endings to good stories: They must leave listeners with a sense that they have understood the story and can remember it long after the action has ended.

Planning Your First Day

If your first class day is typical of most teachers, it will include some or all of the following activities:

> Keeping order before the bell
> Introducing yourself
> Taking care of administrative business
> Presenting rules and expectations
> Introducing your subject
> Closing

Since your responses in these areas may set the tone in your classroom for the remainder of the year, consider them in more detail to see how you can prepare an effective first-day routine.

Before the Bell

As the sole person responsible for your classroom, your responsibility extends not just to when your classes are in session but to whenever school is in session. Consequently, you must be prepared to deal with students before your classes begin in the morning, between classes, and after your last class has ended—or anytime you are in your classroom. Your first class day is particularly critical in this regard, because your students' before-class peek at you will set in motion responses, feelings, and concerns that may affect them long after the bell has rung. Following are a few suggestions that can make these responses, feelings, and concerns positive ones.

To provide a sense of control and withitness, stand near the door as students enter your classroom. In this way you will come in direct contact with each student and be visible to them as they take their seats. Your presence at the doorway, where students must come in close contact with you, will encourage an orderly entrance (and exit) from the classroom. Remember, your class starts when the first student walks through your classroom door.

Another suggestion is to have approximately 8 to 12 rules, divided between conduct and work, clearly visible on the chalkboard, bulletin board, overhead, or in the form of a handout already placed on each student's desk. You may want to prepare rules for the areas in the upper half of Figure 9.4 that you feel will be most critical to your classes during the first few days of school. These rules will formally be introduced later, but they should be clearly visible as students enter your class the first day. This will communicate a sense of structure and organization which most students look for and expect, even on their very first day of school. It will also occupy the attention of early arrivals, who otherwise may be inclined to talk loudly, move about the classroom, or talk with you, interfering with your ability to monitor students who are making the transition from hallway to classroom.

Finally, it is important that you prepare a brief outline of your opening day's routine. This outline should list all the activities you plan to perform that day (or class period), in the order in which you will perform them. A simple 4×6 index card can be used to remind yourself to:

1. Greet students and introduce yourself (5 min.)
2. Take roll (5 min.)
3. Fill out course cards (10 min.)
4. Assign books (15 min.)
5. Present rules (10 min.)
   A. conduct rules
   B. work rules
6. Introduce course content (0–10 min.)
7. Remind students to bring needed materials (2 min.)
8. Close (3 min.)

It is not unusual (considering the tension and anxiety associated with any first day on the job) for you to be forgetful or to get sidetracked on any one event (e.g., introducing yourself), leaving no time for some other important event. Experience suggests that important business (e.g., reminding students of your classroom rules) can be left out or a less logical order of activities chosen when a reminder is not available to keep things on track. In the elementary grades this schedule can be easily amended to include an introduction to the entire day.

Introducing Yourself

You will naturally introduce yourself by giving your name, the subject or class you are teaching, your special areas of expertise, and so on. However, after these more formal introductory comments, you will need to break the ice by showing a part of your personality at the same time that you maintain your role as a teacher. Quite frankly, this is not always easy. Some beginning teachers tend to ramble too much about themselves in an effort to convince their students they are "regular people," while others maintain a cold and stern aura about themselves in order to keep students disciplined and at a distance. Both approaches are extreme reactions that, in the end, often create more problems than they solve. In the first instance students may want to get too friendly too soon, forgetting the discipline and order that school requires, and in the second instance students may stay frightened of you for weeks or even months. Your personality will, and should, unfold in small degrees during the first few weeks of school. There is no need to rush it. However, a small glimpse of the kind of person you are outside of the classroom is often a nice touch for students, who would like to see you as a friend as well as a teacher. A short comment about your interests, hobbies, or special experiences—even family or home life—is often appreciated by students, who at the end of this first day will be struggling to remember just who you are.

Administrative Business

Your first opportunity to meet your students up close will be while taking the roll. This is when you may want to turn the tables and have your students not only identify themselves, but also indicate some of their own interests, hobbies, or special experiences. The time devoted to such introductions tends to be lengthier at the elementary grades than in the junior high and high school, where teacher-student contact is limited to a single period. Also, at the higher grades, interests, hobbies, or special experiences can be more efficiently determined with a brief interest inventory of the type shown in Figure 9.1. The advantage of using this approach is that time can be set aside in the future for looking through the student responses to help in planning future projects and lessons that coincide with your learners' special interests.

Your other administrative duties at this time can be considerable, and in some cases can consume most of the remainder of the class period at the upper grades and a full hour or more at the lower grades. Filling out forms requested by the school and school district, checking course schedules, guiding lost students to their correct rooms, and accepting new students during the middle of the class will make this first class day seem long and unorderly.

Rules and Expectations

Regardless of how much time you must give to administrative tasks during your first day, you should plan on devoting at least some time to a discussion of your classroom rules and of your overall expectations about both conduct and work. This is the time to remove student uncertainties and let them know what to expect. There is no better way to begin this process than by referring to the conduct and work rules that either have been posted for all to see or have been given as a handout.

In addition to your rules, however, there will be related concerns that you will also want to address. For example, for younger students you will want to reiterate certain important school rules (e.g., what to do in the event of sickness, consequences of repeated tardiness or absence, procedures for going to the cafeteria) in addition to your own classroom rules. You will also want to set the tone for the rigor and fairness with which you will grade and for the level of effort you will expect from your students. These comments should tell your students that you will "be fair but tough," "expect a lot but will reward hard work," "give difficult tests but teach you what you need to know in order to get a good grade," and "expect students to do a lot of work but that the work will be interesting." In each of these phrases your high standards are communicated, but so is your understanding and fairness. This delicate balance is the most important impression with which you can leave your students on their first day.

Introducing Your Subject

Although it is unlikely that time will permit the presentation of very much content on the first day, there are several tips that can be given for doing so on the second or third day. First, begin your instruction to the whole class in a direct instruction format. This is a time in which students will not be eager to participate in discussion, nor will they be relaxed enough to give meaningful contributions to inquiry or problem-solving questions. Effective indirect instruction formats depend on the trust and confidence that students have in their teacher, and this trust and confidence will take time to develop. Therefore, the direct rather than the indirect instruction model should be used, at least for the first week or so of classes.

Second, during your first week choose simple content activities that everyone can successfully complete. This will go a long way toward building confidence and promoting enthusiasm for the work that lies ahead. Avoid especially difficult tasks that effectively preclude high rates of success; otherwise, some of your students may experience a fear of failure that can suppress their true abilities long into the school year. In addition, at this time you will not know the dif-

ficulty level that is most appropriate to your learners, and any premature judgments on your part may well have consequences beyond those you intend (e.g., some students reporting to school counselors that they wish to change classes). Following are some examples of first-day activities that can give the flavor of a content area in which most students could demonstrate a high level of understanding and which could be used to begin to convey facts, rules, and action sequences:

> Conducting a brief experiment and asking students what was puzzling or interesting about it (science)
>
> Reading a lively excerpt from a short story and asking students to give their interpretation (English or reading)
>
> Demonstrating a concrete procedure and having students practice it, such as using a calculator, equipment, charts, or tables (math and the sciences)
>
> Describing a typical current event and asking students how it can affect their lives (social studies)
>
> Teaching a few words of conversation and having students try them out (foreign language)

Closure

Your final first-day activity will be to close on a positive, optimistic note. Have a definite procedure for closing in mind (e.g., a preview of things to come, instructions to follow for tomorrow's class, a reminder of things to bring to class), begin closing a full three minutes before the time the bell is to ring, and end with a note of encouragement that *all* of your students can do well in your grade or class.

Summing Up

This chapter introduced motivation and classroom management. Its main points were:

1. *Motivation* is a word used to describe what energizes or directs a learner's attention, emotions, and activity.
2. Motivators can be *internal,* coming from within the individual (e.g., aggressiveness), and *external,* coming from the environment (e.g., peer pressure).
3. Knowledge of a learner's interests, needs, and aspirations can be used to motivate and actively engage a learner in the learning process.
4. An overachiever is an individual whose school achievement is greater than that predicted by tests of intelligence or scholastic aptitude, and an underachiever is an individual whose achievement is less than that predicted. Both underachievement and overachievement often can be attributed to a learner's motivation.
5. Some more formal ways in which instruction can be organized to motivate learners include performance contracts, games and simulations, programmed texts, grouping, volunteering, and grades and tests.
6. Some less formal ways of motivating learners include:

   - Using praise and encouragement
   - Providing explanations
   - Offering to help
   - Accepting diversity
   - Emphasizing reward, not punishment

7. Classroom climate refers to the atmosphere or mood in which interactions between you and your students take place. A classroom climate can be created by the social environment, which is related to the patterns of interaction you wish to promote in your classroom, and by the organizational environment, which is related to the physical or visual arrangement of the classroom.
8. The social climate of the classroom can extend from authoritarian (in which you are the primary provider of information, opinions, and instruction) to laissez-faire (in which your students become the primary providers of information, opinions, and instruction).

9. Your role in establishing authority in the classroom and the social climate can vary and may include

   - a commander-in-chief who carefully controls and hones student behavior by organizing and providing all the stimuli needed for learning to occur,
   - a translator or summarizer of ideas provided by students,
   - an equal partner with students in creating ideas and problem solutions.

10. The social climate of your classroom can also vary depending on how competitive, cooperative, or individualistic you wish the interactions among members of your class to be. Differences among these will be related to opportunities for the expression of student opinion, to the amount of time devoted to student talk, and to the spontaneity with which your students are allowed to respond.
11. Organizational climate pertains to the physical or visual arrangement of the classroom and is determined by the positioning of desks, chairs, tables, and other internal features of a classroom.
12. The degree of competition, cooperation, and individuality in your classroom will be a result of both the social and organizational climate you create.
13. Rules can be divided into those that

    - relate to academic work,
    - relate to classroom conduct,
    - must be communicated your first teaching day,
    - can be communicated later.

14. Rules can be communicated orally, on the board, on a transparency, or in a handout. Rules for the early elementary grades should be presented orally, provided in the form of a handout, and posted for reference. Rules for the elementary grades and junior high school may be recited and copied by students. Rules for the high school may be given orally and then posted.

15. Your inability to enforce a rule over a reasonable period of time is the best sign a change in the rule may be needed.
16. Monitoring students, making transitions, giving assignments, and bringing closure represent four particularly troublesome areas of classroom management.
17. *Withitness* refers to a form of monitoring in which the teacher is able to keep track of many different signs of student engagement at the same time.
18. Problems during transitions most frequently occur when learners are not ready to perform the next activity and do not know what behavior is appropriate during the transition.
19. Homework assignments should be given immediately following the lesson or activities to which they relate and without any unnecessary negative connotations or innuendos.
20. Closing statements should bring a lesson to an end gradually by combining or consolidating key points into a single overall conclusion, summarizing or reviewing key content, or providing a symbol system whereby contents of the lesson can be easily stored and later recalled.

For Discussion and Practice

1. Identify three motivators that could be considered internal and three motivators that could be considered external.
2. Give one example each of an interest, a need, and an aspiration that some of the students you will be teaching are likely to have.
*3. Distinguish between an overachiever and an underachiever as these definitions might be used in your classroom.
4. Ask a sample of schoolchildren that you are observing (or that live near you) to complete the questionnaire in Figure 9.1. If they are in the early elementary grades, ask them the questions orally and then record their responses. From the data provided, identify two curriculum additions that would be responsive to the needs, interests, and aspirations identified on the questionnaire.

5. Provide an example of a performance contract for a poorly motivated learner in your teaching area. Identify the content to be taught, the behavioral outcome to be achieved, the manner in which it is to be obtained, the proficiency expected, and the reward provided if the contract is met.
6. Devise a plan to engage poorly motivated students in the learning process by asking them to help you perform some meaningful classroom activity. Identify the task which you are asking the students to perform and explain why they might want to volunteer to do it.
*7. In addition to contracts and volunteering, identify four other techniques for engaging poorly motivated students in the learning process.
*8. Identify five less formal ways of engaging poorly motivated students in the learning process.
9. Give an example of how an assignment might emphasize punishment and then rephrase your example to emphasize reward.
*10. What are three roles communicating different levels of authority that you can assume in your classroom? How will expression of student opinions, proportion of student talk to teacher talk, and spontaneity of response change as a function of each of these three roles?
*11. Provide example classroom activities that would result in (a) a competitive, (b) a cooperative, and (c) an individualistic classroom climate.
12. Draw three diagrams of the internal features of a classroom, each diagram illustrating how to promote one of the previous three classroom climates.
13. Identify four academic and four conduct rules (that must be communicated your first day of class) that *you believe* are among the most important. Write out a rule for each of these eight areas, exactly as it might be shown to your students on a handout or transparency on the first day of class.
*14. Identify two rules whose retention might be aided if they are communicated in the context of a circumstance or incident with which to associate the rule.
*15. Identify a practical decision rule to be used when a rule should be revised or eliminated.
16. Explain in your own words what the word *withitness* means. Give an example from your own experience of when you (a) displayed withitness

and (b) did not (but should have) displayed it. What were the consequences of these two events?

*17. What are four teaching practices that would help avoid misbehavior during a transition?

*18. What are two ways out-of-class assignments can be made more meaningful and acceptable to your students?

*19. Identify three ways of bringing your lesson to an end that can help students to organize your lesson in retrospect.

20. Identify the characteristics you might reveal about yourself when introducing yourself on the first day of class.

Suggested Readings

Brophy, J. (1981). Teacher praise: A functional analysis. *Review of Educational Research, 51,* 5–32.

A comprehensive review of the research on praise, with many practical applications for when and how to use it to motivate learners.

Brophy, J. & Putnam, J. (1979). Classroom management in the elementary grades. In D. Duke (Ed.), *Classroom management.* Chicago: University of Chicago Press.

An extensive summary of what the research shows makes good classroom managers in the elementary school.

Emmer, E. T., Evertson, C. M., & Anderson, L. M. (1980). Effective classroom management at the beginning of the school year. *Elementary School Journal, 80,* 219–231.

A profile of the teaching practices of effective and ineffective classroom managers during their first week of school.

Emmer, E. T., Evertson, C. M., Sanford, J. P., Clements, B. S., & Worsham, M. E. (1984). *Classroom management for secondary teachers.* Englewood Cliffs, NJ: Prentice-Hall.

A summary of the most practical advice for teachers on how to manage the secondary classroom—

based on the actual classroom observation of effective and ineffective classroom managers.

Evertson, C., & Emmer, E. T. (1982). Effective management at the beginning of the school year in junior high classes. *Journal of Educational Psychology, 74,* 485–498.

The results of an interesting research study in which junior high teachers were observed at the beginning of the school year for their effective and ineffective management styles.

Evertson, C. M., Emmer, E. T., Sanford, J. P., & Clements, B. S. (1983). Improving classroom management: An experiment in elementary school classrooms. *Elementary School Journal, 84,* 173–188.

A report of the results of some effective and ineffective classroom practices on the organization and management of the elementary classroom.

Evertson, C. M., Emmer, E. T., Clements, B. S., Stanford, J. P., & Worsham, M. E. (1984). *Classroom management for elementary teachers.* Englewood Cliffs, NJ: Prentice-Hall.

A companion volume to Classroom management for secondary teachers—*but written for the elementary teacher.*

Homme, L. (1970). *How to use contingency contracting in your classroom.* Champaign, IL: Research Press.

An early but practical guide on how to use performance contracts in the classroom to increase student motivation and achievement.

Kounin, J. S. (1970). *Discipline and group management in classrooms.* New York: Holt, Rinehart & Winston.

One of the first and best books on classroom management—from the originator of the concept of withitness.

Soar, R. & Soar, R. (1987). Classroom climate. In M. J. Dunkin (Ed.), *International encyclopedia of teaching and teacher education.* New York: Pergamon.

An overview of the relationship of classroom climate to teacher and student behavior.

10
Classroom Order and Discipline

Anyone who reads the local newspaper, listens to candidates running for public office, attends school board meetings, or overhears conversations in the teachers' lounge quickly realizes that classroom order and discipline are among the most frequently discussed topics. A teachers' inability to control a class is one of the most frequently cited reasons for dismissing or failing to reemploy a teacher, and beginning teachers consistently rate classroom discipline among their most urgent concerns on the Teacher Concerns Checklist (Borich & Fuller, 1974).

Problems in maintaining classroom order and discipline, however, can be exaggerated. Candidates for public office and some community members may speak from time to time as though discipline in the schools is nonexistent or minimal, while newspapers readily report any incident that does occur. The facts are that major disciplinary problems (e.g., vandalism, violent fighting, physical abuse toward teachers) rarely,

if ever, occur in most schools. Unfortunately, these are the incidents that attract the attention of the media whenever they do occur, and often they are reported to the exclusion of the many positive events that may be happening within a school. This chapter will address some of these major discipline problems, but the primary focus will be on the many less dramatic problems that can wear a teacher down and divert attention from the teaching process.

The previous chapter discussed some of the ways you can anticipate problems before they occur—and plan to avoid them. This chapter will focus on developing systematic procedures for stopping or altering misbehavior that has already occurred. As was noted in the previous chapter, anticipating discipline problems and planning to avoid them is always preferable to dealing with discipline problems once they have occurred. Nevertheless, not all misbehaviors can be anticipated and not all classroom management techniques for avoiding them work every time. Consequently, this chapter is devoted to techniques for dealing with misbehaviors such as

talking out without raising hand

talking back

acting out

tardiness

showing hostility

disrupting others

moving about without permission

failing to complete assignments

ignoring rules

We will also address some of the more serious but less frequently occurring problems:

cheating

vandalism

fighting

substance abuse

Teacher Characteristics Related to Classroom Management

Most of the discipline problems encountered are low intensity, continuous, and unconnected with any larger, more serious event. For example, Kounin (1970) found that about 55% of classroom discipline problems were related to talking and noise; 26% were related to being late, not having homework, or moving about the room without permission; and 17% were related to off-task behavior, such as completing other assignments, reading without permission, or daydreaming. Other researchers have attempted to identify the teacher behaviors that tend to evoke or encourage these types of discipline problems. Other classroom research studies, (Emmer, Evertson, Sanford, Clement, & Worsham, 1984; Leinhardt, 1983; Moskowitz & Hayman, 1976; Emmer, Evertson, & Anderson, 1980) have contributed insightful glimpses of how some teachers often needlessly create disciplinary problems by the way they manage and conduct their classes. From these studies is emerging a behavioral profile both of teachers whose classrooms consistently exhibit discipline problems and of teachers whose classrooms are relatively free of discipline problems. This section will present these two behavioral profiles.

Teachers who had classrooms in which a large percentage of students were off-task, talked without raising hands, talked back, moved about the room without permission, ignored rules, disrupted others, and failed to complete assignments exhibited at least some of the following characteristics.

Extreme Negativity*

Went out today to observe Mrs. _____'s first day of class. She spent the first 15 minutes of class reading the kids the "riot act." By that I mean she told them they had to overcome their poor study habits and laziness because this class would be tougher than all their others. "Tests will be hard, and some may not make it," she said. Class continued with a brief lesson in life science. Teacher seemed to focus on what the kids did not know but should know, using phrases such as, "You should have gotten this in other courses" or "Most everyone at this grade level should already know this." Kids' faces were mostly expressionless; they seemed to leave class wondering when the other shoe would drop.

Teachers in classrooms with high levels of disciplinary problems seemed to want to put students on the defensive from the start. For example, these teachers used phrases such as: "If you disobey the

---

*These and the remaining excerpts are from the Evaluation of Teaching Project (NIE–C–74–0088, Research and Development Center for Teacher Education, The University of Texas at Austin) during which observers were asked to write down at least one critical incident that characterized the classrooms they were observing.

rules in this classroom, and I know some of you will, you will be punished," "Some of you should expect to get failing grades in here," or "Don't underestimate my ability to catch those of you who like to violate the rules." Instead of seeing the bright side of things—or at least hoping the bright side would occur—these teachers seemed determined to create an aura of punishment, difficulty, and failure in their classrooms. It is not clear why these teachers acted in such a manner, but one can speculate that they may have thought that, by casting a scary light on things right from the start, they could prevent misbehavior from occurring. This seemed to correspond with the teachers' lack of confidence in their teaching skills; perhaps by conveying an image of being a stern disciplinarian and a difficult teacher, they may have been trying to provide a convenient cover for their lack of confidence. Whatever the reason for their negativity, it was not difficult for some students in these classrooms to conclude that, since they were so "bad," the teacher might be disappointed if they did not live up to expectations. *These teachers, therefore, may have created their own self-fulfilling prophecy*—one that students made sure would come true.

Exclusive Authoritarian Climate

This is my third observation of _____. Nothing much seems to have changed. Teacher reads from workbook and kids recite answers in unison. Some students, however, seem to purposely shout out wrong or silly answers. Think they may just be bored or are challenging the teacher to find out who they are. Since voices are in unison, teacher had difficulty spotting the culprits. Kids would "lay low" for a time and then shout out another wrong answer. Teacher was noticeably distraught at the disruption but proceeded by pretending not to have heard it. This provoked more kids to join in the game.

Closely associated with teachers' negativity was the rigid, authoritarian climate that usually prevailed in their classrooms. Outward appear-

ances indicated that these teachers seemed to value being a stern disciplinarian even more than being a good teacher. The authoritarian atmosphere in the classroom took the form of high amounts of teacher talk, little or no acceptance or solicitation of student responses, and almost a complete absence of spontaneity. The aim of these teachers seemed to be a desire to be in absolute command at all times and to be the only worthwhile source of anything to be discussed or learned. Again, one suspects that this rigid, almost military atmosphere might have been a cover for anxieties about lacking control. The apparent solution was to arrange instruction in the most rigid of formats to prevent the slightest opportunity for misbehavior to occur; there could be no potentially embarrassing moments when absolute control was not in the hands of the teacher. Although being useful for the teacher, such extreme rigidity provoked rebelliousness in some learners. This strategy might work in a military school, but in the typical public school classroom a climate that is continually authoritarian is often an invitation for some students to test the limits of the teacher's authority. Because there is strength in numbers, these teachers were soon challenged by more than one student; even worse, the teacher's response to this challenge often resulted in an even greater challenge on the part of the students, until a major confrontation arose to create disorder and confusion. There is little doubt among experienced teachers that effective classroom order and discipline *depends as much on the voluntary cooperation of students as it does on a clear communication of rules and the ability to enforce them.* Remember that an overly rigid climate in your classroom—with little opportunity for student talk, student opinion, or spontaneity—may quickly create a warlike climate.

Overreacting

I arrived at _____'s class all ready to give the math posttest. Earlier that morning I had given the Student Questionnaire, and everything had gone quite well—although I was a bit perturbed by the police whistle hanging from the substitute teacher's neck. As I was saying, I arrived for the math posttest and was greeted by thunderous applause which was turning into a standing ovation until the whistle went off and for one split second the room was quiet. It didn't take long for me to see what was happening—there was a contest of sorts going on to see who could make the distraught woman scream the loudest and blow her whistle the most. Kids were leaving their desks, well, not actually leaving, just climbing on top of them and jumping off.

The previous scenario portrays students testing the limits of an overly authoritarian teacher and the teacher fighting back to meet the challenge. This cycle almost inevitably resulted in an overreaction on the part of the teacher. In the problem classrooms it was not unusual for teachers to engage in an emotional outburst as a response to some misbehavior; the teacher's voice would increase in volume and pitch and a shouting match would ensue. More often than not, this resulted from a challenge to the teacher's authority in which students would purposely taunt or attempt to provoke the teacher into making an emotional outburst. One misbehavior often led to another until a cycle of misbehavior began—teacher response to a problem, followed by a student challenge, followed by a more intense teacher response. The only effect of the teacher's emotional response was to escalate the problem. When an emotional outburst (one of the strongest responses a teacher can make) fails to solve the problem, the teacher is left in the uncomfortable position of having few more intense responses. *Although emotional responses may be effective at times, consistent use diminishes their effectiveness at the time they may be needed most.* Because most of these teachers were inconsistent in their use of discipline, they were challenged more often, and it was easy for students to manipulate these teachers into making increased responses to their misbehavior.

Mass Punishment

Went to Mr. _____'s first class after lunch. Students complained about the long homework assignment they were given the previous night that, I take it, not many students finished. Teacher was upset at not everyone completing it, since today's class was to be devoted to students reading their answers to the assignment. Teacher seemed threatened by the apparently large number of students who had not completed the assignment and, so, gave another equally long assignment for tonight. The remainder of the class was devoted to students independently finishing last night's assignment and, if time permitted, beginning on the new assignment. But, since most students had difficulty with the assignment the night before, few students seemed to be concentrating. Others, who completed the assignments, seemed dismayed by being given another long assignment.

When a cycle of misbehavior involving large numbers of students started in these classrooms, a common teacher response was to assign punishment to the entire class. Extra homework in the upper grades and purposeless writing assignments (e.g., writing 25 times "I will always do my assignments" or "I will not talk in class") in the lower grades were the most frequently chosen punishments. The assignment was a response to the misbehavior such that the teacher could be sure that every single student who misbehaved was punished. However, such deep resentment often was felt by the students who did not misbehave that few of them had the enthusiasm to stay on task or to cooperate in the learning task the remainder of the period. Perhaps the teacher assumed that peer pressure from those who did behave would influence the others to conform to classroom rules and procedures. If that was the logic, it has no merit in fact. First, *students who obey often come from a different peer group than those who frequently disobey and, therefore, have little or no influence over the latter either in or out of school.* Second, these peer groups often are so at odds with each other that the disobedient actually derive pleasure from seeing the obedient wrongly punished along with themselves—and may even repeat the misbehavior to derive this same pleasure again. These two social facts explain why mass punishment is seldom, if ever, a lasting solution for misbehavior. Like an emotional outburst, mass punishment escalates the teacher's response to one of its highest levels.

Blaming

Toward the end of class, Mr. _____ was writing on the chalkboard when an alarm to someone's wristwatch went off. He turned and asked whose it was and no one responded. One student looked suspicious but few actually knew whose it was. This student was given an extra set of homework assignments, but complained bitterly—and, so, was given another set of homework assignments. A shouting match of sorts erupted leading to the student being sent to the office. I honestly can't say whether it was this kid or not—but obviously someone was going to catch it.

Another behavior that was observed in these classrooms was the teacher's tendency to blame *someone* for every discipline problem that occurred. These teachers seemed to know who the troublemakers were and blamed them repeatedly even when the true source of the problem may have been in doubt. These students became scapegoats for nearly all the discipline problems that could not be attributed to a clearly identifiable individual. Phrases such as "You're at it again," "You've created trouble in here since the beginning," and "You won't get away with it this time" often were used to identify the supposed culprit responsible for throwing paper, making a noise, or disrupting others behind the teacher's back. Sometimes the true source of the problem was a group of students, which often included the one singled out, and sometimes the true source was unidentifiable. In either case, because

the teacher made an error in judgment, the response of the one being blamed was to quickly and loudly correct the error by attributing blame to others. The troublemaker responded with "It's not me," "It was those two over there," or "I wasn't the only one," engaging the teacher in a tug-of-war to see if the blame could be spread to others. The teacher was in a win-or-lose conflict to prove that the one blamed was actually the one responsible. In the meantime the class has been disrupted by the teacher's preoccupation with a single individual's behavior. *At the root of this problem was the teacher's misguided notion that every misbehavior must always be attributed to someone,* even if it is at the expense of the most likely person responsible. In these teachers' minds there were only winners or losers—and they themselves intended never to be the loser, regardless of the cost of the conflict to classroom morale and instructional time.

Lack of a Clear Instructional Goal

Was in Ms. _____'s class to observe. Lesson was about modern art, I think. Some students talked about the pictures in the text taken from the National Museum of Modern Art. Others talked about making art objects from old car parts—hubcaps, carburetors, that sort of thing. Everyone seemed to have a different idea as to what modern art was—but the teacher did not venture any rules or guidelines. She seemed to want the kids to find them for themselves. Finally, a shouting match erupted between the "old car parts" people and the "painting" people until each side could hardly hear the other. Much of the rest of the period was devoted to returning the classroom to order.

Another characteristic behavior in problem classrooms was the noticeable lack of an instructional goal—at least one that was discernible to the students. These were classrooms in which students often engaged in loosely structured discussions with no apparent direction, agenda, or expected results. Students drifted from one topic to the next without establishing meaningful connections or unifying concepts between and among topics. The students meandered through many different ideas; it sometimes appeared as though large quantities of content were being covered, but in reality each topic was touched upon so lightly that little of substance was ever said. In essence, the discussion had no momentum, and student expectations were unclear about the kind or quality of contribution they should be making. The class became ripe for misbehavior, because little forward momentum existed to keep their attention on task and their energies directed toward an identifiable instructional goal; with no clear goal, some students tended to drift off the subject while others took the looseness of the discussion as a sign that they could turn discussion into argument. It was not unusual during such sessions to find students arguing with each other or with the teacher, or trying to discuss a problem from incompatible points of view. Discipline problems involving excessively loud talking, clowning, moving out of seat, and interrupting others were not unusual during such loosely organized sessions. The message these teachers forgot, or never learned, was that *even the most indirect discussions must be crafted to communicate a structure, an end result, and clear expectations of student conduct.*

Repeating or Reviewing Already Understood Material

Just returned from _____class. They're still reviewing verb conjugations in the workbook. Noise level in classroom seems a bit high, as some students were "whispering" to their friends across the aisle and passing notes around. Seems as though some students are copying from others just so they won't have to complete another exercise. Teacher seems engrossed in paper grading—or doesn't much care.

Another time when discipline problems seemed to occur was when the class was expected to repeat or review material that already had been learned. The name often given to such assignments is **busywork**. This often is given to keep students quiet while the teacher pursues some other, more important, activity; its actual effect, however, can be just the opposite. There is nothing wrong with assigning busywork so that you can have a much needed psychological break, prepare materials for another class, or get some grading finished, *as long as it poses some challenge to your students*. As noted in earlier chapters, assigning work for which students can achieve moderate-to-high levels of success is a prerequisite for actively engaging students in the learning process. However, assigning work for which learners uniformly achieve at high levels of success quickly becomes boring and repetitious. In these instances students often either fail to complete the assignment, or they complete it so rapidly that plenty of time remains for off-task behavior. In these classrooms, discipline problems frequently occurred during long assignments which students quickly recognized as busywork. They responded subconsciously with "What's the point?" and, not being able to find one, shifted their attention to anything in the environment that was more exciting. These teachers failed to realize that *there must always be some mystery, challenge, or curiosity about what is to be learned;* this is lost in the creation of long, easy assignments. That is, there must always be some amount of uncertainty about what the next question or item is and whether or not it can be answered correctly. When all uncertainty is eliminated by a repetitively high success rate, the magnetism that focuses and directs a learner's attention is also eliminated; off-task behavior, including behavior disruptive to others trying to complete the assignment, becomes a more desirable focus.

Pauses and Interruptions

Observed Mr. _____'s social studies lesson today. Lesson seemed to proceed smoothly until the teacher realized that the map he would be using was locked up in the map room. Teacher put a student in charge while he left the room to retrieve the map. Student went to the front of the room but as soon as the teacher left, a few students made fun of her for being "teacher's pet." She got upset and told everyone to "shut up." Noise level went up and commotion began. Teacher returned and spent the next five or so minutes inquiring what had happened and getting the class back to order. Teacher returned without the map —said another teacher must be using it.

Teachers in the problem classrooms also tended to pause or interrupt the flow of instruction more frequently than did teachers in classrooms with fewer discipline problems. Pauses to clean an overhead transparency, to round up graded assignments, to look for reference materials, and to write lengthy assignments on the board were not uncommon. However, once the momentum of a classroom activity is broken, for whatever reason, it is exceedingly difficult to gain it back without valuable loss of class time. Many pauses or interruptions are often a needless waste of time that can be avoided by thinking ahead, such as arranging for needed materials before class or placing assignments on the board during a break or during seatwork. The "withitness" of these teachers was lost during these pauses, and an open invitation was extended for misbehavior. Although not all students will take advantage of such pauses, it only takes a few students—sometimes only one—to place a classroom in disorder. *Awkward gaps, pauses, and interruptions in which eye and visual contact is lost will almost always disengage your students from the learning process.* Two of the most frustrating sources of pauses in your instruction will be unexpected announcements from the school's public address system and unexpected visitors (e.g., counselor, parent, teacher) at your door. In the problem classrooms teachers seemed to lack procedures for handling either of these common occur-

rences. Continuing to move about the room silently during announcements to let your presence be known and asking unexpected visitors either to return after class or to leave a message are some of the ways misbehaviors were reduced in the classrooms that had fewer disciplinary problems.

Dealing With a Single Student at Length

Completed my last observation in _____ class. Students seemed particularly anxious due to it being the next-to-the-last day before the holidays. Things seemed to go well, even given the high noise level, until one student turned to another with an obscene gesture. Both seemed to be about to start a fight so the teacher slammed the book down and lectured them on how their grade in the class would depend on their good conduct. This went into a discussion about today's changing morals and values, which some in the rest of the class thought was humorous. Some laughing and "snickering" could be heard and, finally, the teacher began handing out disciplinary referrals to whomever opened their mouth.

Another characteristic of the problem classrooms was the tendency of the teacher to deal at length with the problem of a single student. The teacher would disrupt the instructional momentum to discipline a student after a breach of classroom rules, usually talking back, acting out, disrupting others, or fighting. These incidents were used as opportunities not only to assign punishment to the offender, but also to give lectures on the implications of the offense (e.g., for getting a good grade, for becoming a good citizen, or for "making it in life"). During the teacher's preoccupation with the misbehaving student, other discipline problems in the classroom often would arise. Sometimes 5 to 10 minutes of class time would elapse while the teacher questioned the offender, lectured him or her on the implications of the misbehavior, and arranged for some form of punishment. Because the teacher's eye contact and attention were on the misbehaving student, there were opportunities for mischief to occur elsewhere in the classroom. As opposed to dealing with individual students at length, teachers in the classrooms with fewer discipline problems had established a set routine to handle the most frequently occurring problems. Frequently they would deal with the problem quickly by *deferring the lecture or punishment phase to after class or school, taking time to only call out the student's name and the offense during class.* Some of the ways these teachers quickly dispensed with a misbehavior and the approximate times expended were:

> silently writing the student's name on the board (5 sec.)
>
> calling out the student's name and assigning a prearranged page number for an exercise (10 sec.)
>
> pointing to the rear of the room and indicating the student must stand there (5 sec.)
>
> moving the student's name from the "good behavior" to "poor behavior" side of the bulletin board (10 sec.)
>
> calling out the student's name and writing a referral to a counselor indicating the nature of the offense (30 sec.)

In each of these instances the disruption to class varied between 5–30 seconds, with few words being spoken. In these classrooms students knew that when their names were called, a visit to the teacher after class or after school for their punishment was mandatory; the disruption to the flow of instruction was minimized. This routine was explained during the first week of school, so all students knew exactly what to expect when their names were called for disciplinary reasons.

Lack of Recognition of Ability Levels

Went to observe Ms. _____'s
Spanish class. Teacher was using the direct

instruction model. Students were expected to respond in Spanish using the correct verb form to her questions, given in Spanish. It was plain to see that when she came to students in the back of the room few, if any, could converse in sentences with the correct verb form—some didn't even try. It seemed as though whenever the action returned to the front of the room two or more students in the back would begin to "socialize" among themselves until the teacher would have to stop and ask them to "be quiet." Things would be quiet for a brief time and, then, the noise level would go up and the whole cycle would start over again. Some students seemed able to keep up but others were most certainly lost.

The teachers in these problem classrooms tended to teach, at least part of the time, over the heads of some of their students. Although these teachers actually may have known the ability levels of their students, this information was treated as if it were irrelevant. These teachers seemed to enjoy being thought tough or difficult; they "poured on the homework" and moved swiftly through the material until time came for a major test—at which time poor grades often were blamed on the students' laziness, lack of interest in the subject matter, or insufficient time devoted to study and homework. As a result, some students had all but given up in these classrooms long before they had been given any real test of their progress. A quarter to a third of the class was having trouble understanding the material and represented a consistent group of troublemakers who often would band together in mischief, making the teacher's progress with the rest of the class more difficult. These teachers rarely reviewed previously taught material or gave progress checks before major tests to determine specific weaknesses that needed to be addressed. *Remedial activities or ability grouping, whereby slow learners could catch up or pursue alternative paths,* seemed not to be considered. On the other hand, the teachers seemed not to notice that they were teaching each day to a smaller and smaller percentage of the class—and that this created an increased amount of pauses for disciplinary action.

Summary of the Characteristics of Ineffective Classroom Managers

Emerging from these classrooms is a profile of teaching practices that tends to be associated with high amounts of discipline problems. When a large number of these practices come together in a single classroom, discipline problems are likely to follow, regardless of what good practices may be occurring in that classroom. Recall the main features of our profile:

extreme negativity

exclusive authoritarian climate

overreacting

mass punishment

blaming

lack of clear instructional goal

repeating or reviewing already learned material

pausing

dealing with a single student at length

lack of recognition of ability levels

Although few teachers can avoid all of these behaviors all of the time, the effective teacher knows their potentially damaging effects on classroom order and discipline. Being consciously aware of these characteristics is the first step to avoiding them.

Effective Teacher Characteristics

Along with these characteristics of problem classrooms, we can also summarize some of the contrasting characteristics of classrooms that exhibited noticeably fewer discipline problems. As could be expected, the teachers in these classrooms tended to exhibit greater levels of withitness; that is, they always placed themselves in the position of *seeing all aspects of the classroom at once* and avoided situations (such as dealing with a single student at length) which could shut them off from the rest of the class. These teachers also were able to perform *overlapping activities,* such as presenting content while at the same time being alert for misbehavior in the back of the classroom, and writing up a disciplinary referral for one student while keeping eye contact on the rest of the class. They also were noticeably *less autocratic and authoritarian* than teachers in the problem classrooms. That is, they allowed more student talk, expressions of opinion, and spontaneity, all of which made the students feel more as though they were participants with the teacher in their own instruction—and, therefore, the students became more willing to accept responsibility for their own learning. These teachers also seemed to realize that no degree of attention to rules and their violations can keep a classroom free of discipline problems unless the teacher first secures the cooperation and goodwill of the students. This often was accomplished by being flexible, allowing *some freedom of student expression and spontaneity,* which promoted an *adultlike cooperative environment* rather than a militarylike autocratic environment. Of course, these classrooms also exhibited *clear rules and directions* for appropriate behavior. Flexibility and freedom were not randomly dispensed but were either given as rewards for good conduct or allowed under clearly established guidelines of acceptable conduct. In addition to students being treated as partners in the learning process, they were given a comprehensive list of rules that told them how to behave and what to expect if they did not do so.

These classrooms also maintained a *balance between direct and indirect instruction.* When the more rigid formality of direct instruction began to affect the students' enthusiasm, the teacher would switch first to the indirect instruction model and then back again; variety and interest in the topic were maintained. In addition, these classrooms maintained a *businesslike pace* that always kept learning stimuli before the students;

there were no awkward pauses when students did not know what to do next. They were kept moving through the material from one activity to the next without hesitation, establishing a momentum that focused their attention on the learning task, which left little time or energy for misbehavior. Once misbehavior did occur, however, it was dealt with quickly; the *assignment of punishment was made later,* so the flow of an instructional activity was not interrupted. Finally, when the pace was found to be too fast for some students, different paces were established through the *formation of ability or activity groups* or through the use of self-paced materials.

These classrooms could be distinguished from classrooms with noticeably more discipline problems by the following:

teacher withitness and ability to overlap activities

less of an autocratic and authoritarian classroom climate

more freedom of student expression and spontaneity

clear rules and directions

balance between direct and indirect instruction

businesslike pace

deferred assignment of punishment

use of ability or activity groups

Now that you have seen some of the teaching practices that can help avoid as well as cause discipline problems, consider more closely your role in solving some of these problems.

Degrees of Teacher Involvement in Solving Discipline Problems

Table 10.1 lists some common discipline problems and teacher responses in the classroom. You will need to consider and prepare procedures for at least some of these. In some cases school rules and school authorities are adequate solutions to a problem (e.g., tardiness, cutting class, plagiarism), but in many other cases your classroom will be the center stage for both the

TABLE 10.1
Some common discipline problems and typical teacher responses

Problems	Teacher Responses
Talking out	Mary, if you have something to say, raise your hand.
Acting out	Bobby, if you don't stop clowning around, you'll be punished.
Talking back	Joan, you know I dislike your talking back to me.
Getting out of seat	Mary, that's the last time I'm going to stand for you leaving your seat to visit.
Note passing	Let me have that.
Noncompliant	I told you three times to open your workbook.
Ignoring rules	You know that make-up assignments must be due the same week they are assigned.
Obscene words or gestures	If I see that again, you'll go straight to the office.
Fighting	Tom and Joe, stop it immediately or you're both in big trouble.
Cheating	Mark, I can see you have another piece of paper under your test.
Stealing	Karl, where did you get this stapler?
Vandalism	Who wrote their initials on this desk?
Substance abuse	Tom, do I smell alcohol on your breath?

problem and its resolution. How you handle these problems will be as important as the nature of the problem itself. To do so you will need to decide on how you will use your authority to bring about a resolution. There are at least three alternatives available to you.

One of these is to decide that you are the ultimate authority. You are the only judge of what occurred, you alone decide on the punishment, and you are the only one available or qualified to determine if the conditions of the punishment have been met. When the learner is unable to take responsibility for his or her own actions or to admit to his or her misbehavior, this approach is the most practical and effective. It may not, however, be the best approach to every situation.

In some situations it may be desirable for you and the student to discuss and agree on the punishment. One approach is for *you to provide* some alternative forms of punishment from which the *student must choose,* thereby giving the student some choice in deciding his or her own fate. Providing students with an opportunity to participate in the punishment phase of the misbehavior sometimes can reduce both their hostility toward you for disciplining them and also the likelihood that the infraction will occur again.

A third alternative is to allow the students to participate in choosing their punishment by *your selection of* a punishment from alternatives that *the student provides.* This may work well with mature students able to judge the severity of the wrongdoing and to suggest punishments accordingly, but may be inappropriate for students who do not take responsibility for their own actions and who may not even be willing to own up to having misbehaved. Contrary to what may be believed, however, experience reveals that when students pose alternatives for their own punishment, the punishments they suggest are often harsher than those assigned by teachers.

Degrees of Severity of Misbehavior

In addition to your use of authority, you will have at your disposal many degrees of severity at which

to respond to misbehavior. You may choose to ignore an infraction if it is momentary and not likely to reoccur (e.g., when a student jumps out of and back into his seat to stretch his legs after a long assignment), or you may call on a school administrator to help resolve the problem. Between these extremes, however, are many alternatives of increasing severity, such as:

Looking at the student sternly

Walking toward the student

Calling on the student to provide the next response

Asking the student to stop

Discussing the problem with the student

Assigning the student to another seat

Assigning punishment, such as a writing assignment

Assigning the student to detention

Writing a note to the student's parents

Calling the student's parents

These alternatives vary in severity from simply giving the student a look of dissatisfaction to involving parents in the resolution of the problem. More important than the variety these alternatives offer, however, will be your ability to *match the correct level of severity to the type of misbehavior that has occurred.* One of the most difficult problems you will encounter in effectively maintaining classroom discipline will be deciding upon a response that is neither too mild nor too severe.

Although all rule violations must consistently be met with some response, the severity of the punishment can and should vary according to the nature of the violation and the frequency with which such a violation has occurred in the past. If you respond too mildly to a student who has violated a major rule many times before, nothing is likely to change in the future. If you respond too severely to a student who commits a minor violation for the first time, you will be unfair. Flexibility is important in the resolution of different discipline problems and must take into account *both the context in which the violation occurs and the type of misbehavior that has occurred.* Table 10.2 presents the common range of responses made to mild, moderate, and severe categories of misbehavior.

Talking out, acting out, getting out of the seat, disrupting others, and similar misbehaviors are dealt a mild response; but when they occur repeatedly, a moderate response may be appropriate. In unusual cases, such as continual talking

TABLE 10.2

Examples of mild, moderate, and severe misbehaviors and some alternative responses

Misbehaviors	*Alternative Responses*
Mild misbehaviors	**Mild responses**
Minor defacing of school property or property of others	Warning
Acting out (horseplaying or scuffling)	Feedback to student
Talking back	Time out
Talking without raising hand	Change of seat assignment
Getting out of seat	Withdrawal of privileges
Disrupting others	After-school detention
Sleeping in class	Telephone/note to parents
Tardiness	Parent conference
Throwing objects	Counselor referral
Exhibiting inappropriate familiarity (kissing, hugging)	
Gambling	
Eating in class	
Moderate misbehaviors	**Moderate responses**
Unauthorized leaving of class	Detention
Abusive conduct towards others	Behavior contract
Noncompliant	Withdrawal of privileges
Smoking or using tobacco in class	Telephone/note to parents
Cutting class	Parent conference
Cheating, plagiarizing, or lying	In-school suspension
Using profanity, vulgar language, or obscene gestures	Restitution of damages
Fighting	Alternative school service (e.g., clean up, tutoring)
Severe misbehaviors	**Severe responses**
Defacing or damaging school property or property of others	Detention
Theft, possession, or sale of another's property	Telephone/note to parents
Truancy	Parent conference
Being under the influence of alcohol or narcotics	In-school suspension
Selling, giving, or delivering to another person alcohol, narcotics, or weapons	Removal from school or alternative school placement
Teacher assault or verbal abuse	
Incorrigible conduct, noncompliance	

that disrupts the class, a severe response may be warranted. Misbehaviors such as cutting class, abusive conduct toward others, fighting, and use of profanity normally would be dealt a moderate response; but when these behaviors represent frequent violations, a severe response may be warranted. Misbehaviors such as cheating, plagiarism, stealing, and vandalism normally are dealt a severe response. Major incidents of vandalism, theft, incorrigible conduct, and substance abuse (in any form or quantity) should immediately be brought to the attention of school administrators rather than being dealt with in the context of your classroom.

Reinforcement Theory Applied in the Classroom

So far it has been suggested that there is more than a single way you can use your authority in managing a discipline problem (e.g., you alone decide on the punishment, you have students share in the responsibility) and more than a single degree of severity with which you can respond (e.g., giving a stern glance, calling parents). There is still more variety in dealing with a discipline problem. In this section you will learn some of the basic principles of reinforcement theory; these determine how learners respond to rewards and punishments, why they respond to them differently, and how you can use them effectively in your classroom.

Reinforcement theory states that any behavior can be controlled by the consequences that immediately follow it. The word *controlled* in this context means that the consequences of a particular behavior or event can change the probability or likelihood that the behavior will occur again. Consider, for example, the following:

Event	Consequence	Future Event
You start going to the library to study.	Your test grades go up.	You begin going to the library more often.
You go to a new restaurant.	You get lousy service.	You never go there again.
You give your boyfriend or girlfriend a word of encouragement before a big test.	He or she gives you a kiss and a hug.	You give a word of encouragement before every big test.

When the consequence that follows an event changes the probability of that event (e.g., test grades go up, you don't go there again, you get more kisses and hugs), reinforcement has occurred.

In your classroom, many events and their consequences will show the effects of reinforcement—whether you intend it or not. It may surprise you that the frequency of some misbehaviors that occur in your classroom are often unintentionally increased through reinforcement. How does this happen? Consider another sequence of events that, unknown to you, may occur in your classroom:

Event	Consequence	Future Event
Johnny cheats on a test.	He gets a good grade.	Johnny plans to cheat again.
Mary passes a note to her boyfriend.	Her boyfriend is able to pass a note back.	Mary buys a special pad of perfumed paper for writing more notes in class.
Bobby skips school.	He earns five dollars helping a friend work on his car.	Bobby plans to skip again the next time his friend needs help.

In each of these instances an undesirable behavior was reinforced (with a good grade, a returned note, five dollars). In these situations the probability that the event will recur was strengthened or increased, because the consequence that followed was perceived as desirable by the student.

Following are some of the ways a teacher can reinforce undesirable behaviors and unwittingly increase their future occurrence:

- A student complains incessantly that her essay was graded too harshly. To quiet her the teacher adds a point to her score, so she complains after every essay for the rest of the year.
- Parents call to complain about their child's poor class participation grade. The teacher starts calling on the student more often, probing and personally eliciting responses, so the student no longer believes that volunteering or raising a hand is necessary.
- A student talks back every time the teacher calls on him, so he is not called on anymore. In order to be left alone, the student does the same in his other classes.

In each of these cases the link connecting the event, the consequence, and the students' perception of the consequence was not apparent to the teacher; reinforcement of an undesirable behavior resulted. For example, in the first instance the teacher may have believed that giving the extra point could do no harm, because a single point probably would not change the student's end-of-term grade. However, the important link for the teacher was not between the teacher's behavior (giving the point) and the student's behavior (going away), but between the student's behavior (complaining) and the teacher's behavior (giving the point). The problem in each of these instances was that the teacher chose to remove the misbehavior in a way that created a consequence that was favorable to the student, thereby actually reinforcing the misbehavior. Notice that in each case the teacher considered the consequence of his actions *only from his own point of view* (e.g., quieting an annoying student, preventing a parent from calling back, avoiding an ill-mannered student) without realizing that

his actions were also reinforcing the very behavior he wished to discourage.

Now that you know how reinforcement theory works, the following sections contain guidelines for making it work for, not against, you.

Rewards

Many different types of reinforcers—or consequences—are available that can increase the probability of a desirable response. These include:

> verbal or written praise
>
> smile, a head nod
>
> special privileges (e.g., visit to the learning center, library, etc.)
>
> time out of regular work to pursue a special project (e.g., lab experiment)
>
> permission to choose a topic or assignment
>
> getting to work in a group
>
> extra points toward grade
>
> "smiley face" stickers on assignments
>
> note to parents on top of a test or paper
>
> posting a good exam or homework for others to see
>
> special recognitions and certificates (e.g., "most improved," "good conduct award," "neatest," "hardest worker," etc.)

Not all of these rewards may be equally reinforcing, however. Some learners may disdain verbal praise, while others will have no need for or intention of ever visiting the library or learning center. Some students like to be called on; others may be too shy to appreciate the added attention. What may be a reinforcement to one student may be completely irrelevant to another. Finding the right reinforcer for a student is often a matter of trial and error; if a reward does not seem to increase the probability of a desirable behavior, it should be changed for another until some success is obtained. Knowing the interests, needs, and aspirations of your learners can save valuable time in finding the right mix of reinforcers. For example, students who are mechanically inclined might enjoy time out looking at issues of *Popular Mechanics* or *Model Airplaner* on file in a Learning Center. For some, time out to read issues of *Vogue, Mademoiselle,* or *Boys' Life* may be equally appealing as a reward for desirable behaviors. You can also ask students for a menu of rewards (e.g., readings, music, magazines), that are in tune with their specific interests. This list might be compiled from an interest survey of the type shown in Figure 9.1; or students could be asked to select rewards from a list you prepare, which ensures that what is chosen will be practical within the context of your classroom.

Punishments

Punishments also can be used to reinforce—or to change the probability or likelihood that a behavior will occur. For example, a teacher can try to keep Johnny in his seat either by giving him an extra assignment every time he is out of his seat or by giving him a trip to the reading center for every 30 minutes he stays in his seat. In the first instance the teacher is giving Johnny a punishment to encourage him to do what's expected, and in the second is giving him a reward to achieve this same end. When a punishment is given to change the probability of a future behavior, it is called a negative reinforcer. Although often misunderstood in the popular literature, negative reinforcement occurs when a punishment—called an aversive—is given explicitly for the purpose of increasing—or reinforcing—the likelihood of a desired behavior. For example, when the buzzer in your car reminds you to put on your seat belt, you have been given an aversive (the buzzer) to increase the likelihood of a desired behavior (putting your seat belt on). A negative reinforcer creates an avoidance response to an undesirable behavior, thereby increasing the likelihood of a desired behavior. On the other hand, a positive reinforcer—or reward—encourages a desirable behavior to recur by dispensing something pleasant or rewarding immediately after the desirable be-

havior has taken place. Punishment as well as reward, therefore, can be used to increase the frequency of a desired behavior.

But negative and positive reinforcers generally are not equally effective in promoting a desired behavior. Given two choices to keep Johnny in his seat—negative reinforcement by assigning extra homework, or positive reinforcement by giving him something interesting to work on—the latter usually will be more successful. The following are several important reasons for this.

Punishment does not guarantee that the desirable response will occur. The extra homework may, indeed, keep Johnny in his seat the next time he is thinking of moving about, but it by no means ensures that he will pursue some meaningful instructional activity while he is there. Daydreaming, writing notes to friends, even pulling Mary's hair may all keep him from being given *that* punishment for the same misbehavior again. Punishment in the absence of rewards can create other undesired behaviors.

The effects of punishment are usually specific to a particular context and behavior. This means that extra homework is not likely to keep Johnny in his seat when a substitute teacher arrives, because it was not *that* teacher who assigned the punishment. Also, *that* punishment is not likely to deter Johnny from pulling Mary's hair, because the punishment was associated only with keeping him in his seat. In other words, punishment rarely keeps one from misbehaving beyond the specific context and behavior to which it was most closely associated.

The effects of punishment can spread to desirable behaviors. If extra homework is truly a negative reinforcer for Johnny, that is, if it is a highly undesirable and painful consequence in his eyes, he may decide never to risk leaving his seat again, even to ask for the teacher's assistance or to use the restroom. Johnny may decide to take no chances about when or when not to leave his seat—or even to trust his own judgment about when an exception to the rule may be appropriate.

Punishment sometimes elicits hostile and aggressive responses. Although any single punishment is unlikely to provoke an emotional response, students receive punishment in various forms all day long, both at school and at home. If your punishment is the "straw that breaks the camel's back," do not be surprised to observe an emotional outburst that is inconsistent with the amount of punishment rendered. This is not sufficient reason to avoid assigning punishment when it is needed, but it is reason to use it sparingly and in association with rewards.

The punishment can become associated with the punisher. If you use punishment consistently as a tool for increasing the likelihood that a desirable behavior will occur, you may lose the cooperation among learners that is necessary for managing your classroom effectively. With this cooperation gone, you will find that the vital link for making management techniques work is lost. *Plan not to solve every discipline problem by using punishment;* otherwise, the punishment could become more strongly associated with you than the desired behavior you wish to encourage.

Punishment that is rendered for the purpose of stopping an undesired behavior, but which is not immediately associated with the desired behavior, seldom has a lasting effect. If the desired behavior is not clear to your students at the time the punishment is administered, punishment will be seen only as an attempt to hurt and not as an attempt to encourage the desired behavior.

At many times during the school day and for many different infractions of school rules, an aversive used to reinforce a desired behavior is the only logical choice. For example, it would be extremely difficult or undesirable to deal with spontaneous infractions of school rules (e.g., cheating, vandalism, obscene language, theft) in any other way than to provide the appropriate punishment that has been decided on for these offenses, as long as the desired behavior is made clear to the student at the time of the punishment. Also, *punishment works best in conjunction with rewards,* as when Johnny is given an extra assignment for jumping out of his seat but also is rewarded with a trip to the reading center for staying in his seat. Even relatively minor classroom misbehaviors (e.g., talking out, sleeping in class, eating in class, throwing objects) must often be followed with punishment, but their recurrence will be less likely when the desired behavior is made known at the time of the punishment and rewarded when it occurs. Some guidelines for using rewards and punishments appropriately are presented in Table 10.3.

Warnings

Warnings can be useful in preventing minor problems from intensifying to a level at which some form of punishment is the only recourse. It is not unusual to provide several warnings for the misbehaviors listed as mild in Table 10.2 before a punishment is dispensed. However, *after two or three warnings a punishment must be assigned,* because waiting any longer will reinforce the belief that you are not serious about administering the punishment and will undermine the integrity of the rule that is being violated. Some moderate misbehaviors may also be given warnings, but behaviors listed as severe are rarely, if ever, given warnings. For these behaviors rewards are too untimely and the consequences of a repeat occurrence too damaging, so punishment should be rendered immediately, *along with a clear indication of the desired behavior.*

Corporal Punishment

Some common forms of punishment are listed in Table 10.2. Conspicuously absent from this list is any form of corporal punishment, such as hitting or paddling a student. Such punishment, although permissible in some school districts when admin-

TABLE 10.3
Guidelines for using rewards and punishments

Rewards	Punishments
1. Give the reward immediately following the desired behavior. ■ Good grade on paper—congratulatory note on top of paper. ■ Insightful answer in class—verbal praise immediately afterward.	1. Let the student know exactly what behavior will be punished, before punishment is given. ■ Rick, if you talk back again, I will assign you the optional exercises for tomorrow. ■ Marty, if you throw a paper wad again, I will write a note home.
2. Be specific about what behavior is being rewarded. ■ Johnny, I want you to stay in your seat the whole period—here is a reading assignment that fits your interests. ■ Mary, I want you to try to read a little faster—let's not grade this one.	2. Give the punishment immediately following the undesired behavior. ■ OK, that's the second time I saw you look at Sue's paper. That's an automatic five points off your test score. ■ That's the second warning about throwing things, Carl. I will have to assign you an extra problem for homework.
3. Be sure the reward is meaningful to the student. ■ Bob, there will be some mechanics magazines waiting at the Learning Center when you're finished. ■ Betty, you can study for that test next period if you have no misspellings.	3. Use the punishment after *every* occurrence of the undesired behavior. ■ Every time I see you sleeping, Bobby, I will assign extra work. ■ For each time I catch you clowning around, you'll have to make up the work for homework.
4. Use a variety of reinforcers so that the reward is always fresh and new. ■ Bob, last time you got to go to the Learning Center. This time you can go to the library. ■ Tom, last week we put you on the all-star list. This week you can work on your term paper.	4. Use punishment only after rewards do not work or is impractical given the severity and spontaneity with which the undesired behavior occurs. ■ I let you sit near your friends last week so you would not fight with Mark. This time I have to write up a referral. ■ I let you go to your locker during class last week, but I'll have to report it as a missing assignment this week.
	5. Be explicit about the desired behavior you want to occur as a result of the punishment. ■ I am giving you two extra homework problems because *I want you to turn in completed homework.* ■ You must *always do your own work,* so I will have to give you a zero for this assignment.

istered by a specifically designated school authority, has not proven particularly effective in deterring misbehavior. One of the reasons for this is that the heightened emotion and anxiety on the part of the student (and of the administrator) at the time of the punishment often prevents a rational discussion of the appropriate behavior that the punishment is supposed to encourage. In addition, these forms of punishment easily can provoke aggression and cause hostility in both students and parents; these can far outweigh the original offense for which the student is being punished. Except in the most hostile of situations (e.g., breaking up a fight to prevent physical injury, disarming a student who is threatening another, or restraining a student from self-injury) you should not have physical contact with a student, either to administer punishment or, in the case of older students, as a reward (e.g., patting a student for doing a good job or placing your arm around a student in times of high anxiety), because such contacts can be easily misunderstood.

The Parent-Teacher Conference

More effective than any form of corporal punishment when a major infraction of a school or classroom rule has occurred will be the parent-teacher conference. This is a time for informing one or both parents of the severity of the misbehavior and for eliciting their active help in preventing the misbehavior. Without the support of the family in providing the appropriate rewards and punishment at home, there is little chance that the relatively small interventions provided at school (including corporal punishment) will have a lasting effect in deterring the misbehavior. Being grounded for the week, having to be in at a certain time, completing extra study time in the quiet of one's bedroom, or performing extra chores around the house *will always have more impact than any aversive that can be administered within the context of a school day,* as long as these family aversives are administered with a full and complete understanding of the desired behavior.

Notifying parents that a conference is desired is usually the responsibility of the principal or a counselor. However, since the request for a conference is the result of a specific problem in your classroom, you will be involved in the preparation of any formal notification to inform parents why a conference is being requested. This notification should consist of a letter sent through the mail containing

1. Purpose of the conference, including a statement of the joint goal of supporting the student's success in school
2. Statement pointing out the integral role of the parent in the discipline management process (this may include a citation from any state or school policy regarding such matters)
3. Date, time, and location of conference
4. A contact person (and phone number)
5. A response form for parents' reply, preferably with a self-addressed stamped envelope

In the event that a request for a conference is made to the student's parents by phone, these same points can be orally presented; it is important that the date, time, location, and contact person for the conference are recorded by the parent at the time of the call.

During the conference you should:

- Try to gain the parents' acknowledgement of and support for their participation in the discipline management process
- Present a plan of action for addressing the problem at home and at school
- Identify follow-up activities (e.g., note home each week indicating progress, immediate phone call if problem should recur, a review of the situation at the next parent-teacher night)
- Document what took place at the conference, including the agreements and disagreements

The Influence of Home and Family on Classroom Behavior Problems

Finally, it is important to note that some of the discipline problems you will face in your classroom will have their origin at home. Living in a fast-paced, upwardly mobile society has created family stresses and strains that could not have been imagined by our grandparents. Their life while growing up was not necessarily any easier than yours or your students'; but it was most assuredly different, particularly with respect to the intensity and rapidity with which children today experience various developmental stages and life-cycle changes. For example, by some estimates boys and girls are maturing a full five years earlier than they did 50 years ago. This means that they are coming under the influence of emotions pertaining to sex, aggression, love, affiliation, jealously, competitiveness, and so on far earlier than perhaps even our own mothers and fathers did.

The average seventh- or eighth-grade teacher is no longer even surprised by the depth of understanding and ability of young students to emulate the attractively packaged images of adult behavior and life-styles (especially as they relate to sex, clothes, relationships, and dominance) so often found in today's media. Although not often recognized, these generational differences are sometimes even more difficult for parents to accept than for you, the teacher. This often leads to major conflicts at home that surface in your classroom as seemingly minor but persistent misbehaviors. There is little influence you can have over home conflicts, except to understand that they originate in the home and not in your classroom. There will be times when no amount of reward or punishment will work, because the source of the problem is within the home and may be far more serious than you suppose— perhaps marital discord, competition among brothers and sisters, financial distress, and divorce. One or more of these family disturbances could easily be occurring in half of the families of the students in any given class. These are not trivial burdens for students, especially when combined with the social and academic demands of school, the uncertainties of a future job or education, and the tension that school-age children always feel between youth and adulthood. When problems persist and your rewards and punishments are to no avail, it is time to consider that some of these family events may be occurring. Although there is no easy way to know what is happening in the lives of your students at home, many students welcome the opportunity to reveal the nature of these problems, *when they are asked*. For some it will be just the opportunity they may have been looking for to shed some of the emotional burden these events are creating in their lives. It is not your role to resolve these problems, but the reasons they are occurring may help put in perspective why your rewards and punishments may not be working and can help you decide whether the problem should be brought to the attention of others (e.g., social worker, counselor, school psychologist) who may be in a better position to help.

Summing Up

This chapter introduced you to some concepts and techniques for maintaining classroom order and discipline. Its main points were:

1. Most classroom discipline problems are low intensity, continuous, and unconnected with any larger, more serious event.
2. Classrooms in which a large percentage of students are off-task, talk without raising hands, talk back, move about without permission, ignore rules, disrupt others, and/or fail to complete assignments are characterized by the following:

   - extreme negativity
   - exclusive authoritarian climate
   - overreacting
   - mass punishment
   - blaming
   - lack of clear instructional goals
   - repetition of already learned material
   - pausing and interruptions
   - dealing with a single student at length
   - lack of recognition of ability levels

3. Classroom order and discipline depends as much on the voluntary cooperation of stu-

dents as it does on the clear communication of rules and the ability to enforce them.

4. Although emotional responses may be effective at times, their consistent use diminishes their effectiveness at the times they may be needed most.

5. Students who obey often come from a different peer group than do those who frequently disobey and, therefore, the former have little or no influence over the latter, either in or out of school.

6. It is not essential that every misbehavior be attributed to someone, even if the most likely person actually is responsible.

7. Even the most indirect discussions must be crafted to communicate a structure, an end result, and a clear expectation of student conduct.

8. There should always be some mystery, challenge, or curiosity about what is to be learned. That is, there should always be some amount of uncertainty as to what the next question or item will be and whether or not it can be answered correctly.

9. Awkward gaps, pauses, and interruptions in which eye and visual contact is lost almost always will disengage your students from the learning process.

10. The punishment phase of a disciplinary action should be left until after class or after school in order to cause the least disruption to the class.

11. Ability grouping can be used with remedial activities to help slow learners either to catch up or to pursue alternative instructional goals.

12. Some characteristics of effective classroom management include the following:

   ■ seeing all aspects of the classroom at once
   ■ overlapping activities
   ■ less autocratic and authoritarian
   ■ some freedom of student expression and spontaneity
   ■ adultlike cooperative environment
   ■ clear rules and directions
   ■ balance between direct and indirect instruction

   ■ businesslike pace
   ■ assignment of punishment later
   ■ formation of ability or activity groups

13. Three ways to apply your authority in dealing with misbehavior are

   ■ you alone judge what occurred and what the punishment should be;
   ■ you provide some alternative forms of punishment from which the student must choose;
   ■ you select a punishment from alternatives that the student provides.

14. The level of severity with which you respond to a misbehavior should match the misbehavior that has occurred.

15. The idea behind reinforcement theory is that any behavior can be controlled by the consequences that immediately follow it. When the consequence that follows an event changes the probability of that event, reinforcement has occurred.

16. Some misbehaviors that occur in classrooms are unintentionally increased through reinforcement, in which case the probability of the misbehavior increases because a consequence that follows the misbehavior is perceived as desirable by the student.

17. Both rewards and punishment can increase the probability of a behavior, although the latter without the former is rarely effective.

18. A reward that is reinforcing to one student may be irrelevant to another.

19. Positive reinforcement is the use of a reward to increase the probability of a desired behavior. Negative reinforcement is the use of an aversive (punishment) to increase the probability of a desired behavior.

20. Punishment in the absence of rewards tends to be less effective in increasing the probability of a desired behavior because

   ■ punishment does not guarantee that the desirable response will occur;
   ■ the effects of punishment are specific to a particular context;

- the effects of punishment can spread to undesirable behavior;
- punishment can create hostile and aggressive responses;
- punishment can become associated with the punisher.

21. After two or three warnings a punishment should be assigned.
22. Corporal punishment is rarely effective in deterring misbehavior.
23. One feature of the parent-teacher conference which accounts for its effectiveness is the involvement of the parent in eliminating the misbehavior.

For Discussion and Practice

*1. Identify the classroom characteristics most commonly associated with poor classroom managers.
2. Give an example of a teacher-student interaction that illustrates each of the characteristics identified in the preceding discussion topic.
*3. Why is obtaining the voluntary cooperation of students in obeying classroom rules important to becoming an effective classroom manager?
*4. Why would the use of repeated emotional responses in dealing with misbehavior diminish your effectiveness as a classroom manager?
*5. Why is mass punishment rarely effective in creating peer pressure that reduces misbehavior?
*6. What would be a reason for not insisting that every misbehavior must be attributed to someone?
*7. What would be some good advice to a fellow teacher who wants to conduct an indirect discussion in his or her class?
*8. Why does repetition of material that already has been learned at high rates of success often create misbehavior?
*9. What are two frequent sources of pauses and interruptions in classrooms? What strategies would you use in combating their effects on misbehavior?
*10. Identify three ways of dealing with misbehavior that defer the punishment phase to a later time.
*11. How can learners who lack the task-relevant prior knowledge to participate in class be given a chance to catch up or pursue alternative paths?

12. Using your own words, write a narrative profile of the kinds of behaviors and classroom activities that would be indicative of an effective classroom manager.
*13. Name three different ways you can use your authority to assign punishment.
14. Identify responses that reflect the severity of the offense for the following misbehaviors. Do not use the same response more than once.

Talking back

Cutting class

Eating in class

Assaulting a teacher

Smoking in class

Sleeping in class

Acting out

Obscene gesturing

Selling drugs

Fighting

15. Give one positive and one negative reinforcer that might be used to get a student to

Do homework

Stop talking

Stop talking back

Turn in assignments on time

Be on time for class

Remember to bring pen and pencil

Not talk without raising hand

*16. Identify five reasons why punishment is rarely effective in the absence of rewards.
*17. Under what two conditions is the use of punishment most effective?
*18. Identify two important objectives for having a parent-teacher conference.

Suggested Readings

Brodinsky, B. (1980). *Student discipline: Problems and solutions*. Arlington: American Association of School Administrators.

A practical handbook written from the perspective of a school administrator about what every teacher should know about classroom discipline.

Charles, C. M. (1981). *Building classroom discipline.* New York: Longman.
A useful book because of its many scenarios on how to handle classroom discipline and to be an effective classroom manager.

Clarizio, H. F. (1980). *Toward positive classroom discipline.* New York: Wiley.
Details the currently most used strategies for establishing a system for classroom order and discipline—very comprehensive.

Deitz, S. & Hummel, J. (1978). *Discipline in the schools: A guide to reducing misbehavior.* Englewood Cliffs, NJ: Educational Technology Publishers.
Similar to others but well-illustrated with examples.

Givener, A. & Graubard, P. S. (1974). *A handbook of behavior modification for the classroom.* New York: Holt, Rinehart & Winston.
A sourcebook of techniques for changing student behavior through the principles of reinforcement theory.

Glickman, C. & Wolfgang, C. (1979). Dealing with student misbehavior: An eclectic review. *Journal of Teacher Education, 30,* 3, 7–13.

An overview and philosophical background to the many approaches to classroom discipline.

Kindsvatter, R. (1978). A new view of the dynamics of discipline. *Phi Delta Kappan,* 322–325.
An analysis of some of the reasons behind classroom discipline problems and how they affect school performance.

Long, N. J., Morse, W. C., & Newman, R. G. (1980). *Conflict in the classroom.* Belmont, CA: Wadsworth.
Covers the theory and practice of classroom management with especially good illustrations of how effective classroom discipline can be achieved.

O'Banion, D. R. & Whaley, D. L. (1981). *Behavior contracting: Arranging contingencies of reinforcement.* New York: Springer.
An authoritative source on the ways to use rewards to create and maintain desirable student behavior.

Wolfgang, C. H. & Glickman, C. D. (1980). *Solving discipline problems: Strategies for classroom teachers.* Boston: Allyn & Bacon.
Down-to-earth treatment of classroom discipline; speaks to the most immediate and pressing classroom management needs of teachers.

11
Teaching Special Types of Learners in the Regular Classroom

This chapter discusses a diverse and heterogeneous classroom that, in addition to including average learners, has various less able, gifted, bilingual, and handicapped learners. While your classroom is likely not to contain all of these types of learners at the same time, it is probable that you will be teaching some combination of them at almost any time. Because these special learners compose a sizable percentage of our school-age population, you are likely to encounter them in any school where you are likely to teach.

The pluralistic culture in which we live, work, and play includes the physically strong and weak, the mentally able and less able, the native and nonnative speaker, the rich and poor, the well-educated and the undereducated, as well as many others who differ from the majority. Unlike many other cultures and educational systems throughout the world, we have welcomed this diversity in our communities and our schools; the mixture of cultures is illustrative of a nation based on

democratic principles. These principles give equal rights, including the right to a free, public education to all learners irrespective of race, creed, intellect, language, or any other physical, cultural, or mental characteristic. These principles also mandate an educational policy that extends educational opportunities to all individuals in the least restricted (least segregated) environment conducive to their maximum development.

This policy and the federal and state laws that undergird it is why this chapter is important to the regular classroom teacher, who may mistakenly believe he or she will have a teaching career devoted exclusively to educating the "average" student. However, in the American school system *average* no longer means the absence of diversity; rather, it increasingly is intended to reflect the diversity of people, cultures, and values that are represented in our communities and the nation at large. The less able, gifted, bilingual, and handicapped learners are only a small part of this diversity, but they are a part that is rapidly redefining the composition and character of the so-called "regular" classroom. This means you must be aware of the special learning needs of these types of learners and be able to execute teaching strategies that can meet their instructional needs. It also means you must be able to manage and teach in a classroom that is no less "average" than the community which exists outside it.

Several observations can be made concerning the special learners discussed in this chapter. The first is that *not all of these learners are independent of each other*. For example, a slow learner may also be bilingual, as can a handicapped or gifted learner; or a learner can be average in one subject and gifted in another. It is even conceivable that one could be both slow and gifted when considering accomplishments in widely different areas of the curriculum, such as math versus art. Many combinations are possible and do exist in our schools; individuals are found in special instructional programs and naturally occurring groups. It may also be true that some learners may be ineligible or overlooked for membership in one group due to their membership in another group. This leads to a second observation, *that any attempt to categorize or group students will necessarily be flawed,* because even when individuals are grouped according to one common characteristic, they will differ on many other characteristics that also affect their behavior. Sometimes the variation in the behavior occurring *within* a group of learners may be greater than the variation found *between* groups of learners. So, why classify learners into categories at all?

Once the flaws inherent in any system of categorizing students are recognized and measures are taken to minimize the importance of category labels, the disadvantages are outweighed by the advantages of categorizing learners into groups; the advantages include the assistance they provide in

1. dispensing state and federal funds that are often earmarked for specific types of learners,

2. developing and organizing instructional materials, texts, and media appropriate for certain types of learners, and
3. training and assigning the most qualified instructional staff to teach certain types of learners.

With these limitations and advantages in mind, this chapter will explore the similarities and differences among these four types of learners and suggest various teaching methods specific to their special learning needs.

The Slow Learner

Contrary to common belief, the slow learner is neither a rare nor a unique individual in the regular classroom. It has been estimated that as many as one third of all students attending school today will drop out before graduation. Of these, more than half could be described as slow learners (Hodgkinson, 1986). Your overall effectiveness as a teacher, therefore, may well depend on your ability to recognize and appropriately teach this group of learners. This section will dispel some common misconceptions about the slow learner, will explain who he or she really is, and will suggest some procedures for becoming aware of and instructing this special group of students.

One common misperception about slow learners is that they are mentally retarded or emotionally disturbed, or that they continually need disciplining. "Slow learner" does not refer to any of these groups or to the student of average intelligence who may fail a subject due to difficulty with the language, lack of sufficient discipline to study, or a lack of interest in school. Indeed, slow learners may be among these groups, but these are not defining characteristics. The student commonly referred to as a slow learner is one who cannot learn at an average rate from the instructional resources, texts, workbooks, and learning materials that have been designated for the majority of students in the classroom (Bloom, 1982). These students need special instructional pacing, frequent feedback, corrective instruction, and/or modified materials, all administered under conditions sufficiently flexible for learning to occur.

Slow learners are usually taught in one of two possible instructional arrangements: The first is classrooms composed mostly of average students, in which case as many as 20% of your class may be slow learners; the second is a class composed of and specifically designated for slow learners. The latter classes are sometimes part of a *track system* in which different sections of math, English, science, and social studies are reserved for less able, average, and more able students. Although the desirability and fairness of various types of tracking systems has been the subject of debate, membership in or eligibility for a track is usually determined on the basis of a student's percentile rank derived from a score on a subscale of a standardized achievement test representing the student's achievement in the subject being tracked. For example, a percentile rank of 30 on an appropriate subscale might be considered the cutoff for admission to a track for less able learners. This would mean that 30% of all the students from across the country who took the standardized test scored equal to or below those admitted to the track. Cutoff percentiles vary considerably across school districts and frequently are supplanted by parental wishes and by administrator and teacher recommendations based upon the past performance of a particular student.

Whether you meet the slow learner in a regular class or in a class specifically devoted to slow learners, you will immediately feel the challenge and the difficulty of meeting the learning needs of this special group. The first and most obvious characteristic you will notice is the limited attention span of the slow learner in comparison to that of more able students. These learners require more than the usual amount of variation in method of presentation (e.g., direct, indirect), classroom climate (e.g., cooperative, competitive), and instructional materials (e.g., films, workbooks, games, and simulations) to keep them actively engaged in the learning process. If this variation is not part of your lessons, these students may well create their own variety in ways that can be disruptive to your teaching.

Other characteristics that are immediately noticeable about slow learners are their deficiencies in the basic skills of reading, writing, and mathematics, their difficulty in comprehending abstract ideas, and perhaps, most disconcerting, their unsystematic and careless work habits. These deficiencies often make instructional lessons geared to the average student too difficult for the slow learner. When a method of presentation and organization of content does not recognize and accommodate these characteristics, the result is often a failing performance and a continuation of a cycle of deficiencies that promotes poor self-concept, misbehavior, and disinterest in school—all of which have contributed to a particularly high dropout rate among this type of learner.

An important aspect of teaching slow learners is knowing the difference between *compensatory* and *remedial* teaching. Recall that these were two approaches to *adaptive teaching* presented in chapter 2. The term **compensatory education** originally referred to the preschool programs of the 1960s, which were designed to compensate for the cultural deprivation of disadvantaged children (Dembo, 1981). Compensatory programs are based on the premise that enriching environmental conditions can influence intellectual and academic development. Compensatory teaching is an approach to instruction that alters the presentation of content by reorganizing it, by transmitting it through alternate modalities (e.g., pictures v. words), and by supplementing it with additional learning resources (e.g., games and simulations), and activities (e.g., group discussions, field experiences) in order to circumvent a student's fundamental weakness or deficiency. This may involve modifying an instructional technique either by including the visual representation of content, using more flexible instructional presentations (e.g., films, pictures, illustrations), or by shifting to alternate instructional formats (e.g., self-paced texts, simulations, experience-oriented workbooks) to compensate for known deficiencies. The objective of compensatory teaching is to deemphasize instructional stimuli that require the use of weaker learning modalities (e.g., verbal, conceptual) and to emphasize instructional stimuli and arrangements that require the use of stronger learning modalities (e.g., visual, tactile).

An alternate approach for the regular classroom teacher in instructing the slow learner is **remedial teaching**. This refers to the use of activities, techniques, and practices that are specifically chosen to eliminate the weaknesses or deficiencies that are known to exist. With this approach deficiencies in basic math skills, for example, would be reduced or eliminated by *reteaching* the content that was not learned at some earlier time. The instructional environment would not be changed in any way, as would be the case with the compensatory approach, and conventional instructional techniques, such as drill and practice, might be employed.

Some important practical and philosophical differences exist between these two alternative strategies for teaching the slow learner. Practically, the compensatory approach is favored because of the instructional time that may be required to reteach an extensive number of basic skills with no guarantee that they will be learned. Because earlier attempts failed to teach these skills, subsequent efforts may meet the same fate once again. The compensatory approach uses currently planned instruction, altering the instructional environment as needed so that basic deficiencies become less important in acquiring new content. Philosophically, the compensatory approach represents a belief that many alternative paths can be taken to acquire new knowledge. One path may emphasize one set of abilities, while another path may emphasize a different set of abilities. The role of the teacher is to be flexible enough to look for and eventually to find a path to learning that works.

Some remediation, however, will always be necessary with the slow learner; some basic skills are so fundamental to subsequent learning that they must be acquired at almost any cost of instructional time. However, for the regular classroom teacher who must deal with students of all ability levels, the remediation of specific deficiencies may be secondary to the acquisition of new concepts and understandings using alternative instructional strategies. It is interesting to note that tracked classes specifically devoted to the slow learner often represent an integration of both the remedial and the compensatory approaches. In these classes deficiencies often are compensated for through the reorganization of subject matter. On the other hand, because these classes are devoted entirely to slow learners where traditional content coverage is abbreviated, more time is allowed for reteaching fundamental skills through drill and practice.

While no single technique or set of techniques is sufficient for teaching the slow learner, some of the following suggestions can serve as a starting point for developing instructional strategies that specifically address the learning needs of the slow learner.

Because the attention span of the slow learner is short, develop lessons around the interests, needs, and experiences of the student as much as possible. These students should be made to feel that some parts of the instruction have been designed with their specific interests or experiences in mind. Oral or written autobiographies at the beginning of the year, or simply inventories in which students indicate their hobbies, jobs, and unusual trips or experiences can provide the structure for lesson plans, special projects, or extra-credit assignments later in the year.

Vary your instructional technique often. Switching from lecture to discussion and then to seatwork provides the variety that slow learners need to stay engaged in the learning process. In addition to keeping the slow learner's attention, variety in instructional technique offers the learner the opportunity to see the same content presented in different ways, thereby increasing the opportunity that the approach will accommodate the different learning styles that may be present among the slow learners and providing some of the remediation that may be necessary.

Incorporate into your lessons individualized learning materials that provide feedback to the learner. Slow learners respond favorably to frequent reinforcement of small segments of learning. Therefore, the use of programmed texts and interactive computer instruction is often effective in remediation of basic skills for slow learners. In addition, an emphasis on frequent diagnostic assessment of the student's progress paired with immediate corrective instruction is often particularly effective.

Incorporate audio and visual materials into your lessons as much as possible. One common characteristic among slow learners is that they often learn better by seeing and hearing than by reading. This should be no surprise, because performance in the basic skill areas, including reading, usually is below grade level among slow learners. Incorporating films, videotapes, and audio into lessons will help accommodate the instruction to the learning modalities that are strongest among slow learners. An emphasis on concrete and visual forms of content will also tend to compensate for the general difficulty of slow learners to grasp abstract ideas and concepts.

Be flexible in developing your own worksheets and exercises when textbook materials are either too difficult or vary markedly from topics that can capture your students' interests. Textbooks and workbooks, when written for the average student, often exceed the functioning level of the slow learner and sometimes become more of a hindrance than an aid. Sometimes only small changes in worksheets and exercises need be made to adapt the vocabulary or difficulty level (e.g., in the case of math problems) to the ability of your slow learners. Also, using textbooks and exercises intended for a lower grade can ease the burden of creating materials that are unavailable at your grade level.

Make peer tutors available for students needing remediation. Peer tutoring can become an effective ally to your teaching objectives, especially when tutors are assigned so that everyone being tutored also has the responsibility of being a tutor. The learner needing help is not singled out and has a stake in making the idea work, since his or her pride is on the line both as a learner and as a tutor.

For slow learners who are severely limited in writing ability, encourage them to express themselves orally as an alternative to preparing a written report. A carefully organized taped response to an assignment might be considered; this has the advantage of avoiding spelling, syntax, and writing errors which could be so pervasive as to eliminate any feeling that an acceptable level of performance could be obtained, no matter how good the content. Many writing assignments go unattempted or only half-heartedly attempted out of recognition that the product produced could not meet even the minimal standards of good writing.

When giving tests, provide study aids about the content to be tested; these help alert students to the most important problems, content, or issues. Study aids serve as advance organizers which eliminate the irrelevant details which slow learners often laboriously study in the belief that they are important. The slow learner usually is unable to weigh the relative importance of competing instructional stimuli unless explicitly told or shown what is and is not important. Example exam questions or a list of the topics from which exam questions may be chosen are important tools for focusing student effort in the appropriate areas.

You may want to consider increasing the learning skills of your students by teaching them how to take notes, how to outline, and how to listen. These skills are acquired through observation by higher ability students but they need to be specifically taught to slow learners.

While all of the five key behaviors—clarity, variety, task orientation, and student engagement in the learning process at moderate-to-high success rates—are relevant to the slow learner, variety in your teaching method and student engagement at high rates of success are among the most important. If you are unable to capture and maintain the attention of your slow learners with a flexible and variable instructional style, little else can transpire in your classroom. And, unless the slow learner is actively engaged in the learning process through interesting concrete visual stimuli, there will be little contact emotionally and intellectually with the content you are presenting. This contact can most easily be attained when you *vary your instructional material often and organize it into bits small enough to ensure moderate-to-high rates of success.*

The Gifted and/or Talented Learner

When a student can read rapidly and comprehend quickly, has an exceptional memory, is imaginative and creative, has a long attention span, and is comfortable with abstract ideas, words like *bright, exceptional, gifted,* and *talented* refer to that student. Not all schools have programs that specifically provide for the learning needs of the gifted and talented, but there is a growing awareness that gifted and talented students represent an important natural resource that must be encouraged, activated, and directed in ways that maximally develop their unique talents and abilities.

Although the size and scope of most specialized school programs, such as those for the handicapped or disadvantaged, make programs for the gifted look pale by comparison, the teaching of the gifted remains an important objective of virtually every school. Because of their importance to your school's objectives and of the distribution of gifted and talented across every social class, community, and type of school, the regular classroom teacher must be aware of the learning needs of this special type of learner. This section will explain some of the characteristics that make a student gifted and talented and some of the ways in which your teaching can be altered to meet the learning needs of this type of learner.

If you were to observe gifted and talented programs in different school districts, you would quickly come to the conclusion that the word *gifted* has many meanings. These different definitions of giftedness have created considerable diversity among both the students called gifted and the instructional programs designed to meet their needs. Gifted students are a population that is every bit as diverse as the slow learners we have previously described. You should learn about some of the ways giftedness is determined and about the diversity of programs that have been designed for the gifted.

As was true of the slow learner, you are likely to meet the gifted learner in one of several instructional arrangements. One of these is a gifted class that is part of a districtwide gifted and talented program. Another is a tracked class specifically intended for the more able student, or, another is a so-called average or regular class composed mostly of average learners but also including varying numbers of slow, more able, and gifted learners. The number of gifted learners in your average class will depend to a large extent on factors that are not within your control, such as the availability of a special program for the gifted in your school, the existence of a formal tracking system of more able learners, and the proportion of gifted learners in the school community in which you are teaching. Whether as teachers of a gifted class, of a more able class with some gifted learners, or of a regular class likely to contain one or more gifted learners, most teachers at both the elementary and secondary levels will come in contact with and have the responsibility for teaching the gifted *during their very first year of teaching.*

It is a mistaken notion that gifted learners, especially compared to the slow learners, are easy to teach. As most experienced teachers of the gifted will attest, nothing could be further from the truth. It is sometimes the case that the experienced teacher who has taught the gifted will prefer *not* to do so again, due to the extra work (e.g., preparing intellectually challenging exams, grading extended essays, dealing with parent expectations) and special demands (e.g., knowing how to use specialized library resources, supplemental materials, and equipment) that often will be required. Hence, the assignment may be given to a beginning teacher who simply may have no choice in the matter.

The truth is that the job of teaching the gifted is as difficult and as challenging as teaching any other type of learner. There are important differences among learning types, but these are differences in kind and not in degree. For example, the preparation required to teach the gifted will be different, but not measurably less, than for a class of slow learners. Likewise, discipline problems encountered with the gifted will be different, but not measurably less, than for other types of learners. The amount of time spent teaching mastery of a concept will not measurably vary among types of learners, because the difficulty level at which the concept is taught must also vary with types of learners. Therefore, teaching the gifted, whether as an intact class in the junior and senior high or as individuals in an average or regular class, should be approached free of any illusions that something less is being required of you. On the contrary, it is more likely that something more of you will be required.

Because the words *gifted* and *talented* often include considerable diversity among these learners, it is important to be aware of the different ways in which gifted students are determined. The most important aspect of determining giftedness is to realize that no one standard or no single definition of giftedness has ever been, or is likely to be, agreed upon. However, the Congressional Record of October 10, 1978, provides a broad definition of gifted and talented:

Gifted and talented children means children, and whenever applicable youth, who are identified at the preschool, elementary, or secondary level as possessing demonstrated or potential abilities that give evidence of high performance capability in areas such as intellectual, creative, specific academics, or leadership abilities, or in the performing and visual arts, and who by reason thereof require services or activities not ordinarily provided by the school (H-12179).

While a consensus exists as to what general abilities and behaviors compose giftedness, there is considerable variation in specific ways of measuring both the degree of ability and also the proper combination of sub-abilities chosen that must be possessed to represent giftedness. The following, however, are some of the most important behavioral ingredients from which an individual school district's definition of giftedness is likely to be composed.

Foremost among the characteristics of giftedness is *intelligence*. As was noted in chapter 2, aptitude in a specific area often is more predictive of future productivity and accomplishments (in that area) than is general intelligence. Nevertheless, most formulae for defining giftedness include general intelligence. This is particularly true in the elementary grades, where it is believed that learners are still in the process of developing their specialized intellectual capacities while their general intelligence is almost completely formed in the critical preschool years. The emphasis on general intelligence for aiding in the identification of giftedness at the elementary level is also a function of the difficulty of measuring specific aptitudes at that age, when many of the words and concepts required for accurately testing specific aptitudes have yet to be taught.

At the junior high and secondary levels, measures of specific intelligence are more likely to be substituted for general intelligence. The most common among these are verbal and mathematical aptitude, scores for which can be derived from most general IQ tests. For example, a sufficiently high score on verbal intelligence could qualify a learner for gifted English but not for gifted math, and vice versa; this gives greater flexibility to the definition of giftedness.

How high must a student score on tests of general or specific intelligence to be considered gifted? This depends upon the school district making the classification. However, it is known how intelligence is distributed among individuals in the entire population. You may recall that intelligence is distributed in the shape of a bell-shaped curve, with most individuals scoring at or about the middle of the curve, which represents an IQ score of 100. From the shape of this curve, we also know that less than 1% of the population receives a score of 145 or higher on an IQ test, about 2–3% scores 130 or higher, and approximately 16% scores 115 or higher. Although these percentages vary slightly depending on the specific test used to measure intelligence, they provide a useful guideline for selecting gifted learners. An IQ score of about 130 or higher generally makes one eligible for gifted instruction (Dembo, 1981). However, in practice, since giftedness is almost always defined in conjunction with at least several other behaviors, admission to gifted programs and classes usually is far less restrictive. Although highly variable among schools and states, it is not uncommon to consider a learner who scores below 130 on an IQ test to be eligible for gifted instruction. It also is possible that IQ may not be considered at all in determining giftedness, in which case the learner would need to exhibit unusual ability in one or more other areas. Since IQ tests rely greatly on the standard language usage known to predominate in the middle class, a school district with a high concentration of low-SES students may not require a high level of tested intelligence, at least not as measured by standardized tests, as a requirement for being gifted. In most cases, however, intelligence is among several behaviors that will constitute giftedness, but rarely is (or should it be) used as the only index of giftedness.

Among the other behaviors frequently used to determine giftedness is the learner's past *achievement,* usually in the area or areas for which gifted instruction is being considered. Prior achievement is measured by yearly standardized tests which cover areas such as math, social studies, reading comprehension, vocabulary, and science. Cutoff scores in the form of percentile ranks are determined in each subject area, with a per-

centile score of 90–95 representing a typical cutoff. Although cutoff percentiles differ among school districts, a cutoff percentile of 90 means that a learner is eligible for gifted instruction if his or her score on the appropriate subscale of a standardized achievement test is higher than those of 90% of all those who took the test.

In addition to intelligence and achievement, indices of *creativity* are often considered in selecting gifted learners. It is the inclusion of this behavioral dimension in defining the gifted which has broadened the definition of this type of learner to include both the gifted and the talented. The significance of this addition is that not all gifted learners may be talented, nor are all talented learners gifted. The phrase "gifted and talented," which is widely used, may mean talented but not gifted, gifted but not talented, mostly talented with some giftedness, mostly gifted with some talent, or both gifted and talented. These alternative categorizations will be more or less possible depending on the inclusion of various indices of creativity among the standards of eligibility. Because creative behaviors generally are considered in selecting gifted students, this type of learner might more appropriately be called "gifted and/or talented."

Some of the observable signs indicating the presence of creativity in a learner include the following:

applying abstract principles to the solution of problems

being curious and inquisitive

giving uncommon or unusual responses

showing imagination

posing original solutions to problems

discriminating between major and minor events

seeing relationships among dissimilar objects

Both recommendations from teachers based upon these and other signs of creativity and also any observable creative products produced by the student (e.g., sculpture, painting, musical score, science fair project, short story) usually compose the creativity component for determining the gifted and talented learner. It is interesting to note that studies have shown only a modest relationship between intelligence and creativity, indicating that creativity is fairly independent of both IQ and achievement.

A fourth behavior sometimes used in selecting gifted and talented learners involves the recommendations from teachers and other knowledgeable sources concerning a learner's *task persistence*. This behavior is difficult to evaluate but often is considered indispensable for satisfactory achievement in a gifted and talented program, because both the quantity and quality of the work are likely to be considerably above what would be expected in the regular classroom. Obviously this trait alone would not be sufficient for qualifying a learner for gifted instruction, but if such instruction is indeed geared to the extremely able student, students will need unusual levels of task persistence to succeed. Some of the behaviors teachers look for in determining task persistence include the following:

ability to devise organized approaches to learning

ability to concentrate on detail

self-imposed high standards

persistence in achieving personal goals

willing to evaluate one's own performance and capable of doing so

sense of responsibility

high level of energy, particularly with regard to academic tasks

It is in evaluating the preceding behaviors that parents play the greatest role in influencing their child's eligibility for gifted instruction. By providing testimony to the school about the ability of their child to work hard, to accept additional responsibility, and to live with increased performance and grading expectations, the parent may convince the school that the learner can indeed profit from gifted instruction. Because prestige accrues to both parent and student from being in a gifted class, you can expect consid-erable pressure from parents to consider students who otherwise might not measure up to established standards of intelligence, achievement, and creativity. In some of these cases it may be necessary to point out why a particular learner would not benefit from gifted instruction and to help secure an alternative placement.

Whether you consider one of your students gifted as a result of previously being assigned to one or more classes devoted to the gifted, or whether you arrive at this conclusion from an independent assessment of his or her intelligence, achievement, creativity, and task persistence, there are several methods for teaching the gifted who, for one reason or another, must be taught among regular students. Some of the following suggestions can serve as starting points for managing and teaching the gifted and talented learner.

Because gifted learners tend to take greater responsibility for their own learning than do average students, choose learning activities that allow them considerable freedom to pursue topics or objectives of personal interest. This will encourage independent thinking while at the same time give the student the extra motivation often required to pursue a topic much more in depth than would be expected of an average student. Along with this, let students know that you are giving them a unique opportunity to, in a sense, create their own curriculum. Some gifted students become disenchanted with school, feeling that nothing in school is relevant to their interests at their intellectual level. By allowing them to pursue and investigate some topics of their own choosing, you will be making them participants in the design of their own learning.

Occasionally plan instructional activities that involve group activities. Gifted students are among those most capable of picking up the ideas of others and creating from them new and unusual variations. Brainstorming sessions, group discussion, panel-type peer interviews, and debates are among some of the ways interactions among students can be started and the ideas and viewpoints of others heard and considered. When carefully organized, this can create a "snowballing" of ideas which can turn initially rough ideas about a problem into polished and elegant solutions.

Plan instructional lessons that include individual and small group investigations of real-life problems that require problem-solving activity. Let your gifted students become actual investigators in solving real-world dilemmas in your content area. This will force them to place newly acquired knowledge and understandings in a practical perspective and to increase the problem-solving challenge. Ask them pointed questions that do not have readily available answers: "How would you reduce world tensions among the superpowers?" "How would you eliminate acid rain?" "How could we harvest the seas?" "How could life be sustained on the moon?" "What would a school for the gifted look like?" Be careful not to accept glib and superficial responses. Make clear that an inquiry must be conducted into the nature of the problem using methods of inquiry as close as possible to those that professionals—scientists, engineers, political scientists—would use in answering the question. Finally, require actual library or laboratory research that produces not just opinions, but also objective evidence leading to a possible answer.

Perhaps more than any other learners, the gifted both are capable of and also enjoy the freedom to independently explore issues and ideas that are of concern to them. You can give them this opportunity by posing a challenging problem and organizing data (e.g., references, materials, and documents) that must be screened by your students for their relevance. Focus the problem in a way so that the learner must make the key decisions about what is and is not important for a solution. This feeling of responsibility and control over the inquiry is essential if it is to be seen by the learner as truly self-directed. Throughout the inquiry the student should feel your support, encouragement, and, most of all, availability to provide additional references and materials relevant to directions they wish to explore.

Because gifted students tend to be verbally fluent, it is sometimes difficult to know whether an articulate response substitutes superficiality and glibness for an in-depth understanding. Fancy words at a high vocabulary level may hide a lack of hard work and investigation. Such responses may even be purposefully composed to intimidate the listener, whether it be the teacher or a classmate. Testing and questioning the gifted, therefore, should be designed to draw out the knowledge and understanding that lies within, in order to separate articulate superficiality from in-depth understanding. Use tests and questions that ask the student to go beyond knowing and remembering facts. Asking your gifted students to explain, analyze, compare, contrast, hypothesize, infer, adopt, justify, judge, prove, criticize, and dispute are means of indicating that more than a verbally fluent response is required. Asking your students to explain the reasons behind their answers, to put together the known facts into something new, and to judge the outcome of their own inquiry are useful means of separating slick responses from meaningful answers.

The Bilingual Learner

There are approximately five million students representing about 10% of the entire school-age population in this country that speak languages other than English as their primary language (Baca and Cervantes, 1984). Although the number of these students varies depending on state and region, you can be expected to meet at least some of them in your classroom. If you teach in some areas of the South, Southwest, and Northeast, as many as a third of your students may not speak English as their primary language.

Most predominant among this group are students of Mexican-American, Puerto Rican, Cuban, and Central and South American heritage. These students generally are considered to be bilingual, which implies that they are proficient in both their native and adopted languages. In reality, however, many of these students are limited English proficient (LEP), which means that they may range from being unable to express themselves at all in English, either orally or in writing, to being marginally proficient in English. Due to the vast and increasing numbers of these students in our population of schoolchildren, they present a challenge that calls for the development and use of instructional materials and techniques that can meet their special learning needs. Because Hispanics constitute the largest language minority in this country, Spanish is used as an example in this chapter, however, the information here applies to all non-English speakers.

While initially only a regional concern, bilingual education has now spread to become a national issue of considerable importance. High rates of mobility, ease of transportation, and rapidly changing employment opportunities have caused the integration of the bilingual learner into the school-aged population of almost every state. This has caused considerable financial and curriculum development demands on individual school districts, where previously little thought or effort had gone into planning for the maximum development of the bilingual learner. The federal government and many state governments have come to the aid of local school districts by providing funds for the development and operation of bilingual programs. Although more than 30 states now either make bilingual programs mandatory or encourage them by establishing guidelines and statewide policies, only 29% of the bilingual programs use both native and English languages for instruction (Zakariya, 1987).

As a result of various federal and state laws and local school district policies, regular classroom teachers are expected to shoulder some of the responsibility for teaching the LEP bilingual learner. Although specialized programs specifically devoted to LEP students have been created in some areas of the country, the LEP student still can be expected to spend at least part of the day *mainstreamed* to the regular classroom. This is in keeping with the general philosophy embodied in federal law that encourages the least restrictive instructional environment for a learner wherever it is deemed conducive to a child's

education. The more instruction that an LEP student can receive in a regular classroom, with the mix of learning types, personalities, and ethnicities represented in the community in which she or he will live and work, the less restrictive will be the instructional environment. It is for this reason that many programs specifically designed for LEP students require the student to spend only part of the instructional day in a concentrated program of bilingual education and the remaining time in the regular classroom.

The term **bilingual education** refers to a mix of instruction through the medium of two languages. This means teaching skills and words in English as well as in another language, which in the United States is predominately Spanish. The primary goal of bilingual education is not to teach English as a second language, but to teach concepts, knowledge, and skills through the language the learner knows best and then to reinforce this information through the second language, in which the learner is less proficient. This raises many related issues: Should the goal of bilingual education be to bring about a transition to the second language as quickly as possible? Or, should some emphasis be placed on maintaining and even improving the learner's proficiency in his or her native language? Such issues arise from the observation that *bilingual* or even *limited English proficient* do not, in practice, mean that the learner is proficient in his or her native language; experience has shown that this very often is not the case. This, of course, not only complicates instruction, because essential skills in vocabulary, syntax, and reading comprehension may be lacking in both languages, but it also raises the issue of whether the bilingual program and schools generally have the responsibility of nurturing and improving the native language in addition to English. Therefore, the linguistic and cultural goals of bilingual education often differ from program to program and among states, which provide the majority of funds for bilingual programs.

As a result of various philosophies concerning the emphasis on transition to a second language as opposed to maintenance of the native language, at least four different approaches have emerged. These approaches have been defined by Baca and Cervantes (1984) as transition, maintenance, restoration, and enrichment.

The **transition approach** uses the native language and culture of the learner only to the extent that it is necessary for the child to learn English. The learner is not taught to read or to write in the native language. The regular classroom teacher in whose classroom there are LEP learners should encourage and sometimes expect such learners to respond, to read, and to write in English. The teacher using the transition approach first discerns the level of English proficiency of the learner and then expects the learner to function in English at or slightly above this level.

The **maintenance approach**, in addition to encouraging English language proficiency, endorses the idea that the learner should become proficient in his or her native language as well. The goal of this approach is to help the learner become truly bilingual, that is, to become fluent in both languages. Such learners have come to be called *balanced bilinguals* to emphasize that their proficiency is limited neither in English nor in Spanish.

Federal funding requirements favor the development of transitional bilingual programs; but local school districts, particularly in the South and Southwest where the Hispanic culture is the most prominent, often supplement federal funds with local resources to meet the dual purposes of a maintenance approach. The implication of this perspective for the regular classroom teacher is that alternative expressions in English and Spanish *must* be accepted as equally valid forms of communication within the classroom. That is not to say, however, that a Spanish response can replace one in English—which clearly would be inappropriate for a non-Spanish-speaking teacher—but that, if the learner wishes, both languages can be used in articulating the same expression. This can be an important aid to the LEP student because thoughts can be organized, formulated, and even expressed in the comfort of the native language and then safely translated into English. Those who have had to express themselves in a foreign language can attest to the helpfulness of this strategy: If they were not proficient in the language and were as yet unable to think in the language, they invariably composed what they wanted to say in English and then replaced the English formulation word-by-word with its counterpart in the other language.

The **restoration approach** to bilingual education is one that attempts to restore the native language and culture of the bilingual student to its purest and most original form. As part of the process of being assimilated into standard American culture, other languages have taken on many abbreviated forms in which words and phrases that are a mixture of both languages often compose regional dialects that are like separate languages by themselves. Even native speakers from other regions sometimes have difficulty deciphering these nonstandard, subcultural expressions. The goal of the restoration approach is to replace these nonstandard dialects with the original form of the language. From this perspective the classroom teacher should discourage the mixing of Spanish and English phrases when they occur in the context of expressing the same idea or thought. In other words, expressions that are expressed alternatively and fully in both English and Spanish may be encouraged, but expressions that are half English and half Spanish are to be discouraged.

A fourth perspective is perhaps most popularly known as an **enrichment approach**. This approach, like the transition approach, has the movement from Spanish to English competence in the quickest time possible as the primary goal of the program. However, in addition to this goal, emphasis is placed on the Spanish culture and heritage while avoiding any direct responsibility for maintaining and improving Spanish language proficiency. The rationale for this approach has come from a desire to follow federal guidelines for the funding of bilingual education (which favor the transition approach) while maintaining a positive attitude and self-concept of the bilingual learner toward his or her native culture. Some argue that native language proficiency must be part of any such attempt, and so this approach sometimes is considered as giving only "lip service" to bilingual education. Regardless of this, it nevertheless strives, through classroom films, publications, clubs, and local cultural events, to create a warm and nurturing atmosphere that conveys acceptance of any minority culture in the school. The implications for the regular classroom teacher following this approach are to convey respect for the cultural heritage of the bilingual student through the arrangement of bulletin boards, transmission of information about cultural events, and the teacher's own attitude.

A recent report by the United States General Accounting Office (1987) included a definition of the many different terms used to describe bilingual programs. This report categorized bilingual programs in the following manner:

English as a Second Language
Programs of bilingual education in which instruction is based on a special curriculum that typically involves little or no use of the native language and is usually taught only during certain periods of the school day. For the rest of the school day, the student may be placed in regular (or submersion) instruction, an immersion program, or a bilingual program.

Immersion
General term for an approach to bilingual instruction not involving the child's native language. Two specific variations of immersion are *structured immersion* and *submersion*.

Structured Immersion
Programs of bilingual education in which teaching is in English but with several special features: (a) the teacher understands the native language and students may speak it to the teacher,

although the teacher generally answers only in English, and (b) knowledge of English is not assumed, and the curriculum is modified in vocabulary and pacing so that the content will be understood. Some programs include some language-arts teaching in the native language.

Submersion
Programs in which students whose proficiency in English is limited are placed in ordinary classrooms in which English is the language of instruction. They are given no special program to help them overcome their language problems, and their native language is not used in the classroom. Also called "sink or swim"; the Supreme Court found this type of submersion unconstitutional (Lau v. Nichols, 414 U.S. 563 [1974]).

Sheltered English
Programs which use a simplified vocabulary and sentence structure to teach school subjects to students who lack sufficient English-language skills to understand the regular curriculum.

Transitional Bilingual
Programs of bilingual education with emphasis on the development of English-language skills in order to enable students whose proficiency in English is limited to shift to an all-English program of instruction. Some programs include English as a second language.

Because many regular classroom teachers can be expected to encounter the bilingual learner either as a full-time student or as part of a "pull-out" program in which part of the student's time is spent in the regular classroom, techniques for teaching the bilingual learner can be an important adjunct to your list of teaching strategies. Some of the following suggestions can serve as starting points for developing instructional strategies for the bilingual learner.

If you do not speak the native language of your bilingual learners (which is the most probable case), you will need to emphasize other forms of communication. These other forms of communication include the visual, kinesthetic, and tactile modalities. You have seen the importance of the *visual mode* in teaching the slow learner, and it is no less important with the bilingual learner. Use pictures, graphs, and illustrations to supplement your teaching objectives wherever possible when bilingual learners are present. Pictures cannot take the place of auditory cues, but they can place these cues in context, making them easier to recognize in relation to an illustration or picture. Infrequently used but equally important are the kinesthetic and tactile modes of communication. The *kinesthetic mode* involves adding movement to the learning process by pointing or tracing so that the learner can feel the motion required to create a particular form, such as a word or letter. The *tactile mode* appeals to the sense of touch, which, in conjunction with auditory cues, can be used to remember concepts and objects when some physical representation of them is available. Thus, a multisensory approach is most appropriate for the bilingual learner using visual, kinesthetic, and tactile modalities wherever possible to reinforce and expand upon auditory communication.

Most bilingual learners learn best from, and are most accustomed to, the rote presentation of instructional material. For example, the "look and say" approach to reading has been found to be more effective than the phonetic approach during the initial stages of reading instruction. Es-

pecially for students who may lack almost any proficiency in English, rote repetition of material, (particularly drill and practice methods) generally is superior to more conceptual presentations of material (which place more emphasis on context, background, perspective, justification, and rationale). Conceptual presentations are subtleties that quickly become lost in the process of translation. Your first step should be to foster the acquisition of facts and their retention in the most visual, concrete way possible.

Small cultural differences, which might otherwise be meaningless, can become extremely important to successful communication whenever one teaches students of another culture. There is no substitute for understanding the culture of the student you are teaching, even though you may have little or no understanding of the language of that culture. For example, several cultural preferences have been noted among bilingual Hispanic learners. One of these is that the Hispanic learner tends to appreciate the cooperation of group achievement to a greater extent than the more competitive aspects of individual achievement. This means that group work, the sharing of assignments, and working as a team are potentially useful instructional strategies for teaching the Hispanic student. In short, it suggests the value of a cooperative classroom climate. Also, the acceptance, warmth, and nurturing of the Hispanic culture are aspects that should not be lost in the classroom. Frequent praise and words of encouragement can set the stage for learning more efficiently than can the sterile recitation of rules and warnings. Also, as pointed out earlier, the bilingual Hispanic learner tends to learn best when physical demonstrations and experience activities supplement verbal presentations. This supports the multisensory approach to instruction that is intended to convey information in multiple ways using various modalities, creating not only alternate paths for learning, but also needed redundancy. In addition, you will find that the Hispanic learner generally will respond better to direct instruction than to indirect instruction or independent seatwork for the acquisition of basic skills; the structure and organization provided with the former supercedes any advantages of the latter.

When selecting or adapting special materials for the bilingual learner, the teacher must carefully evaluate the reading level of the materials and their format. The teacher may find a Spanish version of comparable content, but that does not necessarily mean the materials will be of benefit to the bilingual learner. If you are not fluent in the learner's native language and the materials are in Spanish, others will need to be called upon to evaluate the difficulty level of the material you are considering. It is not unusual to begin selecting verbal material at least several grades below the grade level you will be teaching. After a suitable period of trial use, the materials should again be evaluated and the reading level adjusted accordingly. The format in which the materials are presented is important as well. Material supplemented with graphic illustrations and pictures is preferable to more concentrated prose editions. Notice whether the objects pictured will be familiar to the learners or whether they are specific to the Anglo audience for whom the materials may have been exclusively written.

Know the language ability and achievement levels of your bilingual learners. From school records or your school administrator, find out each learner's

> language most dominant in the receptive mode (e.g., listening, reading),
>
> language most dominant in the expressive mode (e.g., talking, writing),
>
> level of proficiency in the native language, and
>
> past achievement levels in the areas relevant to your instruction.

This information will be invaluable in your selection of special materials as well as in determining the level and manner in which it is most reasonable to begin instructing your bilingual learners. For example, it is not unusual to find bilingual learners who choose Spanish as their dominant means of speaking but English as their dominant means of listening. This information is important because it allows you to speak and be understood in English even though at least some of the learners' communication to you might be in Spanish. Considerable instruction could be provided with little adjustment to your regular instructional plan under such circumstances than if the opposite were true. Knowing your learners' ability and achievement levels will make your initial instructional contact far more effective while potentially avoiding weeks and even months of failing to communicate—and not knowing it!

The Handicapped Learner

As a result of considerable court litigation in the 1950s and 60s concerning the educational rights of handicapped children, it became clear to members of Congress that a coherent national legislative program was needed for directing the education of handicapped schoolchildren. The result of these concerns was Public Law 94–142 (The Education for All Handicapped Children Act of 1975), mandating that a free, appropriate program of public school education be given to all handicapped children in the nation.

This section will review this law and its implications for the regular classroom teacher and alert you to some of the important issues you must consider as a member of an interdisciplinary team responsible for the educational progress of the handicapped learner.

Since the enactment of PL 94–142, "public education for all" has come to mean the responsibility to provide every child of school age with programs and services that are appropriate to his or her educational needs. PL 94–142 extends to all handicapped school-age children the basic constitutional right to be educated and, beyond this, ensures that the public education the handicapped child receives will be in the *least restrictive environment* compatible with his or her educational needs. The special education profession and the public schools have chosen to interpret this law as a mandate to provide minimally restrictive educational and supportive services to the handicapped, whenever possible, *in the context of the regular school program*. Thus, the significance of this law for the regular classroom teacher is that for some types of handicapping conditions and for some instructional objectives, the regular classroom will be the least restrictive alternative for meeting the educational needs of the handicapped.

Over the past few decades handicapped students have been classified and defined in a number of ways. New definitions of handicapping conditions will continue to evolve as more and more becomes known about this subgroup of schoolchildren. However, before the significance of a handicapping condition for public school instruction can be discussed, the question must be asked "What kind of handicap?" To answer this, a number of categories of handicapping conditions have been identified indicating the types of special services and instruction most appropriate to a particular handicapped learner. These categories usually include the physically handicapped, auditorially handicapped, visually handicapped, mentally retarded, emotionally disturbed, learning disabled, speech handicapped, autistic, and multiply handicapped; those are described in Table 11.1.

The purpose of these categories, however, is not to label the handicapped child but to identify specific students whose physical, emotional, and/or cognitive functions are so impaired from any cause that they cannot be adequately or safely educated without the provision of special services. Although these special services are the direct responsibility of the special education program within a school, the regular classroom teacher is expected to provide a contributory and supportive role in the provision of these services by assisting in child identification, individual assessment, Individual Education Plan (IEP) development, individualized instruction, and review of the IEP. Consider what the provision of each of these services means for the regular classroom teacher.

Child Identification

Child identification consists of a school's or school district's procedures for identifying handicapped children who are in need of special education. Students needing such services may never have entered school or could be among those students who are attending school but who have not been identified as handicapped. It is in the identification of these students that the regular classroom teacher may be expected to play an important role.

One stage of this identification is the referral process by which a child comes into contact with and is recommended for special services. Referrals may be made by parents, physicians, community agencies, and school administrators as a result of districtwide testing or screening, but students may also be recommended for special services by the regular classroom teacher. For students who are currently enrolled in regular education, the classroom teacher will be the most likely individual to identify students with needs for special services. In such cases the teacher will become a liaison between the child and the special education staff within a school. In such a capacity you will be responsible for accumulating and reporting to qualified personnel data that can accurately portray

1. the student's current educational status, including attendance records, grades, achievement data, and written accounts of classroom observation,
2. previous instructional efforts and strategies provided the student and the result of those efforts, and
3. data about the learner reported or provided to you by parents.

One of the many skills you will need concerns the distinction between the slow learner and the learning disabled. Slow learners are not included among those considered for special education services under PL 94–142, but instead represent another subpopulation of students who may be recommended for other remedial programs that may be available in a school or school

TABLE 11.1
Categories of handicapping conditions

Physically Handicapped	Students whose body functions or members are impaired by congenital anomaly and disease, or students with limited strength, vitality, or alertness due to chronic or acute health problems.
Auditorially Handicapped	Students who are hearing impaired (hard of hearing) or deaf.
Visually Handicapped	Students who, after medical treatment and use of optical aids, remain legally blind or otherwise exhibit loss of critical sight functions.
Mentally Retarded	Students with significantly subaverage general intellectual functioning existing concurrently with deficiences in adaptive behavior. Severity of retardation is sometimes indicated with the terms profound, trainable, and educable. Not all of the students who are educable are placed in the regular classroom.
Emotionally Disturbed	Students who demonstrate an inability to build or maintain satisfactory interpersonal relationships, develop physical symptoms or fears associated with personal or school problems, exhibit a pervasive mood of unhappiness under normal circumstances, or show inappropriate types of behavior under normal circumstances.
Learning Disabled	Students who demonstrate a significant discrepancy, which is not the result of some other handicap, between academic achievement and intellectual abilities in one or more of the areas of oral expression, listening comprehension, written expression, basic reading skills, reading comprehension, mathematical calculation, mathematics reasoning, or spelling.
Speech Handicapped	Students whose speech is impaired to the extent that it limits the communicative functions.
Autistic	Students with severe disturbances of speech and language, relatedness, perception, developmental rate, or motion.
Multiply Handicapped	Students who have any two or more of the handicapping conditions described above.

district. Learning disabled, on the other hand, is a classification that is included within the population of students for whom PL 94–142 is intended. A student who is learning disabled is one who does not achieve on a level commensurate with his or her age and ability levels. This designation is used when, after learning experiences appropriate to the student's age and ability level have been provided, a lack of achievement is found in oral expression, listening comprehension, written comprehension, basic reading skills, reading comprehension, mathematics calculation, mathematic reasoning, and/or spelling.

A discrepancy between intellectual ability and academic achievement usually is severe enough to qualify a student as learning disabled if

1. the student's assessed *intellectual functioning* is above the mentally retarded range, but his or her assessed educational functioning in one or more of the areas specified is significantly (usually one standard deviation) below the mean for the school district, or
2. the student's assessed *educational functioning* is significantly (usually one standard deviation) below his or her intellectual functioning.

When achievement level is below the mean of the district but is consistent with the student's intellectual functioning, he or she usually is not classified as learning disabled. Many measurement decisions are required in assigning such a designation for a particular learner. Although this decision is made cooperatively by a multidisciplinary team (consisting of regular teachers, special educators, school administrators, parents, and special service staff such as counselors, psychologists, and diagnosticians) the regular classroom teacher is expected to be sufficiently knowledgeable about the learner so that discrepancies between achievement and academic aptitude can be accurately assessed.

Individual Child Assessment

A second process to which you may be expected to contribute is individual child assessment. This is the collecting and analyzing of information about a student in order to identify an educational need in terms of

1. the presence or absence of a physical, mental, or emotional disability,
2. the presence or absence of a significant educational need, and

3. the identification of the student's specific learning competencies together with specific instructional or related services that could improve and maintain the student's competencies.

Although the individual assessment of a child's capabilities falls within the responsibilities of certified professionals who have been specifically trained in assessing the handicapped, the regular classroom teacher is expected to corroborate the findings of these professionals with performance data from the regular classroom. First and foremost among these are formal and informal indications taken from workbooks, homework assignments, weekly and unit tests, and classroom observation of the student's language dominance and proficiency in both the expressive and receptive domains. Often, a teacher's observation and recording of these data suggest that special educators evaluate the validity of the standardized tests that may have been given to the student and whether they may have been given in a language other than that in which the child is dominant.

Corroborative data pertaining to the physical attributes of the student can also be recorded. The classroom teacher may be the only one in a position to observe on a daily basis the ability of the learner to manipulate objects necessary for learning, to remain alert and attentive during instruction, and to control bodily functions in a manner conducive to instruction. In some instances you may provide the only available data source about the ability of the learner to benefit from regular class instruction.

You may be expected to provide data about the sociological and environmental influences on the learner which may, in part, influence her or his classroom behavior. Such data about a learner is often obtained through communications with the family and knowledge of the circumstances leading up to and/or contributing to the student's intellectual and emotional behavior. The extent to which the child's home life and out-of-school support and services contribute to the educative function can provide an important adjunct to in-school data.

Finally, there is the student's intellectual functioning as demonstrated by both verbal and nonverbal performance. Although these behaviors are usually assessed by professionals certified in special education, you may be asked to provide corroborating data pertaining to the child's adaptive behavior, which represents the degree to which the student meets standards of personal independence and social responsibility expected of his or her age and cultural group. Within the context of the regular classroom, you will have many opportunities to observe the social functioning of the child and to gain insights into the appropriateness of this functioning.

Individual Educational Plan (IEP)

A third stage in which you may become involved in the implementation of PL 94–142 is in helping develop an individual educational plan (IEP) for the handicapped students in your classroom. A student receives special education services only after the multidisciplinary team mentioned previously has reviewed data from the comprehensive assessment. Data from this assessment are expected to address the language, physical, emotional/behavioral, sociological, and intellectual functioning of the child. If from this assessment it is determined that the student has a physical, mental, or emotional disability that establishes his or her eligibility to receive special education services, an IEP is written to state short- and long-term objectives for the instructional services to be delivered to the learner and to specify the least restrictive environment in which the instruction is to take place.

The IEP developed for each student by the multidisciplinary team considers a statement of the student's present competencies taken from the overall assessment data, and includes:

1. long-term (annual) and short-term (weekly, monthly) instructional objectives;
2. the specific educational services to be provided the student within the least restrictive environment designated;

3. the dates for the initiation of the services, the approximate amount of time to be spent providing each service, and a justification for the services and settings in which they will be provided; and
4. the criterion for and time of evaluating each long- and short-term objective.

Figure 11.1 illustrates the composition of a typical IEP.

Individualized Instruction

A fourth stage in which you may become involved in the implementation of PL 94–142 is in providing individualized instruction to the handicapped student. This is the day-to-day instruction provided according to the objectives set forth in the student's IEP. This program should be consistent with the needs of the student and with your curriculum. Your activities may include providing any or all of the following:

Specific instructional objectives based on student needs as stated in the IEP

Learning activities appropriate to each student's learning style, presented as specifically and sequentially as needed for the student to progress toward attainment of each instructional objective

Instructional media and materials used for each learning activity, selected on the basis of the student's learning style

An instructional setting that provides multiple arrangements for learning

A schedule of teaching time ensuring the provision of instruction to each handicapped student in individual or group arrangements

Procedures by which the teacher measures, records, and reports each handicapped student's progress

You may also be responsible for writing specific instructional objectives in accord with the student's IEP and the preparation and administra-

FIGURE 11.1
Example Individual Educational Plan (IEP)

INDIVIDUAL EDUCATIONAL PLAN

Student's Name: _Bob Miller_ School: _Oak Hill Elem._ Grade: _4_ Date of Meeting: _2-25-87_

Date of Birth: _12-18-78_ Parent/Guardian: _Tom + Ann Miller_ Address: _25 Ruth Drive_ Phone: _443-2187_

COMMITTEE MEMBERS PRESENT:

Name: _Paula Scott_ Position: _Principle_

Name: _Mary White_ Position: _Spec. Ed Teacher_

Name: _Ann Miller_ Position: _Parent_

Name: _Terry Hull, ph.d_ Position: _Psychologist_

Name: _Jackie Morgan_ Position: _Teacher_

Name: _Suzanne Martin_ Position: _Speech therapist_

	Present Levels of Performance	Learning Strengths	Learning Weaknesses
Word Recognition	1.5	Good auditory learning skills	Short attention span in visual presentations +
Reading Comprehension	2.0		
Spelling	1.9	Knows all basic computation facts	handwriting tasks
Math	3.5	Positive social interaction	
Social Adaptation	4th		Articulation
Other(s) _Speech below age level_			

Based review of all pertinent data, the committee determined that this student DOES/DOES NOT meet eligibility criteria for: _Learning Disabled,_
Speech Handicapped

Recommended Placement: _2_ hrs. per day/week Special Education
_4_ hrs. per day/week Regular Education
_1_ hrs. per day/week Related Services

ANNUAL GOALS	SHORT TERM OBJECTIVES	EVALUATION CRITERIA	SPECIFIC SERVICES	DATE SERVICES BEGIN/END	SUGGESTED MATERIALS	STAFF RESPONSIBLE NAME	POSITION
Increase word recognition to 3.0	Complete Word Drill of Dolch word lists 1 and 2	Sequence and Recognition lists 2nd grade level completion	1/2 hr instruct. in resource room	2/26/87 5/29/87	Dolch word cards Computer game "Word Review"	Mary White	Resource Teacher
Increase reading comprehension to 2.5	Complete S.R.A. series 2nd level	Woodcock-Johnson perform at 2nd grade level	1 hr. instruct. in resource room	2/26/87 5/29/87	SRA Series Scholastic Scope Magazine	Mary White	Resource Teacher
Increase spelling level to 2.5	Complete 2nd level of "Spelling Sounds"	T.O.W.L - Spelled 2.5 level on the Spelling sections	1/2 hr. instruct. in resource room	2/26/87 5/29/87	Speak - White Spell Kit	Mary White	Resource Teacher
Articulate r-blends correctly	Articulate /Ar/ and /br/ correctly	Therapist and Teacher observation of daily speech	1 hr./wk. speech therapy	2/26/87 5/29/87		Suzanne Martin	Speech therapist

tion of teacher-made tests to record student progress toward these objectives.

Review of IEP

A fifth activity in which you may become involved is a review of the IEP. School districts usually have an established set of procedures or a system for reviewing each handicapped student's progress in comparison to the objectives stated in the student's IEP. The purpose of this review is not only to determine the student's progress toward the objectives of the plan, but also to determine the need for modifying the plan and for supplying further special services. A critical aspect of this review is documenting either the movement of a student to a more or less restrictive environment or his or her release from all special educational services.

Recommendations for major changes in the IEP, including changes in the student's placement (for example, to a more or less restrictive environment), is the responsibility of the multidisciplinary team. However, all those involved in implementing the student's IEP are likely to be involved in this review. For example, among the many pieces of information that must be gathered prior to a major change in a student's placement are

> the number of instructional options that have been attempted, including those within the regular classroom

> the appropriateness of the long- and short-range educational objectives, including those written by the regular classroom teacher

> the reliability, validity, and accuracy of the testing that led or contributed to a review of the student's current placement, including testing completed within the regular classroom

In each of these areas, data contributed by you may be critical, because you may be in the most advantageous position to make assessments about the everyday performance of the student. Here,

as elsewhere with the implementation of PL 94–142, the data you provide will be a direct reflection of your effectiveness in the regular classroom.

Several of the previously described service responsibilities required by PL 94–142 (e.g., implementation of the IEP and provisions of individualized instruction) involve the direct instruction of the handicapped learner in the regular classroom. Many approaches to such instruction have been and currently are being used. The following suggestions are some of those that have been found to be particularly useful by regular classroom teachers.

Encourage self-management skills. One of the first things you will notice about some of the handicapped learners in your classroom is their lack of self-management skills. Many low-achieving students consistently use poor organizational strategies; that is, they may work impulsively, hurriedly, and fail to accurately perceive and gauge time, and they may not adequately judge and search for needed information. Part of your role as teacher of the handicapped in the regular classroom is to encourage self-management skills that can lead to greater independence and task completion. This can be accomplished through one or more of the following:

1. the use of study guides that present to the handicapped learner your instructional objectives, the specific assignment you want accomplished, and time lines for completion
2. topical outlines that provide the learner with the order of the content that will be covered in the workbook or class presentation
3. technical vocabularies and glossaries that provide definitions for the more difficult words and concepts to be used
4. brief summaries of the lesson that emphasize what in the lesson is of greatest importance

Each of these teaching aids can assist the learner to better manage the learning task, making task completion more likely.

Use peer tutoring as an instructional strategy. This approach is often indispensable for teaching the handicapped learner in the regular classroom because your time may not always permit dealing directly with the handicapped learner without neglecting other students. This does not mean that peer tutoring can be used as a handy device for avoiding responsibility for teaching the handicapped; but if precise instructional objectives are prepared, tutors from among your regular students are carefully selected and trained, and both tutor and handicapped student are chosen for compatibility and knowledge level, this practice can be an important adjunct to other strategies for teaching the handicapped. It can be an especially effective device when you have a master list on which specific target skills are identified and from which the tutor works in a detailed and systematic manner. It is important to note, however, that tutors should be selected not only for their knowledge of the material to be covered and ability to communicate, but also for their sincerity and commitment in helping the handicapped learner.

Create an atmosphere in which handicapped and nonhandicapped students can learn from each other. One of the primary purposes of PL 94–142 was to bring handicapped and nonhandicapped students into close contact so that they could learn from each other. The nonhandicapped learner may find out just how "average" a handicapped learner is, and the handicapped learner may derive benefits from listening to and learning from someone having different experiences and perspectives. These benefits are never more obvious than when heterogeneous groups of handicapped and nonhandicapped learners are formed explicitly on the basis of their *differences* in skill and ability level. These heterogeneous groups can lead to the more able students spontaneously taking the responsibility for checking the work of the handicapped learners, correcting their errors, reviewing key concepts, and probing for additional responses. They also can provide the social and intellectual interaction conducive to cooperative learning.

Another effective strategy for instructing the handicapped in the regular classroom is the use of learning centers. Sometimes abused and misunderstood, learning centers function much like peer tutoring and heterogeneous groupings when they are carefully thought out and made relevant to your instructional objectives. That is, they can provide valuable instruction to the handicapped learner without your having to neglect the more able learners in the classroom. Centers of instructional resources that include books, audiovisual aids, arts and crafts, graphic illustrations, exercises, study guides, topical outlines, and vocabulary lists can allow students to work independently and at their own pace. These can also provide learners an opportunity to learn through different modalities (visual, auditory, tactile), and can be planned in ways that provide immediate feedback. These are all key elements to successfully teaching the handicapped.

The arrangement of the classroom itself is an important aspect of teaching the handicapped learner. Engagement in the learning process, one of the key teaching behaviors, can be promoted as well as restricted by the arrangement and organization of the classroom. Traditional arrangements place the teacher's desk at the front of the classroom and student desks in formal rows extending outward. This arrangement conveys a teacher-centered classroom in which lectures, supervision, control, and tests are the most predominant student expectations. Unfortunately, this type of arrangement also suggests that all of your students will learn in the same way. When more than a few of your learners are handicapped or depart from the norm in your classroom in any other way (e.g., are gifted or LEP), a more flexible use of classroom space may be called for. A less formal arrangement allows more freedom of movement for those who may wish to benefit from a learning center, independent study carrel, computer terminal, or audiovisual library. It can also more readily accommodate group projects, a heterogeneous grouping of students, and peer tutoring. Because a less structured classroom arrangement can also create considerably more noise and movement at times, making only one or two areas of the classroom into a less structured format may be an initial first step or a necessary compromise.

By some estimates there are over a million micro-computers in the schools today, and this number is expected to soar with each passing school year. The capacity of the microcomputer not only to ease the administrative burden of the classroom teacher but also to actually teach some parts of the curriculum has already been demonstrated. A considerable amount of software for the microcomputer has been developed that can lessen the demands placed upon the regular classroom teacher, particularly in the area of teaching the handicapped: For individualized instruction, assisting in the development of IEPs, testing, and reporting the performance of the handicapped learner. Use of the computer in the regular classroom can substantially lessen the sometimes overwhelming paperwork that the teaching of heterogeneous ability groups entails. You may want to use the computer to provide remediation in critical skill areas, because this is where much of the available computer software is focused. There are programs that instruct in remedial mathematics and spelling, that teach verbs and how to use them in sentences, that correct misspelled words, and even that provide an analysis of common writing errors. You can become familiar with the most current versions of these and other software programs through your school's special education coordinator.

Summing Up

This chapter introduced you to slow, gifted and talented, bilingual, and handicapped learners. Its main points were:

1. The advantages of categorizing learners include the assistance they provide for:

   - the dispensation of state and federal funds earmarked for specific types of learners

   - the efficient development and organization of instructional materials, texts, and media appropriate to certain types of learners, and
   - the training and assignment of instructional staff.

2. The disadvantages of categorizing learners include the fact that sometimes variation within categories of learners can exceed variation between categories, and learners may be ineligible for membership in one group due to their membership in another group.

3. A slow learner is a student who, using instructional resources, texts, workbooks, and learning materials that have been designated for the majority of students in your classroom, cannot learn at the same pace as the majority.

4. It has been estimated that as many as 20% of all students attending school today are slow learners in one subject or another.

5. Slow learners require more than the usual amount of variation in pacing and method of presentation, classroom climate, and instructional materials to keep engaged in the learning process.

6. Slow learners usually have deficiencies in the basic skills of reading, writing, and mathematics, difficulty in comprehending abstract ideas, and unsystematic work habits. These deficiencies tend to make instructional lessons geared to the average student too difficult for the slow learner.

7. Compensatory teaching is an instructional approach that alters the presentation of content by reorganizing it, transmitting it by way of alternate modalities, and supplementing it with additional learning resources; this circumvents a student's fundamental weakness or deficiency.

8. Remedial teaching is an instructional approach that uses techniques and practices specifically chosen to eliminate known deficiencies or weaknesses.

9. Some instructional strategies for addressing the learning needs of the slow learner are:

- Developing lessons around the interests, needs, and experiences of the student
- Varying instructional techniques often (e.g., switching from lecture to discussion to seatwork)
- Incorporating audio and visual materials into lessons that match the strongest learning modalities of your learners
- Developing original worksheets and exercises when existing materials are too difficult or uninteresting to the slow learner
- Modifying the pace of instruction to meet the optimal learning rate of the individual student
- Making peer tutors available for students needing remediation
- Encouraging oral expression, especially for those limited in writing ability
- Providing study aids and advance organizers to alert students to important content or issues
- Teaching notetaking, outlining, and listening.

10. The preparation and time required to teach the gifted may not be measurably less than for teaching any other type of learner—and may be more.
11. Among the behavioral characteristics for defining giftedness are intelligence, achievement, creativity, and task persistence.
12. Variations in the use of these behavioral characteristics to define giftedness have created considerable diversity both among the types of students classified as gifted and in the instructional programs designed to meet their needs.
13. Some of the instructional strategies for addressing the learning needs of the gifted learner are to:

- Allow students to investigate some topics of their own choosing, making them participants in the design of their own learning
- Plan instructional activities that involve group work, such as brainstorming sessions, group discussions, panel type peer interviews, and debates
- Plan instructional lessons that include individual and small group investigations of real-life problems
- Pose challenging problems that allow the learner to make the key decisions about what is and is not important for a solution
- Test and question in a manner that draws out knowledge and understanding and requires more than a verbally fluent response

14. There are approximately five million students representing about 10% of the entire school-age population in this country whose primary language is not English.
15. Bilingual education refers to a mix of instruction through the medium of two languages. Although the word *bilingual* implies proficiency in two languages, it more often applies to limited English proficient (LEP) students, who range between an inability to express themselves at all in English, either orally or in writing, to marginal proficiency in English.
16. Different approaches to bilingual education include:

- The transition approach, which uses the native language and culture of the learner only to the extent necessary to learn English
- English as a second language, which attempts to teach English with little or no use of the native language
- Structured immersion, in which the native language may be used to speak to the teacher but the teacher generally answers in English
- The maintenance approach, which in addition to encouraging English language proficiency endorses the idea that the learner should become proficient in his or her native language as well
- The restoration approach, which attempts to restore the native language and culture of the bilingual student to its purest and most original form

- The enrichment approach, which attempts to move the learner to English proficiency in the quickest time while emphasizing the native culture and heritage

17. Some of the instructional strategies for addressing the learning needs of the bilingual learner are:

- Emphasize forms of communication that use pictures, graphs, and illustrations to supplement teaching objectives
- Emphasize the acquisition of facts and their retention in visual, concrete ways
- Emphasize group achievement more than the competitive aspects of individual achievement
- Adopt instructional materials to the teaching level of your students
- Know the language ability level and achievement level of your learners and select special materials accordingly
- Understand and use cultural differences to enhance the overall learning environment and educational experience

18. Some of the special education functions mandated by PL 94–142 that may involve the regular classroom teacher include child identification, individual child assessment, development of the individual educational plan (IEP), individualized instruction, and a review of the IEP.

19. Some of the instructional strategies for addressing the learning needs of the handicapped child in the regular classroom include:

- Teaching of self-management skills that can increase the student's ability to learn independently
- Use of peer tutoring to teach a specific list of targeted skills
- Use of heterogeneous groups composed of both handicapped and nonhandicapped students to provide the social and intellectual instruction conducive to cooperative learning

- Use of instructional resource (learning) centers to allow students to work independently at their own pace
- Use of a less structured classroom arrangement to promote group projects, heterogeneous grouping, and peer tutoring
- Use of the microcomputer to teach basic skills and content

For Discussion and Practice

1. Explain in your own words what is meant by the phrase "variation in behavior occurring within a category of learners may be greater than the variation found between categories of learners." Using the IQ categories of *average* and *more able*, give an example illustrating your answer.
*2. Give three advantages of categorizing students by learning type.
*3. In your words, give a practical, working definition of a slow learner in your classroom.
*4. What is one source of data a school district probably would use to assign a student to a class of less able learners?
*5. Identify the difference between compensatory and remedial teaching and give an example of each, using content from your teaching area.
*6. What are the four behaviors from which giftedness is most likely to be determined?
*7. What would be one argument against the exclusive use of IQ in selecting students for a gifted program?
*8. Give four different signs of creativity that might be used in determining a student's eligibility for a gifted and talented program.
*9. Give four different signs of task persistence that might be used in determining a student's eligibility for a gifted and talented program.
*10. Describe the language proficiency of a limited English proficient, or LEP, learner.
*11. What is a *balanced bilingual*?
*12. Contrast the structured immersion method with the transitional method for teaching the bilingual student.
*13. In your own words, how do the requirements contained within PL 94–142 affect the regular classroom teacher?

*14. Identify nine categories of handicapping conditions which make a student eligible for special education services.

*15. Describe the difference between a slow learner and a learning disabled learner.

*16. What are four essential features of an IEP?

Suggested Readings

Algozzine, B. & Ysseldyke, J. E. (1982). *Critical issues in special and remedial education*. Boston: Houghton Mifflin.

Based on a large body of recent research, this book explores a number of key concerns to educators who work with students exhibiting learning differences.

Baca, L. M. & Cervantes, H. T. (1984). *The bilingual special education interface*. Santa Clara, CA: Times Mirror/Mosby.

A thorough orientation to the historical background, legal basis, and practical implementation of bilingual services and bilingual special education.

Bloom, B. S. (1982). *Human interactions and school learning*. New York: McGraw-Hill.

The author explores the notion that slow learners have a learning capacity commensurate with that of average learners if only they are instructed at the appropriate pace using mastery learning techniques.

Coleman, M. C. (1986). *Behavior disorder: Theory and practice*. Englewood Cliffs, NJ: Prentice-Hall.

An introductory text on behavior disorders that presents a combination of theory and practical guidelines for classroom teachers.

Dembo, M. H. (1981). *Teaching for learning: Applying educational psychology in the classroom* (2nd ed.). Glenview, IL: Scott, Foresman.

A comprehensive and practical overview of educational theory which provides a basis for understanding educational adaptations for special learners.

Gearheart, B. R. & Weishahn, M. W. (1984). *The exceptional student in the regular classroom*. Santa Clara, CA: Times Mirror/Mosby.

A basic overview of the legal basis for special services and the strategies for programming for mainstreamed exceptional students.

Torrance, E. (1981). Predicting the creativity of elementary schoolchildren and the teacher who "made a difference." *Gifted Child Quarterly, 25,* 55–62.

The role of creativity in the performance of the gifted and how instructional strategies can promote creative behavior.

Wang, M. C. & Walberg, H. J. (Eds.). (1985). *Adapting instruction to individual differences*. Berkeley, CA: McCutchan.

A collection of readings that covers the many unintended problems associated with categorizing and separating students into a variety of programs.

12
Effective Teaching in the Classroom

For the past semester or quarter you have traveled through this book. It has been a long journey and, I'm sure, at times a difficult one. Now it is at an end, but, as with any good journey, it is interesting to look back at some of the sights encountered along the way. Some of these sights appeared in the form of the five key behaviors: *clarity, variety, task orientation,* and *engagement* in the learning process at *moderate-to-high rates of success.* This final chapter will revisit the key behaviors and their catalysts from the perspective of a practicing teacher. This will be your opportunity to see what an effective teacher does with these behaviors and, just as importantly, what an ineffective teacher does with them. To provide a picture of these two types of teachers, this chapter will present both positive and negative indicators of effective teaching as they pertain to the key behaviors. Throughout the discussion there will be references about how the helping behaviors (structuring, questioning, probing, use

of student ideas, and enthusiasm) can be used to achieve the key behaviors.

Clarity in the Classroom

Table 12.1 summarizes some of the behaviors related to clarity. The first two columns in Table 12.1 list indicators of clarity (or its lack) that are likely to be observed among effective and ineffective teachers, and the third column suggests some of the ways a teacher who is observed exhibiting one or more indices of the lack of clarity might improve his or her clarity.

The ability to be clear involves seven important behaviors. Three of these are behaviors that should occur at the *beginning* of a lesson, while the remaining four are those to be implemented *during* a lesson. The three behaviors that should occur at the beginning of a lesson are

TABLE 12.1
Indicators for clarity

	Being Clear (an effective teacher . . .)	Poor Clarity (an ineffective teacher . . .)	Solutions
1.	Informs learners of the lesson objective, (e.g., describes what behaviors will be tested or required on future assignments as a result of the lesson)	Fails to link lesson content to how and at what level of complexity the content will be used	Prepare a behavioral objective for the lesson at the desired level of complexity, (e.g., knowledge, comprehension, etc.). Indicate to the learners at the start of the lesson in what ways the behavior will be used in the future.
2.	Provides learners with an advance organizer (e.g., places lesson in perspective of past and/or future lessons)	Starts presenting content without first introducing the subject with respect to some broader context	Consult or prepare a unit plan to determine what task-relevant prior learning is required for this lesson and what task-relevant prior learning this lesson represents for future lessons. Begin the lesson by informing the learner that the content to be taught is part of this larger context.
3.	Checks for task-relevant prior learning at beginning of the lesson (e.g., determines level of understanding of prerequisite facts or concepts and reteaches, if necessary)	Moves to new content without checking for the facts, concepts, or skills needed to acquire the new learning	Ask questions of students at the beginning of a lesson or check assignments regularly to determine if task-relevant prior knowledge has been acquired.
4.	Gives directives slowly and distinctly (e.g., repeats directives when needed or divides them into smaller pieces)	Presents too much clerical, managerial, or technical information at once, too quickly	Organize procedures for lengthy assignments in step-by-step order and give as handout as well as orally.
5.	Knows ability levels and teaches at or slightly above learners' current level of functioning (e.g., knows learners' attention spans)	Fails to know that instruction is under or over heads of students. Seems not to know when most learners have "tuned out"	Determine ability level from standardized tests, previous assignments, and interests and retarget instruction accordingly.
6.	Uses examples, illustrations, and demonstrations to explain and clarify (e.g., uses visuals to help interpret and reinforce main points)	Restricts presentation to routine verbal reproduction of text or workbook	Restate main points in at least one modality other than the one in which they were initially taught (e.g., visual v. auditory).
7.	Provides review or summary at end of each lesson	Ends lesson abruptly without "repackaging" key points	Use key abstractions, repetition, or symbols to help students efficiently store and later recall content.

- informing the learners of the objective
- providing learners with an advance organizer
- checking for task-relevant prior learning and reteaching, if necessary

Being clear means being understood by your learners, and that may depend as much on what you do *prior* to teaching a lesson as on what you do *during* the lesson. Therefore, these three pre-instructional activities are necessary to establish a *learning set* which focuses your learners in the direction you want to take them. Without this focusing, learners may never notice or be able to grasp what comes after. Consider how this might be done in the classroom.

Often, at the start of a lesson students will not know what behaviors, skills, or concepts they will be expected to learn. Not knowing what to expect can cause anxiety, because in the absence of information, unrealistic expectations that are more frightening than the truth may be created in the minds of your learners. Anxiety, especially high levels of anxiety, can shorten learners' attention spans and provide a timely reason for not tuning you in. Informing them of the objective conveys the expectations you have for them and replaces any unrealistic fears or expectations with realistic ones. If your learners know what to expect and, if it seems reasonable to them, they will want to pay attention and find out more.

At the start of a lesson your learners may not value the content you are about to teach. This lack of value for what you may be teaching may be just the right reason for not paying attention to you. If the content appears to be irrelevant to anything that has gone before or is likely to come after, it becomes just one more burden—and students often gamble that they will not be held accountable for it. Advance organizers can keep your learners from turning you off. Their use makes your lesson important and, therefore, more valued as part of something larger than the lesson itself.

The third pre-instructional activity for achieving clarity needs little introduction, because it has been an important concept throughout this text. Without the mastery of task-relevant prior learn-

ing, a lesson may be incomprehensible to some (if not to most) of the learners. Checking for the required task-relevant prior learning is a behavior that is often neglected by both beginning and experienced teachers. Your lesson can have clarity only to the extent that all or most of your students exhibit the facts, skills, or concepts required for understanding the lesson. To achieve this, you must find out before or at the beginning of your lesson if your learners actually can exhibit the prerequisite behaviors. Many options are available for such an inquiry, from informal oral questions asked randomly of a few students to a more formal checking of homework and workbook assignments. When extensive deficiencies in task-relevant prior knowledge are found, reteaching old but prerequisite content may be more important than teaching the new content scheduled for the day's lesson.

The other dimensions of clarity are

- giving directives slowly and distinctly
- knowing the ability levels of your learners and teaching to those levels
- using examples, illustrations, and demonstrations to explain and clarify text and workbook content
- providing a review or summary at the end of each lesson

These behaviors differ from the first three because, although preparation for them may begin long before the start of a lesson, they pertain to the actual presentation of lesson content. These four practices also represent ways of establishing a clear and understandable dialogue with students. To understand, one must receive the message being sent. As with our three behaviors previously discussed, part of successfully receiving a message is being ready and prepared to receive it. Informing the learner of what is expected, providing advance organization, and checking for and reteaching task-relevant prior learning all help to prepare and make learners ready to receive the message. In addition to these important behaviors, however, it is important to be clear about the message itself. That is, it must be presented in ways that make it intelligible to learners, so that they not only can hear and interpret what you are saying, but also can retain it long afterwards.

One of the most frequently heard criticisms about beginning teachers is that students say they "weren't told (or didn't understand) what to do." Students often are afraid to admit that they could not follow the directions given, either because they simply could not remember all that was said or that it was said so quickly and matter-of-factly that "things just whizzed by." These complaints illustrate that directives pertaining to completing workbook exercises, reading assignments, homework, and drill and practice need to be communicated with the same deliberateness as the lesson content. It is common for beginning teachers to speed up and speak less distinctly when giving directives about what to do, how to proceed, and what rules to follow in completing academic work, and then slow down again when actually teaching the lesson to which the directives pertain. When students cannot follow your directions about how you want them to become engaged in the learning process, they usually will silently proceed on their own, sometimes missing the intent of the assignment. Care must be taken to slow down when conveying instructions, to divide the directives into steps if need be, and to be sure that each step is understood along the way.

The next behavior, knowing your students' ability levels and teaching material appropriate to them, is one of the most difficult to achieve. Because there probably will be several levels of ability (e.g., less able, average, more able) in your class, you may become frustrated by an inability to teach some students. Nevertheless, your clarity will depend in part upon packaging instructional stimuli in the form of oral presentations, visual messages, exercises, and reading assignments that are at the current level of functioning of all of your students. To accomplish this you will need to provide a *range of instructional stimuli* in your classroom that intentionally hit some students and miss others. Learning centers, reference libraries, different types of pictorial dis-

plays, and even alternate texts and exercises that tap into abilities slightly above and below the average learner can help maintain your clarity in a diverse classroom.

The final two behaviors for achieving clarity have several things in common. They both occur well into the lesson, and both (using examples, illustrations, demonstrations, and reviewing and summarizing) are intended to expand upon and clarify the content in the text or workbook, which generally will not be understood completely or uniformly without elaboration. This means that you will have to make this content come alive for your students by putting it into different forms that can highlight its most important features. Oral examples, visual illustrations, and practical demonstrations, *if different than those in the text,* can measurably increase the clarity of your lesson for learners who will be searching for different ways to attach meaning to it and to relate it to their own experiences.

Reviews and summaries at the end of, or interspersed throughout, the lesson can have much the same effect. Recall from chapter 9 that a review or summary need not be a simple parroting back in some abbreviated form of what was taught. Instead, an effective review or summary often recasts content into a form slightly different than the one in which it was originally presented, thereby elaborating upon and organizing earlier content differently for efficient storage and retrieval. This provides learners the opportunity to plug into the content at a different time and also in a different manner. Content unlearned or misunderstood during the lesson can become learned and clarified during summaries and reviews, when the summary and review *go beyond simply repeating the content to repackaging it in a manner suitable for retention and later retrieval.*

Variety in the Classroom

Table 12.2 summarizes some of the behaviors related to variety, which include:

TABLE 12.2
Indicators for variety

	Using Variety *(an effective teacher . . .)*	*Poor Variety* *(an ineffective teacher . . .)*	*Solutions*
1.	Uses attention gaining devices (e.g., begins with a challenging question, visual, or example)	Begins lesson without full attention of most learners	Begin lesson with an activity in a modality that is different from last lesson or activity (e.g., change from listening to seeing).
2.	Shows enthusiasm and animation through variation in eye contact, voice and gestures (e.g., changes pitch and volume, moves about during transitions to new activity)	Speaks in monotone, devoid of external signs of emotion; stays fixed in place entire period or rarely moves body	Change position at regular intervals (e.g., every 10 minutes). Change speed or volume to indicate that a change in content or activity has occurred.
3.	Varies mode of presentation, (e.g., lectures, asks questions, then provides for independent practice [daily])	Lectures or assigns unmonitored seatwork for the entire period; rarely alters modality through which instructional stimuli are received (e.g., seeing, listening, doing)	Preestablish an order of daily activities that rotate cycles of seeing, listening, and doing.
4.	Uses a mix of rewards and reinforcers (e.g., extra credit, verbal praise, independent study, etc. [weekly, monthly])	Rarely praises or tends to use same words to convey praise every time	Establish lists of rewards and expressions of verbal praise and choose among them randomly. Provide reasons for praise along with the expression of praise.
5.	Incorporates student ideas or participation in some aspects of the instruction (e.g., uses indirect instruction or divergent questioning [weekly, monthly])	Assumes the role of sole authority and provider of information; ignores student opinion	Occasionally plan instruction in which student opinions are used to begin the lesson (e.g., "what would you do if . . .?").
6.	Varies types of questions (e.g., divergent, convergent, [weekly]) and probes (e.g., to clarify, to solicit, to redirect [daily])	Always asks divergent, opinion questions (e.g., What do you think about . . .?) without follow up; or overuses convergent, fact questions	Match questions to the behavior and complexity of the lesson objective. Vary complexity of lesson objectives in accord with the unit plan.

- using attention-gaining devices
- showing enthusiasm
- mixing rewards and reinforcers
- varying types of questions and probes
- using student ideas

Look more closely at how each of these behaviors can contribute to the effective use of variety.

The first behavior, using attention-gaining devices, is the first ingredient of a good lesson plan as described in chapter 5. Recall that the attention-gaining devices with which a lesson begins can take many forms including pictures, audio/video tapes, demonstrations, or experiments; or they may be less spectacular, such as posing a challenging question, presenting a dilemma or bewildering situation, or even bringing about the silence that accompanies a unique or interesting visual display. Beginning a lesson in this manner stimulates the learner differently than he or she has become accustomed to during the previous activity. Remember, it is not necessary to try to present the spectacular all the time (although this is always fun to do when the opportunity arises), but it is important to present a change from the instructional stimuli to which the learner has grown accustomed from a previous activity. This not only will wake up the receptive modalities of sight and sound, but also, and just as importantly, it will stimulate the cognitive processes associated with them. Without this awakening and conscious change from the mood and tempo of an earlier activity or class, your learners' attention may never fully be either on you or on your lesson. Attention-gaining devices, therefore, help create natural cycles of highs and lows that make life in classrooms more interesting and less regimented. Although high points of curiosity, interest, and visual impact seldom can be sustained for very long, without them there can be no anticipation and excitement of waiting for the next peak to occur. This is good reason for spreading attention-gaining devices throughout your lesson and for not limiting this important behavior to the start of your lesson.

One of the easiest ways to maintain the momentum of rising and falling cycles of interest, curiosity, and excitement in your classroom is to vary your voice, eye contact, and gestures. When interest is waning in your class and no attention-getting device is readily available to engage your learners' attention, these techniques often can do the job. Although teachers are not (and should not aspire to be) classroom actors and actresses, there is much that a teacher can learn from the field of dramatics. Plays, like lessons, should have opening and closing acts with climaxes and anticlimaxes now and then to keep the audience's attention. How well you plan your script—or lesson—will have much to do with its attention-getting quality. There will be natural variety in the topics and instructional activities that your lesson contains, and that variety can be enhanced by your willingness to accentuate its high points and bolster its low points with changes in your voice, eye movement, and body movement. Simply put, this means that your voice inflection, eye contact, and positioning in the classroom should change often, especially during the high points (e.g., lively group discussion) and low points (e.g., rote recitation from the workbook). Raising the volume of your voice slightly, changing from scanning the front of the class to the back, and repositioning yourself to a new location in the classroom during these times will add to the instructional variety you bring to your learners. These simple signs of your engagement in the learning process are often taken by students as signs of your enthusiasm for wanting to be there.

Researchers and experienced teachers agree that effective teaching involves many different classroom activities. A teacher who did nothing but lecture for an entire period, who only engaged students in prolonged seatwork, or who did nothing but expose students to attention-gaining devices would have difficulty achieving unit outcomes, especially at the higher levels of behavioral complexity. This is not to say that some classes from time to time should not emphasize a single activity, but the majority of classes must offer some variety in the activities with which instructional stimuli are presented. This means that lecturing will be mixed with questions and answers (which may include work at the board), which may be followed by guided practice in which the learners are asked to make their first attempts at responding appropriately in a non-threatening atmosphere. These instructional routines, when thought out in advance and well-executed, form the foundation of effective teaching. In this sense, the variety provided by the different instructional activities is not so much to gain the attention of the students (although we hope they do) as it is to allow them to cognitively process the material in a variety of ways, such as by listening (from lectures), by seeing (from textbooks), and by doing (from workbooks). Different modalities (hearing, seeing, doing) provide the learner with the redundancy that is often needed for mastery learning and present the stimulus material in different contexts, which emphasize the different cognitive abilities that different learners may have to varying degrees. Therefore, a lesson plan that includes some combination of lecture, discussion, question and answer, guided practice, and independent seatwork generally is preferable to one that exclusively emphasizes only one of these instructional alternatives. Varying your instructional routine across two or more of these (but seldom all of them) and varying the combinations chosen from day to day will add the important dimension of variety to your teaching.

One of the first things noticed by a casual observer in a classroom is the teacher's interactions with his or her students. Most obvious among the interchanges that occur are those that concern reward and punishment. Perhaps because everyone seeks rewards of one kind or another in their daily lives, observers are acutely aware of the amount and intensity of the rewards given to learners. Chapter 9 discussed verbal praise as the most frequently used type of reward in the classroom. The reinforcing effect of verbal praise, however, depends on the variety with which it is administered and the other types of rewards with which it is associated. Nothing will be less reinforcing than the phrase "That's good" or "That's correct" when repeated in the same tone of voice hundreds of times with different problems and learners. The phrase soon be-

comes meaningless and loses its ability to reinforce a behavior. It is important, therefore, not only to vary the type, amount, and intensity of the verbal praise you give, but also to branch out and experiment with other types of rewards. What is rewarding to one student may not be rewarding to another, so some experimenting with rewards will always be in order. Using one student's correct answer as a model for the next problem, having the student retrace for the class how the correct answer was obtained, or having peers comment on the correctness of a student's answer are some of the ways verbal expressions and a greater variety of reward can be mixed which may make the reward more meaningful to the student.

Another dimension of variety is associated with questioning and probing. A popular topic for inservice teacher training, the art of questioning and probing is one of the most important skills of an effective teacher. The variety you convey to your students will to a large degree be determined by your flexible use of questioning and probing. The purpose of these related techniques is to draw out of the student a response, sometimes *any* response, that then can be refined and developed into a better or more complete response. Examples in chapters 6, 7, and 8 showed that questions are rarely ends in themselves, but, instead, are beginnings. That is, they provide a platform for engaging the student in the learning process by getting the learner to act on, work through, or think about the material presented previously. Although questions are tools for engaging students in the learning process, to be effective they must be administered flexibly and, often, followed up with probes or other questions that attempt to pierce through the glib, superficial, or inadequate responses that are sometimes initially given to a question. Probes, therefore, are questions that follow questions and are carefully crafted to deepen, enrich, and extend an earlier response.

As was seen in chapter 8, probes can be used to elicit a clarifying response to an earlier question, to solicit new information related to an earlier question, or to redirect the learner into a more productive area. Each of these uses can be a source of variety to add momentum to your questioning behavior—for example, when a solicitation for new information is followed by a request for clarification, which, in turn, is followed by a redirection. These cycles of probes can be executed in waves that return again and again to force learners to act upon and reshape their responses and, most important, their thinking.

The types of questions you ask should show variety as well, alternating between convergent and divergent, although not necessarily in equal amounts. Convergent questions, which usually have a single right answer, are most commonly associated with the goals of direct instruction; while divergent questions, which may have many right answers, are most commonly associated with the goals of indirect instruction. The use of these two types of questions, however, has to do not so much with their association with one or another model of instruction, but rather with their capacity for eliciting behavior at lower or higher levels of behavioral complexity. Recall that convergent questioning often is best suited for eliciting behavior at the knowledge, comprehension, and application levels, and divergent questioning often is best suited for the analysis, synthesis, and evaluation levels.

The final dimension of variety involves the use of student ideas, which is closely related to divergent types of questions having more than a single correct answer. There may be no greater variety than that which occurs in student responses to divergent questions. Because all students are unique individuals, the diversity of their responses to divergent questions is sometimes nothing short of amazing; the proper use of this diversity—or variety—can add an important dimension to your teaching. As noted in chapter 8, this diversity can be a problem as well as a benefit, because unexpected or difficult-to-evaluate responses can sometimes put the teacher on the defensive. A reasonably common response among beginning teachers is to invent a correct answer on the spot to end the awkward pause that frequently follows an unusual and unexpected answer. This is not a proper use of divergent questioning, because one of the purposes of divergent questions is to incorporate student ideas and participation into your lesson. The example dialogue in chapter 7 showed how almost any student answer can be worked into the lesson, pending later clarification and correction. One question (asking students to list some goods and services that a large number of individuals might agree were essential for them to live and prosper) brought many correct answers, albeit not all were equally useful for making important distinctions later in the lesson. The key to eliciting student ideas and opinions is to make the ideas and opinions useful to the goals of the lesson. Soliciting individual student ideas and opinions seldom will be sufficient to provide all the necessary variety in a lesson, if they are not used to create greater understanding for all students. Using this source of variety effectively means taking the contributions of individual students and building from them the more general concepts, patterns, and abstractions that are relevant to the goals of your lesson.

Task Orientation in the Classroom

Table 12.3 summarizes some of the behaviors related to task orientation. Effective task orientation involves:

- Developing unit and lesson plans that reflect the curriculum
- Handling administrative and clerical interruptions efficiently
- Stopping or preventing misbehavior with a minimum of class disruption
- Selecting the most appropriate instructional model for the objectives being taught
- Establishing cycles of review, feedback, and testing

Having effective task orientation begins with being certain that what you are teaching coincides with your school's curriculum, and the single most effective way of assuring this is to base your lessons on the curriculum guide or adopted

TABLE 12.3
Indicators for task orientation

	Being Task Oriented (an effective teacher . . .)	Poor Task Orientation (an ineffective teacher . . .)	Solutions
1.	Develops unit and lesson plans that reflect the most relevant features of the curriculum guide or adopted text (e.g., each unit and lesson objective can be referenced back to curriculum guide or text)	Develops lessons almost exclusively from personal or student interests. Breadth and depth of lesson content fails to distinguish between primary and secondary content in the curriculum guide and text	Key each lesson to a unit plan, the curriculum guide, and the text to test its relevance. Confer with other teachers concerning the most relevant portions of the text and curriculum guide.
2.	Handles administrative and clerical interruptions efficiently (e.g., visitors, announcements, collection of money, dispensing of materials and supplies) by anticipating and preorganizing some tasks and deferring others to noninstructional time	Attends to every administrative and clerical task in detail during the time normally devoted to instruction	Establish a five-to-ten minute restriction on how much time per every hour of instruction you will devote to noninstructional tasks. Defer all other tasks to before or after the lesson.
3.	Stops or prevents misbehavior with a minimum of class disruption (e.g., has preestablished academic and work rules to "protect" intrusions into instructional time)	Attends at length to specific misbehavior; singles out individual students for punishment and lectures on the offense during instructional time	Establish punishments for the most common misbehaviors and post them conspicuously. Identify only the offender and offense during instructional time, deferring punishment to later.
4.	Selects the most appropriate instructional model for the objectives being taught (e.g., primarily uses direct instruction for Type 1 behaviors and indirect instruction for Type 2 behaviors)	Uses inefficient instructional methods for achieving lesson objectives (e.g., frequently attempts to teach facts, rules, and action sequences through discussion or concepts, patterns, and abstractions through drill and practice)	Using your unit plan, curriculum guide, or adopted text, divide the content to be taught into "candidates" for Type 1 and Type 2 objectives. Generally, plan to use direct instruction for the Type 1 content and indirect instruction for Type 2 content.
5.	Builds to unit outcomes with clearly definable events (e.g., weekly and monthly review, feedback, and testing sessions)	Has no systematic milestones toward which to work (e.g., tests on Fridays, major review every fourth Monday) which keep the class on schedule and moving toward a clearly defined goal	Establish a schedule in which major classroom activities begin and end with clearly visible events (e.g., minor and major tests, and review and feedback sessions).

text for your subject or grade. Although these may seem obvious sources of lesson content, a surprising number of teachers stray from them. Without unit and lesson plans the temptation is indeed great to reinterpret adopted curriculum and textbook content into topics of personal interest, for which you may be most knowledgeable, or which your students appear more eager to study. Although revising or reformulating curriculum so that it can be taught at or slightly above your learners' current level of functioning is often necessary, this reformulation should stay true to both the spirit and the letter of the adopted curriculum; otherwise, substituting major topics that are in the curriculum with others that are not will make it less likely that expected outcomes at the unit level will be achieved. Keep in mind that accenting adopted curriculum topics with personal experiences, examples, and illustrations from outside the text or even outside the curriculum often is the mark of effective teaching. But failing to relate these experiences, examples, and illustrations to the adopted curriculum will orient the students away from unit goals and make it less likely they will be achieved. Developing unit plans in which lessons have been checked for relevance to the curriculum guide or text is the first step to maintaining an effective task orientation.

A second behavior for establishing an effective task orientation concerns dealing with administrative and clerical interruptions. In an extensive study of both more and less effective classroom managers at both the elementary and secondary level, Emmer, Evertson, Sanford, Clements, and Worsham (1984) and Evertson, Emmer, Sanford, Clements, and Worsham (1984) found this behavior to be among the most important in determining a teacher's task orientation for the entire class period. This should be no surprise, because it is difficult to return to an instructional task (e.g., group recitation) from a noninstructional one (e.g., passing out materials, checking for supplies); it becomes increasingly difficult to return to the initial state without devoting still more time to getting students back on task. Not only has time been spent on the

noninstructional activity, but just as much time also may have been spent getting learners to return their attention to the instructional activity. It is not surprising that some learners use such pauses or lengthy transitions to keep themselves occupied with misconduct.

Chapter 9 discussed some of the ways to make smooth and efficient transitions; to these can be added the important practice of pre-organizing clerical tasks before class and establishing procedures for handling unexpected interruptions. When clerical tasks are required, such as making a transition from one activity to another (e.g., collecting assignments, passing out new materials, stapling pages of a handout), you can and should complete as much of this work as possible before the class begins. Taking time to collate pages of a handout, staple them, and pass them out in the middle of an instructional activity will be wasteful of valuable instructional time when these activities can be done before the class begins by you or by an early-arriving student. Also, placing supplies and handouts on the students' desks before class (or asking a student to do it) is often preferable to breaking both the flow of what you are doing and your learners' attention even though only a brief moment seems to be required for the task. Remember, a few seconds can turn into several minutes when you include the time it takes the learners to settle back into a concentrated instructional routine.

Although unexpected interruptions such as a messenger appearing at your door or an unscheduled announcement on the public-address system seldom can be avoided, they can be planned for: Establish rules beforehand about what you and your students will do when these events occur. Taking messages but responding to them after class and continuing to move about the classroom silently but in a tasklike fashion during unexpected announcements can often prevent the loss of the valuable minutes of instructional time that might be necessary to bring the class back to order. The less effective classroom managers in the studies by Emmer et al. (1984) and Evertson et al. (1984) often spent inordinate amounts of time returning a class to normal after interruptions, because they often were taken off guard by them and had not planned what to do if such events occurred.

The third behavior for maintaining an effective task orientation involves stopping or preventing misbehavior with a minimum of class disruption. Such an intrusion into your teaching time can be the most devastating; not only because large amounts of instructional time are lost in administering warnings, handing out punishments, and otherwise maintaining control of your classroom, but also because these activities can so drain you of emotional energy that, when the disruption is over, you lack the stamina and enthusiasm to pick up where you left off. Every teacher at every grade level can expect to deal with misconduct, and how it is handled often makes the difference between a classroom that is task oriented and one that is not. The significance of the misbehavior in your classroom must be deemphasized at the time it occurs; you should not ignore it or deal whimsically or halfheartedly with it—but you must *deflect its consequences away from your teaching activity at the time it occurs.* This also means, of course, that you must be prepared to deal with the misbehavior at a later, noninstructional time. In other words, you must learn how to deal with misbehavior at a time and in a context *chosen by you, not by the student,* and thereby take control of the consequences away from the student as quickly and as smoothly as possible. Although such advice is easier to give than to put into practice, there are several important procedures that can help make this become a reality in your classroom.

First, academic and work rules, both posted and orally delivered to your students, will set a tone and climate of classroom organization that can help deter many incidents of misbehavior from ever occurring. Besides these, however, you can defuse and then absorb any misbehavior that does occur into your normal flow of activities, quickly dealing with the misbehavior and moving back into the main flow of instruction; picking up exactly where you stopped at the time of the misbehavior is essential. If procedures concerning misbehavior have been established and com-

municated to students beforehand, you will be able to return to a task orientation almost immediately and with a minimum of disruption. An effective task orientation, therefore, will require establishing an efficient system for *deferring the punishment phase of the misbehavior to noninstructional time,* when your attention can be undivided and the time and arena for discussing the misbehavior can be of your own choosing.

In addition to increasing the amount of class time that is devoted to instruction by preorganizing administrative and clerical chores and establishing procedures for deferring the punishment phase of misbehavior, the fourth behavior for maintaining an effective task orientation requires the efficient use of the time that is devoted to instruction. Inefficient instructional strategies can be as wasteful of your instructional time as are administrative chores and misbehavior, and far more subtly draining. They can be especially damaging to your instructional goals, because at a casual glance efficient and inefficient instructional strategies often look the same. Unless considerable thought is explicitly given to the match between a teacher's objectives and the instructional activities being used to promote those objectives, it is not difficult to be fooled into thinking that great things are happening or are about to happen.

Chapters 6 and 7 devoted considerable attention to two frequently used models of instruction. Although rarely implemented in their pure forms, the direct and indirect approaches to instruction and their respective functions have contributed the means to efficiently teach Type 1 and Type 2 behaviors. These two types of behaviors, representing the acquisition of facts, rules, and action sequences and the learning of concepts, patterns, and abstractions, represent the range of behavioral complexity and types of outcomes found at every grade level and subject. It is not uncommon, however, that beginning teachers (and some experienced ones) attempt to teach *concepts* in the context of drill and practice and to teach *facts* in the context of an inquiry discussion. Although both outcomes could eventually be achieved in either context, the teaching of concepts by rehearsing facts (e.g., memorizing parts of the body to learn about living systems, memorizing the names of the branches of our government to understand what it means to live in a democracy, or memorizing a poem to learn to appreciate poetry) is hardly an efficient means of attaining the concepts of a living system, a democracy, or poetry. The teaching of facts rarely allows for the generalizations and discriminations required for concepts to be acquired, and the teaching of concepts fails to emphasize the unitization and automaticity required for the acquisition of facts. Therefore, matching the type of learning outcome you wish to achieve with the instructional model which most efficiently can accomplish your outcome is an important behavior for establishing an effective task orientation.

The final behavior for task orientation involves establishing cycles of weekly and monthly review and testing, cycles that are built around clearly definable goals (e.g., a test at the end of the month, a review session next week, a demonstration or experiment at the end of the unit). These goals are the types of products that should be made visible to your students and toward which your classroom activities must gradually build with increasing intensity, enthusiasm, and expectation. Such end products will create natural cycles of rising and falling intensity, enthusiasm, and expectation, with the high point of the cycle being just before the expected event and the low point, marking the beginning of a new cycle, immediately afterward. In the upper grades several different cycles may proceed concurrently, as when some classroom activities are preparing students to complete a term paper due next week, while other classroom activities are preparing students to do well on a test to be given at the end of the month. Thus, different cycles may be put in place for tests, assignments, and major projects, and may be staggered so that one cycle is near its highest point when another is near its lowest. This will ensure that a high level of intensity, enthusiasm, and expectation pertaining to one or another clearly defined goal is always present in your classroom.

A brisk instructional pace will be important in accentuating the intensity, enthusiasm, and ex-

pectation as the time for the event arrives. After a major assignment, such as a term paper or test, has been completed, the instructional pace should be noticeably slower than just before the event. This establishes the cycle and makes both the cycle and the goal more apparent to your learners. No one can sustain a high level of intensity, enthusiasm, or expectation for very long without letting down or feeling tricked, so the low point of the cycle serves a desirable function: To regroup, to reflect on past performances, to think about changing study habits, to place content in a broader perspective, and so on. Conversely, a brisker instructional style is a cue to your learners that their performance should begin to change accordingly. These pulses of energy will help maintain a classroom rhythm that will keep your students interested and working with you toward your chosen goals. It will also provide the variety and gentle tension that keeps both students and teachers task oriented.

Engagement in the Classroom

Table 12.4 summarizes some of the behaviors related to engagement. Effectively engaging students in the learning process involves:

- Eliciting the desired behavior
- Providing opportunities for feedback in a non-evaluative atmosphere
- Using group and individual activities as motivational aids, such as performance contracts, programmed texts, games and simulations, and learning centers
- Using meaningful verbal praise
- Monitoring seatwork and checking for progress

Engagement in the learning process begins when the learner is provided with stimulus material with which he or she can practice using the facts, action sequences, or concepts you have taught. Without practice, learning rarely occurs. It is unfortunate that some beginning teachers teach as they themselves were taught in the college classroom, without realizing that vast de-

TABLE 12.4
Indicators for engaging students in the learning process

	Engaging Students Effectively in the Learning Process (an effective teacher . . .)	*Engaging Students Ineffectively in the Learning Process (an ineffective teacher . . .)*	*Solutions*
1.	Elicits the desired behavior immediately after the instructional stimuli (e.g., provides exercise or workbook problems with which the desired behavior can be practiced)	Fails to ask learners to attempt the desired behavior	Schedule practice exercises or questions to immediately follow each set of instructional stimuli.
2.	Provides opportunities for feedback in a nonevaluative atmosphere (e.g., asks students to respond as a group or covertly the first time through)	Formally evaluates the initial practice (e.g., individually calls on students to give correct answer in ways that could be threatening or embarrassing)	Require covert responding or nonevaluative (e.g., group) feedback at the start of a guided practice session.
3.	Uses individual and group activities (e.g., performance contracts, programmed texts, games and simulations, and learning centers as motivational aids) when needed	Fails to match instructional methods to the learning needs of special students (e.g., slow or bilingual learners)	Have individualized instructional materials available (e.g., remedial exercises or texts) for those who may need them.
4.	Uses meaningful verbal praise to get and keep students actively participating in the learning process	Fails to provide reward and reinforcers that are timely and meaningful to the student (e.g., never says why something is "good")	Maintain a warm and nurturing atmosphere by providing verbal praise and encouragement that is meaningful (e.g., explain why the answer was correct). Praise partially correct answers, with qualification.
5.	Monitors seatwork and frequently checks progress during independent practice	Does not monitor student progress during seatwork evenly (e.g., spends too much time with some students failing to observe work of other students)	Limit contact with individual students during seatwork to about 30 seconds each, providing instructionally relevant answers. Circulate among entire class.

velopmental differences lie between the adult and the elementary or secondary school learner. You probably have become accustomed to listening to lectures of an hour or more, during which you were not provided with an opportunity to apply or to use what was being taught. At the college level, where considerable independence and motivation are expected, the instructor may appropriately assume that engagement in the learning process will take place at the convenience and initiative of the individual student as he or she works through the lecture material in the privacy of the study room or the library. This should not be *your* assumption, however, at the elementary and secondary school level. For these learners, lecture and practice must often go hand in hand, separated by minutes rather than days, if learning is to occur. Levels of development, independence, and motivation often are vastly different for the elementary and secondary school learner than for the college student. Engagement in the learning process for the former must be part of the instruction, since the learner at this age is likely not to know how to make the leap from lecture to practice without the active and direct guidance of the teacher. In chapter 5 this process was referred to as "eliciting the desired behavior" and was identified as an important event within the lesson plan. Oral questions, exercises from the workbook, and specially prepared handout problems and model answers, when used under the step-by-step guidance of the teacher, are some of the ways students can be encouraged to think about, work through, or otherwise practice with the material being presented. Such practice should be provided closely in time to the instruction to which it relates and, for complex material, should be interspersed at intervals throughout the lesson—creating cycles of presentation and practice.

In addition to eliciting the desired behavior through guided practice, you will want to provide feedback about the correctness of the elicited response. At this point in the learning process it is important that your feedback be given in as nonevaluative a context as possible to encourage repeated responses and, therefore, en-

gagement in the learning process. A cold "that's wrong" at this stage in the learning process may be just the excuse that a student needs to stop responding to your guided practice. A full-scale evaluation of the lesson and the learners' performances can come later; for now, it is important to get and keep the learners responding to questions, workbook exercises, or handout problems. At this stage of learning crude and often inadequate responses are formed into slightly less crude and more adequate responses, which, in turn, provide the basis for eventually producing finely tuned responses at a high level of accuracy. If behaviors related to the acquisition of knowledge are being sought, this is the time when the processes of unitization (learning the parts) and automaticity (putting the parts together) will be operating; if behaviors related to inquiry or problem solving are being sought, the processes of generalization (learning to go beyond the examples given) and discrimination (learning to separate nonexamples from examples) will be operating. In either case, the feedback must unambiguously inform the learner about the adequacy of any response given, and must do so in a manner that will not embarrass or humiliate the learner in the eyes of others or lower his or her own expectations. Because initial responses to a guided practice exercise may be crude, sometimes funny, and occasionally illogical (in the teacher's eyes), the potential for emotional harm is greatest during this phase of learning. Your job is not to pass judgment but to provide feedback so that the learner can judge his or her own work using the guidance you provide. This can be accomplished by having students respond in unison, by showing answers on a transparency after each problem, or simply by supplying the answer at the end of the designated work time. It is a good idea, however, to request (and occasionally check) that students write out their responses; then you can be certain that they actually engage in the problem solution and not simply wait for the answer to be given.

Chapter 9 discussed the role of motivation; your knowledge of this concept also is important for engaging students in the learning process.

The fact is that for some students, guided practice and nonevaluative feedback are not enough to engage them in the learning process. These learners will need additional motivators in order to become sufficiently energized or excited about learning so that they attempt a first crude response to the practice opportunities you provide. Motivational devices such as performance contracts, programmed learning materials, games and simulations, peer tutoring, volunteering, and learning centers may be useful in getting these students who may represent a sizeable portion of your class to engage in the learning process.

Perhaps most convenient among the motivational devices are individualized learning materials, because often they can be used without interrupting regularly scheduled instruction. Most teachers will not have the time or the flexibility to apply different instructional methods to different types of learners. Teaching two different groups, or even a single group, of problem learners in addition to the regular class often is not a matter of choice for most teachers. Curriculum demands that are often prescribed by the curriculum guide or text make all such dual teaching responsibilities nearly impossible in today's busy classrooms. However, a library of individualized remedial materials can allow for different learning needs to be met in the midst of a heterogeneous class of learners. When performance contracts, programmed texts, games and simulations, and learning centers are individualized, some students can be directed to work independently according to their own, often special, learning needs when others are working on other activities. A teacher who effectively engages students in the learning process will have established a resource library of individualized materials that can be used with special or poorly motivated learners when the need arises. These libraries, however, do not spring up overnight, nor are they likely to be provided entirely by your department or school. Instead, they are accumulated over time by the effective teacher, beginning with his or her first day of teaching.

An important motivation device that is equally applicable to all students is the verbal praise provided after a correct or partially correct answer. Verbal praise in the absence of a genuine accomplishment will be seen quickly by your students as a phony response. Yet, between a glib response such as "Correct," "OK," or "Yep," and an overly emotional response such as "That's wonderful," "Beautiful," or "Brilliant," lies a range of verbal rewards that neither will pass by barely noticed nor will embarrass a student in the eyes of others. Appropriate verbal responses attempt to link a student's response with the exact level of accomplishment attained. For example, instead of simply informing the learner that the response is correct, the learner can be told that the response was correct because ... (e.g., the directions were followed carefully, the correct sequence of events was chosen, care was taken to consult a reference book). Or, instead of informing a learner that a response is brilliant, the teacher can explain about the higher level thought processes that were used to produce such a response (e.g., the answer shows the ability to find relationships among content learned in different chapters). In each of these instances, the emotional impact on the student and the desire to keep engaged in the learning process is greater when verbal praise is provided in the context of the operation successfully accomplished by the student to earn the praise. In this manner, glib phrases such as "Correct," "Good," and "OK" are never worn out, because they are always associated with some unique production by the learner—as when the teacher responds with the reason the response is correct, good, or OK.

Meaningful verbal praise will be especially important in the case of partially correct or correct but hesitant responses. Here, your praise will be important, but it must be tempered with a sign that a better or less hesitant response is desired. To ignore the inadequacy or hesitation in the response in favor of a simple "OK" gives a sign to others that they, too, can provide a less-than-adequate response. In these cases it will be important that the praise is proportional to the adequacy of the response, such as "That's partly correct; now let's see if you can put it all together," or "Good try; now change one thing and you'll have it." Examples such as these point up the subtle difference that can exist between a partially correct answer and a wrong answer; this discrimination often will be a matter of your judgment. It is suggested that your learners' engagement in the learning process will be promoted more by seeing that the glass is half full rather than half empty; likewise, you should praise a partially correct answer with qualification.

Finally, be aware that rarely should you give a response that can be called "meaningful verbal punishment" (e.g., a teacher scolds a learner for a careless response). Not to be confused with reminders to study harder, pay greater attention, think some more, or go over mistakes, which are often desirable stimulants to learning, phrases that ridicule, demean, or draw the class's attention to one's ineptitude rarely, if ever, will lead a learner to change the behavior that led to the careless or incorrect response. In these instances the best approach is to replace an emotional response with constructive tips for finding the right answer or to solicit the answer from another.

The last behavior for effectively engaging students in the learning process involves monitoring and checking. These two processes go hand in hand, because one without the other cannot be effective. Monitoring involves withitness—or systematically observing all aspects of your classroom. It also involves being able to perform overlapping activities in which your learners are actively being observed while you are carrying out other activities. To assure your students that you have withitness, such monitoring should occur during both instructional and noninstructional activities.

During instructional activities such as guided practice and independent seatwork, monitoring should be done within a systematic routine of checking. Rather than monitoring by simply visually scanning parts of the classroom, circulate among students, checking their responses in workbooks or exercises. It is important, however, that this circulating behavior is not seen by your learners as evaluative, but rather as a helpful response to the work being attempted. No one likes to be stared at while working, so a casual glance at this paper and then at another and so on until the entire room is circulated will be more constructive than long interactions with individual students, whose self-esteem and engagement may become stifled by your stay at their desk because this can be taken by others as a sign of unusually poor performance. Interactions with individual students, therefore, should be limited to brief interchanges lasting about 30 seconds and limited to responses that are focused on a particular problem the student is having. This cycle can be repeated many times, of course, in which case you may want to look more closely the second time around. Monitoring and checking for progress, especially during guided and independent practice, are two of the most important tools you can have for effectively engaging your students in the learning process.

Success Rate in the Classroom

Table 12.5 summarizes some of the behaviors related to establishing a moderate-to-high success rate. Engaging learners in the learning process at moderate-to-high rates of success involves:

- Establishing unit and lesson content that reflects prior learning
- Correcting partially correct, correct but hesitant, and incorrect answers
- Dividing instructional stimuli into bite-size pieces at the learners' current level of functioning
- Changing instructional stimuli gradually
- Varying the instructional tempo or pace to create momentum

The first behavior for obtaining a moderate-to-high success rate takes place during unit planning when unit outcomes are identified and a logical sequence of lessons is chosen to achieve those outcomes. Surprising as it may be, many units are planned with little or no consideration given to the ordering in a sequence of events. Although some of your unit outcomes may be achieved by giving your learners content in random order, the cost in instructional time with

TABLE 12.5
Indicators for rates of success

	Moderate-to-High Rates of Success (an effective teacher . . .)	*Poor Rates of Success (an ineffective teacher . . .)*	*Solutions*
1.	Establishes unit and lesson content that reflects prior learning (e.g., planning lesson sequences that consider task-relevant prior information)	Fails to sequence learning in advance to ensure that all task-relevant prior knowledge has been taught before moving to next lesson	Create a top-down unit plan in which all the lesson outcomes at the bottom of the hierarchy needed to achieve unit outcomes at the top of the hierarchy are identified. Arrange lessons in an order most logical to achieving unit outcomes.
2.	Administers correctives immediately after initial response (e.g., shows model of correct answer and how to attain it after first crude response is given)	Leaves students to practice and learn independently immediately after presenting instructional stimuli; waits until next day to show correct responses	Provide for guided practice prior to independent practice and provide means of self-checking (e.g., handout with correct answers) at intervals of practice.
3.	Divides instructional stimuli into small chunks (e.g., establishes bite-size lessons that can be easily digested by learners at their current level of functioning)	Packages instruction in chunks that are too large or small (e.g., teaches too complex of a lesson too early in an instructional sequence)	Break lessons at "bottom" of unit plan into smaller pieces. Use original "lessons" as units or divisions within units.
4.	Plans transitions to new material in easy to grasp steps (e.g., changes instructional stimuli according to a preestablished thematic pattern so that each new lesson is seen as an extension of previous lessons)	Abruptly changes instructional topics and perspectives from one lesson to another without themes and interconnections	Extend unit-plan hierarchy downward to more specific lessons that are tied together above with a single unit theme and outcome. Use the part-whole, sequential, combinatorial, comparative, or the problem centered, hierarchical, or networking approaches for organizing content.
5.	Varies the pace at which stimuli are presented and continually builds toward a climax or key event	Maintains same pace for too long a time, leading to a monotonous and static level of intensity and expectation	Use review, feedback, and testing sessions to form intervals of increasing and decreasing intensity and expectation.

such a haphazard approach is considerable. The result of this type of planning is often expressed as "I've run out of time," or "Couldn't get to topic X," or ". . . too many interruptions this semester to finish the text." Depending on the circumstances, these may or may not be the results of poor unit planning but, more often than not, they could be avoided with good unit planning. Good unit planning means arranging lessons in a sequence that works for, not against, you. Teachers may not be aware that a minor change in the order in which content is taught may create a major savings in instructional time by making each new lesson relate to the previous lesson. This means that task-relevant prior knowledge taught earlier is placed immediately preceding, or as close in time as possible, to the lesson or lessons in which it will be needed. The savings in time results either from not having to reteach the necessary task-relevant prior learning, or from not having to reteach that day's lesson after it appears that the task-relevant information needed for it had not been learned. A considerable amount of your instructional time during a grading period can be consumed with backtracking to remove fact, skill, or concept deficiencies that could have been avoided with better planning at the unit level. Effective unit planning means making each lesson work for you by arranging a sequence of instruction that gradually builds in a logical and systematic order to your unit outcomes. This emphasizes the importance of establishing unit plans in the first place, because without them you run the risk of randomly throwing content at learners, some of whom may be struggling to make the transition from earlier lessons and, finding none, will simply give up or tune out. Make each new lesson a logical extension of the previous lesson; this will help secure moderate-to-high success rates during guided and independent practice.

Another essential behavior for securing moderate-to-high success rates is the provision of timely feedback. During guided practice, in which the desired behavior is being elicited for the first time, correctives should be given immediately after the learner's initial response. The time between practice and feedback has long been considered by educational psychologists to be one of the most important elements of learning. The longer feedback is delayed, the less likely it is to influence the learner's performance on subsequent attempts to produce the behavior. The reasons for this are complex, but essentially the learner must hold a mental image, or print, of the first crude response in memory in order for the feedback to be effective. Unfortunately, mental images fade quickly, especially in young learners, so the effectiveness of the feedback deteriorates rapidly with any delay. In order for the learner to link your feedback to his or her image of the response, the corrective must immediately follow. Earlier chapters discussed several practices for accomplishing this, such as calling out the right answer after each practice item has been completed, displaying a model on a transparency that illustrates how to attain a right answer, or having students check the responses of other students according to some standard provided by you or the text. Note also that feedback using these and related procedures should be administered in a nonevaluative atmosphere. Both immediacy and a nonevaluative atmosphere should be present in order for the feedback to have its greatest effect on revising and refining the response.

In order to achieve moderate-to-high rates of success, feedback should be provided for each and every item given during guided practice. A missed opportunity to correct a wrong, partially wrong, or even correct but hesitant response (which may be correct for the wrong reason) during this critical time can affect success rates during later independent practice (in the form of sustained seatwork, workbook exercises, or homework). Guided practice should continue until a success rate of approximately 60-80% is achieved. Generally, this will only be possible if the correct responses and the reasons for them are provided after every trial response. This will pave the way for a still higher success rate at the end of independent practice, at which time about 90% correct answers should be expected. This higher rate of success, however, rarely can be achieved without first establishing a 60-80% success rate during guided practice, after which feedback during independent practice may be delayed with no ill effects on success rate, such as when correct answers are given at the end of the period or homework is graded the next day.

Our next behavior for establishing moderate-to-high success rates involves sizing unit and lesson plans to fit your learners. To be sure, units need to be chosen to reflect some "whole" that is comprehensible to your learners. But, they also must be sized so that learners still remember the specifics taught at the beginning of the unit when broader concepts and abstractions are taught at the end of the unit. For example, units that ramble through many historical periods, physical laws, mathematical operations, social issues, or elements of composition (no matter how related these periods, laws, operations, issues, or elements may be) will prevent your learners from gaining a sense of direction and from connecting facts, rules, and sequences with the concepts, patterns, and abstractions to which they belong. Experience has shown that, when in doubt, units should be made less encompassing than might be originally desired, simply because the depth and breadth of content that is comprehensible to you will rarely be comprehensible at the same depth and breadth to your learners.

Sizing mistakes at the unit level can come back to haunt you at the lesson level. For instance, if your unit topic is too broad and encompassing, you naturally will be influenced to make the component lessons broad and encompassing in order to cover the unit content in the specified period of time. This is where considerable difficulties can occur at the lesson level in establishing moderate-to-high success rates. As lesson content becomes broader, it must necessarily become less detailed, which often leaves less time for adequate periods of guided and independent practice. There will be a rush to cover the content, and perhaps adequate coverage may be compromised. Also, behaviors at higher levels of complexity may be taught without adequate attention to the task-relevant prior facts, rules, and sequences that may be necessary for attaining

these higher level outcomes. The temptation may be to attempt to walk across mountain tops without realizing that some valleys may have to be crossed as well. The indirect instruction model can play a valuable role in covering concepts, patterns, and abstractions quickly and efficiently, but an entire unit planned exclusively around the indirect instruction model may be a sign that too broad a content area has been intended at the unit level and that some retrenchment may be necessary.

Finally, note that any individual piece of content chosen must be at your learners' current level of functioning if moderate-to-high success rates are to be achieved. When lengthy guided practice sessions or group discussion sessions do not provide 60-80% correct responses, lesson content may be both too broad and too complex for your learners. This would be a sign that your pieces of content may not be bite size and that a lesson may have to be divided into several smaller lessons before it can be digested by your learners. Keep in mind that some unfinished lessons should be continued as subsequent lessons and not relegated to the excuse that "time ran out." This will always be true when the unfinished content represents task-relevant learning for subsequent lessons.

The fourth behavior for establishing moderate-to-high success rates involves the necessary transitions within and between lesson content. Although planning lesson content in bite-sized pieces will aid learners in making transitions between old and new content, this alone will not be sufficient to ensure moderate-to-high success rates. In addition, you will need to organize unit and lesson content in ways that establish some overarching themes that can interconnect different parts of a unit or an extended lesson. In chapters 6 and 7 several methods were suggested by which content might be organized to establish connections across different lessons or parts of a lesson. Although not mutually exclusive, for direct instruction these were the part-whole, sequential, combinatorial, and comparative approaches to organizing content, and for indirect instruction they were the problem-centered, hierarchical, and networking approaches. Each of these approaches represents a means for organizing lessons and content within lessons in order to emphasize relationships between and among various aspects of a topic. Some of these link content together procedurally, as in the sequential or problem-centered approaches; others link content by emphasizing themes and threads running through the content itself, as in the comparative and networking approaches. With either type, however, the effect upon the learner is to make the transitions more comprehensible, to help the learner see that what is being taught now is actually a part of what has gone before and what will follow. This is a valuable outcome for establishing moderate-to-high rates of success in as much as the learner is able to build up an understanding of the topic gradually and in measured steps, as opposed to trying to cram all the bits and pieces together at review and test time. Increasing one's understanding in a stair-step fashion is only possible when there is a direction and continuity linking all the different steps. Without direction and continuity, one quickly loses the underlying theme or connection between the pieces of what is to be learned, and learning is reduced to memorizing the pieces and hoping that they come together. Unless your lessons are organized to come together from the very start, it is unlikely that they will do so in the minds of your learners any time later. These organizational approaches as well as others will serve to make the transitions between lesson topics within reach of every student, even when the lessons are disproprotional in breadth and complexity. Easy and hard lessons may be inevitable, but the transition between them will always be more comprehensive when the common structure of which they are a part is explained to your learners.

The final behavior for establishing moderate-to-high success rates has been mentioned in the discussion of several other effective teaching behaviors. It deserves special mention again, however, with respect to the concept of momentum. This last teaching effectiveness indicator adds a subtle but important feature to establishing cycles of weekly and monthly review and testing. At an earlier point in this text, the practice of teaching was associated with the conducting of a symphony orchestra. One may be surprised at such an odd matching of apparently dissimilar professions, but these two, admittedly very different, occupations may have more in common than either the theatergoer or the student realizes. The thread which binds these two activities together is not, of course, their content, becausemuscial notes have little resemblance to academic subjects (except in music), but rather the simple fact that both the maestro and the teacher must play a melody that will be understood by their respective audiences even if it has never been heard before. This is quite a feat for both the conductor and the teacher, and perhaps it is why each is a member of an extremely challenging profession. How can students be made to understand in the course of an hour-long lesson something they knew nothing about before, and how can the conductor make an abstract and perhaps never-heard-before concerto recognizable to the audience? The secret is in the way the notes or individual pieces of lesson content are put together. How the notes are played against one another is reflected in the tune's melody, and how the individual pieces of content are related to one another is reflected in the lesson's *momentum*. Both teacher and maestro play a melody by juxtaposing familiar notes or familiar facts and concepts in ways that make sense, even though that exact combination of notes or combination of facts and concepts has never been heard before. Obviously, notes cannot just be thrown together to make a symphony any more than facts and concepts can be thrown together to make a lesson. Instead, rules must be followed, discovered over years of painstaking inquiry, that put things together in ways that can be understood by any audience. This book has introduced you to the many and varied rules for effective teaching in the form of techniques (e.g., questioning/probing), strategies (e.g., drill and practice/group discussion), and methods (e.g., direct/

indirect). However, to make your education concerto meaningful you will have to blend these in ways that can be interpreted by your audience. One of the most important ingredients for ensuring that your melody will be listened to and understood is that it has momentum. No one wants to hear the same drab notes played over and over again or even a different set of notes played in the same key with the same rhythm. Momentum is as important to the teacher as it is to the symphonic conductor. Momentum may be the life blood of any good conductor, but it certainly is the life blood of an effective teacher. It is established by varying the pace at which stimuli are presented during the process of reaching a climax or key event. In teaching this can be accomplished first by establishing cycles of weekly and monthly review, feedback, and testing and, then, by gradually increasing pace and intensity as the time for the major event draws near. Playing the same instructional note—or keeping the same monotonous pace—too long may be as boring as listening to a drab and lifeless musical score. Consequently, rising and falling action must be established to set the instruction in motion toward some discernable end, which can be established by scheduling cycles of review, feedback, and testing and by gradually increasing the pace or tempo within cycles in ways that are visible to your learners.

Formative Observation of Effective Teaching Practices

This chapter has discussed many different indicators of effective teaching—28 in all. The chapter ends with a suggestion that you try observing all of these signs in the classrooms you may have the opportunity to visit. At the beginning of Appendix C you will find these 28 behaviors in the form of an observation instrument, on which a simple checkmark can be placed when one of these behaviors is observed. To provide practice in observing some of these indicators of effectiveness, several classroom dialogues have also

been provided in the appendix. You may wish to read these carefully, looking for signs of effectiveness and ineffectiveness pertaining to the five key behaviors, and to record your results on the observation instrument.

A Final Word

It is important to say, as this text ends, that you will have second thoughts (maybe often) about becoming a teacher. The job may be as complex and challenging as that of a symphony conductor but, as we both know, the pay and working conditions are hardly the same—nor will they probably ever be. Rather, it is those indefinable qualities of teaching that draw us to it. Being around the youth and vitality that we know we ourselves will never again have, being able to lead and to guide during the critical developing years of our learners' lives, and being able to instill and share an excitement and understanding for a subject we have come to respect and appreciate, are all part of the best reasons to teach. But even these may miss the most important reason of all for becoming a teacher: Perhaps nowhere else on earth can we be so close to life with all of its excitement, exhilaration, and adversity. The casual traveler, as well as the anthropologist, travels far and wide looking for different cultures, new experiences, novelties, oddities, beauty, strange customs, excitement, and even love and compassion; but there is nowhere that all of these things are woven into such a rich tapestry of life than in the American classroom. The monetary reward for a front row seat may indeed be low, but for countless thousands of us, being able to observe, participate in, and, most important, work to improve this tapestry, will always be worth the cost. Be sure to open your heart and mind to this side of teaching, for which many travel far and wide but often fail to see. And good luck!

Summing Up

This chapter summarized what the effective teacher does in the classroom with regard to the five key behaviors of clarity, variety, task orientation, and engagement in the learning process with moderate-to-high rates of success. Its main points were:

1. To be clear in the classroom, the effective teacher

   - informs the learners of the objective
   - provides learners with advance organizers
   - checks for task-relevant prior learning and reteaches, if necessary
   - gives directives slowly and distinctly
   - knows the ability level of learners and teaches to those levels
   - uses examples, illustrations, and demonstrations to explain and clarify text and workbook content
   - provides a review or summary at the end of each lesson

2. To have variety in the classroom, the effective teacher

   - uses attention-gaining devices
   - shows enthusiasm
   - varies mode of presentation
   - mixes rewards and reinforcers
   - varies types of questions and probes
   - uses student ideas

3. To be task oriented in the classroom, the effective teacher

   - develops unit and lesson plans that reflect the curriculum
   - handles administrative and clerical interruptions efficiently
   - stops or prevents misbehavior with a minimum of class disruption
   - selects the most appropriate instructional model for the objectives being taught
   - establishes cycles of review, feedback, and testing

4. To engage students in the learning process, the effective teacher

   - elicits the desired behavior
   - provides opportunities for feedback in a nonevaluative atmosphere
   - uses group and individual activities as motivational aids when necessary
   - uses meaningful verbal praise
   - monitors seatwork and checks for practice

5. To establish moderate-to-high rates of success in the classroom, the effective teacher

   - establishes unit and lesson content that reflects prior learning
   - corrects partially correct, correct but hesitant, and incorrect answers
   - divides instructional stimuli into bite-sized pieces at the learners' current level of functioning
   - changes instructional stimuli gradually
   - varies the instructional pace or tempo to create momentum

For Discussion and Practice

1. Identify the seven different signs of effectiveness pertaining to the key behavior of clarity. Indicate which, in your opinion, are the most important.
2. Identify the six different signs of effectiveness pertaining to the key behavior of variety. Which, in your opinion, should occur daily, which weekly, and which only monthly?
3. Identify the five different signs of effectiveness pertaining to the key behavior of task orientation. What curriculum resources, in your opinion, should be available during lesson planning to ensure task orientation?
4. Identify the five different signs of effectiveness pertaining to the key behavior of engagement in the learning process. Explain in your own words how engagement in the learning process differs from, but also is related to, task orientation.
5. Identify the five different signs of effectiveness pertaining to the key behavior of success rate. Approximately, what percentage of correct responses should be achieved during guided prac-

tice, and what percentage during independent practice?

6. Identify one sign of ineffectiveness for each of the five key behaviors that, in your opinion, is the most serious for preventing effective teaching.

7. For each of the five key behaviors, identify the single catalytic behavior that would be most helpful in executing that key behavior. The catalytic behaviors are structuring, questioning, probing, use of student ideas, and enthusiasm.

8. Using the Formative Observation of Effective Teaching Practices Instrument as your guide, indicate which of the 28 signs of effectiveness would be, for you personally, (a) the most difficult to achieve and (b) the easiest to achieve. For each of your (a) choices, explain why you think the behavior would be difficult to achieve. What resources, aids, and instructional devices, if available to you, would make these behaviors easier to achieve?

9. If you have the opportunity, observe one or more classrooms over a period of time, and place checkmarks on the Formative Observation of Effective Teaching Practices Instrument (Appendix C) whenever a sign of effectiveness or ineffectiveness is noticed. At the end of your observation add the checkmarks within categories to create frequencies for each of the 28 signs. Now, construct two bar graphs indicating the relative frequencies with which the (a) effectiveness and (b) ineffectiveness indicators were observed.

10. In your own words, explain why the teacher may be more similar to a symphony conductor than to other professionals, such as a doctor, lawyer, architect, or engineer.

11. Apply the Formative Observation of Effective Teaching Practices Instrument to the three classroom dialogues in Appendix C. Compare the results, noting differences in the effectiveness profiles of the three teachers. Share your results in a group session, discussing any differences in profiles with members of your group or class.

Suggested Readings

Biddle, B. (1987). Effects of teaching. In M. J. Dunkin (Ed.), *International encyclopedia of teaching and teacher education.* New York: Pergamon.
An overview of the systematic positive influences on learners that teachers can have in the classroom.

Elliot, J. (1987). Teachers as researchers. In M. J. Dunkin (Ed.), *International encyclopedia of teaching and teacher education.* New York: Pergamon.
An interesting account of how the classroom teacher can, through careful observation and reflection, contribute to modern definitions of effective teaching.

Fogarty, J. E., Wang, M. C., & Creek, R. (1983). A descriptive study of experienced and novice teachers' interactive instructional thoughts and actions. *Journal of Educational Research, 77,* 22–32.
An interesting contrast between two types of teachers showing how the planning and instructional decision-making of the experienced teacher differs from those of the inexperienced teacher—and their potential effects on learners.

Land, M. & Smith L. (1979). The effect of low inference teacher clarity inhibitors on student achievement. *Journal of Teacher Education, 30,* 55–57.
A study exploring the negative effects on student achievement of teachers who exhibit a lack of clarity.

Peterson, P. L. & Clark, C. M. (1978). Teachers' reports of their cognitive processes during teaching. *American Educational Research Journal, 15,* 555–565.
A comprehensive review of what teachers think about during teaching and how some key behaviors are chosen by them for implementation.

Rohrkemper, M. (1987). Proactive teaching. In M. J. Dunkin (Ed.), *International encyclopedia of teaching and teacher education.* New York: Pergamon.
A good summary of some of the most important features of the direct instruction model.

Rohrkemper, M. (1987). Reactive teaching. In M. J. Dunkin (Ed.), *International encyclopedia of teaching and teacher education.* New York: Pergamon.
A good summary of some of the most important features of the indirect instruction model.

Winne, P. & Marx, R. (1982). Students' and teachers' views of thinking processes for classroom learning. *Elementary School Journal, 82,* 493–518.
A report of the retrospective thoughts and concerns of both students and teachers during instruction—with implications for the use of key and catalytic behaviors.

Appendix A

Teacher Concerns Checklist

Francis F. Fuller   Gary D. Borich

The University of Texas at Austin

DIRECTIONS: This checklist is designed to explore what teachers are concerned about at different points in their careers. There are, of course, no right or wrong answers; each person has his or her own concerns.

Sometimes people are tempted to answer questions like these in terms of what they think they should be concerned about or expect to be concerned about in the future. This is not what is wanted here. We would like to know only what you are actually concerned about NOW.

On the following page you will find statements about some concerns you might have now. Read each statement. Then ask yourself: WHEN I THINK ABOUT TEACHING, AM I CONCERNED ABOUT THIS?

If you are *not concerned* about that now, or the statement does not apply, write the number "1" in the box.

If you are *a little concerned,* write the number "2" in the box.

If you are *moderately concerned,* write the number "3" in the box.

If you are *very concerned,* write the number "4" in the box.

And if you are *totally preoccupied* with the concern, write the number "5" in the box. Be sure to answer every item. Begin by completing the following:

1. Name _____ Male _____ Female _____ Age _____
2. Circle the one that best describes your teaching experience:
   1. No education courses and no formal classroom observation or teaching experience
   2. Education courses but no formal observation or teaching experience
   3. Education courses and observation experience but no teaching
   4. Presently student teaching
   5. Completed student teaching
   6. Presently an inservice teacher
3. If you are a student: Freshman _____ Sophomore _____ Junior _____ Senior _____ Graduate _____
4. The grade level you plan to teach (if student) or are now teaching (if inservice): Preschool _____ Elementary _____ Junior High _____ Senior High _____ College _____ Other _____
5. If currently teaching: Average number of students you teach per class: _____

For each statement below, decide which of the following answers best applies to you now. Place the number of the answer in the box at the left of the statement. Please be as accurate as you can.

| 1 | Not concerned | 2 | A little concerned | 3 | Moderately concerned |

| 4 | Very concerned | 5 | Totally preoccupied |

☐ 1. Selecting and teaching content well
☐ 2. Whether the students really like me or not
☐ 3. Increasing students' feelings of accomplishment
☐ 4. Lack of freedom to initiate innovative instructional programs
☐ 5. The nature and quality of instructional materials
☐ 6. Too many students in each class
☐ 7. Motivating students to study
☐ 8. Lack of instructional materials
☐ 9. Rapid rate of curriculum and instructional change
☐ 10. Feeling under pressure too much of the time
☐ 11. Maintaining the appropriate degree of class control
☐ 12. Frustrated by the routine and inflexibility of the situation
☐ 13. The wide range of student achievement
☐ 14. Being in constant demand by students
☐ 15. Doing well when a supervisor is present
☐ 16. Meeting the needs of different kinds of students
☐ 17. Insufficient time to think
☐ 18. Being fair and impartial
☐ 19. Getting a favorable evaluation of my teaching
☐ 20. Diagnosing student learning problems
☐ 21. Lack of opportunity for professional growth
☐ 22. Too many noninstructional duties
☐ 23. Ensuring that students grasp subject matter fundamentals
☐ 24. Working with too many students each day
☐ 25. Challenging unmotivated students

☐ 26. Adapting myself to the needs of different students
☐ 27. Ineffective faculty meetings
☐ 28. Whether students can apply what they learn
☐ 29. Students who disrupt class
☐ 30. Inadequate fringe benefits for teachers
☐ 31. Student health and nutrition problems that affect learning
☐ 32. Insufficient time for rest and class preparation
☐ 33. The psychological climate of the school
☐ 34. Clarifying the limits of my authority and responsibility
☐ 35. Inadequate assistance from specialized teachers
☐ 36. Lack of public support for schools
☐ 37. Chronic absence and dropping out of students
☐ 38. Feeling more adequate as a teacher
☐ 39. Guiding students toward intellectual and emotional growth
☐ 40. Too many standards and regulations set for teachers
☐ 41. Being accepted and respected by my peers
☐ 42. Adequately presenting all of the required material
☐ 43. Slow progress of certain students
☐ 44. Insufficient clerical help for teachers
☐ 45. Helping students to value learning
☐ 46. Whether each student is getting what he needs
☐ 47. Inadequate teacher salaries
☐ 48. Increasing my proficiency in content
☐ 49. Recognizing the social and emotional needs of students
☐ 50. The wide diversity of student ethnic and socioeconomic backgrounds

Appendix B

Chapter 1

1. 1, 2, 1 (or 2), 1 (or 2), 2, 3, 2, 3, 2 (or 1), 3,
   2, 3, 3

3.

Behavior	High SES	Low SES
Individualization	Ask difficult questions	Supplement standard curriculum with individualized materials
Teacher affect	Correct poor answers immediately when student fails to perform	Be warm and encouraging
Overteaching/overlearning	Assign homework	Present materials in small pieces
Classroom interaction	Engage students in questions and answers	Help students immediately when help is needed

Chapter 2

1. a. To match instructional methods to individual learning needs
   b. To understand the reasons behind the school performance of individual learners
2. ▪ High state anxiety: place value of specific assignment in perspective with other assignments
   ▪ Low auditory ability: use visual forms of instruction
   ▪ Gifted: encourage independent thinking
   ▪ Low SES: make available popular reading sources and supplementary learning materials (e.g., visual aids)
   ▪ Poor self-concept: reflect back to students the value of their unique talents
   ▪ High trait anxiety: create a range of acceptable alternatives for a given assignment
   ▪ Unassertive, overassertive, or aggressive: encourage expanded sex roles, avoid sex stereotypes, organize problem-solving activities that define the limits of independent and creative behavior
   ▪ Disruptive peer group: break into more heterogeneous groups for learning exercises
9. Get students to talk about themselves; reward unique talents.

10. a. state   f. trait
    b. trait   g. trait
    c. trait   h. state but also trait
    d. trait   i. trait
    e. state   j. trait but also state
11. It is related to engagement in the learning process and success in an occupation.
12. Exchange some troublesome students with other classes. Form heterogeneous groups composed of members of different peer groups.

Chapter 3

1. a, g, a, g, a, g, a, g, g, g
5. (1) Strengthening of the curriculum in the areas of math, science, English, foreign language, and social studies
   (2) Renewed effort to teach higher order thinking skills
   (3) Raising school grading standards
   (4) Higher college admission standards
   (5) More work in core subjects
6. To teach students how to think
9. ▪ Aims and goals (e.g., texts, curriculum guides, policy reports)
   ▪ Learner needs (e.g., student achievement, workbook exercises, class performance)
   ▪ Knowledge of academic discipline (e.g., subject matter texts)
   ▪ Knowledge of teaching methods (e.g., key and catalytic behaviors)
11. ▪ Front half/back half
   ▪ Girls/boys
   ▪ More able/less able
   ▪ Minority/nonminority
12. ▪ Spreading interactions across categories of students
   ▪ Selecting students randomly
   ▪ Pairing students
   ▪ Coding class notes
13. Self, task, impact
15. First teacher has profile B, second teacher has profile A, third teacher has profile C, fourth teacher has profile D

Chapter 4

1. a. To tie general aims and goals to specific classroom strategies by which the aims and goals can be achieved
   b. To express teaching strategies that serve stated goals in a manner that allows their effects upon the learner to be measured
2. Repetition of the teaching task over time has imprinted experienced teachers with mental images of all the ingredients any well-written objective contains. Also, experienced teachers are much more likely than inexperienced teachers to alter and generalize key instructional elements from one lesson or topic to another.
3. The behavior is observable and measurable; it occurs in a specifiable period of time.
4. The observable behavior, conditions under which it is to be observed, and level of proficiency at which it is to be displayed
5. Teachers tended to focus their concerns on self and task, sometimes to the exclusion of their impact on students.
6. They have widely divergent implications for achieving the desired behavior and for observing its attainment.
7. A, O, A, A, A, O, O, O
8. The circumstances under which the behavior is to be displayed
9. To establish the setting under which the behavior will be tested and, therefore, to guide how and what to study
10. The extent to which the conditions are similar to those under which the behavior will have to be performed in the real world
11. The level of proficiency at which the behavior must be displayed
13. (1) They do not imply that some behaviors will be more or less desirable than others.
   (2) Less complex behaviors do not imply that less preparation, fewer instructional resources, or less teaching time will be required.
   (3) One or more behaviors from the other domains may be required for a behavior to occur.

14. 1. b   4. e
    2. a   5. f
    3. b

Chapter 5

1. Knowledge of aims and goals, knowledge of learners, knowledge of subject matter content and organization, knowledge of teaching methods, tacit knowledge
2. *Systematic* implies orderliness. *System* implies that there are interrelated parts that build to some unified whole.
3. By the way in which individual lessons are sequenced and build upon one another to produce a unified whole
4. ■ Hierarchy helps us see the relationship between individual lesson outcomes and the unit outcome. It also helps us identify lessons that are not too big or too small, but that are just right.
   ■ Constraint helps us see task-relevant prior learning, and it is used to identify the proper sequence of lessons needed to teach the unit outcome.
5. Task-relevant prior learning constrains subsequent learning.
6. ■ Cognitive: analysis, synthesis, evaluation
   ■ Affective: valuing, organization, characterization
   ■ Psychomotor: precision, articulation, naturalization
7. They represent smaller, more detailed portions of content
9. It would take more intermediate levels to arrive at content suitably sized for a lesson.
10. Ability grouping, peer tutoring, learning centers, review, and follow-up materials
11. Mastery learning is when each student displays a high level, if not complete proficiency, of each intended outcome.
12. Gaining attention, informing the learner of the objective, stimulating recall of prerequisite learning, presenting the stimulus material, eliciting the desired behavior, providing feedback, assessing the behavior

13. Presenting the stimulus material
14. Assessing the behavior
15. Eliciting the desired behavior
16. Providing feedback: immediate and nonevaluative
    Assessing the behavior: delayed and evaluative

Chapter 6

1. ■ Type 1: facts, rules, action sequences
   ■ Type 2: concepts, patterns, abstractions
   ■ Type 1 outcomes generally apply to the knowledge, comprehension, and application levels, while Type 2 outcomes generally apply to the analysis, synthesis, and evaluation levels.
2. ■ Knowledge acquisition: facts, rules, actions, sequences
   ■ Inquiry, problem solving: concepts, patterns, and abstractions
3. Full class instruction, questions posed by the teacher, detailed and redundant practice, one new fact, rule, or sequence mastered before the next is presented, arrangement of classroom to maximize drill and practice
4. ■ Cognitive: to recall, to describe, to list
   ■ Affective: to listen, to attend, to be aware
   ■ Psychomotor: to repeat, to follow, to place
5. (1) To disseminate information that is not readily available from texts or workbooks in appropriately sized pieces
   (2) To arouse or heighten student interest
   (3) To achieve content mastery
6. (1) Having students correct each other's work
   (2) Having students identify difficult homework problems
   (3) Sampling the understanding of a few students who represent the range of students in the class
   (4) Explicitly reviewing the task-relevant information necessary for the day's lesson
7. Part-whole, sequential, combinatorial, comparative
8. Rule—Example—Rule

9. To create a response, however crude, that can become the basis for learning

10. It is used to help convert wrong or partially correct answers to right answers by encouraging the student to use some aspects of the answer given in formulating the correct response.

11. (1) Correct, quick, and firm: acknowledge correctness and either ask another question or move on

    (2) Correct but hesitant: acknowledge correctness and review steps for attaining correct answer

    (3) Incorrect but careless: acknowledge incorrectness and immediately move on

    (4) Incorrect: acknowledge incorrectness and then, without actually giving the student the answer, channel student's thoughts in ways that result in a correct answer

14. Review key facts, explain steps required, prompt with clues or hints, walk student through a similar problem

15. 60–80%, reduce content coverage, increase opportunities for practice and feedback

16. To form action sequences; they should increasingly resemble applications in the real world

17. Keep contacts to a minimum, on the average of 30 seconds; spread contacts across most students, avoiding concentrating on a few students.

18. About 95%

19. Gradually increase the coverage and depth of weekly reviews until time for a comprehensive monthly review arrives.

20. Preview them carefully to ascertain their adherence to the six functions of direct instruction.

Chapter 7

1. Inquiry, discovery, and a problem
2. ■ Type 1: facts, rules and action sequences
   ■ Type 2: concepts, patterns, and abstractions

3. The learner indirectly acquires a behavior by transforming stimulus material into a response or behavior that differs from (a) the stimulus used to present the learning and (b) any previous response emitted by the learner.

4. It is not generally efficient or effective for attaining outcomes at the higher levels of complexity involving concepts, patterns, and abstractions.

5. ■ Unitization: the learning of individual facts or rules
   ■ Automaticity: putting the facts or rules together in an action sequence and being able to execute the sequence rapidly and automatically
   ■ Example: learning to read

6. ■ Generalization: classifying apparently different stimuli into the same category on the basis of criterial attributes
   ■ Discrimination: distinguishing examples of a concept from nonexamples
   ■ Example: learning the meaning of *democracy*

7. 1. 1
   2. 2
   3. 1
   4. 2
   5. 2
   6. 1
   7. 2
   8. 2
   9. 1
   10. 2

8. Our memories would become overburdened trying to remember all possible instances of the concept; also, instances of the concept could easily be confused with noninstances.

11. ■ Induction: the process of thinking in which a set of specific data is presented or observed and a generalization or unifying pattern is drawn from the data
   ■ Deduction: the process of thinking in which the truth or validity of a theory is tested in a specific instance

12. Stating a theory, forming a hypothesis, observing or collecting data, analyzing and interpreting the data, making a conclusion

14. ▪ Criterial: clarity, variety, task orientation, engagement in the learning process, moderate-to-high success rate
    ▪ Noncriterial: number of credit hours attained, degree held, number of inservice workshops attended, college grades, years of teaching experience

15. (1) Provide more than a single example
    (2) Use examples that vary in ways that are unimportant to the concept
    (3) Include nonexamples of the concept that also include important dimensions of the concept
    (4) Explain why nonexamples that have some of the same characteristics as examples are nonexamples

16. ▪ Direct instruction: to elicit a single right answer or expose level of understanding
    ▪ Indirect instruction: to help the student search for and discover an appropriate answer with a minimum of assistance

17. Questions that present contradictions, probe for deeper responses, extend the discussion, pass responsibility back to the class

18. Student-centered or unguided discovery learning; in indirect instruction, student ideas are used as means of accomplishing the goals of the prescribed curriculum

19. Encouraging students to use examples and references from their experience; asking students to draw parallels and associations from things they already know; relating ideas to students' interests, concerns, and problems

20. In direct instruction nearly all instances of the facts, rules, and sequences are likely to be encountered during instruction. This is not true during indirect instruction.

21. Orienting students, providing new information, reviewing and summarizing, altering the flow of information to more productive areas, combining ideas and promoting compromise; about once every three minutes

22.
1. direct	6. direct
2. direct	7. direct
3. indirect	8. indirect
4. indirect	9. indirect
5. direct	10. indirect

Both models might be used for the third, fourth, eighth, and tenth topics.

Chapter 8

1. A question that actively engages a student in the learning process
2. Structuring, soliciting, reacting
3. 80%
4. As high as 80%; as low as 20%
5. Interest- and attention-getting, diagnosing and checking, recall of specific facts or information, managerial, encourage higher level thought processes, structure and redirect learning, allow expression of affect.
6. A convergent question is one that tends to limit a response to only a small number of responses or to a single correct response. A divergent question is one for which there is no single best answer; however, divergent questions can have wrong answers.
8. If the learner previously has seen and memorized an answer to this question
9. If the learner arrived at the solution by other than simple recall and memorization, perhaps by reasoning $2 + 2 + 2 + 2 = 8$, which is the same as 2 multiplied by 4.
10. They are unlikely to affect standardized achievement but are likely to increase the learner's analysis, synthesis, and evaluation skills.
16. The time the teacher waits for a student to respond to a question; beginning teachers should work to increase their wait time
17. Raising overly complex questions, not being prepared for unusual answers, not knowing the behavioral complexity of the response desired from a question, providing answers to questions before students can respond, using questions as a form of punishment

Chapter 9

3. An overachiever is an individual whose school achievement is greater than that predicted by a test of intelligence or scholastic aptitude. An underachiever is an individual whose school achievement is less than that predicted.

7. Games and simulations, programmed texts, grouping, volunteering, grades and tests

8. Use of praise and encouragement, providing explanations, offering to help, accepting diversity, emphasizing reward rather than punishment

10. Sole provider of information, equal partner with students in creating ideas and problem solutions, translator or summarizer of student ideas; student opinion, student talk, and spontaneity will increase from the former to the latter

11. (a) drill and practice
    (b) group discussion
    (c) seatwork

14. Visitor at the door, and safety concerning equipment

15. If it cannot be consistently reinforced over a reasonable period of time

17. (1) Allow no talking.
    (2) Allow no more time than is absolutely necessary.
    (3) Make arrangements according to time to be spent, not exercises to be completed.
    (4) Give five- and two-minute warnings.

18. Give reasons for the assignment and give assignment immediately following the content presentation to which it is related.

19. (1) Restating highest level generalization
    (2) Summarizing key aspects of content taught
    (3) Providing codes or symbols for remembering the content

Chapter 10

1. Extreme negativity, exclusive authoritarian climate, overreacting, mass punishment, blaming, lack of clear instructional goal, repetition of already learned material, pausing and interruptions, dealing with a single student at length, lack of recognition of ability levels

3. Classroom rules cannot effectively deal with all potential misbehaviors.

4. The consistent use of an emotional response diminishes its effectiveness at the time it may be needed most.

5. Those who misbehave seldom belong to the same peer groups as those who behave.

6. Sometimes the exact source of a misbehavior cannot be known with certainty. Blaming the wrong person tends to create long periods of class disruption in which the wrongly accused student fights back.

7. Indirect discussions must be crafted to communicate a structure, an end result, and clear expectations of student conduct.

8. There is no mystery, challenge, or curiosity about what is to be learned, and therefore nothing to focus the learners' attention and keep them from more exciting off-task behavior.

9. Visitors at the door and unexpected public address announcements

10. Silently writing the student's name on the board, calling out the student's name and assigning a prearranged punishment, and pointing to the rear of the room and indicating the student must stand there

11. By assigning individuals to ability groups and pursuing remedial activities, such as those provided by programmed materials

13. (1) You alone can be the judge of what occurred, what the proper punishment is, and whether the punishment has been met.
    (2) You provide alternative forms of punishment from which the student must choose.
    (3) You select a punishment from alternatives provided by the student.

16. Punishment does not guarantee that the desirable behavior will occur; the effects of punishment are specific to a particular context and behavior; the effects of punishment can spread to desirable behaviors; punishment can elicit hostile and aggressive re-

sponses; punishment can become associated with the punisher.

17. When the desired behavior is made clear at the time of the punishment and when used in conjunction with rewards

18. (1) To gain support of the parent for assuming some of the responsibility for the discipline management process
    (2) To design a plan of action for addressing the problem at home and at school

Chapter 11

2. (1) Dispensing state and federal funds
   (2) Efficient development and organization of instructional materials, texts, and media
   (3) Training and assignment of instructional staff

3. A student who cannot learn from the instructional resources designated for the majority of students

4. Percentile rank on a standardized achievement test

5. ■ Compensatory: transmitting content by way of alternate modalities in order to circumvent a fundamental weakness
   ■ Remedial: using conventional techniques and practices to repeat instruction that can eliminate the weakness

6. Intelligence, achievement, creativity, and task persistence

7. It might eliminate gifted students whose tested IQs may not reflect their true intelligence

8. Applying abstract principles, being curious, giving uncommon responses, showing imagination

9. Ability to devise organizational approaches; ability to concentrate on detail; self-imposed high standards; persistence in achieving personal goals

10. Anywhere from being unable to express themselves in English to being marginally proficient in English

11. A learner who is equally proficient in two languages

12. Structured immersion allows the student to respond in the native language, whereas the transitional method encourages the student to shift to English as soon as possible.

13. Because of the requirement that the handicapped child be educated in the least restrictive environment, some handicapped learners must be taught in the regular classroom, at least part of the time.

14. Physically handicapped, auditorily handicapped, visually handicapped, mentally retarded, emotionally disturbed, learning disabled, speech handicapped, autistic, multiply handicapped

15. The learning disabled individual is one who is not achieving commensurately with his or her age and ability levels. A slow learner is one who cannot learn from the instructional resources designated for the average learner.

16. Statement of:
    (1) long- and short-term objectives
    (2) specific educational services to be provided
    (3) dates and time periods devoted to each service
    (4) criterion for and time of evaluating each long- and short-term objective

Appendix C

The following instrument contains 28 behaviors alongside which a simple checkmark can be placed when a particular effectiveness or ineffectiveness indicator has been observed (see page 332). Your observations may lead you to check an *ineffective* practice, an *effective* practice, or *both*, in which case a teacher may have exhibited behaviors associated with effective *and* ineffective teaching. The purpose of observing and recording your observations should be to reflect upon what you see for *your own self-improvement,* and not to make summative conclusions about individual teachers, for which your brief period and frequency of observation would be inadequate. We have chosen to call this instrument a "formative" observation instrument to underscore its use in helping to form or mold effective teaching behaviors instead of to grade, test, or evaluate.

Included in this appendix are several classroom dialogues with which you can practice "seeing" some of the behaviors identified on the instrument and discussed in chapter 12.

Dialogue 1

The scene is a hard-to-handle lower track junior high life science class in which the teacher is presenting a lesson on reproductive systems. Her goal is to teach the biological foundations of sexual reproduction required by the curriculum guide. This class is intended as an introduction to a unit on sex education to be taught by the school's physical education teacher the following semester. She has been a teacher for a year and a half, having received her certification in social studies (major) and biology (minor). The following are her opening comments to the class.

TEACHER: I know everyone will be attentive to today's lesson, because it's about the reproductive cycle. (Some snickering can be heard in the back of the room.) Now this is serious stuff, and I don't want any laughing or fooling around. Who knows some ways by which lower forms of animal life reproduce?

TIM: Well, one way we studied last year is by dividing in half.

TEACHER: OK. That is reproduction by fission, in which the parent organism splits into two or more organisms, thereby losing its original identity. It is the way most single-celled animals reproduce. Can anyone think of any other means of reproduction?

TRACY: Sometimes an egg—or something like an egg—gets fertilized.

TEACHER: We're just talking about *lower* forms of animal life.

BILL: Isn't there a way that new life can be created by parts of other things coming together?

TEACHER: Good. You must be talking about a process called conjugation. This occurs when two similar organisms fuse, exchange nuclear material, and then break apart, taking on two different identities. This is the most primitive method of reproduction. Does anyone know of any other ways in which animal life can reproduce?

RICK: You mean like dogs and cats?

TEACHER: No! We're not at that point yet. Well, there is one other—and you should know this, because it's in the text. Many multicellular animals repro-

Formative Observation of Effective Teaching Practices Instrument

Key behavior	Indicators of Effectiveness	Observed (✓)	Observed* (✓)	Indicators of Lack of Effectiveness
Clarity	1. Informs learners of skills or understandings expected at end of lesson			Fails to link lesson content to how and at what level of complexity the content will be used
	2. Provides learners with an advance organizer with which to place lesson content in perspective			Starts presenting content without first introducing the topic in some larger context
	3. Checks for task-relevant prior learning at beginning of lesson and reteaches when necessary			Moves to new content without checking understanding of prerequisite facts or concepts
	4. Ends lesson with review or summary			Fails to restate or review main ideas at the end of the lesson
	5. Gives directives slowly and distinctly; checks for understanding along the way			Presents too many directives at once or too quickly
	6. Knows learners' ability levels and teaches at or slightly above their current level of functioning			Fails to recognize that the instruction is under or over the heads of students
	7. Uses examples, illustrations, or demonstrations to explain and to clarify content in text and workbooks			Restricts presentation to oral reproduction of text or workbook
Variety	8. Uses attention-gaining devices			Begins lesson without full attention of most learners
	9. Shows enthusiasm and animation through variation in eye contact, voice, and gestures			Speaks in monotone and/or is motionless; lacks external signs of emotion
	10. Varies activities with which the instructional stimuli are presented (e.g., lecturing, questioning, discussion, practice [daily])			Uses single instructional activity for long periods at time and/or infrequently alters the modality through which learning is to occur (seeing, listening, doing)
	11. Uses a mix of rewards and reinforcers (weekly, monthly)			Fails to provide rewards and reinforcements that are timely and meaningful to the student

Formative Observation of Effective Teaching Practices Instrument (Concluded)

Key behavior	Indicators of Effectiveness		Observed (√)	Observed* (√)	Indicators of Lack of Effectiveness
Variety con't	12. Varies types of questions and probes	Q convergent divergent			Repeatedly uses only one type of question or probe
		P to clarify to solicit to redirect			
	13. Uses student ideas and participation to foster lesson objectives when appropriate (weekly)				Assumes role of sole authority and provider of information; ignores student input
Task Orientation	14. Develops unit and lesson plans in accordance with text and curriculum guide				Teaches topics tangential to curriculum guide and adopted text; easily gets side-tracked by student or personal interests
	15. Handles administrative and clerical interruptions efficiently				Uses large amounts of instructional time to complete administrative and clerical tasks
	16. Stops misbehavior with a minimum of disruption to the class				Focuses at length on individual instances of misbehavior during instructional time
	17. Generally, uses direct instruction strategies for teaching Type 1 behaviors and indirect instruction strategies for teaching Type 2 behaviors				Uses inefficient instructional methods for achieving lesson objectives (e.g., confuses drill and practice content with group discussion content)
	18. Establishes end products (e.g., reviews, tests) that are clearly visible to students				Fails to establish clearly identifiable weekly and monthly milestones (e.g., tests and reviews toward which the class works)
Engagement	19. Provides for guided practice				Fails to ask learners to attempt the desired behavior or skill after instruction has been given
	20. Provides correctives for guided practice in a nonevaluative atmosphere				Calls attention to the inadequacy of initial responses
	21. Uses individualized or attention-getting strategies to promote interest among special types of learners when appropriate				Does not attempt to match instructional methods to the learning needs of special students

Formative Observation of Effective Teaching Practices Instrument (Concluded)

Key behavior	Indicators of Effectiveness	Observed (✓)	Observed* (✓)	Indicators of Lack of Effectiveness
Engagement con't	22. Uses meaningful verbal praise			Always uses same verbal clichés, (e.g., "OK") or fails to praise when opportunity occurs
	23. Monitors seatwork by circulating and frequently checking progress			Fails to monitor seatwork or monitors unevenly
Moderate-to-high success rates	24. Unit and lesson organization reflects task-relevant prior learning			Fails to sequence lessons based on task-revelant prior learning
	25. Administers correctives immediately after initial response			Delays in checking and correcting wrong responses after initial practice is completed
	26. Divides lessons into small, easily digestible pieces			Prepares lessons with more content or complexity than can be taught in the allotted time
	27. Plans transitions to new content in small, easy-to-grasp steps			Makes abrupt changes between lesson topics; no sign of "dovetailing"
	28. Establishes momentum (e.g., pacing and intensity gradually build toward major milestones)			Lessons lack changes in pacing (e.g., slower pace after a major event building to a faster pace just before a major event); intensity and tempo is static

*Checkmarks may be tallied over repeated observations to accumulate frequencies.

duce by having male and female reproductive cells, which unite to form a single cell called a zygote—which then divides to form a new organism. The word that describes the union of male and female cells is *fertilization*. In this form of reproduction, half the genes in the zygote come from one parent and half from the other.

MARK: That's what sex is all about.

TEACHER: OK . . . shouting out without raising your hand means an extra assignment for tonight. If it happens again, you will have one day in detention. If that doesn't cure you, we will make it two days. Answer all the questions under A, B, and C at the end of chapter 7. Have you learned your lesson?

MARK: I suppose so.

TEACHER: Now, where were we?

BARBARA: We were talking about zions.

TEACHER: They're called zygotes. Now in higher animals—including humans—single species are either male or female, according to whether they produce male reproductive cells or female reproductive cells. Somewhere there's a picture of this in your text. The typical male reproductive cell is a sperm, and the typical female reproductive cell is an egg or ovum.

UNIDENTIFIED STUDENT: We know all that!

TEACHER: That's enough! I don't want to hear anyone . . .

PRINCIPAL: (breaking in over the P.A. system) Teachers, I'm sorry to interrupt, but I have an important announcement. Orders for individual and class pictures must be in no later than 3:00 p.m. today. Failure to place your order by that time means you will not receive pictures for this year. While I have your attention, I would like to tell students to remind their parents that tonight is Parent-Teacher Night, and we would like a good turnout, so be sure to remind Mom and Dad. Thank you. (During the announcement, some students began getting out of their seats and talking with their neighbors.)

TEACHER: Class isn't over yet, so be quiet and let's get back to work. Open your books to the questions at the end of chapter 7. Mark, you take the first one. What is reproduction by fission?

MARK: Fission. Well . . . I'm not sure.

TEACHER: But I just told you; how could you forget so soon? Debbie?

DEBBIE: It's reproducing by cellular division or the splitting of an organism into two parts.

TEACHER: Next, Robert. What's reproduction by fusion?

ROBERT: It's . . . it's when things come together.

TEACHER: Mary, could you give us a better answer?

MARY: It's when two similar organisms fuse, exchange nuclear material, and then divide again, producing new identities.

TEACHER: That's a perfect answer. OK, class, now let's change our focus to how plant life reproduces, because that's in chapter 7 too. Does anyone know how plant reproduction differs from animal reproduction? (There is silence for a few seconds.) OK, then, I'll tell you.

Dialogue 2

For this example we peek into the beginning of an elementary school lesson in arithmetic. The lesson for today is about ratios and proportions and is taught by a teacher who has been at this school for two years and at another school in this same district for three years before that. Math ability does not seem to be high for most members of the class, and the students have been noticeably anxious about an upcoming unit test. Moreover, some of the students may not have grasped all that they should have from some earlier lessons in this unit.

TEACHER: Today our goal will be to study ratios and proportions but using more real-life problems

than in previous lessons. Some of you have had trouble learning how to calculate a ratio, so let's back up and review our skills in division. Who can tell me why division is so important in computing a ratio?

MARC: It's because ratios are nothing but division problems.

TEACHER: Yes, that's right, in the sense that ratios can be expressed as one number over another, like this (writes $\frac{4}{8}$ on board). Now, let's look at this cereal box I have here. Sue, take the box in your hands and tell me how full it is.

SUE: Well, I don't exactly know. It feels pretty heavy— I mean it's kind of full.

TEACHER: What if I asked you to tell me how much *kind of full* is?

SUE: I'd say *kind of* means almost full—well, maybe a little less than almost full (class laughs).

TEACHER: I think the class may have thought your answer was humorous because they would like to know what "a little less than almost full" means. Now, since this is a very typical problem—like the kind people face every day at home and at work— it would be nice to express some things more accurately without the use of words, which tend to be very imprecise when used to describe amounts of things. How might we be more precise, John?

JOHN: Let's form a ratio.

TEACHER: OK. But how do we go about forming a ratio to describe the amount of cereal in this box? Can you tell us some more?

JOHN: Well, we need to know how much the box holds.

TEACHER: That's right. You've got the first step. Now, Tim, what's the next step?

TIM: I don't know.

TEACHER: Mary?

MARY: (silence)

TEACHER: Betty? (after 10 seconds)

BETTY: (silence)

TEACHER: Come on, class. You were all doing so well. Somebody make a guess.

BETTY: (without raising her hand) I think we should compare how much the box holds to how much it has in it.

TEACHER: Never speak out without raising your hand, Betty. So, our second step, Betty, is . . .

BETTY: To measure how much is in the box.

TEACHER: That's right. You have just given us the form of a ratio, maybe without even knowing it. That form is (writes on board):

$$\frac{\text{what is}}{\text{what could be}} = \frac{\text{a little less than half full}}{\text{full}}$$

Now comes the hard part. How will we find numbers to put in the top and the bottom of this division problem? Any suggestions?

DANNY: I have an idea. Let's see how many glasses of water the box holds and then see how many glasses of water it takes to fill the box to where the cereal is.

TEACHER: That's a pretty clever idea, but it may have a few problems as well. Bobby, you have your hand up.

BOBBY: The box isn't going to hold water long enough to do the counting.

TEACHER: Right. And what if the box doesn't fill up exactly at a full glass? We'd have to measure in parts or fractions of glasses, and we haven't come to that yet. Let's look on the box and read how the manufacturer measured what's inside (hands box to Terri).

TERRI: It says, "This box contains six 8-ounce servings measured by volume."

TEACHER: So how many ounces does the whole box contain? Let's review (writes on board); you supply the answers as I go down the list.

$$1 \times 8 = 8$$
$$2 \times 8 = 16$$
$$3 \times 8 = 24$$
$$4 \times 8 = 32$$
$$5 \times 8 = 40$$
$$6 \times 8 = 48$$

So 48 ounces is our total. Now, let's go back to Danny's original idea with the water, but let's measure the contents of the box using ounces. I happen to have an 8-ounce measuring cup. Marc, you pour while the rest of us count.

CLASS: One.

MARC: Where do I empty it?

TEACHER: Let's put it here in the shoe box.

CLASS: Two . . . three . . . four . . . five

MARC: The sixth one's not full.

TEACHER: OK. Read on the side of the cup how full it is.

MARC: It's right at *2* on the cup.

TEACHER: That means 2 ounces. Let's do a little arithmetic. What's our total? Now, who wants to do this problem? (Mary raises her hand)

MARY: Well, we had five full cups, so that's 8 + 8 = 16 + 8 = 24 + 8 = 32.

CLASS: One more.

MARY: Yea, I guess that's only four, so 32 + 8 = 40 and then the 2 at the end makes 42.

TEACHER: OK. Now we have all that we need to create a ratio to describe exactly how full the box was. What does this ratio look like, class?

CLASS: Forty-two over forty-eight (teacher writes):

$$\frac{42}{48} = \frac{\text{what is}}{\text{what could be}}$$

TEACHER: Since you've learned this so well, we will move on to our next topic. But first, I need to get some overheads from my drawer. No talking, except in a soft voice.

Dialogue 3

The following dialogue is from a high school English class for which the curriculum guide specifies a unit on the appreciation of poetry. Because the curriculum guide is vague about how to achieve this outcome, the teacher decides the best way to appreciate poetry is first to learn its fundamentals. To accomplish this he decides to introduce the unit with a lesson on poetic meter. This teacher has taught for a total of eleven years but has been at this school only one year after being transferred from a Chapter I school to fill a midyear vacancy. He begins introducing the lesson with the following:

TEACHER: I want you to listen to a brief excerpt of two popular songs being played on the radio. I think you'll recognize them. Here they are—listen carefully. (Turns tape recorder on until about half of each song is played.)

How many like the first song better than the second? (counts 12 hands) Now, how many like the second better? (counts 18 hands)

Who can tell me what they like about the first song?

DIANA: I like the beat . . . I guess it's the rhythm.

TEACHER: Anyone care to say why they like the second song?

TOM: Well, I like its beat . . . the way it gets you stirred up inside . . . maybe its rhythm . . . just what Diana said, I guess.

TEACHER: I chose these two songs not only because they are both very popular right now and I knew you would recognize them, but because they have two very different beats or tempos. Because a good number of you chose each one, both tempos seemed to work—but in very different ways. Now: If you were to exchange the words of these two songs but keep the original tempos, do you think the songs would still be as popular as they are? Joan, you have your hand up.

JOAN: It just wouldn't work. The songs would sound silly. The words wouldn't match the rhythm, in my opinion.

TEACHER: Well, I think there would be quite a few who might agree with you. These songwriters had to find the right beat to match the words. Although today we will be talking about poetry and not your favorite songs (class groans in jest), the two have much in common. Poets, like songwriters, must find the right rhythm to match the words. In poetry, concepts such as *beat, tempo,* and *rhythm* are represented by a poem's meter. To appreciate a poem—and especially to gain the full emotional impact intended by its author—you must be able to recognize its meter, or rhythm. Today I will describe the different meters used by poets. Listen carefully, because toward the end of the period we're going to have a little fun. Since you all groaned (and I knew you would), I plan to play parts of some of the other popular songs— some of your favorites—and then ask if you see any resemblance between their rhythms and the four types of poetic meter I will now describe. Let's begin by examining what meter is. Anyone care to venture a guess? (Debby raises her hand)

DEBBY: Well, meter is a form of measurement, like in millimeter or kilometer.

TEACHER: That's a good beginning. You've gone right to the root of the word itself. And, surprising to some people, it also is a form of measurement in poetry. So we're off to a good start. Because I don't think anyone would be interested in the length and width of a poem, how is meter used in poetry?

RUTH: Well, could it be to measure its rhythm, or what Diana meant when she used the word *beat*?

TEACHER: Correct. You've made the transfer from measuring something physical with the concept of meter to measuring what we will call *verse*. But maybe we should define verse. Any ideas?

ROLAND: It's like the lyrics in a song . . . the words, kind of . . . but they wouldn't look right if you saw them written out, only if they're sung or read out loud.

TEACHER: Yes. The lyrics in a song have much in common with verse in a poem, because both are the vehicles that convey the author's message. Now, *how* a poet communicates his or her message is just as important as *what* is communicated—just as you pointed out in the two songs I played, when you said the words wouldn't work if sung to the other song's rhythm. The poet has to get the rhythm right, otherwise the words—or verse— might not convey the message. To do this, the poet must choose an appropriate meter, which requires making a number of decisions; it's not as simple as it looks. Today we will look at just one of these, called the *foot*. In the next few lessons we will cover the others, which will lead us to an appreciation of how the poet arranges the number of syllables to a line, creates a pattern among various lines by the use of rhyme, and forms groups of two or sometimes three lines, which are called *stanzas*. So—what's a foot?

RICH: It's what you put your socks over (class snickers).

TEACHER: No talking out without raising your hand. This is a warning, Richard. A foot is the way in which syllables in a line of poetry are accented. A foot consists of one accented syllable accompanied by one or two unaccented syllables. The accented syllable may precede or follow either one or two unaccented syllables in a regularly recurring sequence throughout the line. Let's look at this line on the transparency to actually see what I mean (switches on overhead).

Bŭt tár/riĕs yét / the caúse / fŏr whĭch / he díed.

(writing on board) This symbol "‿" means an unaccented syllable and this "╱" means an accented syllable. What kind of consistent pattern do you see and hear? (reads line)

TOBY: Well, it's kind of sing-song.

TEACHER: What do you mean by sing-song?

TOBY: One unaccented syllable always precedes one accented syllable.

TEACHER: That's right. And, in fact, the poet wanted this line to vary, just as you said, in a down-up or sing-song-type pattern, because that's the rhythm he felt would best convey his message. We will look at the rest of the lines of this poem later to get its full meaning, but for now you've gotten the idea of a foot and of meter. By the way, how many feet are in this line, Toby?

TOBY: Four.

TEACHER: No! You're not being careful. Mary, how many are there?

MARY: Five.

TEACHER: Very good. The pattern repeats itself five times. This type of pattern is called an *iamb* or an *iambic foot*. It is only the first of four different ways of accenting syllables that we will study. Before looking at some examples of these, let's practice recognizing the iambic foot. On the next four lines of poetry, place the accents where you think they should go to create an iambic foot. When you're finished, look up and I'll give you my answers. Oops, someone's at the door. Sue, would you take a message.

SUE: (whispering) It's a counselor.

TEACHER: When you've finished with these four, go on to the iambic exercise marked *D* at the end of chapter 11. Check your work with the answer key in the appendix. I'll give bonus discussion points for those who get them all right. (Goes to door.)

References

Anderson, J. R. (1980). *Cognitive psychology and its implications*. San Francisco: W. H. Freeman.

Anderson, L. & Block, J. (1987). Mastery learning models. In M. J. Dunkin (Ed.) *International encyclopedia of teaching and teacher education* (pp. 58–67). New York: Pergamon.

Anderson, L., Evertson, C., & Brophy J. (1982). *Principles of small group instruction in elementary reading*. East Lansing, MI: Institute for Research on Teaching.

Armento, B. (1977). Teacher behaviors related to student achievement on a social science test. *Journal of Teacher Education, 28*, 46–52.

Ausubel, D. (1968). *Educational psychology: A cognitive view*. New York: Holt, Rinehart & Winston.

Baca, L., & Cervantes, H. (1984). *The bilingual special education interface*. Santa Clara, CA: Times Mirror/Mosby.

Barnes, J. (1987). Teaching Experience. In M. J. Dunkin (Ed.), *International encyclopedia of teaching and teacher education* (pp. 608–611). New York: Pergamon.

Becker, W. (1977). Teaching reading and language to the disadvantaged—what we have learned from field research. *Harvard Educational Review, 47,* 518–543.

Bellack, A., Kliebard, H., Hyman, R., & Smith, F. (1966). *The language of the classroom*. New York: Teachers' College Press.

Bennett, N., Desforges, C., Cockburn, A., & Wilkinson, B. (1981). *The quality of pupil learning experiences: Interim report*. Lancaster, England: University of Lancaster, Centre for Educational Research and Development.

Berliner, D. (1970) Tempus educare. In P. Peterson and H. Walberg (Eds.), *Research on teaching: Concepts, findings and implications* (pp. 120–135). Berkeley, CA: McCutchan.

Bettencourt, E., Gillett, M., Gall, M., & Hull, R. (1983). Effects of teacher enthusiasm training on student on-task behavior and achievement. *American Educational Research Journal, 20,* 435–450.

Bloom, B. (1981) *All our children learning*. New York: McGraw-Hill.

Bloom, B. (1982). *Human interactions and school learning*. New York: McGraw-Hill.

Bloom, B., Englehart, M., Furst, E., Hill, W., & Krathwohl, D. (1956). *Taxonomy of educational objectives: The classification of educational goals. Handbook I: Cognitive domain*. New York: Longmans Green.

Bodwin, F. (1957). *The relationship between immature self-concept and certain educational disabilities.* Unpublished doctoral dissertation, Michigan State University, East Lansing.

Borich, G. & Fuller, F. (1974). *Manual for teacher concerns checklist: An instrument for measuring concerns for self, task and impact.* Austin, TX: The Research and Development Center for Teacher Education.

Brookover, W., Paterson, A., & Thomas, S. (1962). *Self-concept of ability and school achievement. Final report of Cooperative Research Project No. 845.* U.S. Department of Health, Education and Welfare, Office of Education. East Lansing: Michigan State University.

Brophy, J. (1981). Teacher praise: A functional analysis. *Review of Educational Research, 51,* 5–32.

Brophy, J., & Good, T. (1974). *Teacher-student relationships: causes and consequences.* New York: Holt, Rinehart & Winston.

Brophy, J., & Good, T. (1986). Teacher Behavior and Student Achievement. In M. C. Wittrock (Ed.), *Handbook of research on teaching: Third edition* (pp. 328–375). New York: Macmillan.

Brophy, J., & Evertson, C. (1974). *Process-product correlations in the Texas Teacher Effectiveness Study: Final Report* (Research Report 74–4). Austin: University of Texas, Research and Development Center for Teacher Education, (ERIC Document Reproduction Service No. ED 091 094).

Brophy. J., & Evertson, C. (1976). *Learning from teaching: A developmental perspective.* Boston: Allyn & Bacon.

Brown, G., & Edmondson, R. (1984). Asking questions. In E. Wragg (Ed.), *Classroom teaching skills* (pp. 97–119). New York: Nichols.

Bruner, J. (1966). *Toward a theory of instruction.* Cambridge, MA: Harvard University Press.

Bunderson, V., & Faust, G. (1976). Programmed and computer-assisted instruction . In N. L. Gage, *The psychology of teaching methods: The seventy-fifth yearbook of the National Society for the Study of Evaluation, Part I* (pp. 44–90). Chicago: University of Chicago Press.

Civil Rights Commission. (1973). *Teachers and students. Report V: Differences in teacher intervention with Mexican-American and Anglo students.* Washington, DC: U.S. Government Printing Office.

Clark, C. & Elmore, J. L. (1981). *Transforming curriculum in mathematics, science, and writing: A case study of teacher yearly planning* (Research Series

No. 99). East Lansing, MI: Michigan State University, Institute for Research on Teaching.

Clark C., & Peterson, P. (1986). Teachers' thought processes. In M. C. Wittrock (Ed.), *Handbook of research on teaching: Third edition* (pp. 255–296). New York: Macmillan.

Clark, C., & Yinger, R. (1979). *Three studies of teacher planning* (Research Series No. 55). East Lansing: Michigan State University.

Congressional Record. 89th Cong., 2d sess., 1978. P. H-12179.

Corey, S. (1940). The teachers out-talk the pupils. *School Review, 48,* 745–752.

Corno, L., & Snow, R. (1986). Adapting teaching to individual differences among learners. In M. C. Wittrock (Ed.), *Handbook of research on teaching: Third edition* (pp. 605–629). New York: Macmillan.

Crawford, John, Gage, N. L., Corno, L., Stayrouk, N., Mitman, A., Schunk, D., & Stallings, J. (1978). *An experiment on teacher effectiveness and parent-assisted instruction in the third grade. Three volumes.* Stanford, CA: Center for Educational Research, Stanford University.

Cronbach, L., & Snow, R. (1977). *Aptitudes and instructional methods.* New York: Irvington/Naiburg.

Dahllof, U., & Lundgren, U. P. (1970). *Macro- and micro approaches combined for curriculum process analysis: A Swedish educational field project.* Göteborg, Sweden: University of Göteborg, Institute of Education.

Davis, O., & Tinsley, D. (1967). Cognitive objectives revealed by classroom questions asked by social studies teachers and their pupils. *Peabody Journal of Education,* July, 21–26.

Dewey, J. (1938). *Experience and education.* New York: Macmillan.

Doenau, S. (1987). Structuring. In M. J. Dunkin (Ed.), *International encyclopedia of teaching and teacher education* (pp. 398–406). New York: Pergamon.

Dembo, M. (1981). *Teaching for learning: Applying educational psychology in the classroom: Second Edition.* Glenview, IL: Scott, Foresman.

Dowaliby, F., & Schumer, H. (1973). Teacher-centered versus student-centered mode of college classroom instruction as related to manifest anxiety. *Journal of Educational Psychology, 64,* 125–132.

Dunkin, M., & Biddle, B. (1974). *The study of teaching.* New York: Holt, Rinehart & Winston.

Elbaz, F. (1981). The teacher's "practical knowledge": Report of a case study. *Curriculum Inquiry, 11,* 43–71.

Eisner, E. (1969). Instructional and expressive educational objectives: Their formulation and use in curriculum. In W. Popham, E. Eisner, H. Sullivan, & L. Tyler, *Instructional objectives. AERA Monograph Series on Curriculum Evaluation, No. 3* (pp. 1–18). Chicago: Rand McNally.

Emmer, E., Evertson, C., & Anderson, L. (1980). Effective classroom management at the beginning of the school year. *Elementary School Journal, 80,* 219–231.

Emmer, E., Evertson, C., Sanford. J., Clements, B., & Worsham, M. (1984). *Classroom management for secondary teachers.* Englewood Cliffs, NJ: Prentice-Hall.

Epstein, J., & Karweit, N. (Eds.) (1983). *Friendships in school.* New York: Academic Press.

Erikson, E. (1968). *Identity, youth and crises.* New York: W. W. Norton.

Evertson, C., & Emmer, E. (1982). Effective Management at the beginning of the second year in junior high classes. *Journal of Educational Psychology, 74,* 485–498.

Evertson, C., Emmer, E, Sanford, J., Clements, B., & Worsham, M. (1984). *Classroom management for elementary teachers.* Englewood Cliffs, NJ: Prentice-Hall.

Fielding, G., Kameenui, E., & Gerstein, R. (1983). A comparison of an inquiry and a direct instruction approach to teach legal concepts and applications to secondary school students. *Journal of Educational Research, 76,* 243–250.

Fisher, C., Berliner, D., Filby, N., Maliave, R., Cahen, L., & Dishaw, M. (1980). Teaching behaviors, academic learning time and student achievement: An overview. In C. Denham and A. Lieberman (Eds.), *Time to learn.* Washington, DC: National Institute of Education.

Fisher, C., Filby, N., Marliave, R., Cahen, L., Dishaw, M., More, J., & Berliner, D. (1978). *Teaching behaviors, academic learning time and student achievement. Final Report of Phase III-B, Beginning Teacher Evaluation Study* (Tech. Rep. No. V-1). San Francisco: Far West Laboratory for Educational Research and Development.

Fitch, M., Drucker, A., & Norton, J. (1957). Frequent testing as a motivating factor in large lecture classes. *Journal of Educational Psychology, 42,* 1–20.

Flanders, N. (1970). Analyzing teacher behavior. Readings, MA: Addison-Wesley.

Fuller, F. (1969). Concerns of teachers: A developmental conceptualization. *American Educational Research Journal, 6,* 207–226.

Fuller, F., & Borich, G. (1974). *Teacher concerns checklist: An instrument for measuring concerns for self, task and impact.* Austin, TX: Research and Development Center for Teacher Education, The University of Texas at Austin.

Gage, N. (1976). A factorially designed experiment on teacher structuring, soliciting and reacting. *Journal of Teacher Education,* 35–38.

Gage, N., & Berlinger, D. (1984). *Educational psychology: Third edition.* Chicago: Rand McNally.

Gagné, E. (1985). *The cognitive psychology of school learning.* Boston: Little, Brown.

Gagné, R. M. (1977). *The Conditions of Learning, Third Edition.* New York: Holt, Rinehart & Winston.

Gagné, R., & Briggs, L. (1979). *Principles of instructional design.* New York: Holt, Rinehart & Winston.

Gall, M. (1970). The use of questions in teaching. *Review of Educational Research, 40,* 707–721.

Gall, M., & Gall, J. (1976). The discussion method. In N. L. Gage (Ed.), *The psychology of teaching methods: The seventy-fifth yearbook of the national society for the study of education, Part I* (pp. 166–216). Chicago, University of Chicago Press.

Gall, M., Ward, B., Berliner, D., Cahen, I., Winne, P., Elashoff, J., & Stanton, G. (1978). Effects of questioning techniques and recitation on student learning. *American Educational Research Journal, 15,* 175–199.

Good, T. (1979). Teacher effectiveness in the elementary school. *Journal of Teacher Education, 30,* 52–64.

Good, T. and Brophy, J. (1987). *Looking in classrooms* (4th ed.). New York: Harper & Row.

Good T., Ebmeier, H., & Beckerman, T. (1978). Teaching mathematics in high and low SES classrooms: An empirical comparison. *Journal of Teacher Education, 29,* 85–90.

Good, T., & Grouws, D. (1979). Teaching effects: A process-product study in fourth grade mathematics classrooms. *Journal of Teacher Education, 28,* 49–54.

Good, T., & Stipek, D. (1983). Individual differences in the classroom: A psychological perspective. In G. D. Fenstermacher & J. I. Goodlad (Eds.), *Individual differences and the common curriculum* (82nd yearbook of the National Society for the

Study of Education, Part 2) (pp. 9–43). Chicago: University of Chicago Press.

Goodlad, J. (1984). *A place called school,* New York: McGraw-Hill.

Green, J. (1983). Research on teaching as a linguistic process: A state of the art. In E. W. Godon (Ed.), *Review of research in education 10* (pp. 151–252). Washington: American Educational Research Association.

Hansford, B., & Hattie, J. (1982). The relationship between self and achievement/performance measures. *Review of Educational Research, 52,* 123–142.

Harrow, A. (1969). *A taxonomy of the psychomotor domain: A guide for developing behavioral objectives.* New York: David McKay.

Haynes, H. (1935). *The relation of teacher intelligence, teacher experience and type of school to type of questions.* Unpublished doctoral dissertation, George Peabody College for Teachers, Nashville, TN.

Hermann, G. (1971). Egrule vs. ruleg teaching methods: Grade, intelligence and category of learning. *Journal of Experimental Education, 39,* No. 3, 22–33.

Hodgkinson, H. (1986). Today's numbers, tomorrow's nation. *Education Week,* May 14, 14–15.

Hunt, G. (1979). Psychological development: early experience. *Annual Review of Psychology,* 103–143.

Jackson, P. (1968). *Life in classrooms.* New York: Holt, Rinehart & Winston.

Jensen, A. (1969). How much can we boost IQ and scholastic achievement? *Harvard Educational Review, 39* (1), 1–123.

Joyce, B. (1978–79). Toward a theory of information processing in teaching. *Educational Research Quarterly, 3* (4), 66–77.

Kaplan, A. (1964). *The conduct of inquiry.* San Francisco: Chandler Publishing.

Kash, M., & Borich, G. (1978). *Teacher behavior and pupil self-concept.* Reading, MA: Addison-Wesley.

Kim, E., & Kellough, R. (1978). A Resource Guide for *Secondary Teaching* (2nd ed.). New York: Macmillan.

Kounin, J. (1970). *Discipline and group management in the classroom.* New York: Holt, Rinehart & Winston.

Krathwohl, D., Bloom, B., & Masia, B. (1964). *Taxonomy of educational objectives. The classification of educational goals. Handbook II: Affective domain.* New York: David McKay.

Kubiszyn, T. & Borich, G. (1987). *Educational testing and measurement.* Glenview, IL: Scott, Foresman.

La Berge, D., & Samuels, S. (1974). Toward a theory of automatic information processing in reading. *Cognitive Psychology, 6,* 293–323.

Land, M. L. (1987). Vagueness and clarity. In M. J. Dunkin (Ed.), *Encyclopedia of teaching and teacher education* (pp. 292–397). New York: Pergamon.

Land, M., & Smith L. (1979). The effect of low inference teacher clarity inhibitors on student achievement. *Journal of Teacher Education, 31,* 55–57.

Leinhardt, G. (1983). *Overview of a program of research on teachers' and students' routines, thoughts and execution of plans.* Paper presented at the annual meeting of the American Educational Research Association, Montreal.

Levine, D. (1979). Concentrated poverty and reading achievement in seven big cities. *The Urban Review,* Summer, 63–80.

Levine, D. & Havinghurst, R. (1984). *Society and education, Sixth edition.* Boston: Allyn & Bacon.

Levis, D. S. (1987). Teachers' personality. In M. J. Dunkin (Ed.), *Encyclopedia of teaching and teacher education* (pp. 585–588). New York: Pergamon.

Lewin, K., Lippitt, Z., & White, R. (1939). Patterns of aggressive behavior in experimentally created social climates, *Journal of Social Psychology, 10,* 271–299.

Lightfoot, S. (1983). *The good high school.* New York: Basic Books.

Luiten, J., Ames, W., & Aerson, G. (1980). A meta-analysis of advance organizers on learning and retention. *American Educational Research Journal, 17,* 211–218.

Lysakowski, R. & Walberg, H. (1981). Classroom reinforcement and learning: A quantitative synthesis. *Journal of Educational Research, 75,* 69–77.

Martin, J. (1979). Effects of teacher higher-order questions on student process and product variables in a single classroom study. *Journal of Educational Research, 72,* 183–187.

McDonald, F., Elias, P., Stone, M., Wheeler, P., & Lambert, M. (1975). *Final report on Phase II Beginning Teacher Evaluation Study.* Prepared for the California Commission on Teacher Preparation and Licensing, Sacramento, CA. Princeton, NJ: Educational Testing Service.

McKenzie, R. (1979). Effects of questions and testlike events on achievement and on-task behavior in a classroom concept learning presentation. *Journal of Educational Research, 72,* 348–350.

McNair, K. (1978-79). Capturing inflight decisions. *Educational Research Quarterly, 3* (4), 26–42.

Melton, R. (1978). Resolution of conflicting claims concerning the effect of behavioral objectives on student learning. *Review of Educational Research, 48,* 291–302.

Morine, G. (1973). Planning skills: Paradoxical parodies. *Journal of Teacher Education, 24,* 135–143.

Morine-Dershimer, G. (1977). *What's in a Plan? Stated and unstated plans for lessons.* Paper presented at the annual meeting of the American Educational Research Association, New York.

Morine, H., & Morine, G. (1973). *Discovery: A challenge to teachers.* Englewood Cliffs, NJ: Prentice-Hall.

Moskowitz, G. & Hayman, J. (1976). Success strategies of inner-city teachers: A year-long study. *Journal of Educational Research, 69,* 283–289.

National Center for Education Statistics. (1980). *High school and beyond study.* Washington, DC: National Center for Education Statistics.

Newson J., & Newson, E. (1976). *Seven years old in the home environment.* London: Allen & Unwin.

O'Banion, D., & Whaley, D. (1981). *Behavior contracting: Arranging contingencies of reinforcement.* New York: Springer.

Polanyi, M. (1958). *Personal knowledge.* Chicago: University of Chicago Press.

Posner, G. (1987). Pacing and sequencing. In M. J. Dunkin (Ed.), *Encyclopedia of teaching and teacher education* (pp. 266–271). New York: Pergamon.

Public Law 94–142, The Education for All Handicapped Children Act, 20 U.S.C. 1401 et seq., 89 Stat. 773 (November 29, 1975).

Redfield, D., & Rousseau, E. (1981). A meta-analysis of experimental research on teacher questioning behavior. *Review of Educational Research, 51,* 237–245.

Reigeluth, C. (1983). In C. M. Reigeluth (Ed.), *Instructional-design theories and models: An overview of their current status.* Hillsdale, NJ: Erlbaum.

Rist, R. (1970). Student social class and teaching expectations: The self-fulfilling prophecy in ghetto education. *Harvard Educational Review, 40,* 411–451.

Rosenshine, B. (1970a) Enthusiastic teaching: A research review. *School Review, 78,* 499–514.

Rosenshine, B. (1970b). Experimental classroom studies of indirect teaching. *Classroom Interaction Newsletter, 5* (2), 7–11.

Rosenshine, B. (1971a). Objectively measured behavioral predictors of effectiveness in explaining. In I. D. Westbury & A. A. Bellock, (Eds.), *Research into classroom processes* (pp. 51–100). New York: Teachers College Press.

Rosenshine, B. (1971b). *Teaching behaviors and student achievement.* London: National Foundation for Educational Research in England and Wales.

Rosenshine, B. (1983). Teaching functions in instructional programs. *Elementary School Journal, 83,* 335–351.

Rosenshine, B., & Stevens, R. (1986). Teaching functions. In M. C. Wittrock (Ed.), *Handbook of research on teaching: Third edition* (pp. 376–391). New York: Macmillan.

Rowe, M. B. (1974). Wait-time and rewards as instructional variables, their influence on language, logic, and fate control: Part one—wait-time. *Journal of Research in Science Teaching, 11,* 81–94

Rutherford, L. (1986). *Economics in a modern world.* Columbus, OH: Intex.

Ryan, F. (1973). Differentiated effects of levels of questioning on student achievement. *Elementary School Journal, 41,* 63–67.

Samuels, S. (1981). Some essentials of decoding. *Exceptional Education Quarterly, 2,* 11–25.

Scott, J., & Bushell, D. (1974). The length of teacher contacts and students' off task behavior. *Journal of Applied Behavior Analysis, 7,* 39–44.

Sharan, S. (1980). Cooperative learning in small groups. *Review of Educational Research, 50,* 241–271.

Singer, H., & Donlon, D. (1982). Active comprehension problem-solving schema with question generation for comprehension of complex short stories. *Reading Research Quarterly, 17,* 116–186.

Slavin, R. (1980). Effects of student teams and peer tutoring on academic achievement and time on task. *Journal of Experimental Education, 48,* 252–257.

Slavin, R. (1981). Student team learning. *Elementary School Journal, 82,* 5–17.

Slavin, R. (1983). *Cooperative learning.* New York: Longman.

Slavin, R., Leavey, M., & Madden, N. (1982). *Combining cooperative learning and individualized instruction: Effects on student mathematics achievement, attitudes and behaviors.* Baltimore, MD: Center for Social Organization of Schools, Johns Hopkins University.

Smilansky, M. (1979). *Priorities in education: Pre-school, evidence and conclusions.* Washington, DC: World Bank.

Smith, G. (1985). *Understanding Grammar* (pp. 101-103). New York: City Press.

Smith, B., & Meux, M. (1970). *A study of the logic of teaching.* Champaign, IL: University of Illinois.

Smith, E. & Sendelback, N. (1979). *Teacher intentions for science instruction and their antecedents in program materials.* Paper presented at the annual meeting of the American Educational Research Association, San Francisco.

Smith, L. & Land, M. (1981). Low inference verbal behaviors related to teacher clarity. *Journal of Classroom Interaction, 17,* 37–42.

Soar, R., & Soar, C. (1973). *Follow through classroom process measurement and pupil growth (1970–1971, Final Report).* Gainesville: University of Florida, Institute for Development of Human Resources (ERIC Document Reproduction Service No. ED 106 297).

Spielberger, C. (Ed.) (1966). *Anxiety and behavior.* New York: Academic Press.

Stallings, J. & Kaskowitz, D. (1974). *Follow through classroom observation evaluation* (SRI Project URU–7370). Stanford, CA: Stanford Research Institute.

Stallings, J., & Keepes, B. (1970). *Student aptitudes and methods for teaching beginning reading: A predictive instrument for determining interaction patterns. Final report.* U.S. Department of Health, Education and Welfare, Office of Education, Bureau of Research, OEG–9–70–0005. Project No. 9–1–099.

Sternberg, R. (1986). *Intelligence applied.* New York: Harcourt Brace, Jovanovich.

Thurstone, L. (1947). *Primary mental abilities,* Form AH. Chicago: Science Research Associates.

Tobin, K. (1980). The effect of an extended teacher wait-time on science achievement. *Journal of Research in Science Teaching, 17,* 469–475.

Tobin, K., & Capie, W. (1982). Relationships between classroom process variables and middle-school science achievement. *Journal of Educational Psychology, 74,* 441–454.

Tomlinson, P., & Hunt, D. (1971). Differential effects of rule-example order as a function of learner conceptual level. *Canadian Journal of Behavioral Science, 3,* 237–245.

Tyler, R. (1934). *Constructing achievement tests.* Columbus, OH: Ohio State University Press.

United States General Accounting Office (1987). *Bilingual education: A new look at the research evidence.* Gaithersburg, MD. GAO/PEMD–87–12BR.

Walberg, H. (1986). Syntheses of research on teaching. In M. C. Wittrock (Ed.), *Handbook of research on teaching: Third edition* (pp. 214–229). New York: Macmillan.

Wang, M., & Lindvall, C. (1984). Individual differences and school learning environments. *Review of Research in Education, 11,* 161–225.

Weiner, B. (1972). *Theories of motivation: From mechanism to cognition.* Chicago: Markham.

Winne, R. (1979). Experiments relating teachers' use of high cognitive questions to student achievement. *Review of Educational Research, 49,* 13–50.

Wragg, E., & Wood, E. (1984). Teachers' first encounters with their classes. In E. Wragg (Ed.), *Classroom teaching skills* (pp. 47–78). New York: Nichols.

Wyne, M., & Stuck, G. (1982). Time and learning: Implications for the classroom teacher. *Elementary School Journal, 83,* 67–75.

Zahorik, J. (1987). Reacting. In M. J. Dunkin (Ed.), *Encyclopedia of teaching and teacher education* (pp. 416–423). New York: Pergamon.

Zakariya, S. B. (1987). How to keep your balance when it comes to bilingual education. *The American School Board Journal, 6,* 21–26.

Zenger, W., & Zenger, S. (1982). *Curriculum planning: A ten-step process.* Palo Alto, CA: R and E Research Associates.

Subject Index

Author Index

Rowe, M., 211
Ryan, F., 17

Samuels, S., 155, 156
Sanford, J., 9, 13, 236, 250, 306
Schumer, H., 28, 224
Scott, J., 156
Sendelbach, N., 58
Sharan, S., 223
Singer, H., 153
Slavin, R., 159, 184
Smilansky, M., 31
Smith, B., 8, 200
Smith, E., 58
Smith F., 194
Snow, R., 28, 29, 30
Soar, R., 10
Spielberger, C., 39
Stallings, J., 10, 28
Sternberg, R., 33
Stevens, R., 14, 127, 143
Stipek, D., 29
Stock, G., 11
Stone, M., 10

Thomas, S., 40
Thurstone, L., 32
Tinsley, D., 15
Tobin, K., 211
Tomlinson, R., 150
Tyler, R., 83

Walberg, H., 3, 7, 9
Wang, M., 30
Weiner, B., 40
Whaley, D., 222
Wheeler, P., 10
White, R., 229
Wilkinson, B., 11
Winne, R., 14, 197
Wood, E., 224, 225
Worsham, M., 9, 13, 236, 250, 306
Wragg, E., 224, 225
Wyne, M., 11

Yinger, R., 58

Zahorik, J., 16
Zakariya, S., 281

About the Author

Gary Borich grew up on the south side of Chicago, where he attended Mendel High School and later taught in the Chicago suburban school system of Niles. He received his PhD from Indiana University, where he was director of evaluation at the Institute for Child Study (under the direction of Nicholas J. Anastasiow) before joining the faculty of the College of Education at the University of Texas at Austin. Dr. Borich lives in Austin, Texas with his wife (who is a school-teacher) and two children. His hobbies include pottery (pre-Colombian vases) and training and riding Arabian horses.

WE VALUE YOUR OPINION—PLEASE SHARE IT WITH US

Merrill Publishing and our authors are most interested in your reactions to this textbook. Did it serve you well in the course? If it did, what aspects of the text were most helpful? If not, what didn't you like about it? Your comments will help us to write and develop better textbooks. We value your opinions and thank you for your help.

Text Title _____ Edition _____

Author(s) _____

Your Name (optional) _____

Address _____

City _____ State _____ Zip _____

School _____

Course Title _____

Instructor's Name _____

Your Major _____

Your Class Rank _____ Freshman _____ Sophomore _____ Junior _____ Senior

_____ Graduate Student

Were you required to take this course? _____ Required _____ Elective

Length of Course? _____ Quarter _____ Semester

1. Overall, how does this text compare to other texts you've used?

   _____ Superior _____ Better Than Most _____ Average _____ Poor

2. Please rate the text in the following areas:

	Superior	Better Than Most	Average	Poor
Author's Writing Style	____	____	____	____
Readability	____	____	____	____
Organization	____	____	____	____
Accuracy	____	____	____	____
Layout and Design	____	____	____	____
Illustrations/Photos/Tables	____	____	____	____
Examples	____	____	____	____
Problems/Exercises	____	____	____	____
Topic Selection	____	____	____	____
Currentness of Coverage	____	____	____	____
Explanation of Difficult Concepts	____	____	____	____
Match-up with Course Coverage	____	____	____	____
Applications to Real Life	____	____	____	____

3. Circle those chapters you especially liked:
   1   2   3   4   5   6   7   8   9   10   11   12   13   14   15   16   17   18   19   20
   What was your favorite chapter? _____
   Comments:

4. Circle those chapters you liked least:
   1   2   3   4   5   6   7   8   9   10   11   12   13   14   15   16   17   18   19   20
   What was your least favorite chapter? _____
   Comments:

5. List any chapters your instructor did not assign. _____

6. What topics did your instructor discuss that were not covered in the text?_____

   _____

7. Were you required to buy this book? _____ Yes _____ No

   Did you buy this book new or used? _____ New _____ Used

   If used, how much did you pay? _____

   Do you plan to keep or sell this book? _____ Keep _____ Sell

   If you plan to sell the book, how much do you expect to receive? _____

   Should the instructor continue to assign this book? _____ Yes _____ No

8. Please list any other learning materials you purchased to help you in this course (e.g., study guide, lab manual).

   _____

9. What did you like most about this text? _____

   _____

10. What did you like least about this text? _____

   _____

11. General comments:

   May we quote you in our advertising? _____ Yes _____ No

   Please mail to: Boyd Lane
                     College Division, Research Department
                     Box 508
                     1300 Alum Creek Drive
                     Columbus, Ohio 43216

   Thank you!